Psychometric Testing

BPS Textbooks in Psychology

BPS Blackwell presents a comprehensive and authoritative series covering everything a student needs in order to complete an undergraduate degree in psychology. Refreshingly written to consider more than North American research, this series is the first to give a truly international perspective. Written by the very best names in the field, the series offers an extensive range of titles from introductory level through to final year optional modules, and every text fully complies with the BPS syllabus in the topic. No other series bears the BPS seal of approval!

Each book is supported by a companion website, featuring additional resource materials for both instructors and students, designed to encourage critical thinking, and providing for all your course lecturing and testing needs.

For other titles in this series, please go to **www.bpsblackwell.co.uk**

Psychometric Testing

CRITICAL PERSPECTIVES

EDITED BY

BARRY CRIPPS, PhD

WILEY Blackwell

This edition first published 2017
© John Wiley & Sons, Ltd

Registered Office
John Wiley & Sons Ltd, The Atrium, Southern Gate, Chichester, West Sussex, PO19 8SQ, UK

Editorial Offices
350 Main Street, Malden, MA 02148-5020, USA
9600 Garsington Road, Oxford, OX4 2DQ, UK
The Atrium, Southern Gate, Chichester, West Sussex, PO19 8SQ, UK

For details of our global editorial offices, for customer services and for information about how to apply for permission to reuse the copyright material in this book please see our website at www.wiley.com/wiley-blackwell.

The right of Barry Cripps to be identified as the author of the editorial material in this work has been asserted in accordance with the UK Copyright, Designs and Patents Act 1988.

All rights reserved. No part of this publication may be reproduced, stored in a retrieval system, or transmitted, in any form or by any means, electronic, mechanical, photocopying, recording or otherwise, except as permitted by the UK Copyright, Designs and Patents Act 1988, without the prior permission of the publisher.

Wiley also publishes its books in a variety of electronic formats. Some content that appears in print may not be available in electronic books.

Designations used by companies to distinguish their products are often claimed as trademarks. All brand names and product names used in this book are trade names, service marks, trademarks or registered trademarks of their respective owners. The publisher is not associated with any product or vendor mentioned in this book.

Limit of Liability/Disclaimer of Warranty: While the publisher and authors have used their best efforts in preparing this book, they make no representations or warranties with respect to the accuracy or completeness of the contents of this book and specifically disclaim any implied warranties of merchantability or fitness for a particular purpose. It is sold on the understanding that the publisher is not engaged in rendering professional services and neither the publisher nor the author shall be liable for damages arising herefrom. If professional advice or other expert assistance is required, the services of a competent professional should be sought.

Library of Congress Cataloging-in-Publication Data

9781119182986 (hardback)
9781119183013 (paperback)

A catalogue record for this book is available from the British Library.

Cover image: © jijomathaidesigners/Shutterstock

Set in 11/12.5 pt Dante MT Std by Aptara

10 9 8 7 6 5 4 3 2 1

I wish to dedicate this book to the memory of Emeritus Prof Hans Eysenck.

Contents

About the Editor		ix
About the Authors		xi
Foreword		xvii
John Rust		
Preface		xix
Barry Cripps		
Acknowledgements		xxi

Part I **History, Theory and Utility** — 1

Chapter 1 The History of Psychometrics — 3
Craig Knight

Chapter 2 Ride the Horse Around the Course: Triangulating Nomothetic and Idiographic Approaches to Personality Assessment — 15
Barry Cripps

Chapter 3 A Very Good Question? — 29
Peter Saville and Rab MacIver

Chapter 4 Big Data and Predictive Analytics: Opportunity or Threat to the Future of Tests and Testing — 43
Eugene Burke

Chapter 5 The Practical Application of Test User Knowledge and Skills — 65
Gerry Duggan

Chapter 6 The Utility of Psychometric Tests for Small Organisations — 77
Paul Barrett

Part II **Applications and Contexts** — 85

Chapter 7 HR Applications of Psychometrics — 87
Rob Bailey

Chapter 8 Defining and Assessing Leadership Talent: A Multi-layered Approach — 113
Caroline Curtis

Chapter 9 Psychometrics: The Evaluation and Development of Team Performance — 129
Stephen Benton

Chapter 10 Psychometrics in Sport: The Good, the Bad and the Ugly — 145
Dave Collins and Andrew Cruickshank

Chapter 11 Using Psychometrics to Make Management Selection Decisions: A Practitioner Journey — 157
Hugh McCredie

| **Chapter 12** | Psychometrics in Clinical Settings
Hamilton Fairfax | 175 |

Part III Best-Practice Considerations — 185

Chapter 13	The Use and Misuse of Psychometrics in Clinical Settings *Susan van Scoyoc*	187
Chapter 14	Measuring the Dark Side *Adrian Furnham*	197
Chapter 15	Projective Measures and Occupational Assessment *Christopher Ridgeway*	213
Chapter 16	Testing across Cultures: Translation, Adaptation and Indigenous Test Development *Lina Daouk-Öyry and Pia Zeinoun*	221
Chapter 17	Personality Testing in the Workplace: Can Internet Business Disruption Erode the Influence of Psychology Ethics? *Earon Kavanagh*	235
Chapter 18	A Practitioner's Viewpoint: Limitations and Assumptions Implicit in Assessment *Jay Roseveare*	251
Chapter 19	When Profit Comes In the Door, Does Science Go Out the Window? *Robert Forde*	263

Part IV Psychometrics and the Future — 267

| **Chapter 20** | The Future of Psychometric Testing
Robert McHenry | 269 |

Index 283

About the Editor

Dr Barry Cripps
BSc, BEd, PhD, CPsychol, CSci, FBPsS, HCPC Registered

Barry's doctorate is in the social psychology of sport, focusing his research on team interaction in professional soccer. Career moves followed into the BPS/DOP and the role of Director of Training for a test publisher. Barry has had a portfolio career focusing on individual, team and organisational work in industry and sport. Barry is a Founder Member of the BPS Division of Sport and Exercise Psychology. He was the winner of the Distinguished Contribution to the Field of Sport and Exercise Psychology Award presented at the Inaugural Conference of the DSEP, December 2008. He has lectured in psychology and business with the Open University, the University of Plymouth and Exeter University, and was a Visiting Professor at the University of Commerce, Tianjin, China. Barry serves as an external examiner in business psychology. Barry is Newsletter editor of the South West Branch, South West Review. He is particularly interested in personality, assessment, psychometrics, clinical hypnosis, and performance psychology; he has produced two books and is co-author of the personality questionnaire, *Eysenck, Cripps & Cook Occupational Scales*. His consultancy is based in Exeter, Devon.

About the Authors

Rob Bailey is an occupational psychologist specialising in the use of psychometric assessments in the workplace. His career has encompassed training clients in the use of psychometrics, development of psychometric products, and consultancy work with clients. Rob joined SHL (now CEB) in the head office research and development team in 1999, then in the UK consultancy business. In 2005, he joined OPP Ltd, developing products based on the 16PF personality questionnaire, for recruitment and development applications. Although Rob's chapter was written during his employment at OPP, he is now working for Talent Q Ltd's product and innovation team.

Paul Barrett received his PhD in personality psychometrics from the University of Exeter. He was a research scientist and co-director of the Biosignal Lab at the University of London's Institute of Psychiatry for 14 years, Chief Scientist at two of the UK's high-security forensic psychiatric hospitals, Chief Psychologist at Mariner7 (Carter Holt Harvey plc, NZ), Chief Research Scientist at Hogan Assessment Systems Inc. (US), and adjunct Professor of Psychometrics within the University of Auckland Business School, NZ. Currently he is Chief Research Scientist at Cognadev (UK and South Africa), an Honorary Professor of Psychology at the University of Auckland and Adjunct Professor of Psychology at the University of Canterbury (NZ).

Stephen Benton graduated in psychology from Brunel University and joined the Acoustics Research Group at Chelsea College, University of London on a SERC scholarship to conduct PhD research into the psychophysical properties of low-frequency noise, later moving to University College London to take up a post-doctoral fellowship in visual pschyophysics. After this he joined the University of Westminster (UW), where he has researched and lectured in various aspects of human factors as applied to the improvement of individuals' quality of life and performance. This work provided the platform for his creation in 1997 of the first business psychology postgraduate programme in Europe. In 2001 he was appointed Director of the Business Psychology Centre at UW. Stephen was awarded the title of Professor of Business Psychology in 2009, the first in the UK.

Eugene Burke is an independent consultant, adviser and commentator on HR analytics, assessment and talent management. He was the Chief Science and Analytics Officer at CEB and has held positions in R&D, product development, product management and consulting services. In his earlier career, he was a military psychologist with the Royal Air Force, the United States Air Force and NATO, and was Principal Psychologist with the London Fire Brigade, where he established the Brigade's Occupational Psychology Unit. He has authored a number of tests and assessments, including the Verify Suite of Online Ability Tests and the Dependability and Safety Instrument. He is the author of the Pilot Aptitude Tester (PILAPT), the most widely used assessment system for selecting military and civilian pilots.

David Collins has published over 300 peer-reviewed publications and 60 books or book chapters. His research interests include performer/coach development, expertise and the promotion of peak performance. As a performance psychologist, he has worked with over 60 world or Olympic medallists, and with professional teams and performers. Current assignments include football, rugby, judo, boxing, ski and snowboard and adventure sports, and work with military and business organisations. Dave is a director of the Rugby Coaches Association and of iZone Driver Performance, a Fellow of the Society of Martial Arts, of ZSL and of BASES, an Associate Fellow of the British Psychological Society and an ex-Royal Marine.

Andrew Cruickshank has researched and published in areas of professional sport psychology practice, elite team culture, management and leadership, coaching, and individual and team performance. On an applied level, Andrew is currently the Senior Sport Psychologist for British Judo and a consultant in professional rugby and elite golf, and is involved with a range of other programmes and clients in elite performance. Previously a professional footballer with Hibernian FC in Scotland, Andrew is also a UEFA licensed coach.

Barry Cripps. See 'About the Editor' above.

Caroline Curtis is the former Head of Executive Talent, Succession and Development at global banking group Santander. Her combined experience as a chartered psychologist, a qualified coach and a senior HR leader has enabled Santander to move forward hugely in terms of how it identifies and manages its talent, developing and deploying innovative talent models and ways of working with business stakeholders. These achievements are recognised both by external awards and by a strong presence on the external speaking circuit.

Lina Daouk-Öyry is an Assistant Professor of Organizational Psychology at the Olayan School of Business at the American University of Beirut. Her research focuses on test adaptation across cultural boundaries and on understanding the structure of personality in the Arab world, mainly through the psycholexical investigation of the Arabic language. Lina is also the Director of the Evidence-based Healthcare Management Unit (EHMU), a cross-disciplinary research and service unit aimed at generating knowledge and evidence that is necessary for the effective and efficient application of management principles within the healthcare industry. As such, her research also focuses on evidence-based management in the healthcare industry from an organisational psychology perspective. Lina obtained her MSc in Organisational Behaviour and her PhD in Psychology (focus on psychometrics) from City University London.

Gerry Duggan is a registered occupational psychologist with 35 years' experience in the field of psychological assessment and testing. After studying at Macquarie and Sydney Universities in Australia, Gerry worked as a test constructor on behalf of the University of New South Wales, where he designed selection tests for train drivers, railway station attendants and apprentices. As the Assessment Partner for TPS Developing Organisations Ltd, Gerry designs international assessment and development programmes for major companies in the engineering, financial, pharmaceutical and service sectors. Gerry works on behalf of the BPS as a verifier of those wishing to assess the capability of applicants for the Register of Qualifications in Test Use.

Hamilton Fairfax is a chartered counselling psychologist and professional lead for a psychology and psychological therapies service in adult mental health, Devon NHS Partnership Trust, South Devon. He has worked in the NHS for more than 15 years. He is also the Research Lead for the Division of Counselling Psychology, BPS. His interests include mindfulness, personality disorder, OCD, therapeutic process and neuropsychology; he has published and presented in these areas. He is also a senior research lecturer on the University of the West of England Counselling Psychology doctorate course. He is honoured to have been named Practitioner of the Year 2014 by the BPS.

Robert Forde has worked in a variety of roles in educational, business and military settings, as well as in prisons. His work has included research, clinical assessment, and staff selection and training in both public and private sectors. For the last 15 years he has been in private practice, mainly working as an expert witness providing evidence of criminal risk to courts and parole panels. His doctoral research on the use of risk assessment in parole decisions was completed in 2014, and has aroused considerable interest (see http://etheses.bham.ac.uk/5476). In 2014 he was appointed the first Consultant Forensic Editor of Assessment & Development Matters. He has now retired from active casework, and is currently writing a book on psychological practice.

Adrian Furnham was educated at the London School of Economics, where he obtained a distinction in an MSc Econ., and at Oxford University, where he completed a doctorate (DPhil) in 1981. He has subsequently earned DSc (1991) and DLitt (1995) degrees. Previously a lecturer in psychology at Pembroke College, Oxford, he has been Professor of Psychology at University College London since 1992. He has lectured widely abroad and held scholarships and visiting professorships at, amongst other institutions, the universities of New South Wales, the West Indies, Hong Kong and KwaZulu-Natal. He has also been a Visiting Professor of Management at Henley Management College. He has been made Adjunct Professor of Management at the Norwegian School of Management (2009). He has written over 1000 scientific papers and 80 books.

Earon Kavanagh earned his PhD in social constructionist organisational psychology at Tilburg University and an MBA in organisational change leadership. He later embarked on post-doctoral studies in personality testing through completion of the BPS Test Specialist credential. He has practised counselling for over two decades, has taught over 50 courses in counselling psychology programmes and business programmes, and is a member of the Society for Industrial and Organizational Psychology. His interests include the intersection of psychology with business, and competitive strategy.

Craig Knight is a chartered psychologist, a business change specialist and an Honorary Research Fellow at the University of Exeter. He is a founding Director of Haddleton Knight. His PhD was in the psychology of working and living space. Subsequent published studies with colleagues consistently demonstrate that – compared with current best practice – the psychological application of design and management principles can improve well-being by up to 40 per cent and workplace productivity by up to 32 per cent. Craig is also a psychological therapist and counsellor. He is a member of the Health and Care Professions Council and of the British Society for Clinical and Academic Hypnosis.

Rab MacIver is R&D Director at Saville Consulting, a Willis Towers Watson company. In this capacity he is responsible for the research, development and localisation of all Saville Consulting assessment products, including the Wave online personality questionnaires, aptitude assessments and bespoke multimedia situational judgement tests. At the start of his career, Rab worked at SHL with Peter Saville, managing the revision to the Occupational Personality Questionnaires and reports. On joining Saville Consulting, Rab again worked with Peter, this time to lead the development of the Wave questionnaires. Rab's particular passion throughout his career has been for investigating, developing and validating approaches which lead to assessments which provide more accurate forecasts of work performance and potential.

Hugh McCredie, CPsychol, Chartered FCIPD, AFBPsS spent a career lifetime as an HR practitioner, specialising in senior management assessment and development. He collected predictor and performance data which he analysed, first, to improve selection and development methods for clients, and, subsequently, to submit successful MSc and PhD theses to Aston and Manchester Business Schools, respectively. His voluntary appointments include Vice-Chair of the Psychometrics Forum, for whom he initiated and organises the annual 'New Frontiers in Psychometrics' event. Hugh authored *Selecting & Developing Better Managers* (2010), and is the most frequent contributor to the BPS periodical *Assessment & Development Matters*.

Robert McHenry was Executive Chairman of OPP Ltd, a people assessment company based in Oxford. He is now an independent practitioner. For most of his professional life, Robert has pursued two parallel careers. As an occupational psychologist, he worked for ten years as a consultant for many well-known global corporations before founding OPP Ltd and becoming CEO, a post he held until 2011. At the same time, he carried on an academic career, and taught experimental psychology at Oxford University from 1974 to 2011. He is currently working on bringing rigorous talent assessment to a wider audience through devices like the smartphone. Robert has a doctorate in experimental psychology from Oxford University and is a registered occupational psychologist in the UK. He is a past president of the Occupational Psychology Division of the BPS and served on the board of the BPS for five years. In 2013, he was elected to an Honorary Fellowship at Oriel College, University of Oxford.

Christopher Ridgeway has had four strands to his career. He has been an international HR director, the CEO of a global occupational psychology, strategic HR and organisation change consultancy, a business school academic in the US, Africa and the UK, and a coach and facilitator to boards. Chris has specialised in talent management and individual and corporate change. He has written seven books and 80 papers. Chris is a chartered occupational and counselling psychologist.

Jay Roseveare is a business psychologist specialising in personal and career development, leadership coaching and occupational assessment, following an early career in operational and change management to managing director level. His research into leadership loneliness led him to design and test an instrument to predict individual effectiveness in isolated situations and earned him a Professional Doctorate in Occupational Psychology from the University of East London in 2006. He is a chartered psychologist and an Associate Fellow of the BPS, a specialist in Test Use (Occupational) and a EuroTest User (Occupational).

Peter Saville is acknowledged as a worldwide authority in the field of industrial psychology. His picture hung in the National Portrait Gallery in London as the first work psychologist to be awarded the Centenary Lifetime Achievement Award from the BPS for Distinguished Contributions to Professional Psychology. Consultant to over 300 organisations, Peter has written and presented over 250 papers and books, appeared on TV and radio internationally and presented speeches and keynotes in over 65 countries. He founded Saville and Holdsworth (SHL) with Roger Holdsworth in 1977, taking it to full flotation on the London Stock Exchange in 1997. At SHL he devised the original Occupational Personality Questionnaires (OPQ). In 2001 Peter was voted one of the UK's top ten psychologists, the only occupational psychologist included. Peter later developed the Wave Questionnaires at his second company, Saville Consulting, founded in 2004. Already a Fellow, in 2012 he was awarded an Honorary Fellowship of the BPS, joining an eminent list including Freud, Jung, Murray, Skinner and Chomsky. His citation stated, 'he brought science to the workplace and set the global gold standard in psychometric testing'. He is Visiting Professor at Kingston University, London.

Susan van Scoyoc is a chartered counselling and health psychologist, registered with the Health and Care Professions Council and working in independent practice with S&S Van Scoyoc (UK) Ltd. She is a trainer and supervisor with a particular interest in the use of psychometric assessments in clinical and legal settings. Her focus on the use of psychologists as expert witnesses, along with her extensive training of psychologists in this field, was recognised by the BPS when she was named Practitioner of the Year by the Professional Practice Board.

Pia Zeinoun is an Assistant Professor of psychology at the American University of Beirut. Her research centres on the development of culturally appropriate instruments that can measure constructs which are both culturally relevant and universally recognised. She is particularly interested in test usage in the Arab region. Pia is the co-founder and head of the Psychological Assessment Center at the American University of Beirut Medical Center's Department of Psychiatry, where she also carries out clinical assessments of children and adolescents. Pia has also taught university courses in research and in assessment. She holds a doctoral degree in psychology from Tilburg University. Before that, she had a Fulbright sojourn at Illinois State University, where she obtained a master's degree in Clinical and Counseling Psychology.

Foreword

Modern psychometrics has come a long way since the turn of the century, and this book presents a broad spectrum of ideas, both revised and new, that are having an increasing impact on the worlds of work and health. The distinguished authors present a crucible of ideas, ranging from the subject's grounding in ancient Chinese and Greek thought, through the scientific revolution in statistics instigated by the early twentieth-century psychometricians, to modern innovations that apply machine learning and artificial intelligence techniques to the analysis of online digital footprints. Both theory and practice are represented, providing something for all interested in how their subject is developing in the modern world.

But psychometrics as a discipline has had a very troubled past, containing, yes, some enormous successes but also some great tragedies. The same technology that, 100 years ago, introduced IQ testing to military recruitment and university entrance, giving us the new meritocracy that underpins modern education, also gave us the disastrous dead ends of eugenics and scientific racism. Between them, these two had almost wiped psychometrics off the map by the end of the century. What had proved to be fair to individuals was showing massive discrimination between groups, spuriously justified by evolutionary pseudoscience during the race/IQ debate. We owe our subject's recovery to the persistence of those who realised that tests, selection, and by consequence rejection, were something that affected everyone, and if we didn't do our best to make them reliable, valid, but also fair, then who would? We also owe a great debt to James Flynn, whose perseverance in spreading the message of the Flynn Effect did what it always had the potential to do, back-footed the proponents of bell-curve thinking that had stood in the way of progress for the less advantaged. And we also owe just as much to the many dedicated practitioners, represented here, whose recognition of the worth of their trade kept the discipline alive through this difficult period.

Is this raking over old coals? Well, it could be were not another impending challenge confronting us. The story of the last century was one of unintended consequences – ability testing, the SAT, the 11+ and grammar schools were to be the lynchpin of a modern industrial society. They were not intended to generate an underclass – but they did. And, once created, we, or most of us, had not intended to condemn its participants to accusations of congenital inferiority, but many did. In the words of Samuel Taylor Coleridge, "If men could learn from history, what lessons it might teach us! But passion and party blind our eyes, and the light which experience gives us is a lantern on the stern which shines only on the waves behind". The internet has given us social networks that bind us together, and AI tools that unite the internet of things and can make our lives so much easier. But it also has the potential to give us Big Brother and Skynet. Both of our major contemporary tools, online digital footprint analysis and computer adaptive testing, are lying across the tracks for both trajectories. Our destiny is in the hands of the practitioners of our trade. More power to their elbow in the difficult times ahead.

John Rust, 19th December 2016

Preface

When I was approached by a commissioning editor at Wiley-Blackwell to author a book on psychometric testing I was excited by the challenge and flattered by the invitation. I quickly realised that the size of the task for a sole author was completely outside my capability, but to edit a book consisting of chapters contributed by the current 'thought leaders' would be a possibility, and so, here we are.

During the whole of my career as a psychologist I have worked alongside, and communicated, met and discussed with, so many colleagues, academics, teachers, practitioners and publishers in the field of psychometric testing that I could not possibly count them all. What surprised and humbled me is that when I put out a call to colleagues for support in editing this book in September 2014, their response was magnificent, as you will soon read. It has been a pleasure and a privilege to work with these colleagues and I thank them sincerely.

It seems to me important for psychologists, as indeed it was for Socrates, to ask questions in order to find out about what it is to be a person, what attributes differentiate humans from other animals and indeed each other? As differentiation is obvious in so many ways the next question is: can we measure these differences? Differences in intelligence, ability, personality, motivation and interests have formed the earliest set of enquiries. Finally, how can we use this knowledge to advantage in our work and for the benefit of our clients?

Possibly the earliest stream of development in testing has been in education, enquiring into what we know about intelligence and use to develop theories of learning with its associated pedagogy and teaching technology. Testing in schools has now moved into the early years in the UK.

As has often been the case in other fields such as engineering, early developments in testing were sponsored by the military. It seems fairly obvious that in the selection of an officer to command a submarine or pilot a supersonic aircraft, any process would need to be extremely rigorous. Once measures and tests had been written by pioneers, not necessarily psychometricians, the gates were open and a whole test publishing industry has been set up. The industry developed its own language and adopted technical terms that have moved into everyday use.

Psychometricians and statisticians have refined instruments to sophisticated levels of validity and reliability. It is now *de rigueur* for companies to use psychometric tests in order to select and develop their people.

This book summarises the critical viewpoints of leading experts and thought leaders in the field of psychometric testing. The brief was to offer a critical view of psychometric testing, strengths and limitations derived from contributors' extensive, evidence-based experience and scientific research, application and enquiry.

Chapters are arranged in a logical order, from theory to practice. Kurt Lewin's apt phrase, 'There's nothing as practical as a good theory', summarises this logical order, in all its diverse instrumentation and application.

Final chapters look to the future, the dynamic, ever-changing world of testing via the Internet and smartphone technology.

What stands out for me as I read is to enter, as a privileged observer, the personal world of experienced practitioners and authors engaged in publishing, teaching, coaching, consulting and the advising industry globally.

Some editors when writing their preface would single out certain chapters, or indeed précis them all. I have deliberately not done this because all the chapters, in my opinion, are 'jewels in the crown of psychometric testing'.

Dip in and out as you please. Enjoy the read…

Barry Cripps
Exeter, Devon, 2016
drbarrycripps@btinternet.com

Acknowledgements

My thanks go to Darren Reed, Liz Wingett and the publishing team at Wiley-Blackwell …

To all the authors/subscribers without whom there would be no book …

To my wife Ann who has mopped my brow on many occasions …

To my good friend Peter Saville, supportive as ever at crucial times …

Part I History, Theory and Utility

1 The History of Psychometrics
Craig Knight

He had the personality of kipper; on an off day.
Joan Collins

Think about the people you know for a moment. Have you ever wondered how Chris manages to maintain a sense of equilibrium under even the most testing circumstances, or why Sam is more irritating than a starched collar? Why are some people like balm to a wound, while others look to start a fight in an empty room? And wouldn't it be useful if you could predict people's behaviour patterns *before* an event rather than ruefully mopping up afterwards?

Humans have been speculating on and assessing their own variables since Cain weighed up Abel, often with the success of somebody nailing fog to a wall. If it's hard to judge those we claim to know best, just how can you assess the personality of a good accountant, manager or leader? Of course Tibetan Buddhists re-select the same leader on an eternal basis. The rest of us have to make a more or less educated assessment of the candidates available.

It is this assessment that is central to psychometrics. If we accept the definition of psychometrics as 'the science of measuring mental capacities and processes' (en.oxforddictionaries.com, 2016) then the *quality* of that science becomes the predictor of its success.

As we will see, psychometrics is a flawed discipline. Its advocates can be vociferous and wrong. Vaunted predictive capabilities go unchecked and snake oil oozes from the cracks of many psychometric creations. No matter how persuasive the personality advocate and how beguiling the evidence, we do well to remember that nobody ever equates to a yellow circle, a traffic light or a bear. Only decent instruments – probably in the hands of trained assessors – can link skills, propensities and personalities to jobs, proclivities and outcomes.

Well-researched psychometrics can test for the qualities required in a boardroom or back office or bakery. So while these tools – like all tools – arrive in various shades of imperfection, their lack during times of recruitment and appraisal can be costly. This chapter will explore the origins and development of psychometrics, its uses and abuses. It will close by reading the runes of future developments.

GREAT MEN AND THEIR HUMOUR

From when time was in its cradle people have believed that personality traits can be divined. The gift of leadership was particularly prized. Leaders were said to have natural charisma and ability which others instinctively lacked. Even as infants leaders waved their rattles like sceptres (Haney, Sirbasku & McCann, 2011). Thus followers innately looked to trail behind, while women were 'fitted to be at home as is their nature' (Buss & Schmitt, 2011). Scientifically illiterate though these ideas may be (Haslam, 2004), moot them in the Red Lion and witness the levels of assent amongst the crowd. The idea of a born leader remains powerfully salient. With due deference to Meir, Thatcher and Merkel, as Carlyle had it (1841, p. 47), 'The history of the world is but the biography of great men'.

However, even a cursory look at different leaders' personalities reveals considerable variety within the camps. Alexander the Great's propensity for megalomania would have sat poorly with Nelson's service ethic; Kublai Khan's extravagance is unlikely to have appealed to Karl Marx, while Mahatma Gandhi's peaceful resistance would probably leave Emperor Hadrian somewhat perplexed. Discussion over the cornflakes would have been tense. And the same differences of approach are found amongst carpenters, midwives and tennis players. So how does any instrument assess for role, aptitude and skill?

PERSONALITY AND THE FOUR HUMOURS

Many of the chapters of this book will explore how various instruments gauge aspects of personality. Even between the most widely respected psychometric tools the number of perceived personality traits varies widely and runs from five to 32. However, originally there were just four.

It is a matter of conjecture whether a belief in the need for bodily balance was developed by the Indian Ayurveda system of medicine or by the Ancient Greeks. What is certain is that the concept of four distinct bodily fluids – hydraulically interdependent and all influencing human nature – survived from Hippocrates through Galen and the Roman Empire, right through to the Renaissance. Indeed we retain much of the terminology today. To be *sanguine*, *choleric*, *phlegmatic* or *melancholy* is to echo a system of personality assessment that resonates through the centuries (Figure 1.1).

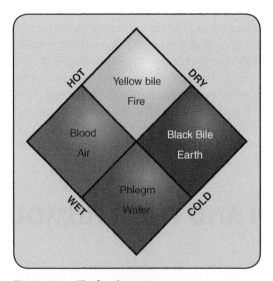

Figure 1.1 *The four humours*

A surplus or deficiency of any one of four elemental bodily fluids – or *humours* – was thought to directly affect one's feelings and health. All four humours may originate from just one bodily fluid: blood. In the open air blood sedimentation shows a dark, thick clot at its base (black bile), and erythrocytic cells (or red blood) sit on top below a layer of white blood cells which could easily have been labelled as phlegm. Phlegm was not the expectorated gloop we know today. Finally a top pool of yellow liquid (yellow bile) completes the basic substances which were thought to comprise the corporeal human.

An excess of yellow bile was expressed through overt aggression, an issue said to be associated with an agitated liver. Even now we will call somebody who is peevish and disagreeable 'liverish' or 'bilious', while alternative medicine often insists that anger remains a symptom of a disturbed liver (Singh & Ernst, 2008).

Meanwhile those said to have an excess of what the Greeks called *melaina kholé*, or black bile, were said to be suffering from 'melancholy' or depression. An excess of phlegm was thought to be behind a stolid, fixedly unemotional approach to one's affairs, and gave rise to the modern phlegmatic personality.

In contrast to the other three humours an excess of blood carried clear personality benefits. People who are *sanguine* (from the Latin *sanguis*, 'blood') have always been cheerful, optimistic and confident.

Each individual had their own humoral composition, which they shared to a greater or lesser degree with others. This mix of humours precipitated personality in a view that held good from Hippocrates to Harvey via Ancient Rome and Persia. Indeed, this holistic approach is still used in *personality type* analysis today, where psychometricians are keen to label individuals with marks of similarity (Pittenger, 1993).

Thus, while it is considered pseudo-scientific to tell somebody that they possess a mostly phlegmatic personality (Childs, 2009), you are very likely to hear that you have the temperament of a team worker, or of an introvert, or that you have a blue/green personality. You may even be assigned a group of incongruous-sounding letters such as ENTJ from the globally dominant Myers–Briggs Personality Type Indicator. Amongst other attributes ENTJs are 'born leaders' (personalitypage.com, 2015). And we see the ancient terminology being recycled in the twenty-first century, even when it is known to be psychologically flawed. So are some modern interpretations any less pseudo-scientific than their rather longer-lasting forebears (Sipps, Alexander & Friedt, 1985)?

THE BEGINNINGS OF MODERN PSYCHOMETRICS

The history of psychometrics intertwines with that of psychology. Its modern incarnations have two main progenitors. The first of these concentrates on the measurement of individual differences; the second looks at psychophysical measurements of similarity.

Charles Darwin's (1809–82) *The Origin of Species* (Darwin, 1859) explained why individual members of the animal kingdom differ. It explored how specific characteristics show themselves to be more successful and adaptive to their environment than others. It is these adaptive traits that survive and are passed on to successive generations.

Sir Francis Galton (1822–1911) was a Victorian polymath whose panoply of accomplishments encompassed sociology, psychology and anthropology. He was also related to Charles Darwin and was influenced by his half-cousin's work. Consequently Galton wondered about various adaptive traits in human beings. Not content with merely studying the differences, however, Galton wanted to *measure* them.

In his book *Hereditary Genius* (1869), Galton described how people's characteristics make them more or less *fit* for society and for positions within it. Galton – often called 'the father of psychometrics' – was drawn to measuring intelligence, as was Alfred Binet (1857–1911) in France (Hogan & Cannon, 2007). This work was later taken up by James McKeen Cattell (1860–1944), who coined the term *mental test*.

As Darwin, Galton, Binet and Cattell developed their measures of fitness and intelligence, Johann Herbart – a German philosopher and psychologist – was also working to scientifically unlock 'the mysteries of human consciousness' (Wolman, 1968). Herbart was responsible for creating mathematical models of the mind in his field of psychophysics. Psychophysics influenced Wilhelm Wundt, who was often credited with founding the science of psychology itself (Carpenter, 2005). Thus Herbart, via Wundt, and Galton, via Cattell, have strong claims to be the pioneers of modern psychological testing.

THE TWENTIETH CENTURY

The twentieth century saw psychometrics become increasingly reliable, valid and robust. Louis Thurstone, founder and first president, in 1936, of the Psychometric Society, developed the *law of comparative judgement*, a theoretical approach to measurement that owed much to psychophysical theory. Working with statistician Charles Spearman, Thurstone helped to refine the application and theory of factor analysis, a statistical method that explores variability and error without which psychometrics would be greatly diminished and considerably less accurate (Michell, 1997).

Working at the same time, Hungarian psychiatrist, Leopold Szondi was in something of a revolt against this forensic but narrow statistical treatment of people's psyche. He did not believe that the make-up of something as complex, changeable and irrational as a human being could be captured by a series of focused numbers, no matter how thorough the statistics that underlay them (Szondi, Ulrich & Webb, 1959).

In developing his own, eponymous test, Szondi instead tried to capture as much of the essence of the spirit of humankind as possible by widening the assessments that were made. The test's goal was to explore the innermost recesses of our repressed impulses. Constructs were elicited by assessing the levels of sympathy or aversion engendered by showing clients specific photographs of psychopaths. The client was expected to point to the person she or he would least like to meet on a dark night and explain why (Szondi et al., 1959).

Szondi held that the characteristics of – and emotions in – others that bother us are those that most disturbed us early in our lives. That is why we repress these factors in ourselves. His test is said to address fundamental drives which classify the entire human system but in a more qualitative manner than instruments offered by his psychometrician contemporaries.

In this gestalt approach Szondi is closer in spirit to Hermann Rorschach, the Swiss Freudian psychiatrist and psychoanalyst. Rorschach developed perhaps the most famous psychological instrument the world has seen. The Rorschach inkblot test assesses clients' perceptions of a series of patterned smudges, some of which are shown in Figure 1.2 (Wood, Nezworski,

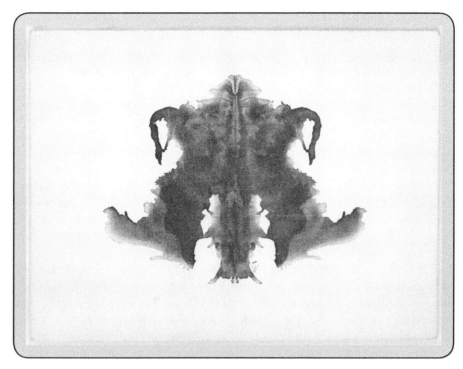

Figure 1.2 *Ink blots from the Rorschach test. © Zmeel Photography/iStockphoto*

Lilienfeld & Garb, 2003). There were ten original inkblots, which Rorschach presented on separate white cards, each approximately 7 × 10 inches in size, each with near-perfect bilateral symmetry. First, the client interpreted the shapes in a *free association* phase. 'Oh, that one looks like a prehistoric moth …', and so forth. Then the cards were presented in a fixed order, and held, rotated and pored over by the client, who was quizzed at each stage. Responses were tabulated.

Rorschach wanted his test to act as a series of pegs upon which aspects of human personality could be hung. The interpretation of Rorschach is both complex and contested. Rorschach interpreters are effectively on probation for up to four year before being considered sufficiently competent to handle the test alone. Nevertheless some critics consider the interpretation of odd blobs nothing more than pseudo-science (Wood et al., 2003). Even so, the Rorschach test, like Freud, the man who inspired Rorschach himself, may be flawed and a little past its peak, but it continues to be very influential – one of the tests most used by members of the Society for Personality Assessment (Gacano & Reid, 1994).

MEASUREMENT, CONTROVERSY AND THEORETICAL DEVELOPMENT

The split between the preferred types of psychometric assessment grew. At the same time, the importance of accurate psychometric measurement became ever more key and contentious. Even the definition of measurement itself caused argument.

In 1946 Stanley Smith Stevens defined measurement as 'the assignment of numerals to objects or events according to some rule' (Michell, 1997). At first glance this definition benefits from a certain vagueness, useful to some social scientists but slightly and importantly different from the definition used by physical science, where measurement is 'the estimation or discovery of the ratio of some magnitude of a quantitative attribute to a unit of the same attribute' (Michell, 1997).

An opposite view quickly formed. This was that as physicists and psychologists were both scientists there should be no convoluted semantic differences between how they measure their inputs, throughputs and outputs (Hardman, 2009).

While picking up the niceties of measurement can be a little like eating consommé with a fork, the different theories themselves are happily salient. *Classical Test Theory* grew from the combination of three mathematical developments and the genius of Charles Spearman in the early twentieth century (Novick, 1966). First, there was the realisation that there are errors when people are measured. If, before an assessment, you have slept like a contented elephant and eaten a hearty breakfast, you are likely to feel and perform differently than had you rolled in from an all-night party, unwashed, unrested and unfed. Second, it is not always possible to predict where the error will occur (you might perform brilliantly when hung over) and, third, some aspects of your performance are usefully correlated while others are not. You may, for example, be happier in the morning than in the afternoon, so your happiness and the 24-hour clock are correlated *and* linked. However the freshness of the morning milk also correlates with your moods, but the correlation is incidental and unlinked.

By harnessing the mathematics to the psychometrics, Classical Test Theory was able to improve the predictive power of psychological testing. It used people's performances to feed back into the reliability and validity of the instruments. It made useful estimates as to how psychometric performances would translate into real-world successes (Novick, 1966).

However, a major flaw in Classical Test Theory is that the characteristics of the test taker and the characteristics of the test itself are impossible to separate. Each can only be interpreted in the context of the other. Furthermore, the standard error of measurement (which is the difference between what you would score on a test in ideal conditions – your true score – and the score you did achieve in the conditions prevailing at the time of the test) is assumed to be the same for everybody, regardless of mood swings or innate personality stability.

During the 1950s and 1960s three men working, independently but serendipitously, on parallel research led to the development of *Item Response Theory*. Danish mathematician Georg Rasch, American psychometrician Frederic Lord and Austrian sociologist Paul Lazarsfeld developed a framework for evaluating how well psychological assessments work, and how valid specific items within these assessments may be.

Item Response Theory is also known as *latent trait modelling*. This is because IRT models the relationship between concealed, or latent, traits within a test taker and the responses that a test taker makes to test items. Thus somebody's sociability can be assessed by asking questions such as 'Do you enjoy meeting people?' and 'Do you take the initiative in making new friends?' (Cook & Cripps, 2005).

Traits, constructs or attributes therefore do not need to be directly observed, but can be inferred from the responses given. Item Response Theory is argued to be an improvement over Classical Test Theory (Uebersax, 1999). IRT is said to provide a basis for obtaining an estimate of comparisons between related but different groups with varying levels of ability.

For example, a chemistry graduate's knowledge of her or his subject can be examined via a university test. The result can then be reliably compared to the test result of a senior school pupil sitting a similar but easier examination. By contrast, Classical Test Theory relies on comparisons with a norm group (a norm group is a collective representation of a relevant group, such as 'graduates', 'taxi drivers' or 'senior managers'), so that while there are comparisons within groups, there is no *relative* comparison between groups.

Item Response Theory is especially popular in education. It is used in designing, comparing and balancing examinations across disciplines and age groups. It is, perhaps, at its best in computerised adaptive testing where questions change with and mould to the test taker's ability level (Lord, 1980).

While Classical Test and Item Response Theories compete for psychologists' and statisticians' attentions, *Generalisability* – or *G – Theory* is now staking its claim. In the 1960s another Swiss psychologist, Jean Cardinet, began to explore the specificity and generalisability of data (Cardinet, 1975). G Theory looks at the reliability of measures under specific conditions.

In practice, generalisability allows researchers to explore what would happen if aspects of a psychometric investigation were altered. For example, an opinion poll company could now discover whether assessments of voting intention varied much depending on whether 10, 100, 1,000 or 1,000,000 politically active adults were interviewed. Implications for time and money are plain.

These advancements may not be as clear-cut as they first appear. Classical Test Theory still tends to dominate psychometrics. Most instruments remain norm-based, with comparisons between norms fraught with unreliability. Similarly the most popular statistical packages still present and prepare data in ways, and to standards, that Charles Spearman would recognise. So what of the instruments themselves?

TOOLS FOR THE JOB

The first modern psychometric instruments measured intelligence. Probably the best-known of its type was the Binet–Simon IQ test. At the end of the nineteenth century the French Government introduced universal education. Significantly underperforming children were categorised as *sick* and removed to asylums for their own welfare (Nicolas, Andrieu, Croizet, Sanitioso & Burman, 2013). In 1899, working with Théodore Simon, a psychologist and psychometrician, Alfred Binet looked to develop a way of identifying 'slow' rather than sick children, so that they could be placed in special education programmes instead of being separated from society (Avanzini, 1999).

By testing a wide range of children across many measures, Binet and Simon developed a baseline of intelligence. Their original goal was to find one, clear indicator of intelligence, of general mental excellence. In this, they failed. Instead children were compared within categories and age groups (Fancher & Rutherford, 2012). Binet and Simon were able to set common levels of achievements, and from here developed benchmarks for high and low achievers. They produced a portable, generalisable test that is still in use in modified form today. This categorisation of intelligence within the Binet–Simon test (which became the Stanford–Binet test in 1916) may be seen in Table 1.1 in both its present and its original classification (Bain & Allin, 2005).

Table 1.1 *Stanford–Binet IQ classification 2015 versus final Binet–Simon IQ classification 1916*

Stanford–Binet (2015) IQ range	IQ classification	Binet–Simon (1916) IQ range	IQ classification
145–160	Very gifted or highly advanced		
130–144	Gifted or very advanced	Above 140	Near genius or genius
120–129	Superior	120–140	Very superior intelligence
110–119	High average	110–120	Superior intelligence
90–109	Average	90–110	Normal, or average, intelligence
80–89	Low average	80–90	Dullness, rarely classifiable as feeble-mindedness
70–79	Borderline impaired or delayed	70–80	Border-line deficiency, sometimes classifiable as dullness, often as feeble-mindedness
55–69	Mildly impaired or delayed	Below 70	Definite feeble-mindedness

There is a distinct problem in comparing IQ scores across even a few decades. By convention, the average IQ score is set to 100. When tests are revised – as good practice demands – a new cohort of people take the test. Because of the passage of time, new test takers tend to be from younger generations than their predecessors. In almost every case new average scores are significantly above 100 and means have to be revised (Flynn, 2009). The average rate of increase seems to be about three IQ points per decade in the Western world (Marks, 2010). In other words, an average person sitting the 1916 Binet-Simon IQ test in the year 2016 would register a true score of 130.

So, given the apparent growth in intelligence, average members from the Binet– Simon IQ test in 1916 would be 'borderline impaired' compared to today's average cohort (see the scales and labels shown in Table 1.1). Meanwhile, Napoleon Bonaparte and Benjamin Franklin must have had IQs that would barely challenge a modern Border collie. It is not difficult to see that there may be a slight flaw in this logic!

Better nutrition is a popular explanation for rising intelligence scores. However, given that what constitutes good nutrition is debatable – and that today's diet is probably too fat- and sugar-rich compared to that of earlier generations – this explanation does not fit the evidence well (Marks, 2010). Similarly, longer school careers may account for some but far from all the variation (Flynn, 2009).

Perhaps the answer lies with modern humans' familiarity with everyday quiz type documents. This means that as a whole we are more *au fait* with conundrums in general and with dealing with abstract notions in particular (Mackintosh, 2011). Mackintosh's argument also helps to account for large cultural variations in test performance which are largely ironed out with time and exposure (Dickens & Flynn, 2002).

PSYCHOMETRICS, WAR AND A PEACETIME DIVIDEND

As with invention so with psychometrics; war is a great driver of innovation. The recruitment of men for the Great War was so inept as to have been a potentially significant contributory factor to desertion, shell shock and slaughter (Mazower, 1999). It was the Americans who tested their soldiers for IQ in 1917 using Army Alpha and Beta tests (for literate and illiterate soldiers respectively). Plotting IQ and literacy against suitability may have been coarse, but it was an improvement on what the British, French and – before the war at least – the Germans had done. It is argued that it was the Americans and their new strategies that helped bring the First World War to a speedier conclusion than would otherwise have been the case (Mead 2000).

Putting, as far as possible, the right soldiers into challenging conditions was a maxim employed by the Duke of Wellington, forgotten by the technologically reliant Victorians and then rediscovered during the Second World War, which saw greatly increased psychological intervention (Reid, 1997). The American Army and Navy General Classification Tests (AGCT and NGCT respectively) replaced the Army Alpha and Beta tests used on the Western Front over 20 years earlier. As a consequence aptitude replaced literacy as a deployment device. The new psychometrics used a broad spectrum of applied psychology to drill into individuals' personalities and to test mental acuity. Data from these psychological tools were used to improve instruction and training. Today the US armed forces use the multiple-choice Armed Services Vocational Aptitude Battery (ASVAB), originally introduced in 1968. The ASVAB features written and computerised tasks, which test talent across a range of ten disciplines including mechanical acuity, electronics, mathematics and English (Hogan & Cannon, 2007).

Over the past century, the British armed forces have moved forward at different speeds. The army lagged behind both the senior and junior services during the world wars, when new recruits were subjected to the most basic training. The Navy, however, insisted on finding skilled seamen, while the Royal Air Force (initially the Royal Flying Corps) has always used challenging recruitment regimes which include physical, mental and intelligence checks (Ballantyne & Povah, 2004).

When National Service was abolished in the UK in 1960, military recruitment standards were tightened and made more rigorous. Today the Army Recruiting and Training Directorate

(ARTD) has an estimated annual budget of approximately £700m with which to enlist candidates and train all ranks. The British Army Recruit Battery (BARB) test is a psychometric array to match the American model. It is designed to steer recruits towards their most suitable roles and predict 'trainability'. Candidates who pass BARB are interviewed, after which those who pass the interview face a two-day assessment centre at an Army Development and Selection Centre (ADSC) (Reid, 1997). And what is an assessment centre? For that we need to turn the other side of the trenches and look at the defeated forces of Kaiser Wilhelm II.

Assessment centres date back to the aftermath of World War I when Germany, now a republic, decided to select its serving officers differently. In 1914 the German officer class had been drawn from the ranks of the nobility, which by the early 1920s had become a more restricted and less trusted elite (Ballantyne & Povah, 2004). The army was only allowed to enlist men for twelve years of service and was restricted in size. It therefore needed to pick the most able, promising candidates. Step forward German psychologist Dr Wolfgang Simoneit, who developed novel methods of identifying the best candidates.

Under Simoneit's aegis the army looked for four major attributes: leadership, adaptability across different situations, mental perspicacity and the ability to work as part of a team (Morgan, 1955). Simoneit developed a range of techniques, the application of which allowed him to judge how well candidates displayed selected competencies.

Everything an applicant said or did was – in theory at last – linked to a competency area. So aspirant officers were exposed to stresses they might face in the field, such as imagined provision shortages, poor communications, even the deaths of key command personnel supposedly killed in action. Would candidates be able to extract the facts from a reticent colleague during a role play? Could they present their ideas cogently to a forceful senior officer, and how did they interact with their peers?

Simoneit had a team of fellow assessors who would compare their opinions of the knowledge, skills, abilities and attitudes displayed. How did men's personalities alter under stress? Did they show more, or less, intelligence when the pressure was on? Were these people trustworthy, capable and inspirational (Morgan, 1955)?

MOVING FORWARD, MIND THE SNAKE OIL

From its ancient origins, psychometrics has been fired in the ovens of war and now proliferates in business. At the top end of the recruitment market, AT&T was one of the first commercial organisations to take up the idea of military-style recruitment in the 1950s. Today the big four accountancy firms make extensive use of psychological analysis within their businesses: 80 per cent of managerial recruitments across the Fortune 500 and FTSE 100 companies depend on psychometric tools, while 68 per cent of *all* employers in Western Europe and the USA now use some form of psychometric assessment as part of their recruitment and development processes (Sponton & Wright, 2009). This growth seems likely to continue. Given increasingly esoteric job roles, the need to uncover the latent talents will call for ever more forensic examination of characteristics, preferences and ability (Cook & Cripps, 2005).

But beware.

Personality and ability assessment depend upon instruments being both reliable and valid. Your wristwatch may be reliable but it is not a valid tool with which to measure your personality. Meanwhile a questionnaire drawn up on the back of an envelope after a discussion with colleagues is likely to be neither reliable nor valid. Validity means that an instrument is consistent and actually measures that which it is supposed to measure.

Many excellent organisations can provide such tools. Companies such as SHL (formerly Saville and Holdsworth Limited), Psytech and ECCOS offer tools of significant worth. Meanwhile bodies like the American and British Psychological Societies maintain the standards required to apply and interpret psychometric data to a high level.

However, the market remains unregulated. Dear reader, you yourself could jot down 40 questions about work, based on your own experience, and publish your list tomorrow, calling it, for the sake of argument, the *Crawchester Psychometric Inventory (or CraPI)*. You could develop your own scoring index, hire a glossy publisher and produce a good-looking, saleable but entirely spurious instrument that lacks market research, science and statistical support. It would be unreliable and invalid. And it would be one of many such tools on the market.

An invalid psychometric instrument is business poison, whereas a good psychometric is a litmus test. Valid psychometric tools used together can significantly improve recruitment, assessment and development. For this we owe a good many thanks to those Ancient Greeks.

REFERENCES

Avanzini, G. (1999). *Alfred Binet*. Paris: Presses Universitaires de France.

Bain, S. K. & Allin, J. D. (2005). Book review: Stanford–Binet intelligence scales, fifth edition. *Journal of Psychoeducational Assessment*, 23, 87–95.

Ballantyne, I. & Povah, N. (2004). *Assessment and development centres* (2nd edn). Aldershot: Gower.

Buss, D. M. & Schmitt, D. P. (2011). Evolutionary psychology and feminism. *Sex Roles*, 64(9–10), 768–87.

Cardinet, J. (1975). International Test Commission: Application of the Liège recommendations for the period 1971–4. *International Review of Applied Psychology*, 2(1), 11–16.

Carlyle, T. (1841). *Heroes, hero-worship, and the heroic in history*. London: James Fraser.

Carpenter, S. K. (2005). Some neglected contributions of Wilhelm Wundt to the psychology of memory. *Psychological Reports*, 97, 63–73.

Childs, G. (2009). *Understand your temperament*. New York: Rudolf Steiner.

Cook, M. & Cripps, B. D. (2005). *Psychological assessment in the workplace: A manager's guide*. Chichester: John Wiley.

Darwin, C. (1859). *The origin of species*. London: John Murray.

Dickens, W. T. & Flynn, J. R. (2002). The IQ paradox: Still resolved. *Psychological Review*, 109, 764–71.

Fancher, R. E. & Rutherford, A. (2012). *Pioneers of psychology*. New York: W. W. Norton & Company.

Flynn, J. R. (2009). *What is intelligence? Beyond the Flynn effect*. Cambridge: Cambridge University Press.

Gacano, C. B. & Reid, M. J. (1994). *The Rorschach assessment of aggressive and psychopathic personalities*. Hillsdale, NJ: Lawrence Erlbaum.

Galton, F. (1869). *Hereditary genius*. London: Macmillan.

Haney, B., Sirbasku, J. & McCann, D. (2011). *Leadership charisma*. Waco, TX: S & H Publishing.

Hardman, D. (2009). *Judgment and decision making: Psychological perspectives*. Hoboken, NJ: Wiley-Blackwell.

Haslam, S. A. (2004). *Psychology in organizations: The social identity approach* (2nd edn). Thousand Oaks, CA: Sage Publications.

Hogan, T. P. & Cannon, B. (2007). *Psychological testing: A practical introduction*. Hoboken, NJ: John Wiley & Sons.

Lord, F. M. (1980). *Applications of item response theory to practical testing problems*. Mahwah, NJ: Erlbaum.

Mackintosh, N. J. (2011). *IQ and human intelligence*. Oxford: Oxford University Press.

Marks, D. F. (2010). IQ variations across time, race, and nationality: An artefact of differences in literacy skills. *Psychological Reports*, 106, 643–64.

Mazower, M. (1999). *Dark continent: Europe's twentieth century*. London: Penguin.

Mead, G. (2000). The doughboys: America and the First World War. London: Penguin.

Michell, J. (1997). Quantitative science and the definition of measurement in psychology. *British Journal of Psychology*, 88, 355–83.

Morgan, W. J. (1955). *Spies and saboteurs*. London: Victor Gollancz.

Nicolas, S., Andrieu, B., Croizet, J.-C., Sanitioso, R. B. & Burman, J. T. (2013). Sick? Or slow? On the origins of intelligence as a psychological object. *Intelligence*, 41(5), 699–711.

Novick, M. R. (1966). The axioms and principal results of classical test theory. *Journal of Mathematical Psychology*, 3, 1–18.

Personalitypage.com (2015). *Portrait of an ENTJ*. https://www.personalitypage.com/ENTJ.html. Accessed 13 August 2015.

Pittenger, D. J. (1993). Measuring the MBTI … and coming up short. *Journal of Career Planning and Employment*, 54, 48–52.

Reid, B. H. (1997). *Military power: Land warfare in theory and practice*. London: Frank Cass.

Singh, S. & Ernst, E. (2008). *Trick or treatment: Alternative treatment on trial*. New York: W.W. Norton.

Sipps, G. J., Alexander, R. A. & Friedt, L. (1985). Item analysis of the Myers–Briggs Type Indicator. *Educational and Psychological Measurement*, 45, 789–96.

Sponton, J. & Wright, S. (2009). *Management assessment centres pocketbook*. Alresford: Management Pocketbooks.

Szondi, L., Moser, U. & Webb, M. W. (1959). *The Szondi Test in diagnosis, prognosis, and treatment*. Philadelphia, PA: J. B. Lippincott.

Uebersax, J. S. (1999). Probit latent class analysis: Conditional independence and conditional dependence models. *Applied Psychological Measurementt*, 23(4), 283–97.

Wolman, B. B. (1968). *Historical roots of contemporary psychology*. New York: Harper & Row.

Wood, J. M., Nezworski, M. T., Lilienfeld, S. O. & Garb, H. N. (2003). The Rorschach Inkblot Test, fortune tellers, and cold reading. *Skeptical Inquirer*, 27(4), 23–8.

2 Ride the Horse Around the Course: Triangulating Nomothetic and Idiographic Approaches to Personality Assessment

Barry Cripps

RATIONALE

This chapter discusses three theoretical positions of personality enquiry contributed by Hans Eysenck, Carl Jung and George Kelly, and the three accompanying personality instruments which follow and have been developed from their work.

In my practice as a psychologist, I work with clients in the field of 'performance psychology', a term I coined some 30 years ago.

My work supports clients by helping them manage the challenges and difficulties that they experience when they are doing their job in management, the arts or sport, and helping them make the necessary changes in order to move on to achieve successful performance outcomes. By 'performance' I mean virtually any human act, generally in front of others, such as overcoming stage nerves, passing the driving test, surviving a stressful (usually temporary) event, overcoming a phobia, conquering exam nerves, competing in sport at any level, relationship issues, recovery from injury in sport, and managing anxiety induced by an individual set of self-perceptions.

I like to work with my clients in a series, usually three or four, of brief one-to-one therapy consultations in my rooms.

As part of initial 'history taking' and opening rapport, I adopt a triangulation approach of applying three psychometric instruments, and use the analysis in discussion with the client to gain knowledge and formulate an agreed therapeutic protocol from which to proceed. 'One test good, three tests better' (apologies to George Orwell).

The approaches I have chosen with which to assess clients in the early stages of a consultation follow two traditions in psychology: a normative, nomothetic approach using two personality instruments, and an idiographic, one-to-one, in-depth, personal construct approach. In psychometric terms I take three pictures of my client from three entirely different positions in order to open up rapport and formulate a way forward.

According to Rom Harré (2006, p. 181), James Thomas Lamiell succinctly reveals 'the conceptual confusions and logical fallacies in the way these [personality research] issues were resolved by mainstream psychologists in the 20th century'.

Harré points out that the distinction between idiographic and nomothetic styles in research was first made in 1898, by Windelband (1898[1998]). 'In a nomothetic approach we seek general laws applicable to all.... In the idiographic approach we seek adequate descriptions of individuals in all their particularity. It is important to realize that though we may make use only of concepts applicable to all people, they may be present in unique degree or form in each person' (Harré, 2006, p. 181). Any confusion between the two is possibly due to the distinction between Gordon Allport's 'common attributes', for example body height, which is common to all, and average height or the 'average property'. A group of people share the common attribute of body height but no single member need have that average height.

My first, normative, nomothetic approach looks at my client and the way that he or she fits onto the map drawn by the test constructor Eysenck, Cook, Cripps, Occupational Scales (ECCOS), a trait measure adapted from the internationally respected Eysenck Personality Scales (Eysenck & Eysenck, 1991). The second approach looks at the way my client fits onto the map drawn by the Myers–Briggs Type Indicator, derived from Jung's Theory of Type, a type measure of personality.

The third, idiographic approach, via George Kelly's Personal Construct Psychology, looks at how my client makes sense of their world and personally interprets events, drawing their *own map* and laying out their own hierarchical set of personal constructs.

So initially, when working with a client, I take three pictures, as it were three snapshots, one inspecting personality traits, the second looking at the personality type and the third looking at how my client constructs their reality and interprets their personal world via a Repertory Grid. The combination of history taking and psychometric analysis provides, in my opinion, a sound psychometric base for us to move forward.

I offer now a critique of some of the theories underpinning both the chosen psychometric approaches and instruments and the rationale for their use.

Theory in psychology provides the foundation for exploration and testing of ideas, and evidence to support those ideas that lead to the advancement of the science of psychology. Researchers never prove a theory; in psychological science there is no such phenomenon as proof. Researchers in the field merely add their findings to support hypotheses constructed to demonstrate the efficacy of the underlying theoretical perspective. Theory is tested via the scientific method – 'the road to developing a successful psychology' (Kline, 1998, p. 3) – but, as on many other journeys in science, that road is not smooth.

One way to find out about people is to ask them, but in order to do this we need a common language and one such common language is, in short, the language of the subject of this book, psychometric testing. In summary, if we want to find out about the personality of a person we can ask them to describe themselves via the language of psychometrics or via inspection of their personal constructs.

There is a considerable body of theory underpinning psychometric testing in all its forms; theorists and researchers abound. Enquiries into mental states of intelligence, ability, personality and many other human attributes go back hundreds, indeed thousands, of years. Craig Knight takes his look at the history of psychometrics in Chapter 1.

'It is a little-known fact that psychometrics as a science began in Cambridge between 1886 and 1889. The first laboratory dedicated to the subject was set up within the Cavendish Physics

Laboratory in the University of Cambridge by James McKeen Cattell (not R. B. [Cattell]!) in 1887' (Rust, 2008).

Hans Eysenck wrote in 1967, 'Attempts to measure intelligence have passed through several stages since Galton tried to use the measurement of sensory processes to arrive at an estimate of the subjects intellectual level (1883), and McKeen Cattell (1890) employed tests of muscular strength, speed of movement, sensitivity to pain, reaction time and the like for a similar purpose. These largely abortive efforts were followed by the first stage of intelligence measurement properly so called; it may with truth be labelled the *"g"* phase because both Spearman (1904) and Binet and Simon (1905) stressed the importance of a *general factor of intellectual ability*, Binet contributing mainly by the construction of test items and the invention of the concept of mental age, Spearman contributing mainly by the application of correlational methods and the invention of factor analysis' (Eysenck, 1967, p. 81).

It is reasonably clear to participants what we are testing when we ask them to complete a test of numerical or verbal ability. Each item, for example 'What number is the next in this series, 1, 3, 5, 7 …', clearly identifies the intentions of the test user in a totally transparent way. Each test item identifies a level of cognitive processing or a mental ability of the participant with respect to understanding number and measuring numerical ability. The test results from each participant can be ranked on a scale identifying those who score more highly than others. Assumptions are then made that the highest scorer has the highest level of numerical ability, and so it is possible to compare people, for example to identify high scorers and low scorers. So it is then that ability tests will discriminate between people, those who can and those who can't. In practice there is a great leap of faith as we next assume that high scorers will perform more effectively in the workplace than low scorers. The leap of faith is that test results will automatically transfer to productivity behaviour, a huge leap indeed and another story for another time!

The classic trio of verbal ability, numerical ability, and diagrammatic reasoning measuring spatial ability has been captured by test constructors and used by occupational psychologists for many years for the various purposes of general assessment, selection, development, promotion boards and so on. The results of these tests are matched against a job analysis; how much of these abilities are required in the particular job becomes one of the yardsticks in decision making. The assumption is made that those test takers who perform well on a test of ability will also perform well when sitting at their desk in the workplace. Ability test results are often claimed to be the most useful and valid metric for predicting future performance.

Ability test constructors take a psychometric approach using statistics, means and standard deviations in order that test users can compare participants (normatively) in order to make HR decisions; results are calculated according to the curve of normal distribution and the law of error, thus following a nomothetic tradition.

With regard to testing per se, gauging a participant's ability to answer a question correctly, to 'test' them as described above, is not what all psychometric tests do. We can't say that a personality or motivation questionnaire is necessarily a 'test' of personality or motivation in the same way that an ability test is a test of ability, for they are measuring totally different attributes. It is obvious that when a participant scores more highly on a test of numerical ability their score is 'better' than a participant's whose score is lower. However, it cannot be said when measuring, say, extraversion that someone who scores more highly on that scale is a better extravert than someone who scores lower. Personality scales, although they may record higher or lower scores out of 10 (sten scores, from 'Standard Ten'), do not rest on the same assumptions as ability scales.

Personality instruments are often not as transparent to the test taker as cognitive ability tests. Because of the complexity of analysing the responses in a personality questionnaire, screening out the personal bias of the analyst and being aware that a person's score may vary over time and even over the time of day are potential pitfalls. That old chestnut 'error of measurement' also comes to the fore in both ability and personality instruments. Because people will not sit still for long enough to be measured, observed results differ from one moment to the next.

Computer analysis of results and subsequent computer-written reports can remove the subjective bias of the analyst. However, computer-written reports are often guilty of a rather anodyne, 'one size fits all' approach.

When sitting a test of, say, verbal ability, the participant is quite aware of what attribute is being tested, or looked for; such transparency is self-evident. Ability tests are very difficult to fake; indeed there is no point in trying to fake, as the participant's answer is either right or wrong. Personality inventories on the other hand are more open to faking via impression management; that is, the participant may give socially desirable responses in order to present themselves as what they judge to be the personality fit required by the selectors. Although items in personality questionnaires are not transparent in the same way as items in ability instruments, the participant can usually see through them or attempt to understand what aspects of their personality are being uncovered. We can imagine the unconscious battles going on in a test taker's thinking when trying to outguess, or give the perfect desired response, in order to secure the job. It is possible to fake, lie or give socially desirable responses in a personality measure. Personality test constructors are up to this challenge and generally have means at their disposal to minimise faking.

It would seem then that personality is a much more complex attribute to measure than ability. So perhaps a better term to use with respect to personality is 'exploration'. 'Personality exploration' is hardly a marketable term and so 'personality test' or 'questionnaire' is perhaps more appropriate, and that is what they are called in common parlance.

A personality questionnaire is a perfectly sound mechanism for exploring personality, but it is essential to involve the participant during the feedback of results if only for confirmation or disconfirmation of results that are, in the same way as ability tests, subject to the laws of error. In the early stages of consultation with my client it helps open rapport, and above all build trust, to discuss the results of whatever personality questionnaire is used.

Personality instruments generally look at personality traits or types which can be related to possible behaviour in the workplace, and so can't really be called tests. The relationship between personality and behaviour is of course tenuous. Personality is more 'what we are' and behaviour 'how we act or what we do', and the links, if any, are contextual and situational.

Personality questionnaires and ability tests are as different as chalk and cheese, but they are both classed as psychometric tests.

The scores on a numerical test under normal testing conditions are, ipso facto, reasonably stable and not contextually dependent, whereas scale scores on a personality instrument can be mood- and situationally dependent. Personality questionnaires face the unalterable fact that 'people will not stand still long enough to be measured'.

Scale scores on all instruments should be regarded as expectations or hypotheses and subject to movement. Psychometricians allow for this movement of course in their calculations of the standard error of measurement, a statistical term used to explain the fact that the observed score in all tests can vary from day to day and even by the time of day.

During the recommended 20-minute feedback discussion the participant should therefore be given to understand that, although their scores can vary from day to day and by time of day, their score on that day or at that time, the score we see in front of us, is the 'observed score'. Their 'true score' is a theoretical entity only.

Tests of ability and normative personality questionnaires, because they are measuring human attributes, obey the law of common error. Personality scales, for example Extraversion–Introversion, are often produced with the use of statistics – generally factor analysis – to fit the participant onto the test constructor's scale according to the normal distribution. It matters not whether the test constructor's name is Binet, Cattell, Eysenck or Saville, the test taker fits themselves onto the test constructor's map. There are as many maps as there are cartographers, and there are as many test scales as there are test constructors.

Up to this point in my discussion of the approaches to test construction, whether the tests are of ability or personality they all obey the general law of error and so are nomothetic. The participant is fitted onto the scale produced by the test constructor or, in Hans Eysenck's most appropriate observation, onto the 'bed of Procrustes', but hopefully not as painfully!

The distinction between idiographic studies (one person at a time in depth) and nomothetic studies (abstracting commonalities from a population) was well known to Eysenck. Certainly his own, laboratory-tested, psychophysiological theory of personality, confirmed via confirmatory factor analysis, led to the development of his internationally recognised Eysenck Personality Questionnaire.

The psychophysiological theory of the Eysencks largely concerns the Extraversion–Introversion and Stability–Neuroticism orthogonal dimensions. The Eysencks demonstrated and confirmed the presence of E-I and S-N via laboratory experimentation and factor analysis. The P-Psychoticism or Tough-minded, Lie or Social Desirability scales formed part of the 1975 EPQ. Impulsiveness, Venturesomeness and Empathy (IVE) scales, described in the late 1970s, were published in the Eysenck Personality Scales (EPQ-Revised IVE) (Eysenck, H. J. & Eysenck, S. B. G., 1991). With respect to the psychiatric nature of the terms used by Eysenck in the original manual of the Eysenck Personality Scales, i.e. the terms 'neuroticism' and 'psychoticism', Eysenck comments on page 6 of the Manual of the Eysenck Personality Scales, 'we have suggested that in the interests of communication with users who are not familiar with the underlying theory the terms "neuroticism" and "psychoticism" be dropped, and the terms "emotionality" and "tough mindedness" be substituted'. Similarly with respect to the renaming of the Lie Scale as 'social desirability', the authors Cook and Cripps (Cook, Cripps, Eysenck & Eysenck, 2007) took it upon themselves to call this scale 'social desirability' in line with the scale naming then current in other instruments.

In their attempt to link personality dimensions with the main body of experimental and theoretical psychology, the Eysencks (Eysenck, H. J. & Eysenck, S. B. G., 1991) looked closely at Extraversion and Neuroticism (otherwise emotionality or stability–instability), both closely related to the inherited degree of lability of the autonomic nervous system. Eaves, Eysenck and Martin (1988) suggested that genetic factors contribute more to individual differences in personality than do environmental ones.

Extraversion, according to Eaves, Eysenck and Martin, 'is closely related to the degree of excitation and inhibition prevalent in the central nervous system; this balance … is largely inherited (Eaves, Eysenck, Martin 1988), and may be mediated by the ascending reticular formation (Eysenck 1967)' (Eysenck, H. J. & Eysenck, S. B. G., 1991, p. 3).

Deductions have been made from general and experimental psychology regarding the expected behaviour of extraverted and introverted participants in a great variety of laboratory experimental investigations. A summary of this work is given in H. J. Eysenck and M. W. Eysenck (1985).

The methodology, the use of underlying psycho-physiological theory as demonstrated in laboratory studies by the Eysencks to identify the presence of personality traits, and the employment of confirmatory factor analysis to validate them, are scientifically robust and unique. Most other researchers have not, however, been as methodically thorough in their enquiries designed to uncover personality traits. Capitalising on the Eysencks' discoveries, other test constructors have largely omitted scientific laboratory work and moved forward to employ exploratory factor analysis and correlation to derive and produce unnamed scales, adopting a purely psychometric and statistical approach.

Count and Bowles (1964, p. 99) comment that 'applying statistical techniques respectively to a sampling of simplex units and to a sampling of complex units is two different things. ... A correlation coefficient is a confession of ignorance. The magnitudes of two statistical quantities are found to vary somewhat regularly and, concomitantly. ... [This] suggests quantitatively a putative relationship; the explanation still lies ahead, unprobed. In the social sciences, too often such quantifications abet the illusion of more result than actually is there. A statistical agnosticism is no valid substitute for hypothesis and theorem.'

The Eysenck Personality Questionnaire (EPQ) has been revised and developed from earlier personality questionnaires: the Maudsley Medical Questionnaire (Eysenck, 1952), the Maudsley Personality Inventory (Eysenck, 1959), the EPI (Eysenck & Eysenck, 1964), and finally the Eysenck Personality Scales (EPS Adult) (Eysenck, H. J. & Eysenck, S. B. G., 1991). As indicated above, the EPS Adult or EPQ Revised-IVE added the P or Psychoticism (renamed Tough–tender-mindedness), Impulsiveness, Venturesomeness, Empathy and Lie/Social Desirability scales.

The main application of the Eysenckian instruments has been in the clinical, educational and industrial fields.

S. B. G. Eysenck, Cripps and Cook (2007) have produced the Eysenck, Cripps, Cook, Occupational Scales, now available as ECCOS Online, a version developed from the EPQ-Revised (1991) for the occupational domain.

What it is important to point out in this critical view of psychometric testing is the difference in structure between Eysenck's measures (i.e., psycho-physiological plus confirmatory factor analysis) and the literally hundreds of other instruments purporting to measure personality using artefactual factors derived solely from concepts teased out by exploratory factor analysis.

In summary, the reason for my choice of the Eysenckian models to assess the personality of my clients in the early days of an intervention is that they are based on sound psycho-physiological scientific enquiry first, followed by rigorous confirmatory factor analysis. The latter statistical factor-analytic procedures bring ECCOS into line with the normative, nomothetic traditions of trait measures of personality, the first leg of the assessment triangle.

The normative psychometric approach to the study of personality looks to compare an individual with the traits or dimensions common to everyone, as discussed above, following general laws. As has already been stated, this is a nomothetic approach. In the past 30 years a growing consensus has begun to reduce the number of trait scales down to five, known as the 'Big 5' (or the Five Factor Model (FFM)): extraversion, agreeableness, conscientiousness, emotional stability and openness to experience, explored by Peter Saville in 1984 and expressed in the Pentagon instrument by Saville and Holdsworth Ltd. ('The Pentagon model measured five scales and was possibly the first dedicated measure of the Big Five factors of personality, pre-dating Costa and McCrae's NEO-PI-R by a year. The Octagon, Factor and Concept versions of the OPQ, (the Occupational Personality Questionnaire developed by Peter Saville and others at Saville and Holdsworth Ltd) measured respectively 8, 16 and 30 scales.' 'Peter Saville' in Wikipedia; accessed 18 November, 2016.)

Peter Saville (personal communication) factor-analysed the 16PF in his PhD thesis (Saville, 1977). He used the Promax rotation method on a general-population, specially sampled group of British Adults, tested in their own homes (N=2,000). R. B. Cattell gave it 'lavish praise' (he wrote that it was the best standardisation he had encountered, even by American standards). The Big 5 factors emerged then – not 9 as Paul Kline later wrote. The thesis provides good support for the idea that the 16PF could be broadly described by the Five Factor Model. Furthermore, George Sik and Saville (1992) did 'further work on factoring 32 facets of personality of the OPQ on a further large industrial sample and found that Drive/Ambition emerged as a 6th factor. This has been found by other authorities like L. Hough in the USA. We published this solution as the successor to Pentagon and called it "Images"' (Saville, personal communication).

However, since then it has come to be believed that these factor-analytic methods have tended to underestimate the number of personality factors. For example, Extraversion is now commonly broken down into Affiliation and Dominance, and Conscientiousness into Detailed Conscious and Drive. So although the FFM is nowadays seen as a very useful overarching academic taxonomy it is not the best predictive taxonomy. 'Facets' or subdivisions of the FFM seem to predict better in the workplace as discussed later by McRae and Costa (1987).

From the nomothetic standpoint the Big 5 are considered by some to sufficiently describe the main traits, facets and aspects of any personality.

The first main approach by instruments in personality psychometrics such as 16PF measures 'traits'. A personality trait could be, simply, anxious, sociable or aggressive. The second main classification of personality is found in instruments that cluster traits together into broad personality types. These include measures such as the Myers–Briggs Type Indicator, which follows the ideas of Carl Jung in his theory of type.

To quote from the MBTI manual (Myers & McCaulley, 1985, p. 1) 'The MBTI is based on Jung's ideas about perception and judgement, and the attitudes (or orientations towards life) in which these are used in different types of people.' And further, 'The purpose of the Myers-Briggs Type Indicator (MBTI) is to make the theory of psychological types described by C. Jung (1921/1971) understandable and useful in people's lives. The essence of the theory is that much seemingly random variation in behavior is actually quite orderly and consistent, being due to basic differences in the way individuals prefer to use their perception and judgment' (ibid.). The Theory of Type after Jung is interpreted by the MBTI as expressing the specific dynamic relationships between the scales leading to the descriptions and characteristics of 16 'types'. A clone of the MBTI published by Psytech International, the Jung Type Indicator (Psytech International, 2008) similarly uses participants' preferences to place them within a combination of Extravert and Introvert, Sensing and Intuition, Thinking and Feeling, Judgement and Perception, leading to the construction of 16 type categories.

Administering and analysing a Type measure becomes the second leg of my assessment triangulation of clients and presents an entirely different picture from that of the normative trait measure.

At the other extreme of trait and type descriptions, Gordon Allport (1937) found over 18,000 separate terms describing personal characteristics. While some of these are common traits (that could be investigated nomothetically) the majority, in Allport's view, referred to more or less unique dispositions based on life experiences peculiar to ourselves. He argues that they cannot be effectively studied using standardised tests, that is through trait and type psychometric instruments. What is needed, Allport suggested, is a way of investigating them idiographically.

The psychologist who developed a unique method of doing this was George Kelly (1955) with his role construct repertory grid. The idiographic approach to testing in contrast to a nomothetic approach is self referential, purely ipsative and derived usually from the completion of a repertory grid. Kelly's role construct repertory grid and its methodology follow the theoretical paradigm of Personal Construct Theory.

Rom Harré (2006, p. 62) comments that Kelly was a psychologist 'whose declared aim was to bring a "new psychology" to life. ... Kelly saw himself in opposition not only to Freud's psychodynamics but also to the way that the psychology of individuals had been deleted from the project of a scientific psychology. He came to favour idiographic enquiries over nomothetic methods. He tried to restore the study of individual people against the prevalent focus on the extraction of general trends from statistical data', and further says that 'Kelly was almost brutally sidelined from the mainstream of American psychology. *The Psychology of Personal Constructs* must be one of the most important "unread" books in the history of the subject. It is a treasure house of sophisticated observations on the philosophy of science, as well as a subtle and carefully delineated presentation of a "new psychology of the person".'

The Rep Grid, as it is commonly known, is a quantitative method of expressing qualitative personal constructs, or ways of interpreting our personal world. It converts the participant's constructs about their world into a hierarchical order, potentially opening up discussion between psychologist and participant. Because of the unique way each of us constructs our reality, analysis of personality via an idiographic approach does not permit comparison between people.

Fransella and Bannister (1977, p. 5) note that 'Kelly devised repertory grid technique as a method for exploring personal construct systems. It is an attempt to stand in others' shoes, to see their world as they see it, to understand their situation, their concerns.' They continue, 'Kelly believed that we strive to makes sense out of our universe, out of ourselves, out of the particular situation we encounter. To this end each of us invents and re-invents an implicit theoretical framework which, be it well or badly designed, is our personal construct system.'

Thus, the Repertory Grid is completely self-referential, ipsative and personal, measuring the way we interpret the world and construct our own reality. Standard psychometric personality tests ask us to register our responses on the scales produced by the test designer, that is, to place ourselves on the personality map drawn by the test constructor. Responses to Kelly's repertory grid are entirely different; here the participant draws their own map, a map in the 'range of convenience', as Kelly calls it, a repertoire of personal values, attitudes, beliefs, feelings about others.

CONCLUSION

Having now over 30 years' experience of working with people in psychology and starting by measuring their personality, I maintain that, by analysing participants' responses to a trait instrument, a type instrument and an idiographic technique, I can explore my client/participant in depth. I feel that after taking down their history by triangulating their personality using reliable and valid measures I can usually begin to help them resolve those issues that have put them into my consulting or training room, whether in the arts, industry, education or sport, and furthermore that in discussion with my client I can gauge their suitability for a particular work post in a selection exercise, give support and insight in a team exercise and further support their goals in a personal development, counselling and coaching situation. In these three ways I, as a test user, can more fully calculate whether further investment in this particular participant will benefit the individual, the company or organisation sponsoring the testing enquiry. I rather like the film analogy of a one-frame snapshot view of a person versus a much longer movie.

Whatever test, method or technique psychologists and those in HR use to help make decisions about the future, the main question in my view is one of ethics: how is the instrument being analysed, interpreted and fed back ethically to all involved? To use a motor car analogy, it is possible to drive one of the best cars in the world, such as a Rolls Royce, very badly.

Of course, psychometric testing is not the be-all and end-all solution to HR decisions about applicants in the workplace. The BPS Psychometric Test Centre recommends that tests are used together with as much other data about participants as possible: application form, track record, CV, assessment centre exercises (as many as 6–8 exercises) and so on. Utility analysis demonstrates that a thorough selection procedure that includes psychometric testing can pay for itself six times over in the first year. 'Failure to select the right employees, by contrast, goes on costing the employer money year after year' (Cook & Cripps, 2005, p. 260).

As a consultant working with managers in industry, actors in the theatre and athletes in sport and exercise psychology, I include psychometric testing in my initial history taking with clients in order to offer indications about formulating their development. I will usually take three pictures of my client, looking at their personality through three different-coloured lenses, as it were. I describe this process fully in Appendix 1, 'Triangulation: A case study illustration of the personal development of an equestrian'.

My case has been put as a psychologist working with people generally one to one. Psychometric testing, because of its truly scientific background and when applied skilfully, is a most valuable technique in my kitbag. It allows my client and me to open up a conversation and work on easily understood common ground leading towards the resolution of client issues and hopefully a predictable increase in performance outcomes. Psychometric testing using a triangulated approach following a trait, a type and an idiographic protocol is a good friend to us both.

REFERENCES

Allport, G. W. (1937). *Personality: A psychological interpretation*. New York: Holt, Rinehart and Winston.

Cripps, B. (2006). Personality assessment, balancing the scales: Self or other construction. *Selection and Development Review*, October, 3–8.

Cook, M. & Cripps, B. (2005). *Psychological assessment in the workplace: A manager's guide*: Chichester: John Wiley and Sons.

Cook, M., Cripps, B., Eysenck, H. J. & Eysenck, S. B. G. (2007). Eysenck Cripps Cook Occupational Scales, technical manual. The ECCOS Partnership. www.eccos.co.uk.

Count, E. W. & Bowles, G. T. (eds) (1964). *Fact and theory in social science*. Syracuse, NY: Syracuse University Press.

Eaves, L., Eysenck, H. J. & Martin, N. G. (1988). *Genes, culture and personality: An empirical approach*. New York: Academic Press.

Eysenck, H. J. (1952). *The scientific study of personality*. London: Routledge & Kegan Paul.

Eysenck, H. J. (1959). *Manual of the Maudsley Personality Inventory*. London: University of London Press.

Eysenck, H. J. (1967). Intelligence assessment: A theoretical and experimental approach. *British Journal of Educational Psychology*, 37(1), 81–98. (Originally delivered at a symposium on New Aspects of Intelligence Assessment at the Swansea Meeting of the BPS on 3 April 1966. First published online 13 May 2011.)Eysenck, H. J. & Eysenck, M. W. (1985). *Personality and individual differences: A natural science approach*. New York: Plenum Press.

Eysenck, H. J. & Eysenck, S. B. G. (1964). *Manual of the Eysenck Personality Inventory*. London: University of London Press.

Eysenck, H. J. & Eysenck, S. B. G. (1991). *Manual of the Eysenck Personality Scales (EPS Adult)*. London: Hodder and Stoughton.

Fransella, F. & Bannister, D. (1977). *A manual for Repertory Grid Technique*. London: Academic Press.

Harré, Rom (2006). *Key thinkers in psychology*. London, Thousand Oaks, CA & New Delhi: Sage.

Kelly, G. A (1955). *A theory of personality: The psychology of personal constructs*. New York & London: Norton.

Kline, P. (1998). *The New Psychometrics: Science, Psychology and Measurement*. London & New York: Routledge.

McRae, R. R. & Costa, P. T. (1987). Validation of the 5-factor model of personality across instruments and observers. *Journal of Personality and Social Psychology*, 52, 81–90.

Myers, I. B. & McCaulley, M. H. (1985), *Manual: A guide to the development and use of the Myers–Briggs Type Indicator* (ed. R.Most). Palo Alto, CA: Consulting Psychologists Press.

Psytech International (2008). Jung Type Indicator. http://psytech.com//Assessments/JungTypeIndicator. Accessed 7 October 2016.Rust, J. (2008) The birth of psychometrics in Cambridge, 1886–1889. http://www.psychometrics.cam.ac.uk/about-us/our-history/first-psychometric-laboratory. Accessed 23 September 2016.

Saville, P. (1977) A critical analysis of the 16PF. PhD thesis, Brunel University.

Saville, P. & Sik, G. (1992). *The Images Personality Questionnaire*. London: SHL.

Windelband, W. (1898[1998]), trans. J. T. Lamiell. History and natural science. *Theory and Psychology*, 8, 5–52.

APPENDIX 1

Triangulation: a case study illustration. Applying psychometrics in performance psychology: the personal development of an equestrian.

ANDY AND COBALT, SHOW JUMPERS

Andy telephoned expressing difficulties he was having with his confidence level during the last 2014 show jumping season. The indoor season from September to March saw Andy winning four tournaments. After Christmas 2014, however, he reports his performance as being very erratic, up and down. His coach suggested that he could benefit from talking to a sport psychologist and he found me through my website.

During our first session, and after an extended interview gathering historical data, I explained that it is my practice to take several assessments including three psychometric assessments. Two of these assessments, ECCOS Online and the MBTI, could be done outside of the consulting room; one, however, could be recorded there and then. I proceeded to elicit constructs looking at how Andy interprets his personal world of show jumping.

Psychometric Assessment Number One

ECCOS, the Eysenck, Cripps, Cook, Occupational Scales (2007), is derived from Eysenck's Personality Questionnaire-Revised, IVE (1991) and contains seven scales.

Analysis

Andy's score of sten 7 for tough-mindedness fits well into the competitive sport arena. Tough-mindedness is a valuable personality trait for a competitive sports person. A suggestion that he is not particularly worried about what other people think of him or his performances also fits well.

Because his team is very small – coach, horse and himself – any difficulties fitting into a team are not there; he does not have others around him offering distractions, which is as he wants it. His fluidity score, measuring anxiety, may help him in his preparation for events, particularly in anticipating what may go wrong. Scores for impulsive and venturesome scales are above average, indicating a propensity for making changes for each competition depending on ground conditions, level of competition, starting order, weather and many other variables.

Indicators from ECCOS which may help future performance in the show jumping ring are:

- Control fluidity and pre-competition nerves; channel them into performance set and focus.
- Check risk taking; channel it into control.

Psychometric Assessment Number Two

This is MBTI, a type instrument.

Andy reports himself as an Introvert, Sensing, Thinking, Perceiving type.

Introvert   (supporting ECCOS Introversion) happy to be on his own working with his mare, Cobalt.

Sensing   able to focus on the present and on the concrete information fed into his sensory system during high pressure moments in the jump ring.

Thinking   basing his decisions on logic and on objective analysis of cause and effect.

Perceiving   maintaining a flexible and spontaneous approach to his sport.

Analysis

A cool onlooker, a quiet and reserved observer able to pick out what will work with him and Cobalt in the show jumping ring, Andy thrives on action and is quite fearless. Andy analyses local weather conditions in the ring and other competitors' times, and judges the pace at which he can safely negotiate a clear round. Able to focus on the present, the here and now, he knows exactly what he must ask of Cobalt. Andy is intensely loyal to his horses; he builds confidence and trust, resulting in successful performance. Mutual trust between horse and rider cements their symbiotic relationship.

Psychometric Assessment Number Three

This is a Repertory Grid.

I prepared a Repertory Grid called Sport Values Questionnaire. Using the triadic system of the repertory grid, Andy considered 11 people in his world of show jumping and construed the differences between them.

According to Kelly, personal constructs are bipolar and organised in a hierarchical way. Andy's hierarchical arrangement of how he would like to be as a show jumper, and how he would *not* like to be, is as follows:

- Calm under pressure–irate
- Maintaining a positive attitude–doubting
- Ignoring failure–dwelling on failure
- Working through difficulties–giving up
- Producing his horse for the future–winning at all costs
- Dedication–lazy
- Being totally focused in the ring–'whatever' attitude
- Being forgiving with his horses–rough with horses
- Respecting his horses–acting aggressively
- Maintaining a professional approach–no backbone
- Calculated–ruthless.

Clearly Andy favours the emergent pole of the construct and the above is his hierarchical ranking outlining the constructs he feels will help him get to the top.

Analysis

Being calm under pressure and maintaining a positive attitude will be transmitted to Cobalt to instil trust and confidence. Having built trust, mutual respect and confidence, Andy and Cobalt can work through difficulties and handle the pressure of competition, essential in any competitive sport. Being forgiving with Cobalt and respecting her brilliant skill and competence as a jumper will cement the symbiotic relationship essential for success. Finally, maintaining a professional approach to horsemanship will help Andy move towards fulfilling his ambitions.

TRIANGULATION OF INSTRUMENTS

Indications of areas where psychological support can help are:

- Maintenance of own standards and values; not being concerned what other people think (apart from coach and significant others).
- Controlling anxiety and turning it into performance set, motivation and need to achieve.
- Ability to read the situation during a round and knowing when to raise the pace.
- Ability to focus on the here and now.
- Ability to analyse error and work in training to fix it.
- Capitalising on being calm under pressure, maintaining a positive attitude, ignoring failure and working through it.
- Respecting and forgiving Cobalt.
- Maintaining professional standards.

These attributes, strengths and limitations form the basis of a psychological support programme when added to interview data, past performance record, goal setting and monitoring of every performance.

Andy is on the very edge of success at the highest level of British show jumping. He and Cobalt have been placed in the top five in their class in the last six competitions.

3 A Very Good Question?

PETER SAVILLE AND RAB MACIVER

IT IS THE WAY YOU WRITE THEM

Psychologists relish their theories on interpreting personality questionnaire scales but pay less attention to the items upon which they are based. As a result psychologists are often poor item writers. Good market researchers, on the other hand, care less about theory but are more skilled item technicians. Why might this situation have evolved? Psychologists, and indeed many HR professionals who use tests, like to be seen as the external consultant or in-company expert on the interpretation of scales, so adding to their kudos. Market researchers, on the other hand, compete face to face, organisation to organisation, in predicting consumer habits, which results in a more pragmatic approach.

There is an apocryphal story in market research about two priests who are discussing whether it is a sin to pray and smoke at the same time. The first says that he thinks it is a sin. The second thinks it is not. So they agree to go to their respective superiors to gain a higher opinion. When they meet again, the first priest says that his superior regarded smoking while praying as a sin. The second said that his superior was adamant that it was not a sin. So the second priest said to the first, 'What did you ask your superior?' He replied, 'I asked my superior if it was a sin to smoke when praying.' 'Ah,' said the second priest. 'My superior said it was fine. But I asked, is it a sin to pray when smoking?' The way one phrases a question can make a very large difference to the answer one receives.

One hears countless examples in day-to-day life of questions asked in a way which will clearly bias a reply. At a recent rugby match, on calling for a video replay of a disputed try, the referee was heard to ask the relevant official, 'Is there any reason why I can't give a try?' This is likely to gain a different response to the simpler question 'Was that a try?'

Similarly, questions can be written in psychometrics and surveys which steer the respondent to virtually only one conceivable answer. In the local high street of one of the authors of this paper, he was asked to complete a questionnaire by an interviewer which started with the question 'Now, you are interested in your children's education, aren't you?', an old technique used by door-to-door encyclopaedia sales people to gain entry to your house and make the sale. So what influence does item phrasing have in psychometric testing?

LEVELS OF AGREEMENT

The most common item format in personality questionnaires is the *normative Likert scale*, where one is required to answer an item with one of a number of options, normally five:

1) **I have a lot of friends.**
   - Strongly disagree
   - Disagree
   - Uncertain
   - Agree
   - Strongly agree

2) **I frequently think up good ideas.**
   - Strongly disagree
   - Disagree
   - Uncertain
   - Agree
   - Strongly agree

3) **I get anxious before important events.**
   - Strongly disagree
   - Disagree
   - Uncertain
   - Agree
   - Strongly agree

To many, data originating from such Likert normative scales are absolutes and enable direct comparison between people. This clearly is nonsense. Without destroying the normative approach completely, let us consider the problems presented by this normative test item format.

With such items, the respondent is faced with a number of quandaries. With the first item, who qualifies as a friend? Does one's partner? Mum and Dad? How close to the person do they need to be before they regard them a friend? And how many people constitute a lot of friends? Two, three, five or even ten? In the case of Facebook, we are informed that the average 18–24-year-old female has some 650 friends; for males it's significantly lower. Yet, in psychological research, adults state that they only have two or three close friends.

In item 2, what constitutes 'frequently'? As early as 1944, R. H. Simpson found that 'frequently' meant over 80 per cent of the time to some students and fewer than 40 per cent to others. So are these questions absolutes? Is direct comparison between people really that easy? Probably not.

Dealing with item three, we come to the issue of *social desirability responding*. As Wiggins (1986) pointed out, the belief that every respondent is out to deceive us in selection is almost certainly false. Nevertheless, on normative items, people are known to present themselves in a favourable light. According to Paulhus (1984), social desirability responding takes two forms. The first is self-deception, called factor alpha, and impression management, known as factor gamma. Factor gamma is out-and-out lying, often referred to academically as impression management. Factor alpha is the natural tendency for people to give a desired answer, which they may well believe themselves but which projects them in an unrealistically favourable light. They often believe themselves to be less heavy than they really are, drink less alcohol than they really do (Robertson and Heather, 1986), and bathe more often than they actually do. If we were to calculate the volume of all the baths and showers that people claim to take, we would have little water in our reservoirs. Even when people are asked which newspaper they generally read, the consumption of quality broadsheet newspapers is considerably overestimated in comparison with newspapers based on tabloid journalism. Rather than ask an individual what they generally read, market researchers will often ask 'What did you read today?' Such a question, asking about a specific behaviour, normally gives them more accurate data.

Intriguingly, it is more often the better-adjusted, the less anxious and the more optimistic who are inclined to produce inflated views of themselves, showing exaggerated alpha responses. This is despite the fact this may show less valid self-insight (Roth and Ingram, 1985;

Sackeim, 1983). There exists a slight negative correlation between inflated self-insight and intelligence. Those who are more self-critical in response tend to be of somewhat higher general mental ability, though the correlation is not large.

Eysenck (1975), in his measures of extraversion, introversion and later psychoticism, tried to avoid the problem of social desirability responding by giving the respondent only two options, 'Yes' and 'No'. This proved uncomfortable to some test takers, who would put an offending cross between the two options, so making up their own three point-scale (Saville & Blinkhorn, 1976)!

Normative items also suffer from *central tendency response set*. Some respondents consistently answer down the middle of the scale, giving answers around points two, three and four in the five-option scale, while others almost exclusively give the extreme responses of five (strongly agree) and one (strongly disagree). Again, this makes the strict inter-person comparison between people enormously difficult. Market researchers know this problem well. It is said that northern Europeans tend to use the middle of the scale when making ratings, while southern Europeans are more inclined to use the extremes. Comparing the habits between countries is an eternal headache when using the normative format alone.

As a practical example of central tendency bias, Sir Richard Branson, the outstanding entrepreneur, on taking a version of the authors' normative questionnaire, responded on virtually every question with an extreme one or five response, meaning that normed scores in his profile generally ranged from one extreme to the other. In comparison, when Major General Sir Jeremy Moore completed the same questionnaire, he never once used the one or five extreme item responses. On being asked about this he replied. 'Well, I either agree or disagree. But, if you'd like to call my "agree" responses "strongly agree" and my "disagree" answers "strongly disagree", then please do.' On this basis, his personality profile opened up with many more extreme high and low normed scores on his profile. On normative formats, a great deal depends on how much one emphasizes the style in which the person should approach the questionnaire and whether the respondent is inclined to use extreme responses or not.

It has also been observed with regard to interest inventories measuring occupational choice that some students respond that they are interested in every activity or job, while others are uninterested in virtually everything. Faced with such interest profiles the career counsellor using normative item scales can be at a loss as to how to deal with their counsellee. Perhaps they might ask the respondent to rank the activities in order of what they find most and least preferable?

Interest inventories also have the problem of fantasy responses: those students who have not obtained a single GCSE, but say they wish to go on to be a veterinary surgeon or a doctor, and those standing six feet two inches tall (1.9 meters) and weighing 198 pounds (90 kg) with the ambition of becoming a professional jockey. There are those who express a strong interest in football in an occupational interest inventory, yet merely watch the occasional match – this compared with others who also express a strong interest but play twice a week, train three times a week, and run and captain the team. Can we directly assess these identical responses as being comparable in interest on an absolute scale?

WHAT IS THIS QUESTION ASSESSING?

In the early days of the psychometric assessment of personality by questionnaire, there was an obsession about candidate distortion. This led to the development of questionnaires with so called 'subtle' or manifestly bizarre content; a trend which persists to the present day. Examples from actual questionnaires include:

1. The sight of pus disgusts me.
2. I have a fear of being buried alive.
3. I believe in the second coming of Christ.
4. There is something wrong with my sex organs.
5. Would you rather be Jack the Ripper or Dr Crippen?
6. There is no love or companionship in my family.
7. I would rather be a Bishop than a Colonel.
8. Under certain circumstances there is nothing I would not do.
9. I would like to be a formula one driver.
10. I prefer the beauty of a poem to that of a well-made gun.
11. I'd rather keep my desk tidy than kiss a member of the opposite sex.
12. I would love to go to an orgy.

Of the items above, the item on being a Bishop versus a Colonel was once put forward as an example of an item that was immune to distortion. When put to some 100 managers, 98 indicated that if they were distorting, they would answer with the response 'Colonel'. Presumably they believed that wishing to be an officer of high military rank would be preferable in management selection to being a member of the clergy. Clearly this item has enormous problems and is best avoided, not least as it involves matters of religious faith.

Is it any wonder that questionnaires containing such content became the butt of humorists' jokes, putting, in many people's eyes, self-report personality questionnaires in the area of pseudo-science? What makes psychologists include such ridiculous, dated and even sexist items in some questionnaires? Indeed, the use of items similar to these has led to expensive court action in the USA, as they are an irrelevant intrusion into privacy. The use of items from instruments such as the Minnesota Multiphasic Personality Inventory (MMPI), designed for the diagnosis of mental health conditions but used inappropriately in the world of work, has resulted in companies losing literally millions of dollars in legal action. As Buzzard (1971) quoted, 'I don't know … they may be alright … they always seem to me to overestimate the self-knowledge of the subject and underestimate his or her sense of humour.'

THE ANSWER IS NO, OR IS IT YES?

Next is the issue of using negatively phrased items in questionnaires, such as 'I am not the sort of person who readily appreciates the beauty of nature'. When Saville and MacIver inspected the negatively phrased items among the normative items of the Occupational Personality Questionnaires (Saville, Holdsworth, Nyfield, Cramp & Mabey, 1984) they found significantly lower alpha reliabilities for the negatively praised items than for those positively expressed. They postulated that negatively phrased items were more semantically complex or more difficult to comprehend, or even that the word 'not' in the item was simply missed, leaving a situation where an intended 'disagree' response on a Likert scale was recorded as 'agree'. If this should happen on as few as two items, the score would vary significantly and the error would seriously invalidate the resulting personality scale score. The second observation from this study was that the positive items were capable of measuring a greater number of different, discrete behaviours than the negative items. Negative items, then, can both reduce the level of precision of measurement and cause the complexity of personality to be underestimated.

The authors have a distinct dislike of statements resulting from personality questionnaires which would seem to be true of virtually every human being. In a study of 1,000 students, MacIver and Saville showed the percentage of people who would agree that statements commonly given in published personality questionnaires applied to them. The list is given below:

- **99.3%** – You are fair-minded
- **98.6%** – You are kind
- **96.5%** – You are thoughtful
- **97.2%** – You are reasonable
- **99.3%** – You are co-operative
- **99.3%** – You value honest communication
- **97.9%** – You value sincere appreciation and recognition for a job well done
- **97.9%** – You like to be on good terms with other people, and will generally react to them in a friendly and open way

Feedback on statements such as this often result in the well-known Barnum or Forer (1949) effect. Barnum was a circus owner who is said to have coined the phrase 'there's a sucker born every minute'. Notice that every statement is positive, that is, complimentary to the individual. People tend not to like negative feedback, even if it is true. It is upon this fact that poor questionnaires flourish.

Questionnaires sometimes contain scales that are bipolar in nature although they do not actually represent true opposites. Many scales, for example, have the arts at one end and the sciences at the other. Yet in a study of 237 people by Saville, MacIver, Kurz and Hopton (2008), the correlation between interest in the arts and interest in sciences was found to be zero. They are not simple opposites at all, yet in many questionnaires they are wrongly shown as opposite ends of a vector. From general observation, one finds that scientists like Einstein, Leonardo da Vinci, and more recently the physicist and TV presenter Professor Brian Cox, have commented on the closeness of the arts to the sciences and indeed mathematics. Treating the Thinking and Feeling scales of the Myers–Briggs Type Indicator (MBTI), as separate rather than forced-choice items, Saville and MacIver found not the expected negative but a positive correlation of approximately +0.4 between them. People who are Thinkers are more, not less, likely to be Feeling types. Thinking and Feeling are quite simply not opposites.

LONGER ITEMS, LONGER SCALES?

Then there is the issue of ambiguous items, which are rife throughout the questionnaire world. A particular problem are items that contain the 'little words': 'and', 'but', 'if', 'always', 'never', etc. How often can one say one 'always' or 'never' behaves in a given way? One frequently comes across items of the type 'I'm a sensitive person and one who show my feelings.' This is two questions, not one. One may be sensitive but not show it. Despite the common myth that longer items work better, shorter items are generally superior for measuring personality scales. One study showed a −0.4 correlation between the number of words in the item and how well it measured the scale it was designed to measure. Having many items in a scale can also actually weaken validity, as shown by Burisch in 1997 when writing on test length:

> Results from three different subject samples extend earlier findings that lengthening a scale beyond some point can actually weaken its validity. A near-optimal algorithm selected the most valid aggregate of items from a common pool. Findings were then cross validated in a second sample. From the procedure emerged fairly short scales with acceptable cross validities, but only if the item pool had been prescreened for content saturation. Under these circumstances, even extremely short scales of two to four items each, which had survived double cross validation, suffered hardly any loss of cross validity. In a third sample they outperformed standard scales eight times as long. (p. 303)

The work of Burisch on the advantage of short scales which 'hit the target' over lengthy ones is supported by Lie (2008) in the *Journal of Clinical Sleep Medicine*. It was shown that one can screen for excessive daytime sleepiness, as effectively as with a day of physiological/psychological tests, with the simple psychometric item 'Give me your daytime sleepiness, where 0 is the lowest and 10 is the highest'. Cronbach (1970) reported that in predicting if soldiers were more combat-effective in hot or cold climates, simply asking 'Would you prefer to be in a hot or cold climate?' was as effective as three days of physiological/psychological testing. We psychologists at times do love to complicate things!

Burisch (1984a) showed that questionnaires based on a complex theoretical background had no higher validity than those that were more simply constructed with a given aim in mind. Call us anti-theoretical if you like, but Occam's razor still applies.

As Neal Schmitt (Morgeson et al., 2007) put it, 'If you are going to use personality measures, make sure you know what the outcome is and direct your personality measure development toward that outcome, then you not only are more likely to have validity, but you are also likely to be able to defend the use of that test if it is challenged.'

In developing Saville Consulting Wave® Professional Style we put to bed the myth that longer scales are necessarily better, undermining the Spearman–Brown prophecy formula, which implied that longer scales are necessarily more reliable. This is simply not the case.

WHAT TO ASK?

In writing items for personality scales, one needs to be aware that there can be a distinct difference between the following:

> I am **good at** checking details.
>
> I **enjoy** checking details.

One can find that some candidates are actually quite good at error checking but do not wish to spend the rest of their lives doing it. In the Saville Consulting Wave Questionnaire (Saville, MacIver & Kurz, 2012) a distinction is made between items that indicate behaviour for which a person feels they have a talent and items that show what motivates them to behave in a particular way. They will often coincide but not always. One can have a talent for something but a low motivation to do it. If this talent is an important job skill, there may be a problem with motivation. If that skill is irrelevant to the job, then ignore it. On the other hand, if one has high motivation but low talent in a job-relevant behaviour, this could be a development area for the individual. Such knowledge is enormously useful in feedback and counselling psychology. We suggest that one should not confuse an ability for a certain activity and the motivation to carry it out. Very few questionnaires make the distinction between the two. They consist of a hodgepodge of items that indicate liking or being good at, and ambiguous, attitudinal and spuriously bipolar items which ask people to mark themselves on a scale between two alternative 'poles' which are not in fact opposites. Angleitner, John and Löhr (1986) found that the well-known 16PF personality questionnaire they studied was particularly guilty of containing such content, as did Saville in 1977.

We suggest that the items in personality questionnaires should not go into Freudian, Jungian or other clinical constructs, which have little relevance in the workplace, but be phrased in terms of relevant job competences and behaviour. Rather than abstract psychoanalytic concepts, use, as Morgeson et al. (2007) suggested, work-relevant competencies described in behavioural terms.

Questionnaire scales with great names or that are based on an interesting new theory don't magically forecast outcomes in the real world better as a result of the inclusion of those names. To paraphrase electoral politics, 'It is the items, stupid!'

Scales which are carefully written, with real thought, precision and expertise and with items whose inclusion is based on the right criteria, will make for questionnaires that make better forecasts of real-world criteria. In turn, such scales will drive more effective decisions and provide users with increased return on their investment. In the development of the Saville Consulting Wave Questionnaire, strict writing guidelines and review criteria were established. The items must be:

> **Targeted** – A clear objective in the development of Wave was to base items on a clear understanding of what 'good looks like'. Items were designed to be unipolar, with higher scores indicating more effective performance. Exemplars of individuals with particular traits were used as part of this process to identify whether each item was worded effectively. For example, one of the facets is labelled 'discreet' and its items deal with 'maintaining confidentiality'. The item writers sought individuals whom they had observed behaviourally to be lower on this trait to check that they would not positively endorse the statement in the item. Care was also taken to avoid focusing on concepts that were likely to have negative correlations with overall job performance and potential ratings. Aspects of adapting approaches – associated with emotional resilience and agreeableness – were, for example, amended to reflect more proactive, pro-social behaviours.
>
> **Simple** – The items were written and reviewed to be as simple a construction as possible to measure the trait being targeted. Frequently used words were preferred to less frequently used ones. One concept only is measured by an item, so conjunctions such as 'and', 'or' or 'but' are avoided.

Short – Long items tend to have lower reliability, which will impact on their validity. Wherever possible Wave Styles items were written short and then shortened. However, extremely short or one-word items, such as an adjective like Sociable, can fail to convey subtlety and precision of meaning when a narrow trait is being targeted. The longest item in the Wave Styles questionnaires has 11 words and the shortest has three words. The mean number of words in an item is 6.7.

Comprehensible – An important feature of any item is that reviewers and respondents understand and agree upon its meaning.

Direct – There was no attempt in Wave Styles items to conceal their meaning or make them indirect or opaque. Indeed, they were deliberately written with a high degree of 'directness' or transparency so that the respondents are clear what they are being asked and are not surprised later by their results. Opaque or indirect items can lack face validity for the respondent and mean that a scale requires many more items to measure the concept reliably and validly.

Avoiding idioms and metaphors – Items such as 'I like to beat others', used by Saville (1984) in the original Concept Version of the OPQ were taken literally in some cultures, to mean to physically beat others. Another problematic item was 'Chancing your arm', which is British slang for taking a risk. It simply did not translate well to different cultures, which meant its removal from the decision making scale. Few idioms or metaphors translate successfully across languages and cultures and can lead to the gross misinterpretation of an item. They are best avoided.

Positively phrased – Items that employ negation by using words such as 'not' typically have lower reliability and are prone to respondent response error due to misreading. Negative items can help in controlling acquiescence responding, but their inclusion can result in lower reliability.

Self-referent – Items ask respondents to rate and rank their own motives and talents. Items that ask for opinions or attitudes, such as 'I think a team needs a leader', were avoided.

Behavioural – The items focus on behaviours that are more or less observable. Talent items look for direct expression of these behaviours in terms of action, and motive items focus on the individual's needs and preferences which make particular behaviours more likely. This behavioural approach makes responses more verifiable, as the traits should correlate with effective expression of these behaviours which can be observed and rated by others.

Avoiding stereotypical or biased content – Care was taken by reviewers and item writers to avoid items that might focus on specific knowledge or experience which a particular protected group may have less or limited access to. As a matter of course opinions on and attitudes to specifics of the real world (such as particular people or events) are avoided. Items are specifically reviewed by international reviewers with consideration to culture, country of origin, ethnicity, age, gender, sexual orientation and religious belief.

Non-bizarre – Item content was not designed to be strange or sensational, or present hypothetical scenarios, whether they are likely or unlikely to be faced by the respondents in their working life.

Non-clinical – Items that refer to mental or physical disorders or that describe mental or physical symptoms that may indicate a clinical abnormality were avoided. The items are designed to be relevant and acceptable to typical working adults. Items that could be perceived as an invasion of privacy with regard to mental health issues were also avoided.

- **Work-relevant** – The items in the Saville Consulting Wave Styles predictor (trait) model and criterion (competency) model were written and reviewed to be work-relevant and positive with regard to achieving overall effectiveness at work.
- **Internationally relevant**   The items chosen were reviewed to be in simple business English and easy to translate. Individuals from over 50 countries were involved in the item trialling and review process. Words with a common spelling in US and UK English were used whenever possible, but separate versions were created when items contained spelling differences that it was not possible to change.

Finally, it is critical to have a professional item-writing team working actively together, considering prototypes and reviewing and refining items. Writing many more good items than you need allows the selection of the best items for the questionnaire, and if you can then select from those the items which research shows best forecast the criteria, so much the better. Most questionnaires select items that work with the other items in the scale. In the development of Saville Consulting Wave, over 4000 items were written, of which 428 were selected by the item-writing team as the very best. Finally, the 216 items that best forecast individual behavioural competencies and overall effectiveness according to independent ratings were included in the final instrument.

DON'T RATE, RANK?

In view of the issue of bias in normative items, some questionnaire authors have preferred the ipsative or ranking format in presenting (and subsequently scoring) items, as demonstrated below.

Please rank the following statements in order of which is most true of you (1) to least true of you (5).

A.	I care about other people.	4
B.	I succeed at most things I do.	2
C.	I produce creative ideas.	1
D.	I deal well with detail.	5
E.	I am confident in social situations.	3

In this example, the respondent is stating that 'producing creative ideas' is most true of them, 'succeeding at most things they do' comes second, and 'dealing with detail' is least true. In practice, so that a high numerical value represents a higher score on any given trait, the rankings are often simply reversed. That is, in this example option C would be scored with a value of five, option B with a value of four and option D with a value of one. This has no effect on the item responses other than to make them easier to handle on interpretation.

Generally speaking, one does not want a facet which is ranked low to have a high score, merely as a matter of convenience.

This, the ipsative method of item presentation and scoring, can help control the social desirability, central tendency and other biases found with Likert and other normative scales. However, it introduces the problem that the sum of the raw scores in a questionnaire is a constant for all individuals (Clemens, 1966). This has led some to claim that ipsative measures cannot be used to make comparisons between people, that is, they are intra-individual, rather than inter-individual, assessments.

The strongest attack on Ipsative measures was that by Johnson, Wood and Blinkhorn (1988) in the article 'Spuriouser and spuriouser: The use of ipsative personality tests'. They stated four 'uncontroversial' facts regarding ipsative tests. (1) They cannot be used on an individual on a scale-by-scale basis. (2) Correlation of scales cannot legitimately be factor-analysed in the usual way. (3) Reliabilities on ipsative tests overestimate the actual reliabilities of the scales. (4) Validities are overestimated; indeed correlations between ipsative scales and external criteria are uninterpretable.

Investigating these claims, Saville and Willson (1991) demonstrated with simulated data that ipsative scores could be factored soundly, that the reliability data were not overestimated and that, under moderate conditions of central tendency bias in normative items, ipsative scores actually correlated better with hypothetical 'true' scores than the normative form. When replicated on real data, on a sample of 243 respondents, a very high correlation was found between ipsative and normative scores on a questionnaire consisting of 30 scales of personality. Ipsative scaling did not produce spuriously high reliability, and both normative and ipsative data showed sensible and significant correlations with external rating criteria. When the complete matrix was inspected, the like-to-like scale correlations between ipsative and normative scales were invariably higher than the correlation of any one scale with any other scale. For example, the correlation of the scale 'Social Confidence' in the normative and ipsative versions of the questionnaire was higher than the correlation with any of the remaining 29 personality scales. The odds of this happening by chance are indeed very remote. The data suggest that those 'significant others' who made the independent ratings of the individual's behaviour could distinguish as many as 30 aspects of personality, giving support to the view that raters are capable of distinguishing more than just five aspects of personality – the Big Five, otherwise known as the Five Factor Model (FFM) of personality.

Commenting on the papers challenging ipsative scoring, Cronbach (personal communication, 1991) wrote: 'This overstates the complaints. Ipsative scales can be used for comparing individuals scale by scale. The interrelations can be factored soundly. Reliabilities are entirely sound when properly interpreted; there is no overestimation that I know of. I see no reason for regarding validity coefficients as overestimates.'

If normative and ipsative approaches to measuring personality have their relative advantages and disadvantages then intuitively it would make good sense to use both formats in a questionnaire. In the days of pencil and paper testing this would have been particularly onerous, in terms of completion time. Saville, in 1992, produced the CM7 version of the Occupational Personality Questionnaires (OPQ), but it took over two hours to complete, which was commercially unviable. With the coming of internet administration, where the computer can assign ranks to normatively endorsed items, and with the use of well-written, short items, as many as 108 facets of personality in the Saville Consulting Wave could be assessed in a little over 35 minutes.

In 2008, Saville, MacIver, Kurz and Hopton published the results of their 'Project Epsom', which compared the validities of a range of well-known personality questionnaires on a sample of 308 participants. The seven most popular questionnaires all showed significant and potentially useful correlations with work performance. However, the Saville Consulting Wave Professional Styles Personality Questionnaire, using both ipsative and normative measurements in one instrument, outperformed all the other questionnaires in terms of validity. The results are reproduced in Figure 3.1.

More recently, Salgado, Anderson and Tauriz (2014) conducted a meta-analysis on the validity of different personality questionnaires, using normative, ipsative and quasi-ipsative formats. A quasi-ipsative questionnaire is one like Saville Consulting Wave which includes a ranking format but where the sum of the raw scores is not a constant for all individuals. They found that personality questionnaires in personnel selection were substantially more valid than was previously thought. The traditional opinion among researchers in I/O psychology is that normative Likert-type scales have superior predictive validity to ipsative inventories. But their research findings suggest this is not true for quasi-ipsative inventories. In comparison with ipsative and normative personality inventories, quasi-ipsative personality inventories showed higher predictive validity regardless of occupational group.

In summary, to answer the 'very good question' of the title, personality questionnaires can and do produce useful validity coefficients with incremental validity over cognitive measures, particularly when they are based on skilfully written and selected items and both ipsative and normative formats are incorporated into their design.

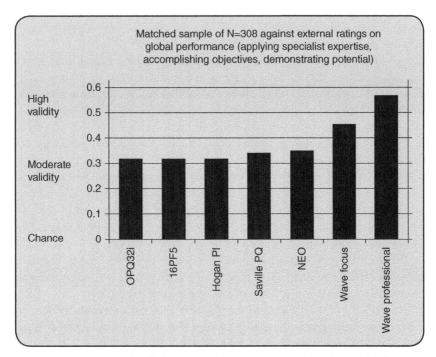

Figure 3.1 *Validity of Saville Consulting Wave Professional Styles Personality Questionnaire, using ipsative and normative measurements in one instrument, compared with five other personality questionnaires. (Source: Saville, MacIver, Kurz and Hopton (2008), p. 7)*

REFERENCES

Angleitner, A., John, O. P. & Löhr, F.-J. (1986). It's *what* you ask and *how* you ask it: An item-metric analysis of personality questionnaires. In A. Angleitner and J. S. Wiggins (eds.), *Personality assessment via questionnaires* (pp. 61–107). Berlin: Springer-Verlag.

Burisch, M. (1984). Approaches to personality inventory construction: A comparison of merits. *American Psychologist*, 39(3), 214–27.

Burisch, M. (1997). Test length and validity revisited. *European Journal of Personality*, 11, 303–15.

Buzzard, R. B. (1971). Obituary to Sir Frederic Bartlett. *Occupational Psychology*, 45(1), 1–6.

Clemens, W. V. (1966). *An analytical and empirical examination of some properties of ipsative measures.* Psychometric Monographs, 14. Richmond, VA: Psychometric Society.

Closs, J. (1973). *Manual of the APU Occupational Interest Guide (Standard & Advanced Forms).* London: Hodder & Stoughton.

Cronbach, L. J. (1970). *The essentials of psychological testing* (3rd edn). New York: Harper & Row.

Johnson, C. B., Wood, R. & Blinkhorn, S. F. (1988). Spuriouser and spuriouser: The use of ipsative personality tests. *Journal of Occupational Psychology*, 61, 153–62.

Lie, D. (2008). A single subjective question may help screen for excessive daytime sleepiness. *Journal of Clinical Sleep Medicine*, 4, 143–8.

Morgeson, F. P., Campion, M. A., Dipboye, R. L., Hollenbeck, J. R., Murphy, K. & Schmitt, N. (2007). Reconsidering the use of personality tests in personnel selection contexts. *Personnel Psychology*, 60(3), 683–729.

Paulhus, D. L. (1984). Two component models of socially desirable responding. *Journal of Personality and Social Psychology*, 46, 598–609.

Robertson, I. & Heather, N. (1986). *Let's drink to your health!* Leicester: British Psychological Society.

Roth, D. L. & Ingram, R. E. (1985). Factors in the self-deception questionnaire: Associations with depression. *Journal of Personality and Social Psychology*, 48(1), 243–51.

Sackeim, H. A. (1983). Self-deception, self-esteem, and depression: The adaptive value of lying to oneself. In D. Masling (ed.), *Empirical Studies of Psychoanalytic Theories* (pp. 101–57). Hillsdale, NJ: Erlbaum.

Salgado, J. F., Anderson, N. & Tauriz, G. (2015). The validity of ipsative and quasi-ipsative forced-choice personality inventories for different occupational groups: A comprehensive meta-analysis. *Journal of Occupational and Organizational Psychology*, 88(4), 797–834.

Saville, P. (1977). A critical analysis of Cattell's 16PF questionnaire. PhD thesis, Brunel University, London.

Saville, P. & Blinkhorn, S. (1976). *Undergraduate personality by factored scales.* Windsor: NFER.

Saville, P., Holdsworth, R., Nyfield, G., Cramp, L. & Mabey, W. (1984). *Occupational Personality Questionnaire manual.* Thames Ditton: Saville-Holdsworth Ltd.

Saville, P & Hopton, T. (2014). Psychometrics @ Work. Saville Consulting Ltd, London.

Saville, P., MacIver, R. & Kurz, R. (2010). Saville Consulting Wave® Professional Styles Handbook. Saville Consulting Group: Jersey. First Edition.

Saville, P., MacIver, R., Kurz, R. & Hopton, T. (2008). Project Epsom: How valid is your questionnaire? A summary of a comparison of personality questionnaires in measuring performance at work. London: Saville Consulting.

Saville, P., MacIver, R. & Kurz, R. (2012). Handbook to Saville Consulting Wave Focus Styles. Saville Consulting Group: Jersey.

Saville, P. & Willson, E. (1991). The reliability and validity of normative and ipsative approaches in the measurement of personality. *Journal of Occupational Psychology*, 64(3), 219–38.

Shephard, D. (1966). Metric structures in ordinal data. *Journal of Mathematical Psychology*, 3, 287–315.

Simpson, R. H. (1944). The specific meanings of certain terms indicating different degrees of frequency. *Quarterly Journal of Speech*, 30(3), 328–30.

Wiggins, J. S. (1986). Epilog. In A. Angleitner & J. S. Wiggins (eds.), *Personality assessment via questionnaires* (pp. 225–34). Berlin: Springer-Verlag.

4 Big Data and Predictive Analytics: Opportunity or Threat to the Future of Tests and Testing

EUGENE BURKE

THE CONTEXT FOR TESTING HAS CHANGED AND CONTINUES TO CHANGE

This chapter is not about a specific test, psychometric method or psychological model through which test scores are interpreted. Those topics are adequately covered by other contributors to this book. This chapter is about the wider technological and social context in which testing operates and will operate in the coming years, a context that has changed significantly since the beginning of this century and more specifically in just the past few years.

Technology has been and continues to be a key factor that both enables and shapes testing science and practice. As an example, just a few years ago was the debate about unproctored Internet testing (UIT) and whether cognitive ability tests could be delivered via the Internet while avoiding threats to their validity from cheating (Burke, 2009; Lievens & Burke, 2011; Tippins et al., 2006).[1]

Yet few today, whether testing professionals or end users, would be surprised that an ability test, a personality questionnaire or a Situational Judgement Test (SJT) is delivered via UIT. The capacity of technology to enable online testing and the desire of clients for a 24/7/365 capability, convenient for candidates and allowing clients to compete more effectively and efficiently for talent, essentially forced the science of testing to develop solutions to the issue of test security and candidate verification.

Indeed, the very medium, the Internet, that was seen to create challenges and even threats to effective testing practice itself provided the means through which innovations to defend the validity of tests and test scores have been developed and deployed (see Bartram and Burke, 2013, for a discussion of these issues in relation to employment testing, including ability and personality assessments; see International Test Commission (ITC) Guidelines on Computer-Based and Internet Delivered Testing, 2005, 2014, for how technology and client demand have impacted on testing best practice).

While it is not the subject of this chapter, another example of the impact of technology on testing is the increased interest in simulation-based assessments (see Fetzer & Tuzinski,

2013, for a review). These new forms of assessment represent both a shift in technological capability and a shift in the wider life context of potential candidates. Who, these days, is not aware of interactive games?

Mobile is another technology that is shaping test development and deployment by virtue of the fact that many potential candidates do not own a laptop or a PC and operate with mobile (cell) phones, smartphones and tablets (see, for example, the blog posted by HR Avatar, 2015, and, later in this chapter, how research at the University of Cambridge is exploring how to embed 'assessment' in smart mobile technology).

My point is that technology, end users (such as employers seeking to use testing to improve their talent management processes) and candidates all frame the context in which tests are developed and deployed. In this chapter, I will focus on a very specific shift in that context that offers both opportunities and potential threats to testing. That shift is the advent of Big Data and the data sciences more popularly known as predictive analytics (Davenport & Kim, 2013; Fitz-Enz & Mattox, 2014; Linoff & Berry, 2011). See table 4.1 for an explanation of some Big Data terms.

Table 4.1 *Some key terms in the Big Data and analytics world*

Big Data terms …	… and what they mean
Big Data	A term used to refer to large volumes of data available to enable organisations to optimise investments in organisational structures, technology, operations, marketing and sales, and, more recently, HR. Big Data is generally described through attributes known as the five V's: Volume, Variety, Velocity, Veracity and Value.
Predictive analytics	The use of data, statistical algorithms and machine-learning techniques to identify the likelihood of future outcomes based on historical data.
Talent analytics	Also known as HR Analytics, Workforce Analytics and People Analytics, refers to the application of benchmarking, data modelling and, at the highest levels of maturity, predictive and prescriptive analytics that provide organisational leaders, HR and talent management professionals with decision diagnostics for managing HR processes and human capital investments.
Data mining	A subfield of computer science concerned with discovering patterns in large data sets and using methods that combine artificial intelligence, machine learning, statistics, data visualisation and database systems to extract information and transform it into an understandable structure for further use.
Neural networks	A term used in machine learning for statistical learning models inspired by biological neural networks and used to help explain patterns and relationships in data that are difficult to identify through more common linear and rule-based heuristics and methods.
Text analytics	Processes used to derive information from text sources to find key content across a larger body of information, for sentiment analysis (what is the nature of commentary on an issue?), explicative analysis (what is driving that commentary?), investigative analysis (what are the particular cases of a specific issue?) and classification (what subject or what key content pieces does the text talk about?).

Of course, analytics and data have always been fundamental to the development of tests and assessments, and large data sets have always been an advantage to effective test development and validation. So, why are Big Data and predictive analytics different? I will offer two (of many possible) answers.

The first of my answers is that organisations worldwide are exploring and exploiting algorithms that predict our consumer profiles and purchasing choices, our political profiles and voting intentions, and our medical profiles and future health needs. Predicting job and career success, intention to stay with a company or even whether an employee may present a risk to a company (what has become known as 'human capital risk') is a natural extension of the application of predictive analytics. As we will see, it is an extension of analytics that is already happening.

The second of my answers is that these trends are coming from outside the disciplines of psychology and psychometrics, both of which remain relatively obscure to many end users and senior stakeholders, the people who hold the purse strings for funding test development and purchasing tests and testing programmes. These trends are being driven by interest among marketing, finance and business strategy functions who may not be data scientists themselves but have certainly read about the potential value of Big Data for driving organisational success. Imagine the interest of those who read that Big Data can improve productivity by five or six per cent (Brynjolfsson, Hitt & Kim, 2011), or $300 billion (£194 billion[2]) in value to US health care and $250 billion (£161 billion) to the EU's public administration (larger than the then GDP of Greece; figures taken from Manyika et al., 2011).

Add to that books, films and articles linking predictive analytics to success in sports. The book *Moneyball: The Art of Winning an Unfair Game* by Michael Lewis, published in 2003, brought analytics to the attention of the sports fan by showing how analytics (or 'sabermetrics'[3]) helped a cash-strapped baseball team to surprising success.[4] Fans of the 'beautiful game' and of the English Premiership football league have seen teams such as Arsenal pay a reputed £2 million ($3.1 million) to add predictive analytics capabilities in support of their aspirations for sporting success (Hytner, 2014).

Exposure like this in the popular media has inevitably whetted the curiosity of executives and managers as to the possibilities of Big Data and predictive analytics for helping them solve their business problems and their people issues.

In short, Big Data and analytics have and will continue to have an impact on the science and practice of testing. The question is how? Is it an opportunity and a springboard for the wider use of tests, and a catalyst for innovation in test development? Or is it, as some commentators are suggesting, the end of testing as we know it today?

CHAPTER PLAN

My focus will be on employment testing and assessment, whether for recruitment and hiring, development and coaching, succession planning and senior appointments, or workforce planning and organisational design. In my view, the impact of Big Data and predictive analytics cuts across all of these HR needs and, looking at the opportunities for testing, also opens up applications for test data to more strategic applications such as workforce planning. Later in this chapter, we will explore the use of test data in predictive benchmarking of populations, whether those populations are groups of employees, entire organisations, an industry sector or entire nations.

I will first outline what the shift to Big Data and analytics has been to date, the drivers for that shift, and trends in the employment or talent management space. This shift has seen significant changes in the test vendor landscape as larger technology and consultancy companies have acquired test vendors to extend their reach into the HR customer base and mark out dominant positions in the market for talent management products and services.

Next, I will explore a significant threat: new entrants to the testing space with data-mining tools and models that lead to the substitution of tests with data-driven algorithms. I have characterised this threat as the 'ultimate candidate-friendly test' whereby the candidate does not actually sit a test. I will also explore some of the pitfalls that beset that threat such as potential discrimination and lack of cause–effect theory. Despite those pitfalls, I will show that the threat of substitution is a very real one.

I will then go on to explore three more positive scenarios for testing in a world of Big Data and analytics:

- **Analytics as a value-add to testing** in which the use of test data in the form of predictive benchmarks and the use of data sciences to unpack outcome (criterion) measures extend the value of testing for end users.
- **Testing as a value-add to analytics** in which models, theories and test data enable more effective applications of data analytics approaches to understanding both the potential of employees and barriers to realising that potential.
- **Analytics as a platform for the evolution of testing** in which the interest in Big Data and data analytics provides new opportunities for applications of psychometrics and psychological models in fields such as marketing and well-being.

THE ERA OF BIG DATA AND DATA ANALYTICS

Recent years have seen testing, and more widely psychometrics, gaining traction as a standard suite of tools to enable more effective decisions in hiring, managing and developing employees. In June 2015, testing (principally personality assessment) made it as a feature in *Time* magazine that valued the testing industry at $2 billion (£1.29 billion) (Gray, 2015).

Some in the employment testing industry would see that press coverage as a long-overdue recognition of the value of testing, and that is not to be denied. What the press coverage also signifies is the growth of an ecosystem around the testing of products, technologies and services in the Big Data market, of which talent management is but one segment within which the employment test industry sits.

To give a sense of the weight of that market in influencing the world in which testing science and practice co-exist, and compared to the value *Time* magazine placed on the testing market, in 2014 Forbes valued the Big Data market at $27.4 billion (£17.7 billion) (Columbus, 2014). That is 13.7 times the size of *Time*'s estimate of the size of the testing market. Within that Big Data market, the talent management market was valued by Bersin by Deloitte at $6 billion (£3.9 billion) driven primarily by talent management software vendors (Jones and Wang-Audia, 2014). As one would expect, Big Data as a market comes with some very big financials (see Figure 4.1 for a sense of the comparative numbers involved).

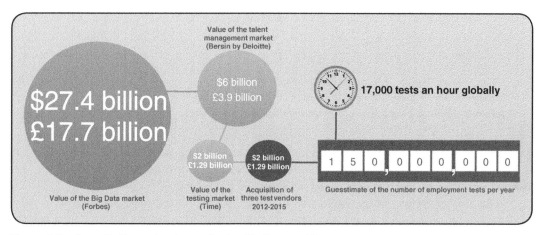

Figure 4.1 *Some Big Data related to testing in a Big Data world*

Why mention these financials in a book about testing? Those financials show how the market for testing products has changed, how Big Data and predictive analytics, through the market segment of talent analytics, are influencing the flow of finances to test development and, as we will see later in this chapter, where psychometrics research is moving today.

The significance of that influence is evidenced by the acquisition of three test vendors (or, as some would call them, using their more traditional label, test publishers) by technology and consultancy firms over the three-year period between 2012 and 2015. Those acquisitions amounted to a more than $2 billion (£1.3 billion) investment (BusinessWire, 2012; IBM, 2012; Moss, 2015).[5] In other words, that investment over three years in just three test vendors equates to *Time* magazine's valuation of the testing market in 2015.

Why are these technology and consultancy companies making these very substantial investments? I will offer three reasons.

- From a **commercial perspective**, to add to and consolidate their customer install base and company footprint in the talent management market within and across geographies.
- From a **capability perspective**, to offer stronger end-to-end integration of talent management services and products (or as some would call them, 'talent workflows'). In effect, to become a one-stop shop for talent management solutions.
- From a **Big Data and talent analytics perspective**, which is an extension of the capability reason, to add test and assessment data to other HR and talent management data streams and create even Bigger Data (see Figure 4.1 for a sense

of how large Big Test Data might be),[6] and to add to the firm's predictive analytics capabilities psychological research and psychometrics know-how, including the predictive modelling of employee performance and engagement.

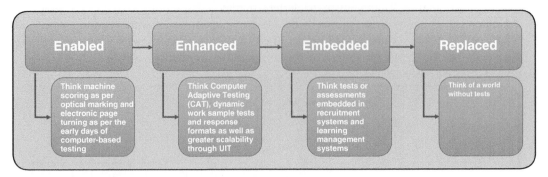

Figure 4.2 *Technology and testing, from enablement to replacement*

For the remainder of this chapter, I will focus on the third of these reasons and explore how these market forces, as well as wider technological and social forces, are shaping the very notion of what we may come to call a 'test' in the future.

That impact is characterised in Figure 4.2, which is offered to summarise an evolutionary path through which technology has supported the capability to administer and deploy tests more efficiently, provided the opportunity to deploy more sophisticated psychometric scoring algorithms and increase the scope of testing programmes (such as through UIT), and led to the embedding of tests in talent workflows such as applicant tracking systems (ATSs) and learning management systems (LMSs). Ultimately, and going back to the question addressed in this chapter, Figure 4.2 flags a possible end-point of this evolutionary path in the eventual replacement of tests as we know them today by other data-analytic substitutes.

THE ULTIMATE CANDIDATE-FRIENDLY TEST: THE ONE YOU DON'T HAVE TO TAKE!

One of the key concerns of organisations in an ever more competitive market for acquiring and retaining employees is the candidate's experience of any HR process, including tests and assessments (see Burke, Mahoney-Phillips, Bowler & Downey, 2011, for a discussion of this in test solution design and of the ever-narrowing assessment window). In addition to promoting organisational branding through the look-and-feel of an HR process workflow, such as a recruitment process and an applicant tracking system (ATS), the effort required of and the convenience of the process for the candidate, as well as their perceptions of a 'test', are key factors that are now weighted heavily by stakeholders when they design an online HR process. And those stakeholders are no longer restricted to HR. Today, brand managers and colleagues from marketing are often as important in the decision making that influences the use of tests as the test-savvy HR professional or the in-house psychologist.

Staying with a recruitment process as an example, organisations typically require candidates to supply background information, and many use social media to engage and maintain relationships with candidates throughout the recruitment process.[7] In addition to that data, candidates are busy generating online data through their professional network sites (e.g. LinkedIn) and social media sites (e.g. Facebook) to create a 'digital footprint'. They may also be members of a number of other specialised networks through which they generate data (we will look at an example for programmers a little later in this chapter).

It is these sources of data that provide the basis for the ultimate candidate-friendly test in the sense that this data is created through normal online activity and through the expected requirements of applying for a job. Using this data, there is no separate and discrete event called a test. The argument from those that see the utility of testing as having come and gone is that organisations can create predictive algorithms from this data, negating the need to administer a test.

Let us look at a couple of these applications of analytics and Big Data that are already available, and more specifically how US companies are using data-mining and text-mining software to screen job applicants. Wells Fargo has explored the use of predictive analytics using a more traditional biographical data, or biodata, approach alongside testing (Kuehner-Hebert, 2015, which uses the term 'biometric data'). The research claims that 65 questions covering the number of jobs held to date, the length of tenure in those jobs, promotions to date and highest level of educational attainment have improved retention rates among bank tellers and personal bankers by between 12 and 15 per cent.

So far, not so new, perhaps, if you are familiar with the history of biodata questionnaires (Stokes & Mumford, 1994). But consider the application of biodata-like approaches to less structured and largely textual data, such as data generated by social media activity. This is what the *Wall Street Journal* reported in 2012 in describing how Xerox had turned to an analytics company to model its recruitment data and improve both its screening processes and the productivity of new hires (Walker, 2012). Among the data points linked to stronger job performance were that that person lived near the job, had reliable transport and used one or more, but not more than four, social networks. Note that the number of social networks is now factoring into an algorithm predicting job performance. We will come back to social and professional online networks that feature in predictive algorithms.

In the same article, findings reported for a different unnamed client showed that 'a lengthy commute raises the risk of attrition in call-center and fast-food jobs. The online process asks applicants for call-center and fast-food jobs to describe their commute by picking options ranging from "less than 10 minutes" to "more than 45 minutes." The longer the commute, the lower their recommendation score for these jobs'.

Those with a knowledge of the history of testing may be dismissive of these examples of predictive analytics as old wine in new bottles, and point out that they run the same risks that a long line of published scientific research has flagged for biodata questionnaires. These include a tendency towards 'dustbowl empiricism' (finding connections that lack any clear cause–effect explanations or models); the risk that scores suffer from short-lived criterion validities because they lack a robust theory to back them up; and the risk of leading naive end users into adopting pre-screening metrics that are subsequently found to discriminate against minorities and groups protected by employment law.

Take the example of how close to the workplace a candidate lives. Then think about the implications if the neighbourhoods close to the workplace have a very specific demographic profile that is low on the likelihood of someone being an ethnic minority member or of a given gender or age group. Despite those risks, these applications are seen as offering sufficient value for yet another recent acquisition within the talent management market of a predictive analytics company for $42.5 million (£27.4 million; Cornerstone On Demand, 2014).[8]

A couple of other examples of how predictive analytics and Big Data are playing in the HR space help to explain why these applications of analytics are attracting this level of investment and, as we will see, serious investigation by psychometrics researchers.

The next example comes from a 2013 *New York Times* article entitled 'How big data is playing recruiter for specialized workers' (Richtel, 2013), which describes the following scenario:

- A software programmer receives an email notifying him or her of a job opening in a physical location close to where they live (remember, proximity to the workplace has been found to be related to retention rates of new hires).
- The email outlines a position that seems very suited to the recipient's skills and, after all, the job is within easy commuting distance.

Why wouldn't the recipient respond to the email and engage in the application process? But, how did that email originate and why was it sent to this particular person? Let's play the backroom scenario out a little more:[9]

- Programmers will often sign up to online peer groups and submit their computer code for peer review. That gives analytics companies a source of data and, with the right algorithms, the opportunity to score examples of a person's code and rank them against others in a given professional segment (e.g. a specific type of computer code).
- Programmers, along with everyone else, tend to subscribe to professional and personal network sites, thereby creating other sources of data about their background (including the types of biodata mentioned earlier) and location as well as information about the type of person they are (their Likes on Facebook, for example).
- Data on people's online profiles collated from several sources can be used to aggregate people against job types and segment them according to location, salary potential and the types of working environments they are most likely to enjoy.
- Now we need to bring the two parties together, which is effectively the business model here, that of an aggregator and an intermediary. To do that, we need clients who are looking for certain skills and we need potential candidates who match those skills. The clients can be found through web searches and inquiries about job openings.
- Given that we have already solved the problem of finding people to supply to the client, now we can bring the two parties together by first emailing the potential job applicant to see if they are interested. What is more, we can pre-screen the candidate before we send that email, using the quality of their code and their proximity to the client's location among other data points.
- But we can do more than that. If we are able to obtain and score the data available from professional and social media websites, we can also send the client a profile of the candidate to accelerate pre-screening and frame a more informed job interview should both parties move to that point.

So there is no test per se, and a largely automated process substantially increases the efficiency and reduces the cost of sourcing and screening candidates. All of this is, of course, subject to permissions from the various parties involved.[10] Readers of this book will (I hope) ask about the evidence of validity that supports such a process; the addition of validity evidence is the next logical step in the evolution of this form of candidate-friendly test, and one that psychometric researchers are actively involved in.

What if we were able to tap into unstructured data, such as text from social media sites, and score that data using a well-established psychometrics and psychological model such as the Big 5 (a model that seems appropriate given that this is a chapter looking at the impact of Big Data on testing)? That is exactly what researchers at Cambridge University, Stanford University and Microsoft have been doing (Kosinski, Stillwell & Graepel, 2013; Park et al., 2015; YouYou, Kosinski & Stillwell, 2014).

In this series of studies, the researchers mined and analysed Facebook Likes and explored how their findings correlated with measures of the Big 5 personality constructs, using the international Personality Item Pool (IPIP; Goldberg et al., 2006) and with fluid intelligence as measured by Raven's Standard Progressive Matrices (Raven, Raven & Court, 2004).

The results showed modest but nonetheless meaningful correlations between the indices developed from Facebook Likes and the psychometric measures. Correlations of the former with Big 5 measures ranged from 0.29 for Conscientiousness, through 0.3 for both Agreeableness and Emotional Stability, to 0.4 and 0.43 respectively for Extraversion and Openness to Experience (Kosinski et al., 2013). Hardly results in the realm of alternate forms reliabilities, perhaps, and the study was constrained by the reliabilities observed for the measures of the Big 5 used in the study. For intelligence, the observed correlation was 0.39, which is remarkable when you consider that an abstract reasoning task is being predicted by whether a Facebook Like included words such as Harley Davidson (lower intelligence test scores)[11] or science and Mozart (higher intelligence test scores).

Subsequent analysis showed that, despite these modest correlations, the coding and scoring of Facebook Likes provided rather impressive levels of accuracy in predicting people's personality profiles compared to others' judgements of Big 5 profiles.

Facebook friends were asked to rate a participant's personality using a ten-item version of the IPIP Big 5 scales. In this study, the computer algorithms correlated with participants' self-rated Big 5 profiles at 0.56 when 227 Likes were available, and the correlation rose to 0.66 when 500 or more Likes were available to generate a Big 5 profile from social media data. In comparison, the correlation between self-ratings on the Big 5 and others' ratings varied from 0.58 for a spouse and 0.50 for a family member, to 0.45 for a friend or housemate and 0.27 for a work colleague. This study also looked at correlations with thirteen outcomes and traits associated with personality including life satisfaction, depression, political orientation, self-monitoring, impulsivity, values and interests, field of study, substance use, physical health and social network characteristics. The computer algorithms outperformed human ratings for 12 of these 13 outcomes (YouYou et al., 2014).

IBM has been pursuing a similar line of research with the Personality Insights application (Mahmud, 2015). This application accepts text and provides a narrative report on the writer's personality profile to support targeted marketing, customer care, résumé writing and even more effective online dating. Both this application, which requires between 3,500 and 6,000 words of input,[12] and the Cambridge–Microsoft research, where accuracy improves with over 500 Likes, are data-hungry formative technologies. Even so, they both serve as examples of how Big Data, analytics and psychometrics have already merged to explore new models and methods for capturing people's profiles that may well evolve into the ultimate candidate-friendly test.[13]

I have already pointed to a few of the challenges facing these applications of Big Data and analytics in an employment setting. As many of the researchers in this field point out, the ultimate candidate-friendly test based on publicly available online data also has a number of ethical hurdles to clear before wider adoption is likely. Yet the potential is there, and the threat that these new developments will replace what we know as tests today is real, as one industry analyst with a test development background recently observed (Handler, 2013):

> There are a number of emerging trends in hiring right now that center around the currency of the new millennium: *data*. The impact of our ability to collect, organize and interpret data is rapidly changing all areas of the economy. Should employment be any different? There are three ways in which data is slowly killing the employment test as we know it. …
>
> 1. People born in the past decade or so, along with all persons to come, will begin accumulating a personal digital fingerprint that will be associated with them from cradle to the grave. While there may still be some things that can be kept private, most everyone's every move, preference, and connection will become publicly available to anyone who is interested. …
>
> 2. Also gaining in popularity at present are many types of data that people directly create and groom for specific purposes related to employment. Consider if you will the LinkedIn profile, which is now becoming the de facto resume. It is fluid and fully deconstructible for use in hiring situations. It has all the info needed by an employer to gauge your ability to contribute to their cause. …
>
> 3. Change is coming when it comes to performance data. Workforce analytics is here to stay and at its core resides data of all shapes and sizes. … Once the post-hire data stream becomes more available, we should be prepared to find all kinds of new predictors of value.[14]

I am not quitting my day job as a testing guy just yet. But things are changing fast and those of us in the testing business are going to be tested ourselves. … Yes, tests may be involved somewhere in the data stream, but they will cease to be the only focus when it comes to predicting job success.

THREE OTHER SCENARIOS FOR TESTING IN A BIG DATA AND ANALYTICS WORLD

Whatever your emotional or ethical reactions to what I have called the ultimate candidate-friendly test are (and some readers may be excited by the prospect for innovation in psychometrics and testing practice), research and development that brings together psychometrics, psychological theory and models, Big Data and predictive analytics is certainly going to increase. There are many possible scenarios for how these potential synergies will play

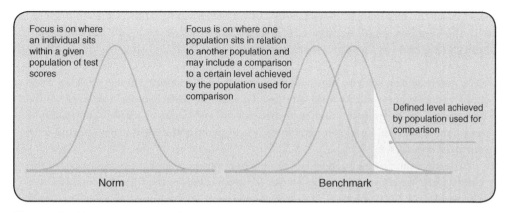

Figure 4.3 *Norms and benchmarks*

out. I will explore three which offer a much more positive future for the test as we know it today, as well as opportunities for the value of test data to be recognised and leveraged in a Big Data world.

Analytics as a value-add to testing

In this scenario, one application is the use of test data to create predictive benchmarks for use by end users to help them understand what may be driving an issue or to check their assumptions about the likely return from an HR investment.

Those in the testing world will typically interpret a test score by using a norm to understand where an individual sits in relation to the test scores of comparable individuals. Benchmarks are occasionally used in addition to norms to help guide interpretations such as how an individual or a group of individuals compares with a target group such as a specified population of sales personnel or a given management or leadership group. Figure 4.3 summarises the difference between a norm (within-population comparison) and a benchmark (a between-population comparison).

In manufacturing and service settings, a benchmark serves to measure whether a process is achieving desired levels of performance and where improvements are required. Assuming that a test score is supported by validity evidence (Messick, 1995), and specifically by criterion validity evidence, then the aggregation of test score data to form benchmarks offers the potential to show not only how one population compares to another, but also whether employees can be expected to achieve a given level of performance when compared to the benchmark population.

That interpretation is supported if a criterion-centric approach to interpreting tests scores is adopted (Bartram, 2005). For example, personality and cognitive ability scores can be combined using regression weights to form composites that talk to the likelihood of desired workplace behaviours being observed and, if the research supports such an interpretation, to the levels of job performance that can be expected if those behaviours are observed (see Burke, 2008 for a discussion of this use of test scores).

Burke (2013) describes the use of aggregated test score data based on these principles for benchmarking an organisation's employees against external populations such as occupational groups, industry sectors or groupings of organisations (such as the Interbrand

Global 100 or the FTSE 100), as well as by country or by geographical region.[15] Here is an excerpt showing this use of aggregated test score data in action, using the upper quartile (the highest-scoring 25%) as the performance comparison:

> [W]e undertook an analytics study for a client in the cable industry in the US. They came to us with two questions: how do we show the value we deliver to our business from the assessments we are using for front line retail manager and customer service agent, and how do we know whether our recruitment processes are giving us the talent that we need to drive our retail operations?
>
> To answer the first question and establish a framework for looking at the quality of this client's hires, we reviewed analytics studies for seven clients in the US and a total analytics sample of over 3,000 employees in retail management and customer service. The trends across those clients showed that employees in the upper quartile on our talent metrics for retail manager and customer service agent had shorter time to competence as compared to other employees (19% faster for the customer service role), incurred lower costs and generated higher revenues per employee (a weighted average of $154k more revenue per year per manager and agent), and were seen as offering greater potential for progression in the business (in one case and for retail manager, 20 times more likely to be seen as having the potential for a more senior role).
>
> These trends show that being in an upper quartile on a CEB talent metric such as fit to retail manager or to customer service agent does lead to better staff performance and a higher impact of people on business outcomes. Our client in the cable industry was satisfied that this upper quartile approach was useful and so they conducted their own analysis using this approach. They found that those people in their business in the CEB upper quartile for the customer service agent metric showed a difference in over $300k more revenue per employee per year when compared to other employees, and a much higher retention rate to the end of the first year's employment (16% lower voluntary turnover). ...
>
> Let's return to ... their second question: how do we know whether our recruitment processes are giving us the talent that we need to drive our retail operations? Building on the link between a CEB talent metric (in this case, fit to retail manager or customer service agent), answering this question also shows how CEB talent metrics speak to the effectiveness of a talent process such as recruitment. If higher CEB talent metrics predict higher organisational returns, then the greater the proportion of people attracted with higher scores on a CEB talent metric, the more effective that process is going to be in supporting an organisation in achieving its goals.
>
> To answer the cable client's second question, we looked at the talent they had attracted over a year to the retail manager and customer agent roles. Using that upper quartile to define top talent for these roles, the analytics showed that this client had outperformed the labour market for their industry by 154% for the quality of talent attracted for front line manager (of those attracted to the retail manager role, 56% were in that upper quartile against the talent pool for North America), but were on par for the quality of talent attracted to the customer service agent role (actually, the proportion of customer service agent applicants attracted over that year and that were in the upper quartile range was just short of 25%). Simple headline – keep the process running for front line manager (maintain) and take the learning across from that to customer service agent as this is where the impact is likely to be greatest in driving revenues and margins in retail operations (take action). (pp. 1–2).[16]

How does this example of aggregated test score data show the value-add to testing from Big Data and analytics? One way is that it raises the value of test scores beyond assessments of individuals and brings that value into the scope of strategic-level HR and organisational issues. That shows there is value beyond the typical transactional use of scores from employment tests in screening new hires or diagnosing the development needs of an existing employee, both of which have value but on a much narrower scale.

A second way that this adds value to testing is by bringing together information on the talents of people and populations, and predictive relationships such as work and organisational outcomes, in a single talent metric. Whether it be in the form of a benchmark on not, talent metrics that speak to the potential of people *and* to whether desired outcomes will be achieved are a very powerful basis for generating insight for organisational leaders and managers.

A third is the senior audience who is likely to be exposed to test data in this form which, if visualised and presented in ways familiar to that audience (e.g. graphical displays that they would typically see in reports, presentations and dashboards used to track finance, marketing and operational performance), offers the opportunity to communicate the power of test data to provide deep insights based on the root causes, i.e. people, of why outcomes are achieved and why they are not.

Analytics and data sciences can add value to testing in other ways. One is the use of data science methods such as neural networks in the analysis of test data and in the design of tests themselves, an application that is already 20 years old (Rust & Golombok, 2009). In his observations on the threat of Big Data and analytics to testing, Handler (2013) refers to the growth of workforce analytics and how it is helping to build more sophisticated models from the data within organisations on performance as well as on mobility and change in workforces over time. This is an exciting prospect for testing researchers and testing professionals as it provides a much richer and easier navigation of the criterion space critical to building the validation evidence in support of tests.

Testing as a value-add to analytics

The one significant weakness of much use of Big Data and analytics in unveiling insights into employees and HR processes is the lack of strong theoretical models to frame and guide much of that effort. That may seem unduly critical to a reader who practises in the field of HR Analytics, but developing models within single organisations based on the narrower context that a single organisation offers does run the dual risks of dustbowl empiricism and errors in believing that Y (an outcome) is caused by X (a data point), when a stronger and more widely tested theory might well show that Y is driven or moderated (or mediated) by a different variable altogether. This is something that psychologists and psychometricians are all too aware of, largely because of the many examples over the histories of those disciplines of theories found to be subject to those errors.

Whatever the sophistication of Big Data algorithms, they need data to be codified into meaningful variables. We have already seen how models such as the Big 5 and a test of intelligence have been used as variables to guide analytics research and development. A very real value-add of testing to analytics is in providing frameworks and meaningful construct definitions of variables as well as reliable methods for measuring those constructs.

Test data provides a means to isolate cause-and-effect relationships so that a more informed view can be developed of the root causes of performance, the impact of employee churn on the capabilities, and human capital risk. For example, an analyst may have an array of data and results that help him or her to make sense of the current state of performance in an organisation. Potential contributors to the levels of performance observed will include resources available to employees, including technology (i.e., levels of capital investment made by the organisation), the way in which work is organised and how performance targets are tracked through the organisation (i.e., work design), and external factors such as the levels of market competition and customer profiles (or analogous factors in the not-for-profit and government sectors). A key set of variables will also be the talents (abilities, skills and other characteristics) of the employees, and here test data offers immense value in isolating the factors to focus on to improve performance and showing how these different factors interplay and can be optimised (or not).

To realise that potential for tests in an analytics world, tests may have to become significantly more efficient in the way that they capture data, and that may mean challenging some of the tenets of the conventional wisdom of today's testing science and test design. One such tenet is obsession among test researchers and practitioners with internal reliability (e.g. Cronbach's Alpha) and with test lengths that maximise that form of reliability. That means employment tests that measure narrower constructs, and that are developed as criterion-referenced rather than normative measures (as one example of moving from conventional test designs) and for indices of test score quality other than the conventions of reliability commonly used today.[17]

This scenario may, perhaps, prove to be only a waypoint on the road to the redundancy of tests as we know them today. It does, however, give testing a place in the analytics world and a voice to influence the transition to 'testing' as it might become in the future. That brings us to the last scenario in which Big Data and analytics provide the platform for the evolution of tests and testing science.

Analytics as a platform for the evolution of testing

I have already mentioned that Big Data and analytics may provide the catalysts for new test designs and for new psychometric methods through which we evaluate the information value and validity of tests. In this last scenario, I will briefly describe another driver for the evolution of testing and outline how tests, as they are today or could be tomorrow, may be embedded in everyday technologies.

One of the technological trends that have captured the excitement of the press as well as the wallets of consumers worldwide is wearable technology, such as the Apple Watch and the Google Glass, to mention but two (BBC, 2014). These devices point to a future in which disruption to social interactions is reduced as the need to use more invasive technologies, such as hand-held or smartphones, may decline. They will contribute, and indeed are contributing, more data to the Big Data streams that already exist and they are also spurring further developments in predictive analytics.

One such development is image analytics, which, like text analytics, comprises methods for classifying and extracting meaning from unstructured data in the form of images. Today's applications lie mainly in marketing and advertising, in refining the algorithms that track our behaviours as consumers online (for example, what does what we are looking at say about our purchasing preferences?) and in refining how products are packaged and advertised (including the design of the stores we make our more traditional purchases from).

The use of images or image features in testing is, again, not new, as shown by the Color Code Personality Test, which takes sixty seconds to complete and which captured the attention of US news media (Jones, 2010; Sadka, 2004). Before you dismiss this example as something from pop psychology, consider that the outputs are described in the form of colour-types and the inputs are a series of forced-choice questions. Now consider if those inputs and outputs were reversed so that the colours or images were the 'test items' that drove the scores and the narrative outputs describing people's profiles and likely behaviours. Now imagine that those inputs come from ambient and wearable technology rather than any conscious effort to provide responses to test items, and you begin to see the prospect that image analytics holds for evolving testing science and the practice of testing.

A little too far-fetched and futuristic? Well, consider a research programme announced on the website of the Psychometrics Centre at the University of Cambridge.[18] This programme, known as CitizenMe, aims to provide users with greater control over their digital identities through greater transparency of the use of their personal data by companies. Within that, the project also aims to extract emotional and psychological data from text and language stored on users' devices as well as social media data and other open-sourced databases. Ultimately, the aim of this strand of the research programme is to provide a predictive algorithm that provides insights into the psychology and emotions of the user. Adding image analytics to this line of research is a relatively small step for data scientists.[19]

AS A WISE PERSON ONCE SAID, 'THE FUTURE IS DIFFICULT TO PREDICT'

That quote is widely attributed to the Nobel Prize-winning physicist Niels Bohr and is a sensible warning about any aspirations to being a futurist. This chapter was written without any such aspirations as the trends shared in this paper are already a reality or close to becoming so.

The reader may note that as I described each of the four scenarios above, the text devoted to each scenario reduced. This is because I have sought to work within the available data and not to stretch my contribution too far beyond what is foreseeable from technologies and from psychometrics research already underway. If those scenario descriptions are uneven, then perhaps they reflect the comment by the author William Gibson, 'The future is here – it's just not very evenly distributed.'

This chapter was written with the intention of showing how a very significant change in the technological, organisational and social context of our world has very substantial implications for testing. It was also written in the hope that Big Data and predictive analytics will act as a spur to innovations in test development and application, and as a channel for wider appreciation of the value of psychology and psychometrics.

Testing is already embedded in the HR workflows of many organisations for assessing individuals pre- and post-employment. It has become part of the business-as-usual for managing people. Some organisations are beginning to realise the wider value of test data through benchmarks and as variables in predictive analytics. Those organisations see how valuable test data is as a data stream alongside data streams from HR, finance, sales and marketing[20] in helping them to unlock operational improvements, revenue growth and customer loyalty. Here, then, is an opportunity for test data to attain the same respect among senior managers and executives that they have for marketing and finance data in this world of Big Data.

That said, a world of the ultimate candidate-friendly test, that is, a world without tests as we know them today, is an entirely feasible one. For me, that conjures two possible outcomes for the 'test'. There is the world I have described in which Big Data and predictive analytics completely substitute for tests and, at best, testing sciences are absorbed into the wider data sciences gaining ground today.

There is an alternative world in which testing science and practice evolve to be the creative means through which that candidate-friendly test is developed and realised. The end product is probably not a test but a psychological data stream that sits alongside other data streams to enhance both organisational and employee success.

After all, isn't psychometrics a data science synonymous with innovation and doesn't testing practice have a long history of problem solving? And haven't both continuously and successfully responded to a constantly changing world? I like to think they have and that they will continue to do so.

NOTES

1. Also referred to as maximal performance tests, these tests contain items or questions to which there is only a single correct response. Because of this, they are seen as particularly susceptible to people learning answer keys and to people sitting a test on behalf of others. The first of these two issues raises the need to safeguard item content. The second issue raises the need to verify candidate identity. Other forms of tests and assessments, such as personality questionnaires and Situational Judgement Tests (SJTs), are also subject to validity threats, but cognitive ability tests became the focal point for the debate on UIT in the opening decade of this century. For some commentators, the perceived ability to game tests is a strong reason for developing Big Data applications to replace them.
2. Figures in US dollars have been converted to British pounds by the author at the conversion rate available at the time of writing this chapter. The rate was £1 to $1.55. This rate was also used to convert financials reported in British pounds to US dollars.
3. 'Sabermetrics' is a term for metrics applied to predicting performance in baseball, but it has come to be more widely associated with metrics that challenge conventional wisdom on what drives outcomes.
4. To gauge the success of the book, consider that the film made over $111 million (£72 million) at the box office and a further $34 million (£22 million) in domestic DVD and Blu-ray sales, giving a total revenue of $145 million (£94 million). As a benchmark for comparison, those revenues from the *Moneyball* film represent between 56% and 426% of the publicly available (at the time of writing) annual revenues of larger and smaller well-known brands among employment test vendors.
5. These are but three acquisitions chosen because of the prominence of the brands and product ranges of the acquired companies. Other acquisitions would extend the

total financial value of acquisitions made in recent years beyond the figure of $2 billion (£1.3 billion) quoted.
6. In Figure 4.1, I show a 'guesstimate' of the number of employment tests administered each year globally and every hour. These are tests administered for recruitment and selection, development and succession planning as well as for high-potential employee and leadership identification, to mention but a few of the possible administrations. By employment tests, I mean cognitive ability tests, personality and similar assessments, SJTs, competency assessments and skills tests. My guesstimate is based on the published number of administrations of two of the larger global test vendors, CEB SHL Talent Measurement and IBM-Kenexa, and on an assumption that they occupy around 40% of the total employment testing market worldwide.
7. Post-hire, organisations will have access to a wealth of data about their employees. In a world of Big Data, that would include a raft of communications data, relational data between employees and even social media data in addition to the more formal types of HR data captured by HR information systems (HRIS), performance and development systems and learning management systems (LMS).
8. The company purchased was listed as one of the ten most innovative companies in Big Data in the same year that it was acquired (Fast Company, 2014). It is, or was, the very analytics company that advised Xerox as described in the *Wall Street Journal* article.
9. This scenario is based on personal communication with the company involved. The company's website is https://www.gild.com/. Accessed 25 September 2016.
10. There are inevitably a number of ethical and data protection issues involved in the applications of Big Data and analytics described. For the sake of brevity and because these issues are covered by numerous publications and codes, I have chosen to acknowledge this as a serious issue in this footnote to allow space in the chapter to focus on the threats posed and opportunities offered by testing science and practice.
11. A finding which drew a rather voluminous critical response from Harley Davidson owners when presented on prime-time US TV.
12. At the time of writing, a demo of the application that will allow you to submit your own text can be accessed via https://watson-pi-demo.mybluemix.net/. Accessed 25 September 2016.
13. Case study – CareerWhiz (21 July 2015) provides an example of a similar application that uses LinkedIn information to provide advice on career paths, including jobs to seek and skills to acquire. http://www.slideshare.net/DaniilShash/case-study-careerwhiz. Accessed 25 September 2016.
14. The numbers are inserted by the present author.
15. See Burke and Glennon (2012) for how this approach to benchmarking can be used to analyse the supply of leadership talent globally and innovation talent by country, as well as the supply of business-critical skills. Also see Burke, Vaughan and Glennon (2013) for a discussion of benchmarks in the form of 'talent metrics'.
16. For those who are curious about using the upper quartile as a performance benchmark, Aguinis and O'Boyle (2014) provided a critique of the presumption that outstanding performance follows a normal (Gaussian) distribution and observed that 'sales managers typically find that 80% of unit sales are attributable

to 20% of their workforce. ... An examination of multiple industries at multiple time points suggests ... the top decile of performers contributing an average of 30.1% of the total production, whereas the top quartile produce an average of 50%' (p. 324).

17. One example of narrow band tests are criterion-focused occupational scales or COPS (Ones and Viswesveran, 2001a, 2001b). In my own work, a COPS approach was used to develop a five-minute test to screen for safety-critical and customer service roles. The research showed that similar constructs drove outcomes in both settings, although in one the validities were negative in sign (higher scores related to lower accident rates) and in the other positive (higher scores related to higher customer satisfaction). Further development of this test as a source of benchmarking data showed that the small item pool could be divided into two subscales related to different workplace behaviours and still maintain validities comparable to those reported in published scientific articles. All of these scores had modest internal reliabilities, simply because this form of reliability is inappropriate for this particular design of test (Burke, Vaughan and Ablitt, 2010).

18. A summary, 'Innovate UK: Regain control of your online digital footprint', can be accessed via the following link, which also provides access to the CitizenMe app: http://www.psychometrics.cam.ac.uk/research/innovate-uk. Accessed 26 September 2016.

19. Consider that the origin of Item Response Theory (IRT) is frequently traced back to Frederick Lord's PhD in 1952, and yet the applications of IRT, including computer-adaptive testing (CAT), took decades to be realised and implemented. The developments in data sciences mentioned in this chapter are, in several cases, less than a decade old and already being applied.

20. Merging different data streams or databases to solve organisational challenges is widely referred to as 'blended analytics' and is taken as a sign of the analytics maturity of an organisation.

REFERENCES

Aguinis, H. & O'Boyle, E. (2014). Star performers in twenty-first century organizations. *Personnel Psychology*, 67, 313–50.

BBC (2014). Wearable technologies. Online video posted on 25 February. http://www.bbc.co.uk/programmes/p01sg4f4. Accessed 25 September 2015.

Bartram, D. (2005). The Great-Eight competencies: A criterion-centric approach to validation. *Journal of Applied Psychology*, 90, 1185–1203.

Bartram, D. & Burke, E. (2013). Industrial/organizational testing case studies. In J. A. Wollack & J. J. Fremer (eds.), *Handbook of Test Security* (pp. 313–32). New York: Routledge.

Brynjolfsson, E., Hitt, L. M. & Kim, H. H. (2011). Strength in numbers: How does data-driven decision making affect firm performance? *Social Science Research Network (SSRN)*, 22 April. http://dx.doi.org/10.2139/ssrn.1819486.

Burke, E. (2008). Coaching with the OPQ. In J. Passmore (ed.), *Psychometrics in coaching: Using psychological and psychometric tools for development* (pp. 87–114). London: Kogan Page.

Burke, E. (2009). Preserving the integrity of online testing. *Industrial and Organizational Psychology*, 2, 35–8.

Burke, E. (2013). *CEB talent analytics: Answering the critical questions about the potential of your people and the effectiveness of your talent management processes*. Washington, DC: CEB. https://www.cebglobal.com/content/dam/cebglobal/us/EN/regions/uk/tm/pdfs/White%20Paper/talent-analytics-white-paper-uk.pdf.

Burke, E. & Glennon, R. (2012). *The SHL talent report: Big Data insight and analysis of the global workforce*. Thames Ditton: SHL.

Burke, E., Mahoney-Phillips, J., Bowler, W. & Downey, K. (2011). Going online with assessment: Putting the science of assessment to the test of client need and 21st century technologies. In N. T. Tippins & S. Adler (eds.), *Technology-enhanced assessment of talent* (pp. 355–79). San Francisco, CA: Jossey-Bass.

Burke, E., Vaughan, C. & Ablitt, H. (2010). *Dependability and Safety Instrument (DSI) Version 1.1: Technical manual*. Thames Ditton: SHL.

Burke, E., Vaughan, C. & Glennon, R. (2013). Employment testing and assessment in multinational organizations. In K. Geisinger (ed.), *APA handbook of testing and assessment in psychology* (vol. 1, pp. 579–609). Washington, DC: American Psychological Association.

BusinessWire (2012). Corporate Executive Board (CEB) to acquire UK-based SHL for $660 million. http://www.businesswire.com/news/home/20120702006383/en/Corporate-Executive-Board-CEB-Acquire-UK-Based-SHL#.VgbqiPlViko. Accessed 25 September 2015.

Columbus, F. (2014). Roundup of analytics, Big Data & business intelligence forecasts and market estimates. *Forbes*, 24 June. http://www.forbes.com/sites/louiscolumbus/2014/06/24/roundup-of-analytics-big-data-business-intelligence-forecasts-and-market-estimates-2014/. Accessed 25 September 2015.

Cornerstone OnDemand (2014). Cornerstone OnDemand signs definitive agreement to acquire Evolv. Press release, 7 October. http://finance.yahoo.com/news/cornerstone-on-demand-signs-definitive-agreement-211200715.html. Accessed 25 September 2015.

Davenport, T. H & Kim, J. (2013). *Keeping up with the quants: Your guide to understanding and using analytics*. Boston, MA: Harvard Business Review Press.

Fast Company (2014). The world's 10 most innovative companies in Big Data. 10 February. http://www.fastcompany.com/most-innovative-companies/2014/industry/big-data. Accessed 25 September 2015.

Fetzer, M. & Tuzinski, K. (2013). *Simulations for personnel selection*. New York: Springer.

Fitz-Enz, J. & Mattox, J. R. (2014). *Predictive analytics for human resources*. Hoboken, NJ: John Wiley and Sons.

Goldberg, L. R., Johnson, J. A., Eber, H. W., Hogan, R., Ashton, M. C., Cloninger, C. R. & Gough, H. G. (2006). The international personality item pool and the future of public-domain personality measures. *Journal of Research in Personality*, 40, 84–96.

Gray, E. (2015). How high is your XQ? Your next job might depend on it. *Time*, 22 June.

Handler, C. (2013). Employment tests are becoming irrelevant for predicting job success. ERE. 8 May. http://www.eremedia.com/ere/employment-tests-are-becoming-irrelevant-for-predicting-job-success/. Accessed 25 September 2015.

HR Avatar (2015). 5 pre-employment test trends you need to know about. 14 January 2015. https://www.hravatar.com/ta/blogs/28/5-preemployment-test-trends-you-need-to-know-about.html. Accessed 25 September 2015.

Hytner, D. (2014). Arsenal's 'secret' signing: Club buys £2m revolutionary data company. *The Guardian*, 17 October. http://www.theguardian.com/football/2014/oct/17/arsenal-place-trust-arsene-wenger-army-statdna-data-analysts?CMP=twt_gu. Accessed 25 September 2015.

IBM (2012). IBM completes acquisition of Kenexa. 4 December. www-03.ibm.com/press/us/en/pressrelease/39501.wss. Accessed September 25 2015.

International Test Commission (2005). ITC guidelines on computer-based and internet delivered testing. Document reference: ITC-G-CB-20140617. https://www.intestcom.org/files/guideline_computer_based_testing.pdf. Accessed 25 September 2015.

International Test Commission (2014). The ITC guidelines on the security of tests, examinations, and other assessments. Document reference: ITC-G-TS-20140706. https://www.intestcom.org/files/guideline_test_security.pdf.

Jones, D. (2010). Favorite colors test shows CEOs are different; take the test. *USA Today*, 2 February. http://usatoday30.usatoday.com/money/companies/management/2010-02-08-ceocolors08_ST_N.htm. Accessed 25 September 2015.

Jones, K. & Wang-Audia, W. (2014). The market for talent management systems 2014: Talent optimization for the global workforce. Bersin by Deloitte. 26 June. http://www.bersin.com/Practice/Detail.aspx?docid=17684.

Kosinski, M., Stillwell, D. & Graepel, T. (2013). Private traits and attributes are predictable from digital records of human behavior. *Proceedings of the National Academy of Sciences*, 110, 5802–5. http://www.pnas.org/content/110/15/5802.full.pdf.

Kuehner-Hebert (2015). Predictive analytics for hiring. *Predictive Analytics Times*, 21 May. http://www.predictiveanalyticsworld.com/patimes/predictive-analytics-for-hiring-0521153/. Accessed 25 September 2015.

Lewis, M. M. (2003). *Moneyball: The art of winning an unfair game*. New York: Norton.

Lievens, P. & Burke, E. (2011). Dealing with the threats inherent in unproctored Internet testing of cognitive ability: Results from a large-scale operational test program. *Journal of Occupational and Organizational Psychology*, 84, 817–24.

Linoff, G. S. & Berry, M. J. A. (2011). *Data mining techniques: For marketing, sales, and customer relationship management* (3rd edn). Indianapolis, IN: Wiley.

Mahmud, J. (2015). IBM Watson Personality Insights: The science behind the service. IBM developerWorks. 23 March. https://developer.ibm.com/watson/blog/2015/03/23/ibm-watson-personality-insights-science-behind-service/. Accessed 25 September 2015.

Manyika, J., Chui, M., Brown, B., Bughin, J., Dobbs, R., Roxburgh, C. & Byers, A. H. (2011). Big data: The next frontier for innovation, competition, and productivity. *McKinsey Global Institute*, May.

Messick, S. (1995). Validity of psychological assessment. *American Psychologist*, 50, 741–9.

Moss, R. (2015). Towers Watson acquires Saville Consulting. *Personnel Today*, 27 April. http://www.personneltoday.com/hr/towers-watson-acquires-saville-consulting/. Accessed 25 September 2015.

Ones, D. S. & Viswesveran, C. (2001a). Integrity tests and other criterion-focused occupational personality scales (COPS) used in personnel selection. *International Journal of Selection and Assessment*, 9, 31–9.

Ones, D. S. & Viswesvaran, C. (2001b). Personality at work: Criterion-focused occupational psychology scales used in personnel selection. In B. W. Roberts & R. Hogan (eds.),

Personality Psychology in the Workplace (Decade of Behavior) (pp. 63–92). Washington, DC: American Psychological Association.

Park, G., Schwartz, H. A., Eichstaedt, J. C., Kern, M. L., Kosinski, M., Stillwell, D. J., Ungar, L. H. & Seligman, M. E. (2015). Automatic personality assessment through social media language. *Journal of Personality and Social Psychology*, 108, 934–52.

Raven, J., Raven, J. C. & Court, J. H. (2004). *Manual for Raven's Progressive Matrices and Vocabulary scales*. San Antonio, TX: Harcourt Assessment.

Richtel, M. (2013). How big data is playing recruiter for specialized workers. *New York Times*, 27 April. http://www.nytimes.com/2013/04/28/technology/how-big-data-is-playing-recruiter-for-specialized-workers.html?pagewanted=2&_r=4&ref=business. Accessed 25 September 2015.

Rust, J. & Golombok, S. (2009). *Modern psychometrics: The science of psychological assessment*. Hove: Routledge.

Sadka, D. (2004). *The Dewey Color System: Choose your colors, change your life*. New York: Three Rivers Press.

Stokes, G. S. & Mumford, M. D. (1994). *Biodata handbook: Theory, research, and use of biographical information in selection and performance prediction*. Palo Alto, CA: CPP Books.

Tippins, N. T., Beaty, J., Drasgow, F., Gibson, W. M., Pearlman, K., Segall, D. O. & Shepherd, W. (2006). Unproctored internet testing in employment testing. *Personnel Psychology*, 59, 189–225.

Walker, J. (2012). Meet the new boss: Big Data. Companies trade in hunch-based hiring for computer modeling. *Wall Street Journal*, 20 September. http://www.wsj.com/articles/SB10000872396390443890304578006252019616768. Accessed 25 September 2015.

YouYou, W., Kosinski, M. & Stillwell, D. (2014). Computer-based personality judgments are more accurate than those made by humans. *Proceedings of the National Academy of Sciences*, 112, 1036–40. http://www.pnas.org/content/112/4/1036.full.pdf?with-ds=yes. Accessed 26 September 2016.

5 The Practical Application of Test User Knowledge and Skills

GERRY DUGGAN

INTRODUCTION

There are few disciplines in the world of psychology where the domains of the theoretical and practical jostle for the same space in the way that they do in psychological testing. In essence, testing is a practical pursuit, but it is underpinned by voluminous theory in the areas of both psychological knowledge (e.g., theories relating to personal constructs, traits, cognition and behaviour) and psychometric processes (e.g., factor analysis, psychophysics, item response theory). As Dillon (1997, p. 1) notes, 'the credibility of a test is determined in large measure by the extent to which the test is grounded in a theory of the domain and is developed in the context of the rules of measurement'.

In the United Kingdom, a test user with a recognised qualification (e.g. the British Psychological Society *Test User* qualification) may have had as little as one day of face-to-face training (and perhaps two or three days in total). With that, they can have access to a wide range of testing materials which they can use to make critical decisions which can have a significant impact on both the lives of test takers and the effectiveness of organisations. It can be difficult for even the most experienced practitioners to apply all their learning when they are faced with the day-to-day pressures of many testing situations. How much harder must this be for the relatively 'new kids on the block', who may still be getting their heads around some of the more esoteric concepts raised in their test training?

This chapter is designed to help new test users to broaden their horizons in test use and to be comfortable with and enhance their use of both psychological and psychometric theory, so that their testing experiences, and the testing experiences of those with and for whom they work, are enriched.

CHOOSING TESTS

Many of the providers of psychological test training programmes are also commercial organisations which also sell tests. It is not uncommon for test trainers to focus completely on their own tests in their training programmes. The result is that many test users become locked in to the tests and systems of the test publisher who trained them. They may not be aware of any tests other than those sold by this test publisher. They may not even be aware that other tests, many other tests, are available to them as a holder of their qualification.

Purely from a coverage point of view, test users should be aware of as wide a range of tests as possible, as this offers a broader tool kit when they are considering which is the right test for a particular need. It is good practice to ensure that one has good coverage in terms of one's test options. An important part of this practice is to consider what it is that a particular test measures, and this is not always evident from the name of the test. 'Verbal' and 'numerical' do not convey sufficient detail of the ability or aptitude that is relevant, say, to job performance, and test users should take great care that they choose a test that measures the precise ability they wish to assess.

For example, the range of numerical tests can include reasoning, estimation, number facility and checking. Verbal tests can include reasoning, comprehension, vocabulary, word agility, grammar and spelling. It is the responsibility of the test user to determine exactly what ability they need to measure and to be sure that there is evidence – beyond the test name – that the tests they are considering do measure that ability.

It is for this reason that UK test qualifications offered by the British Psychological Society insist that test users can 'describe the major theories of intelligence, differences between them and issues relating to them' (British Psychological Society, 2016, p. 7). Having a solid appreciation of, say, the differences between crystallised and fluid intelligence can help the test user to understand the kinds of problem-solving strategies that an individual may need to complete a specific job task. Understanding the differences between abilities and aptitudes can help to decide whether on-the-job training is likely to fill perceived gaps in capability.

Undertaking training leading to BPS qualifications helps to avoid potential omissions in understanding psychological and psychometric theory. It allows the test user to consider different approaches to testing and instruments which are constructed in a variety of ways. It ensures that practical and ethical questions such as 'Who owns my test data?' and 'Is it fair to use this test in this situation?' are foremost in the test user's mind. When choosing tests, it helps to recall the need to ask about test shelf-life, costs, practical administrative considerations and, above all, whether this test does what you need it to do.

Here are some tips for choosing tests:

1. Register with a number of test publishers and build up your own list of 'useful' tests that may relate to the testing situations you face.
2. When selecting a test for a particular purpose, consider tests from at least two sources.
3. Besides the name of the test, check the test publisher's technical manuals and other information to ensure it is measuring the ability you really need for the purpose. If possible, examine the section in the test manual that precisely describes the ability the test is measuring.
4. Wherever possible, look at the items in the test and analyse precisely what the test taker has to do to answer the questions correctly. Does this align with the kinds of activities that the person needs to demonstrate to be successful in a job role?
5. Check the psychometric properties of the test: the reliability and validity data, the diversity and size of the published norm tables, information about sub-group performance, etc.

6. Be wary of published validation studies. Under what circumstances were the studies completed? Who conducted them? Do the statistics indicate a sufficient level of validity (not just a statistically significant finding) to justify you spending money on the test?

INTERPRETING TEST RESULTS

It always seems a little unfair that so much effort in choosing, administering and scoring an ability test should result in so little information, most often a single raw score. Of course, norm tables are used to provide percentile ranks and standard or transformed scores (T-scores, stens etc.). However, it feels as though more useful information should result from what might be over an hour of effort from the test administrator and test taker.

Some test trainers will warn against reading too much into other 'raw' data, such as how many test items a test taker completed, but useful information can be found there. It would be particularly useful to know whether a person is fast or slow compared with a relevant norm group, but test publishers seldom provide that information. It is still useful to consider how many items a test taker has completed and the percentage of items he or she has correctly answered. Where more than one test has been completed, a picture of speed and accuracy can be built up by looking at the results for each test. It is, however, worth remembering that there is generally little difference in test scores, whether speeded or unspeeded, in terms of a test taker's relative standing (Kline, 1993, p. 162).

Similarly, it can be useful to look at individual subtest scores, where available, to see whether there are patterns in the kinds of items that a person answers correctly and those they don't. Of course, one must be careful of reading too much into subtest scores. For a start, the reliability of a subtest may be quite low because of the smaller number of test items (a test with more items will be more reliable than a test with fewer items, other things being equal). Also, where a test is timed, it may be that items towards the end of the test are not completed, which reduces the potential score of the later subtests.

Despite these cautions, building an understanding of an individual's capability through a more forensic examination of how they completed the test will generally be more valuable than simply reporting a single figure that compares the person with other, similar people. Of course, this is less practical when one is testing large numbers of people, but it can be helpful when one is trying to identify the most suitable applicant from a small pool or testing for development purposes.

Some tests are designed to provide more than a single meaningful score. For example, tests of decision making, such as the ABLE Series Critical Information Analysis test, can include the overall number of correct answers, a count of the times when a test taker makes a decision without sufficient information (errors of omission) and the number of times they utilise unnecessary information in their decision making (errors of commission) (Blinkhorn, 1997). This data can form the basis of a rich conversation with a test taker about the kinds of decisions they need to take in job roles, their ability to manage ambiguity and their willingness to take risks.

Quite often, a trained and qualified test user is presenting test results to somebody who has no formal background in testing. In those circumstances, it is the responsibility of the test user to present the testing outcomes in a way that is clear, jargon-free and accessible to their 'customer', who may well be a test taker or a member of a client organisation (for example a recruiting manager).

An important part of test training is report writing, as it is in this context that the test user's interpretation of the test scores really adds value. Reports should give the test taker or the client an understanding of the meaning of the test results in terms of the initial reason for testing. One part of this is being helpful by reporting the person's level of ability as compared to populations that the customer can envisage. This is often one limitation of norm groups.

The test user is trained to use norm groups that are 'relevant' to the test taker, but it may be hard for a person who is receiving the test user's report to envisage the population that is a 'composite group of school leaver applicants to a range of industries aged 15–18' or a 'group of applicants to a range of positions in the paper and printing industry'. More specific groups may have very low sample numbers, which, in itself, compromises the value of using the norm group. It is not unheard of for popular tests to have norm groups consisting of as few as a dozen people. One only needs to use one's knowledge of the *standard error of the mean* to appreciate why these norm groups would be unlikely to offer a reliable representation of a significant population.

One way of helping a report reader to 'position' the test taker's level of ability is to offer comparison against several different norm groups. Some test publishers already offer computer-generated reports which show a person's score in comparison to non-graduates, undergraduates and graduates, for example. Depending on the quality of the norm samples, it may well be appropriate to offer comparisons against, for example, senior managers (the role that the person is applying for) and directors. For some organisations, comparisons across both the private and public sectors may be helpful in giving the test customer some reference points to work with. The point of norms is to provide a reference against which a test score can be compared. It is the test user's job to ensure that the person who needs the test results can visualise what this score means.

People who aren't trained in test use may be unsure how confident they can be that the test results are telling them something that can be relied upon. It can be frustrating, as a trained test user, to hear that somebody 'isn't a fan of psychometric testing' (Freedman, 2010) – as if testing were a matter of faith or popularity rather than a matter of scientific evidence. (Interestingly, in the author's experience, the people who have no faith in testing often have unlimited faith in their own interviewing ability.)

It can be a problem that test users are not always very clear in explaining how confident one can be of the value of the test score as a measure of the person's actual ability. Consider how we would feel about being told, when buying a car, that the salesperson is 68% confident that the car will get you at least ten miles before breaking down. Imagine if a financial adviser told us that he or she is 95% confident that the return on our investment will be somewhere between an 80% gain and an 80% loss. These examples may be far-fetched, but some psychological test reports are hardly any better. A basic understanding of the standard error of measurement and how this is used to create confidence intervals (which is one of the BPS areas of competence) provides us with the knowledge to clarify these issues.

Take the example of a well-used verbal reasoning test with a stated reliability coefficient of around 0.8. The standard deviation of the sample group is around 7.5 raw score points. The standard error of measurement works out to be around 3.35 raw score points. We can be 95 per cent confident that the true ability of somebody who scores around the mean for this group puts them between the 30th and 80th percentiles of the norm group (95% confidence limits for the 'true score' are $2 \times SE_m$ (standard error of measurement) either side of the obtained score). This estimate of ability is far too wide to satisfy a manager who wants a much more accurate assessment. It simply isn't particularly helpful to the organisation that wants to know whether the person they are about to employ (on a significant salary) can actually do the kinds of verbal tasks that the job entails.

Obviously, one way of providing more useful information is to choose more reliable tests, and norm groups which allow for a closer estimate of true ability. Another might be to consider whether or not the concept of '95% confidence' is a reasonable one for psychological testing.

Some highly regarded and well-used medical tests are relatively unreliable (visual scans, some blood tests). Others are reliable measures of sometimes unstable conditions (blood pressure, glucose levels). In both cases, the perceived unreliability of the test has not stopped them from being valuable indicators. The way they are often used is as screening processes to move people to the next level of testing.

Of course, this is how we tend to use psychological tests also, but maybe we need to be clearer to our customers about exactly what claims we are able to make with our tests. Rather than trying to defend a fairly unobtainable level of confidence, we may be more helpful if we let the recruiting manager know that we can be about 70% confident that our test taker has, say, more verbal reasoning ability than 60% of undergraduate students and 40% of applicants to managerial roles. In effect, we are feeding back to the manager the person's results, the comparison of the result against several norm groups, an indication of the reliability of the test, and the level of confidence we can have in the test scores, all in one go.

The interpretation of reliability shouldn't stop at the reliability coefficient (Kline 1998). In practice, reliability tells us how confident we can be in the test results, and this is what we need to communicate to those people who have requested that a test or tests be used. We need to help people who are not specifically trained in test use to recognise what the test results are, and are not, telling them. Over-interpretation is probably a bigger problem than under-interpretation, and test users have an obligation to ensure that the 20 or 30 minutes that a person takes to complete a test isn't given more weight in deciding the future of a person than it deserves.

Here are some tips for interpreting test results:

1. Look at all of the information that the test results offer and try to understand what it tells you about all of the aspects of the ability measured.
2. Consider using a range of comparison (norm) groups to give a fuller view of where a person stands in relation to relevant others.
3. Use the information you know about a test (reliability, SE_m, distribution of norm tables) to build a picture of confidence in the test results that you can share with the test customer.
4. Be clear about what the test results do and do not tell you, so that you can be clear about the appropriate weighting that should be given to test results.
5. Think about what might follow a test (for example an assessment centre-type exercise) to support (or not) a test result.

FEEDING BACK TEST RESULTS

In most test training courses, there is a dedicated face-to-face session where test takers are provided with feedback of their test scores in detail. In practice, depending on the number of people who have been tested, the will of the testing organisation to arrange feedback and, sometimes, the wishes of the test takers to receive feedback, the 'ideal' feedback session is not always possible.

Some feedback sessions may be shorter than ideal. Others may have to take place over the telephone, still others in writing. Some psychologists feel that it is inappropriate to share numerical scores with test takers; others feel that it is their right to see their scores. Still others feel that providing written feedback without a face-to-face interpretation is not good practice.

It is up to the test user to arrange the best outcome possible. Quite often, this needs to be arranged before the testing session itself so that the feedback arrangements can be communicated clearly to the test takers. Where testing is being done on behalf of a third party, the test user should endeavour to negotiate suitable feedback arrangements as part of the testing programme.

Where an ideal feedback session, for whatever reason, isn't possible, the test user needs to choose how best to use the information available to the advantage of the test taker. Computer-generated reports can make this task easier, but even a short interpretation that helps the test taker to pull out the salient points from the report can be very helpful.

Oral feedback sessions, where the person giving the feedback works through a number of results, detailing the figures without any interpretation, are not overly helpful. The test user must consider what is their added value in the feedback process.

Take, for example, the feeding back of a 30-scale personality measure. Even the most tenacious listener's attention will fade as the results are provided one after another, scale after scale, sten score after sten score.

In preparing for feedback, it is useful to consider the questions:

- What is it useful for this person to know?
- What can I tell them that will help them in the future?
- What is the most they can take away from this session, and how can I help them achieve that?

The focus should be immediately on the person and not on the test or measure. It is then the test user's responsibility to work with the person to identify what is important to them and what the test results say that can inform a discussion in that area. The BPS test user standards are quite clear that, in feedback, the test user should 'provide the candidate with opportunities to ask questions, clarify points, comment upon the test and the administration procedure and comment on the perceived accuracy and fairness or otherwise of the information obtained from the test'. It is incumbent on the test user to 'facilitate a feedback discussion which shows an appropriate balance of input between the test user and test taker' (British Psychological Society, 2016).

At the start of a feedback session, particularly for a personality questionnaire, it can be very enlightening, as well as helpful in establishing rapport, to ask questions such as:

- What did you think of the questionnaire as you completed it?
- How well does it appear to represent you?
- What aspects of your profile/results would be most interesting to you to explore?

Using the results to build hypotheses which are then discussed with the person is a good way to build a conversation which is rich and relevant for them. Looking at trends in the results is likely to be much richer than working through individual scales, and it allows the parties to work together to build up a picture which resonates with how the person sees themselves and how their abilities or personality traits are reflected in their behaviour.

With a self-report inventory, which is the format of most personality measures, it is important to remember that the results are an indication of how the person views themselves. It is not an objective measure of personality traits. The results are only as good as the responses to the questions. Where a person says 'I don't recognise myself in that statement', it is worth exploring how or why they answered the questions in the way they did, rather than immediately dismissing the response.

Conversations arising from these kinds of discussions can provide information about the 'psychological context' the person used when completing the questionnaire. For example, they may well see themselves as very different in work and in outside-work situations, and it may be worth exploring why this is. There may be good enabling behaviours that they use in one context, for example, that they could use to good effect in a different context.

Throughout the feedback process, it is important that the test user is still aware, and ready to use their understanding, of the psychometric properties of the instruments they are using. Particularly with multi-scale personality measures, where scales might be made up of a handful of items, the reliability of the scale and the confidence with which one can interpret scale scores should be scrutinised, and test users should have as full an understanding as possible of how the test scores are derived. The following example demonstrates this need.

One well-used personality measure has a scale which is made up of around 30 questions. The reported reliability statistics for the scale are fairly respectable, with coefficients of just above 0.8 and a standard error of measurement of just over 2 raw score units. The real problem with this scale is the distribution of scores in the norm group (and probably the reference population at large) and how that affects the computer-generated narrative that is produced.

Because of a much-skewed distribution of scores at the top end, a person would need to answer less than a handful of the questions in a 'not like me' way to find themselves around the bottom third of the norm group. These might be questions such as 'I know what I want to be' or 'I am a happy person'. The narrative that would accompany this score (which represents 'like me' answers to around 85 per cent of the questions) states that the person is 'somewhat lacking in leadership potential'.

Seeing this comment in a report when one is applying for a senior management role can be quite devastating, especially if the person knows that the employing company is seeing this too. The test user has an obligation to be able to explain to the person and the company how little confidence can be placed in the narrative statement. It is easily within the 95 per cent confidence limits to say that the person is at the 99th percentile, where the narrative report would say they 'have high standards of accomplishment and seek leadership roles'.

The point in this example is neither to denigrate the personality measure referred to nor to cast aspersions on narrative reports. Computer-generated reports have their place and serve a useful purpose. However, qualifications in the UK require test users to be able to 'critique computer generated reports to identify where modifications might be needed to take account of feedback and to improve contextualisation' and to 'take responsibility for the final report, whether written by the test user or computer generated' (British Psychological Society, 2016, p. 31). To be able to offer a thorough and realistic critique of reports, the test user must have a good understanding of the psychological constructs and the psychometric properties behind the measure. In effect, as the test user, you are asking the (test) questions and it is your responsibility to ensure that the answers are being interpreted and fed back correctly.

Here are some tips for providing feedback:

1. Use the test taker to provide context around the feedback session. What is valuable for them?
2. Work with the person to look for trends and patterns in the results. Explore hypotheses and agree meaning with the test taker.
3. Add value from your knowledge of the tests, what they measure and their psychometric properties.
4. Make sure that the person has a 'take-away' – something of added value from the feedback process beyond an oral recital of the printed report or profile.

PUTTING FORWARD THE CASE FOR TESTING (OR NOT TESTING)

Feeding back to those who have requested the testing is also an important part of the test user's role. We have discussed some of the relevant issues surrounding this in the previous sections of this chapter, but there is one area where feedback tends to be lacking: test utility.

It is somewhat baffling that a company will spend many weeks building a business case for the purchase of a new piece of machinery, gathering information about the features and benefits of different models, asking for free samples or trial periods and so on. They will then employ a senior manager for the company on the strength of one or two interviews which have very low demonstrable validity. Asking the company to spend even a relatively small amount of money on an ability test or personality measure can be met with concerns about the expense or even how the applicants might feel about being asked to do them.

One way of convincing recruiting managers of the value of tests is to explain how much the test can increase their chances of selecting good recruits. The Taylor–Russell approach is a good way to get this message across. Taylor and Russell (1939) examined the relationship

Table 5.1 *Proportion of potential recruits considered satisfactory for different test validities and percentile cut-off scores.*

Test validity	Percentile cut-off score used to select recruits				
	0	20	40	60	80
0.1	50	51	53	54	56
0.3	50	54	58	62	67
0.5	50	57	63	70	78

Source: Taylor & Russell, 1939. Reproduced with the permission of APA.

between test validity and the practical effectiveness of tests in terms of selecting good candidates. In effect, they explored how the validity of the test, combined with the proportion of people selected on the basis of test scores, can increase the probability of selecting a good person, compared to not using the test at all.

Look at the sample from the Taylor–Russell tables in Table 5.1. The figures in the body of the table show the chance of selecting good candidates using tests with different levels of validity. This table is based on a base rate of 50%. This means that, if we didn't use this test, the chances of selecting a good person would be 50%, or 50–50. Obviously, we could increase our base rate by making sure that our advertising is well targeted, or perhaps by screening CV's effectively. As the first column shows, if we disregarded the test results our chances of selecting a good recruit would remain at 50% regardless of how valid the test was.

Let's say we are using a highly valid test with a validity coefficient of 0.5. Now, let's assume we have five applicants for the job and we test each of them. Even if we use the test results just to screen out the lowest scorer (20th percentile), the table suggests that we have already increased our likelihood of selecting a good recruit to 57%. If we were to use the test to select only the top scorer, our chances of selecting a good recruit would increase to 78%. The use of the test has increased our chances of selecting a good recruit from 50% to 78%. Selection processes with even higher validities (e.g., the use of assessment centres) can have even more dramatic effects on the probability of selecting good people, although they can be much more expensive than testing.

Test users have an opportunity, in the feedback process, to communicate to recruiting managers the impact that using the test has on the likelihood of them choosing good employees for the company. If they wish, they can provide an actual pounds and pence business case for using tests, using utility equations, but, generally, offering clarity about how tests can deliver more certainty in an uncertain process is welcomed by managers. In effect, we are saying that the test can improve the chances of a good hire by this much for this cost. Cook and Cripps (2005, p. 260) discuss utility fully.

Of course, we may also be right to show that an expensive selection process might not be advisable, as it may not significantly increase the probability of a good hire. Full-day assessment programmes or expensive personality questionnaires may not be suitable for selecting applicants for roles where the 'value' of a good recruit over a less good recruit does not justify the cost of the selection process. Sometimes the test user has to use their knowledge of utility theory to make these kinds of calls and explain to those who are not familiar with tests why they are making their recommendations.

Of course, the validity of using a test in a particular situation is key to deciding whether or not to use any assessment instruments. It is to this subject that we turn in the final part of this chapter.

VALIDITY IN PRACTICE

When one uses a test in a particular instance, it is not really possible to know exactly how valid the use of that test is, as nobody has ever used that test in exactly that situation before. They may well have used the test in very similar situations, and we can certainly use the findings of any validity studies done in such situations to inform us of the likely validity in the specific situation in which we are now using the test. However, it isn't exactly the same, and it is up to the test user to identify any similarities and differences and make an estimate of how valid the use of the test is in their situation.

Tests don't 'possess' validity. The question 'Is the test valid?' is not really viable, as the most appropriate answer is 'It depends on what you want the test to do'. If we consider validity as a measure of the use of the test rather than as a property of the instrument itself, we will usually find ourselves on much safer ground when justifying the use of that test.

The theory of validity has seen a blossoming of the number of different 'types' of validity in recent years. Now, the qualifications for test users in the UK require a knowledge of face, faith, content, construct, criterion (predictive and concurrent) and consequential validity. Construct validity is seen as a central pillar upon which all the other validities rest, as, without knowing what the test measures, one is unable to make rational choices about the use of the test.

Looking back to the beginning of this chapter, one can see that being clear what the test measures and how this relates to job requirements is central to building a case for the validity of using the test in a particular case. Construct validity statistics from a test manual can be helpful in this. Looking at the kinds of tests that the scores of a test correlate with and the kinds of tests its scores do not correlate with helps one to build an understanding of what it is that the test is really measuring.

For example, if we see that the scores on a new numerical reasoning test correlate highly with scores on both verbal and mechanical reasoning tests but not highly with scores on numerical calculation or numerical estimation tests, it is reasonable to infer that the test is measuring a more general reasoning ability in a numerical context rather than a more global facility with numbers. We can then look back at the job role and ask ourselves what, specifically, is required of the job holder.

Predictive validity can be an easy concept to grasp in theory but a difficult process to deliver in practice. On the face of it, it should be easy. Keep test results (securely) on a spreadsheet. Add a column of performance data. Correlate the two columns. Make any corrections required (for example, to take into account the unreliability of the criterion measure). Job done! However, it is seldom straightforward in practice.

A common problem is the gathering of performance measures which have a clear rational connection to the constructs measured by the test or questionnaire. Identifying zero correlation between a test of verbal reasoning and the neatness of an officer's uniform (which may well be a very reasonable measure of job performance) does nothing to demonstrate the validity (or invalidity) of using the test. Test users may need to be creative in identifying and measuring those aspects of job performance that the test is designed to predict. Logical leaps by managers notwithstanding, tests don't measure everything and, therefore, can't predict everything.

Consequential validity is an interesting concept. It concerns looking at the overall use of an assessment tool and determining whether its use has negative consequences that might outweigh the positive benefits. In-company 'development' programmes present a situation where this can be observed. If the use of assessment tools, in this circumstance, could create ill will and, potentially, a backlash against using tests in the future, it may be that the longer-term disadvantages for the organisation will outweigh the benefits for the group in question. For this reason, it is always good practice to be clear with an organisation how test results will be used, how feedback will be managed, how negative outcomes will be handled and so on.

CONCLUSION

Test theory and test practice do dovetail well, but it isn't always clear how to utilise the former to enhance the latter. Hopefully, this chapter provides some insights (admittedly from a practitioner rather than a theoretician) into how one can go back to the text books and the training manuals and bring some of that learning forward into the daily testing practices with which one is involved.

The following tips are offered as a way of embedding some of the theory I learned while training to be a test user.

1. When faced with a problem test scenario, identify the different areas of knowledge that you need to be able to handle it effectively.
2. Clarify the questions you need to answer to solve the problem.
3. Do the research, identifying relevant information or studies which provide some of the answers you need.
4. Don't shy away from statistical concepts or calculations. If you don't understand them, get somebody to explain.
5. Always come back to the question 'Does my solution make sense?' If not, don't be afraid to re-evaluate what you are doing and change it.
6. Finally, good luck!

REFERENCES

Blinkhorn, S. (1997). *Critical Information Analysis manual and user's guide*. Oxford: Oxford Psychologists Press.
British Psychological Society (2016). Occupational test user standards: Guidance for assessors for the qualification – Test user: Occupation, ability.

Cook, M. & Cripps, B. (2005). *Psychological assessment in the workplace: A manager's guide.* Chichester: John Wiley and Sons.

Dillon, R. F. (1997). *Handbook on testing.* Westport, CT: Greenwood Press.

Freedman, H. (2010). The psychometric testing myth. *The Guardian*, 12 April. The Careers Blog. https://www.theguardian.com/careers/careers-blog/the-psychometric-testing-myth-harry-freedman. Accessed 26 September 2016.

Kline, P. (1993). *The handbook of psychological testing.* London: Routledge.

Kline, P. (1998) *The new psychometrics: Science, psychology and measurement.* London and Philadelphia, PA: Routledge.

Taylor, H. C. & Russell, J. T. (1939) The relationship of validity coefficients to the practical applications of tests in selection. *Journal of Applied Psychology, 23,* 565–78.

6 The Utility of Psychometric Tests for Small Organisations

PAUL BARRETT

Consider the evidence bases/validity coefficients for personality, EQ/EI, and other variants of psychometric tests presented in test manuals, academic articles, presentations at conferences; virtually all are drawn from large corporate organisations, government departments, the police and armed forces. For employee selection scenarios at smaller organisations, 'validity generalisation' is invoked so as to assure these particular clients that even they can benefit from psychometric testing of prospective candidates. But can they really? The issue here is whether the expected positive benefit indicated by a validity coefficient computed over large numbers of cases within one or more corporates is at all noticeable by a smaller organisation which may be employing fewer than 20 new employees each year.

What I want to look at is the likely real-world consequence of using psychometric tests for a small organisation, in terms of whether any such organisation would ever notice the claimed performance consequences which are meant to be accruing from the use of such tests.

For this exercise, in order to gain a clearer picture of the utility (or otherwise) of using psychometric tests in small organisations, I will need to model what will happen for thousands of such employers using a percentile cut-score on a test to screen out or screen in candidates.

Although it is possible to factor in realistic constraints on sampling, such as

- how many people are actually available as serious potential 'candidates' for a job,
- what happens to that 'candidate availability' over time as more and more organisations seek to select from that subset while job turnover puts some candidates back into the market,
- the variations in candidate 'quality' in terms of 'prospective job performance',
- whether discrete or composite 'profile' cut-scores are used, or just a single 'primary' scale,
- how test scores are used; for example, as the basis of subjective narrative-report interpretations,
- test-score and performance-outcome distributions not being 'normal', but rather skewed-beta or Pareto,

these constraints require more complex modelling that is beyond the focus of this chapter.

THE CURRENT MODELLING CONSTRAINTS AND PARAMETERS

- Test validities are varied between 0.2, .03, and 0.4.
- Interview and other kinds of selection process validity is assumed to be a fixed constant at 0.2.
- Interview and other selection methods validity adds [0.1] to each level of test validity (because it is reasonable to assume that there will be some overlap between a test score and what can be judged about a person's test score from a variety of other information about a candidate).
- Number of employees to be selected: 5 or 10.
- Both test scores and performance are assumed to be normally distributed, with sample values for both attributes expressed as *integers*.
- Test scores are generated for a typical 15-item attribute scale, with Likert response range between 0 and 4 per item, giving a measurement range between 0 and 60, in integers.
- The mean population test-score is [38], with standard deviation of [7].
- Test cut-scores (select-in *at or above*): 30th [=34], 50th [=38] and 70th [=42] percentiles.
- Performance outcome 'ratings' vary between 0 and 100, with the mean 'population' rating as [60], and standard deviation of [10].
- Candidates are grouped into five predicted performance groups based upon their performance rating:
  - 'Poor' [*below* 25th percentile = 53].
  - 'Below average' [*at or above* the 25th and *below* the 40th percentiles = 53, 57]
  - 'Average' [*at or above* the 40th and at or *below* the 60th percentiles = 57, 62]
  - 'Above average' [*above* the 60th and *at or below* the 75th percentile = 62, 67], and
  - 'Excellent' [*above* the 75th percentile = 67].
- 5,000 organisation-samples of new employees are randomly drawn from the appropriate bivariate distribution for each of the 27 possible conditions (3× test validities × 3× cut-scores × 3× numbers of selected employees).
- A 'contrast' condition for each psychometric test-score validity condition is reported for a sample drawn with no prior knowledge of psychological test scores. This condition represents candidate selection using existing methods other than psychometric testing, with an implicit validity of 0.2.
- Each empirical bivariate data distribution consists of 100,000 cases of data (*rounded integers*) sampled randomly from the parameter-specific bivariate normal distributions.

THE SAMPLING SEQUENCE

1. Randomly select 5, 10, or 20 'new employees' from an empirical bivariate distribution with specified validity, where each candidate's test score meets or exceeds the specific test cut-score threshold. Do this 5,000 times, tallying the numbers of 'selected' employees classified within each performance group.
2. Express the numbers in each group as a percentage of the total employees selected. For example, for selecting 5 employees, the total number selected is 25,000. For selecting 10 employees the total number selected is 50,000.
3. Contrast these summary results with those generated from sampling within the 'contrast' bivariate distribution where cases are sampled entirely at random from the entire applicant distribution.

Model 1: Test score validity 0.2 and projected employee job-performance group-classification; three test cut-score thresholds

Figure 6.1 shows the average selection rates across the five predicted job-performance groups, for a test score validity of 0.2, with a 0.1 lift in validity due to additional non-psychometric

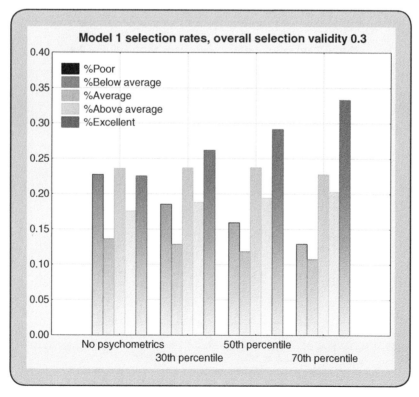

Figure 6.1 *Selection rates for Model 1*

selection procedures (an overall selection validity of **0.3**). Three test cut-scores are utilised: at or above the 30th, 50th, and 70th score percentiles. The contrast group labelled 'no psychometrics' represents selection using an employer's totality of existing selection processes, assumed to possess a validity of 0.2.

Model 2: Test score validity 0.3 and projected employee job-performance group-classification; three test cut-score thresholds

Figure 6.2 shows the average selection rates across the five predicted job-performance groups, for a test score validity of 0.3, with a 0.1 lift in validity due to additional non-psychometric selection procedures (an overall selection validity of **0.4**). Three test cut-scores are utilised: at or above the 30th, 50th, and 70th score percentiles. The contrast group labelled 'no psychometrics' represents selection using an employer's totality of existing selection processes, assumed to possess a validity of 0.2.

Model 3: Test score validity 0.4 and projected employee job-performance group-classification; three test cut-score thresholds

Figure 6.3 shows the average selection rates across the five predicted job-performance groups, for a test score validity of 0.4, with a 0.1 lift in validity due to additional non-psychometric

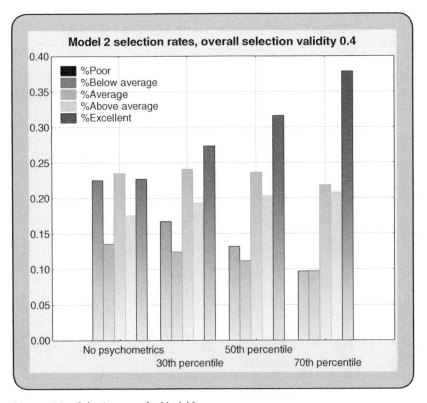

Figure 6.2 *Selection rates for Model 2*

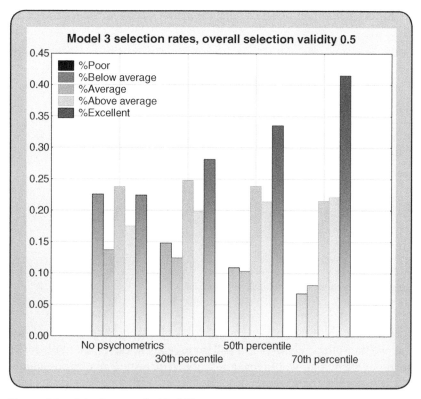

Figure 6.3 Selection rates for Model 3

selection procedures (an overall selection validity of **0.5**). Three test cut-scores are utilised: at or above the 30th, 50th, and 70th score percentiles. The contrast group labelled 'no psychometrics' represents selection using an employer's totality of existing selection processes, assumed to possess a validity of 0.2.

Although the graphs show clear trends in terms of rates of expected job-performance category employees, what's important here is seeing the actual numbers of employees selected given these rates, where only a few employees might be selected and employed over a year. Tables 6.1–6.3 show the numbers of selected new employees across two predicted performance groups: *Below average* and *Average & above*, using the selection rates in Figures 6.1–6.3, contrasted with the 'no psychometrics' selection group.

What might we conclude?

1. Using a selection test with a validity of 0.2 looks to be of marginal impact unless you select above a substantive percentile (at least above the 50th percentile). The likelihood is that, if screening candidates using a lower percentile, few employers would notice any 'stand-out' difference at all in the quality of employees they hired using a psychometric test as an initial candidate screen.

Table 6.1 Expected numbers of new employees across job-performance categories (5 selected)

Selection rule	0.3 overall selection validity		0.4 overall selection validity		0.5 overall selection validity	
	Below average	Average & above	Below average	Average & above	Below average	Average & above
*No psychometrics	2	3	2	3	2	3
At or above 30th percentile	2	3	1	4	1	4
At or above 50th percentile	1	4	1	4	1	4
At or above 70th percentile	1	4	1	4	1	4

Note: * The *No psychometrics* condition has a validity of 0.2 overall.

2. Using a selection test with a validity of 0.3 is of lesser utility unless you select at or above the 50th percentile). But still there really doesn't look to be the kind of 'stand-out effect' that would make psychometric testing an obvious addition to an already implemented selection process.
3. Using a selection test with a validity of 0.4 looks more noticeable in its effects, although again it's not until you increase the cut-score percentile that the benefits really accrue. But this is beginning to look like a 'will make a substantive difference' result.

Table 6.2 Expected numbers of new employees across job-performance categories for Model 1 (10 selected)

Selection rule	0.3 overall selection validity		0.4 overall selection validity		0.5 overall selection validity	
	Below average	Average & above	Below average	Average & above	Below average	Average & above
*No psychometrics	4	6	4	6	4	6
At or above 30th percentile	3	7	3	7	3	7
At or above 50th percentile	3	7	2	8	2	8
At or above 70th percentile	2	8	2	8	1	9

Note: * The *No psychometrics* condition has a validity of 0.2 overall.

Table 6.3 *Expected numbers of new employees across job-performance categories (20 selected)*

Selection Rule	0.3 overall selection validity		0.4 overall selection validity		0.5 overall selection validity	
	Below average	Average & above	Below average	Average & above	Below average	Average & above
*No psychometrics	7	13	7	13	7	13
At or above 30th percentile	6	14	6	14	5	15
At or above 50th percentile	6	14	5	15	4	16
At or above 70th percentile	5	15	4	16	3	17

Note: * The *No psychometrics* condition has a validity of 0.2 overall.

4. Overall, from this very constrained analysis, I think it would be fair to conclude that a small organisation wanting to improve its employee selection using screening psychometrics should use tests with job-performance validity coefficients of at least 0.3, with screening cut-scores at or above the 50th percentile.

Important caveats

1. Although the figures in Table 6.1 look better for any selection above the 30th percentile and test validity > 0.2, bear in mind these data are rounded integers. For example, the actual average value for Below average, at or above the 30th percentile, is 1.46 (rounded to 1). But this is getting a bit too numerically picky given the host of simplifying assumptions outlined in the preamble of the modelling.
2. It's easy for me to make recommendations about using more discriminating cut-scores, but the reality is that this strategy only works where sufficient candidates apply for a position who might exceed that cut-score threshold. What may happen is that by selecting a very discriminating cut-score, the employer sees no candidates at all. But the dilemma then arises that adopting a less discriminating cut-score also diminishes the impact of the psychometric screening.
3. This modelling assumed linear relations between the psychometric test scores and job performance. Yet we know that for attributes like Conscientiousness non-linearity is more evident than not (Carter, Guan, Maples, Williamson & Miller, 2015; Le et al., 2011; Lam, Spreitzer & Fritz, 2014). So simply using the results from this computational investigation may prove unwise when it comes to selecting candidates on those attributes shown to demonstrate curvilinear relationships with job performance outcomes.
4. What's also missing from this analysis is the cost–benefit analysis which factors in the cost of using psychometrics. But with many organisations offering instant 'have

credit card – can test' options for screening-style assessments, such costs are likely to be trivial. However, whether any of these 'instant' assessments possess validity coefficients of any veracity is a moot point. Without those validities, a client is forced to take a 'punt', which, as this modelling shows, may result in no added advantage to how they currently select their new employees.

IN CONCLUSION

This was just a simple 'back of a matchbox' look at whether a small organisation might benefit at all from using screening psychometrics in its selection processes. Given the assumptions stated at the outset of the article, and the caveats at the end, I think a small organisation might obtain significant 'noticeable' financial benefit if it uses psychometric tests which possess evidence of at least moderate validity (0.3 and above) *and* a discriminating cut-score. The modelling used here could be greatly refined, adopting realistic usage and candidate–market–behaviour effects similar in approach to those used by Sturman's (2000) powerful investigation into the realistic versus advertised benefits of conventional utility analysis (that is, after several real-world adjustments, the modelling showed a 96% reduction of the standard utility-formula-projected 'saving'). And such 'intervention-effect' modelling need not be confined to the potential deployment of psychometric tests, but could be applied also to the deployment of expensive leadership and employee development interventions in large corporates, where costs may be insubstantive and outcome expectations are based upon the 'plausible reasoning' claims made by providers rather than on substantive empirical evidence bases.

NOTE

This chapter was originally printed in *Psyche*, the Newsletter of The Psychometrics Forum, Edition 74, Summer 2015.

REFERENCES

Carter, N. T., Guan, L., Maples, J. L., Williamson, R. L. & Miller, J. D. (2015). The downsides of extreme conscientiousness for psychological well-being: The role of obsessive compulsive tendencies. *Journal of Personality*, 84(4), 510–22. http://onlinelibrary.wiley.com/doi/10.1111/jopy.12177/abstract?campaign=wolacceptedarticle. InPress, 1–46.

Le, H., Oh, I.-S., Robbins, S. B., Ilies, R., Holland, E. & Westrick, P. (2011). Too much of a good thing: Curvilinear relationships between personality traits and job performance. *Journal of Applied Psychology*, 96(1), 113–33.

Lam, C. F., Spreitzer, G. & Fritz, C. (2014). Too much of a good thing: Curvilinear effect of positive affect on proactive behaviors. *Journal of Organizational Behavior*, 35(4), 530–46.

Sturman, M. C. (2000). Implications of utility analysis adjustments for estimates of human resource intervention value. *Journal of Management*, 26(2), 281–99.

Part II Applications and Contexts

7 HR Applications of Psychometrics

Rob Bailey

INTRODUCTION

This chapter will evaluate Human Resource applications of psychometric assessments, including needs analysis before psychometric use, selection, personal development, team building, increasing motivation and career guidance. It will examine the evidence base for HR use of psychometrics and which kinds of psychometric instruments are best suited to which kinds of application.

Psychometric assessments have a major contribution to make to Human Resources activities; when used properly, they can measure a wide range of attributes needed in the workplace, from manual dexterity to mental arithmetic to personality and the most deeply held values of an individual. When used badly, psychometrics can give a false level of assessment, leading to poor or even discriminatory decisions. This chapter gives an overview of the field of psychometric testing as most often practised by HR professionals, takes a look at common pitfalls and makes some suggestions for how to avoid them; it is followed by recommended further reading.

The chapter will cover the following topics:

- A rationale for using psychometrics in HR
- The most common uses of psychometrics in HR
- The range of psychometric instruments that support HR activities
- Deciding which psychometric instrument to use

Finally the reader is pointed to suggested further reading.

RATIONALE FOR THE USE OF PSYCHOMETRICS IN HR

Psychometric assessments can potentially:

- *Improve decision making*, for example by helping identify the most promising candidate from a large pool of applicants. Generally an assumption is made that a candidate who scores more highly on a test of, say, numerical ability will perform well in the job.

- *Increase the cost-effectiveness of selection processes* by gathering information about candidates in an efficient manner compared with alternative, labour-intensive methods, such as manual sifting of applicants. For further information about how to calculate the likely financial cost–benefit utility analysis, see Cook and Cripps (2005).
- *Reduce bias in selection.* One of the most frequently used methods in the recruitment process, the traditional selection interview, is commonly afflicted by bias; for example, interviewers tend to warm to people similar to them and tend to give poorer assessments to people of different backgrounds (see, e.g., Rivera 2012), even if they would make excellent employees.
- *Create a good impression for the candidates.* Few people are likely to say that they enjoy being assessed, particularly when it comes to completing difficult aptitude tests. However, many candidates expect and believe it to be fair and objective to be asked to complete a psychometric test (e.g. Hausknecht, Day & Thomas, 2004), particularly if they are applying for senior positions in prestigious companies.
- *Leave an auditable record of the recruitment decisions.* This can not only increase transparency, which can appeal to responsible recruiters, but it may also create a rich set of data that can enable an employer to check the effectiveness of their recruiting methods.

If the use of psychometric questionnaires did not offer such benefits, then their use would be questionable. Managers should always ask themselves, 'Do we need to test?' Managers intending to use tests in the workplace should have a clear idea of what their chosen psychometrics are likely to achieve, ideally with a clear application, purpose and outcome. The following questions should have satisfactory answers:

- What specific applications do you want to use the psychometrics for?
- What problem will they address?
- What outcome is expected? For example: an improvement in the quality of recruits, a reduction in the cost of the recruitment programme, and a reduction in the number of employees who leave in their first year.

A psychometric assessment should be able to offer the HR user additional information over and above other methods. If they do not, there is little point using them.

Also, psychometric instruments rarely have any value when used on their own. For example, if a role requires an accredited professional qualification, then a candidate with excellent psychometric results, but not the qualification, is clearly unsuitable. Finally, it must be borne in mind that all psychometric data is self-reported and should be used alongside other selection methods.

COMMON HR USES OF PSYCHOMETRICS

Smith and Smith (2005) list the four most common uses of psychometrics in the workplace as recruitment, development, research and auditing.

Recruitment

Probably the most frequent application of psychometric tests is in the recruitment and selection process. Three elements should be considered, namely job analysis, assessment protocol, and the application of this protocol to candidates. I refer to this as the 'funnel of recruitment' (Figure 7.1).

Sifting or screening out

In situations where there are a very large number of applicants, a sift-out approach enables employers to reduce the numbers by excluding clearly unsuitable applicants. A common example of such an assessment is an online numerical reasoning task for graduate roles in finance. Poorly performing applicants would not be invited to further stages of the recruitment process.

Typically, sift-out stages use high volumes of low-cost psychometrics. The advantage of this approach is that much of the process can be automated (for example through online administration and scoring of the instruments); therefore the effort and cost of the recruitment process are reduced.

The disadvantages of this process are several. First, with online testing candidate validity is always paramount; how do recruiters know that the person taking the test online is actually the person turning up for interview?

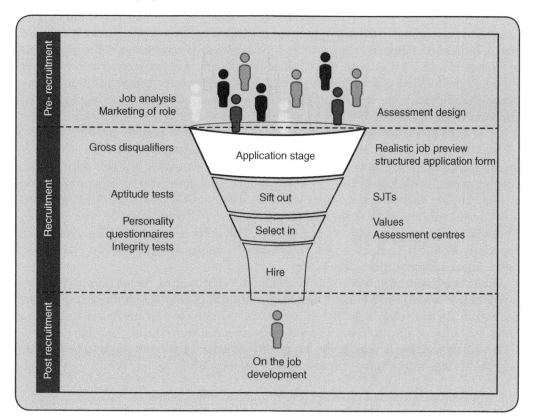

Figure 7.1 *The funnel analogy of recruitment*

Secondly, during the sifting process, recruiters must always be aware of the potential sources of adverse impact that can arise from psychometric testing and other assessment methods (e.g. Cook & Cripps, 2005). Adverse impact occurs when there is a substantially lower rate of selection of members of different demographic groups (for example, race, sex or ethnic group) in hiring, promotion or other employment decisions. It should be noted that adverse impact does not necessarily mean that the selection process is unfair: if a minority group does not contain enough people able to demonstrate a skill essential for the role, it would be unfair not to recruit more suitable majority-group members. However, such a situation would be concerning: genuine differences between groups might need to be addressed through education, skills training or strategic interventions; some of this could be done via organisations minded to improve minority-group opportunities, some could only be addressed through strategic government initiatives. Several types of aptitude measures that could be used for sifting out can cause adverse impact against legally protected groups of people, including ethnic minorities, disabled people and older people. They may also lead to gender discrimination.

The issue with some psychometrics is the unfortunate difference in performance across different groups. For example, in UK or US assessments, black candidates, on average, score lower on numerical aptitude tests. Women also on average tend to perform less well than men on numerical tests, but may outperform men on verbal tests. These differences persist despite considerable effort from many test publishers to create tests that are as unbiased as possible.

Reasons for the ethnic differences are complex. Some authors controversially suggest that this reflects inherent differences between races (e.g. Rushton & Jensen, 2005); however, other researchers point to the disadvantageous differences in social, economic and educational opportunities for minority groups (e.g. Dickens & Flynn, 2006; Suzuki & Aronson, 2005). The second argument is supported by meta-analysis (a combination of many studies) by Woods, Hardy and Guillaume (2011), who found that the gap between scores from different ethnicities has dropped over the last few decades and that this corresponds to an increase in opportunities for minority groups. This pattern contradicts the idea that cognitive differences are inherent and extends the nature–nurture debate.

In the definition of adverse impact, the word 'substantially' is open to question: what is a substantially different selection rate? Thankfully, guidance is available in the form of a rule of thumb known as the *80% rule* or the *Four-Fifths rule*. The rule enables a simple calculation of whether or not the selection of minority-group members is disproportionately low, for example:

If a company hires 60% of its white job applicants, but only 20% of its black applicants, then the ratio of hires is 60:20. In other words, this is 33% (calculated by dividing 20 by 60). This falls well short of the 80% rule, suggesting that there is a repeated bias against black applicants. Note that the rule does not require equal numbers of applicants of each ethnicity, only comparable proportions of selection.

Ideally, the Four-Fifths rule would be applied at every stage of the recruitment process, and therefore would need to be calculated at the first sifting-out stage, at the interview stage and then at the final offer stage. The Four-Fifths rule is a simple measure that will give some initial indication of any problems with adverse impact in a recruitment campaign.

To control for adverse impact, the design of recruitment processes needs to be carefully considered. The main ways to reduce adverse impact are to:

- Select assessments that show no or little difference in performance between groups.
- Use assessments only if they have been shown to be relevant to performance in the role.

- Place these assessments as far into the recruitment process as possible. There may be an all-too-human wish to cut out as many people as possible at an early stage in order to save time and money; however, the greater is the number of people sifted through such assessments early in the process, the more likely it is that adverse impact will ensue. In the later stages of assessment, an employer is likely to have invested considerable cost in each candidate; by this point the employer is less likely to want to reject a candidate on the basis of one assessment result alone, and more likely to take a more rounded view of the candidate's results. If decision making at a later stage of recruitment is based on a mix of assessment methods, some of which (such as personality inventories) cause less adverse impact, adverse impact is less likely to occur.
- Use conservative (more lenient) cut-off scores to differentiate between acceptable and unacceptable performance on the assessments. Typically, a conservative cut-off might be at the 30th percentile to remove the bottom third of performers. See the breakout box and Figure 7.2 for an illustration of why.

In Figure 7.2, the impact of a high cut-off score is clear: the vast majority of the minority group are rejected, including some performing at an average or above-average level on the assessment. At the same time, a much larger proportion of the majority group are taken through to the next stage. Setting a lower cut-off score means that greater numbers of each group are progressed to the next stage, while ensuring that poorer performers are excluded.

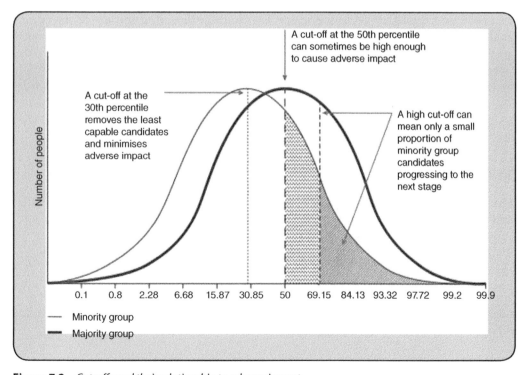

Figure 7.2   *Cut-offs and their relationship to adverse impact*

Selecting in

Once a short-list of candidates has been agreed, assessments can be used that have a selecting-in approach to decide which of several suitable candidates to choose. This is typically a stage with low numbers of pre-sifted candidates and is likely to be a more expensive, more labour-intensive stage of recruitment. At this stage, psychometric assessments may be employed that require completion under supervised test conditions, greater expertise to administer, or increased time to feed the results back to candidates.

Assessments not suitable for recruitment

Some psychometric assessments have not been designed for use in recruitment, so should not be used for this purpose (although they may be suitable for the personal development of people within a role).

For example, the Myers–Briggs Type Indicator (MBTI) (Myers, McCaulley, Quenk & Hammer, 1998), on the recommendation of the authors, is a questionnaire *only to be used in development situations*. It provides broad indications of a person's likely personality type, but not the level of detail appropriate for recruitment.

Some psychometrics could be used in recruitment, but their use would be questionable, for example Big Five questionnaires that only measure five broad traits of personality.

Although many psychologists agree that personality comprises five broad traits (Extraversion, Openness to experience, Conscientiousness, Agreeableness and Neuroticism), a questionnaire that only measures these broad traits may not provide enough detail to support informed choices. Block (1995) has argued that they are too broad to be useful. Other researchers (e.g. Hough, 1992) have shown that the Big Five need to be split into more detailed traits before they can be linked to specific job requirements (for example, Extraversion is frequently broken into traits including impulsiveness, social confidence and warmth towards others; it may be that when a surgeon is being recruited the social confidence is valued, but not the other two qualities). There are so many questionnaires available which measure with finer detail than the Big Five (e.g. the 16PF (Cattell, Cattell & Cattell, 1993), OPQ, NEO-PI-R (Costa & McCrae, 2008), Saville Wave (Saville, MacIver & Kurz, 2009)) that there is little reason not to use one of those for improved decision making.

Development

In the field of personal development, psychometric assessments serve two main purposes: to enable greater self-awareness for an individual and to help employers to develop their staff for improved performance.

Career guidance

Career counselling can occur at all stages of an individual's working life, including the period when young adults first consider which occupations might appeal to them. Many questionnaires are suitable for career counselling:

- **Career interest questionnaires** help a candidate to think about which occupation they are likely to find most rewarding.

- **Aptitude tests** can give an indication of the potential to reason with verbal, numerical or abstract data or to learn specific skills and abilities.
- **Values questionnaires** can not only inform people of their own values, or moral and ethical concerns, but also help them consider which organisations are likely to have compatible values.
- **Dexterity tests** will indicate a person's current level of dexterity (which could potentially be improved with practice).
- **Personality assessments** can show the likely fit between a person's natural behaviour, the demands of different occupations and the culture of the organisation. Where there are mismatches, dissatisfaction and tension may occur as a result of trying to fit a candidate into an unnatural pattern of behaviour; where there is a match, individuals are more likely to experience job satisfaction, organisational commitment and less intention to leave (Verquer, Beehr & Wagner, 2003).

A battery of assessments similar to those listed above may help redundancy/outplacement counselling, particularly if individuals are considering a change of career after redundancy.

In the middle of an individual's career, psychometrics may have a role to play in several of the ways described below.

Coaching

Opening out discussion in the early stages; identifying areas where the coachee may be exhibiting positive and negative interpersonal styles.

Team formation and team building

When working with teams, personality trait or type questionnaires can be used. The rich detail that can be provided by trait-based questionnaires can sometimes prove difficult, as team members might need to try to spot and remember patterns between team members on 16 to 36 traits. This is where type-based questionnaires, such as the MBTI, can provide simpler and more memorable summaries of the composition of a team.

Leadership development

Many psychometric questionnaires exist to measure a wide variety of participants' approaches to leadership. Theories of effective leadership differ greatly, so users may need to identify psychometrics designed to measure the styles of leadership most likely to work for a particular individual, team or organisation.

Interpersonal effectiveness training

Psychometrics promoting better understanding of others (e.g. emotional intelligence questionnaires) can help people become more aware of their strengths and of limitations in their interpersonal skills, and can therefore form a basis for training or coaching interventions.

Increasing motivation and engagement

By better understanding values, motivation (via motivation questionnaires) and personality, it may be possible to communicate more effectively with employees or to adapt elements of their jobs and benefit from increasing their motivation in the workplace.

Talent management

By assessing the cognitive capacity, strategic thinking and typical behaviour of employees, companies can estimate which of their employees shows the greatest potential to advance beyond their current roles. Although excellent performance in a current role might be indicative of this, psychometrics can provide clues about an individual's potential in areas not yet tested by their job.

Research

The use of psychometrics within a group business will generate a lot of data. Provided permission has been given by test takers, this data can prove valuable for research. For example, a validation study could be conducted to identify which psychometric test correlates the most with effective work performance within a particular organisation; this is often called venture marking. It can mean that recruitment processes can be refined by retaining the most useful assessments and dropping any that do not show any relationship to on-the-job performance.

Test publishers may agree to do such studies for free, as this gives them useful evidence that their questionnaires are effective workplace assessments.

Auditing

Use of questionnaires across a whole department or organisation can help to identify useful patterns. For example, HR professionals looking for ideas for improving retention and reducing turnover may benefit from using psychometrics to assess company culture, run satisfaction surveys or collate data on the personality and values of employees.

WHAT KIND OF PSYCHOMETRIC INSTRUMENTS SUPPORT HR ACTIVITIES?

Broadly speaking, psychometric assessments used in HR can be categorised according to three qualities of the individuals that they assess:

Can do – can those being assessed do the job?

Will do – are they motivated to do the job?

Will fit in – does their personal style match the culture of the organisation or team?

Can do

A great deal of research has been done to see how well different selection methods predict job performance. A summary of this research is shown in Figure 7.3. The numbers are the result of a meta-analysis (a compilation of the results of many studies) by Smith and Robertson (2001). A meta-analysis is far more reliable than any single study, as it shows corroboration from many different, independent investigations.

The figures show validity, which ranges from 1 – a perfect relationship between a measure and what it aims to predict – to 0, a random relationship; in psychometric measurement, a coefficient of 1 is unrealistic. Work sample tests, unsurprisingly, show the strongest relationship with performance in a role – only about 30% accurate, however, presumably because they are a simulation of that role. Graphology (handwriting analysis) shows an almost random relationship with work performance: 4% accurate.

The research clearly shows which assessment methods are more likely to help to identify the potential for good future job performance. Thus it is a reasonable guide to the methods that should be favoured, or rejected.

The assessments may include aptitude tests, work sample tests, job knowledge tests, Situational Judgement Tests, risk questionnaires and integrity tests, which are discussed in more detail below.

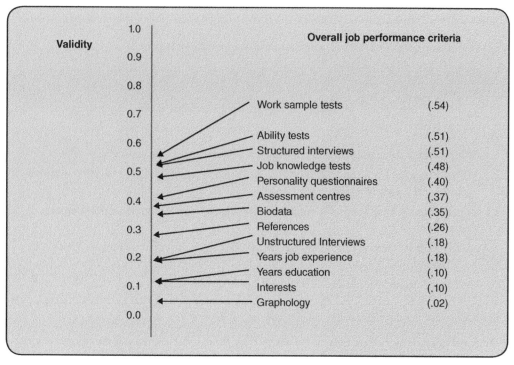

Figure 7.3 *The relationship between different selection methods and job performance. Adapted from Robertson and Smith (2001)*

Aptitude tests measure a wide variety of human potential: reading, spelling, checking, numerical reasoning, verbal reasoning, diagrammatic reasoning, mechanical reasoning, logical reasoning, spatial reasoning, manual dexterity, physical strength and fitness.

Among these, verbal reasoning tests aim to measure how well someone can understand, evaluate and manipulate information that has been presented in words. The example in Box 7.1 has been written as an illustration of the sort of question to expect; it is not from a published psychometric test.

A sample verbal reasoning test — BOX 7.1

Read the passage below and answer the questions that follow:

The spread of the internet has made cybercrime and related fraud, such as identity theft, so prevalent that many major businesses are likely to come under some form of attack. Criminals can strike from outside the company or work from within as employees, making background checks increasingly important in situations where confidential information is to be handled. A number of high-profile cases have shown that even when criminals find it difficult to gain access to organisations, employees themselves are often exposed to the risk of identity theft through the loss by organisations of disks, memory sticks and laptops that contain sensitive information.

Internet usage, legislation and new digital technology have all affected the data protection policies of major companies. One popular security measure, in companies that handle sensitive data, is to avoid hiring temporary staff to cover roles dealing with confidential information. Rather, trusted employees from other departments are seconded to cover the job until the regular worker can return.

Answer questions Q1 to Q4, saying in each case whether the statement is

(A) True

(B) False

or (C) There is insufficient information in the passage to say whether the statement is true or false.

Q1. Changes to company data protection policies are due to a single cause.

Q2. The greatest threat to an individual's security comes from the loss of computer media that contain sensitive information.

Q3. Individuals are still at risk of identity theft, even when criminals do not actively target a company.

Q4. One popular method of ensuring data security is to avoid using temporary staff in certain situations.

(The correct answers are 1. B, 2. C, 3. A and 4. A.)

Numerical reasoning tests aim to measure how well someone can understand, evaluate and manipulate numerical information presented in a variety of formats. Many positions in the workplace demand the ability to understand numerical, statistical or financial information and therefore a variety of different question types have been developed over the years.

The example in Box 7.2 has been written as an illustration of the sort of question to expect; it is not from a published psychometric test.

A sample numerical reasoning test — BOX 7.2

Product sales report: Wholesale office supplies

	October 2008		November 2008		December 2008	
Products	Volume of sales (number of units sold)	Total value in £	Volume of sales (number of units sold)	Total value in £	Volume of sales (number of units sold)	Total value in £
Note pads (pack)	32	80	40	150	48	200
Envelopes (pack)	45	585	40	440	60	600
Staplers (pack)	12	240	14	280	18	340

The table shows a product sales report at a wholesale office supplier over a period of 3 months. The products sold are packs of envelopes, note pads and staplers.

1. In which month was the total value of sales the highest?

A	B	C	D
Cannot say	October	November	December

The correct answer is D, which is arrived at by adding the total value of all product sales together.

Work sample tests simulate a situation that could be encountered on the job. For example, a manager might need to prioritise an inbox of emails comprising customer complaints, or a proof reader might need to correct errors in a passage of text. Work sample tests, with a typical validity coefficient of 0.54 (see more about how to interpret this below), are one of the methods most likely to predict future job performance.

Job knowledge tests assess specific job knowledge. For example, a car salesperson might need to answer questions about the kinds of finance packages available for car buyers. Job knowledge tests have a high validity (typically 0.48). However, they suffer from a type of bias known as *opportunity bias*. This is because they assess knowledge that has been attained through employment and will therefore have a bias towards people with existing job experience. What they cannot do is to assess individuals with limited job experience but a great deal of potential, so an employer might miss the opportunity to spot, and then employ, a potential high-flier. This opportunity bias is of particular importance when employing people who are in the early stages of their career, for example recent graduates, many of whom will not have had the opportunity to learn within employment. Therefore a job knowledge test might be entirely unsuitable for such a candidate pool.

Situational Judgement Tests (SJTs) present candidates with scenarios and a set of options related to each scenario. If the test asks which of the options *would be most effective*, then it tends to measure cognitive performance (aptitude). If the tests ask candidates to say which of the options is closest to *what they would actually do*, the SJT is more likely to measure personality. Although some off-the-shelf SJTs are available from test publishers, they are frequently tailor-made for specific companies. SJTs have been shown to have reasonable validity, but unfortunately they can still show adverse impact. In a meta-analysis of US studies, Whetzel, McDaniel and Nguyen (2008) showed that SJTs tended to favour older candidates, whites and women. They found that adverse impact was stronger for SJTs requiring cognitive skills to arrive at a correct answer, but was lower for SJTs where the questions were measuring more behavioural traits. The favouring of older people is likely to be due to their greater exposure to the kinds of problems found in the workplace.

Risk questionnaires can give an insight into the likely risk-taking behaviour of candidates. For example, an individual might be asked to rate how confident they were that they were right when answering a numerical question; if they overestimate their accuracy, this may be indicative of a risk-taking style. These questionnaires may be of use for roles such as financial traders, who can cause high losses through risky behaviour.

Integrity tests work in a variety of ways; some will measure admissions of less acceptable behaviour, others look for preferences or behavioural patterns associated with unreliable, aggressive or dishonest activities. Although it might appear naive or ironic to expect people to honestly admit to anti-social or dishonest behaviour, many questionnaire takers do; hence the ability of these assessments to signal concerns over some candidates. Because of the sensitive nature of what they ask, candidates may feel more discomfort about and opposition to completing these questionnaires. (See Chapter 14 in this volume by Adrian Furnham, 'Looking at "the Dark Side"'.)

As mentioned above, it will not always be possible to use the most valid assessment. For example, a Job Knowledge Test might be inappropriate when recruiting graduates with little work experience.

Generally, using more than one assessment (e.g. a personality assessment and a cognitive ability test), can increase validity. However, a word of caution: the validity for combining assessments is rarely simply additive, as they often assess overlapping qualities. As an illustration only, when personality and cognitive assessments are used, validity increase will not be $0.4 + 0.51 = 0.91$; it is more reasonable to expect a moderate increase, say to around 0.55.

Another note of caution: the use of psychometrics will not replace the need for careful decision making over job applicants or individuals on development courses. Although a great deal of research and scientific endeavour underpin the assessments, their correct use requires judgement, not a blind reliance on the numbers they produce. They should always be combined with other information about individuals.

Non-psychometric information

Of the psychometric assessments above, the majority aim to estimate an individual's future potential (aptitude) to perform well in a specific job or jobs. Not many of them measure past attainment, for example job knowledge. Examples of non-psychometric assessments that measure attainment are exam grades and vocational qualifications.

Other sources of information about whether or not the candidate *can do* the job include certificates, licences and prerequisite experience.

If any of the above is essential for the job, but not possessed by the candidate, it is obvious that the candidate is not suitable for the role unless the employer is confident that any missing qualifications can be obtained within a reasonable timescale and cost. When such characteristics are used to rule out an applicant they are known as *gross disqualifiers*. They may include physical capabilities; for example, some forms of colour-blindness will make people ineligible for employment as a pilot.

There are several reasons why so many assessments focus on aptitude, rather than upon attainment:

- the evidence base: in Figure 7.3 we see that some past attainments, such as years of work experience, have very low levels of validity for predicting work performance; many aptitude tests have higher levels of validity;
- opportunity bias: this was explained above in relation to job knowledge tests;
- the fact that majority of candidates in the selection pool may have the required grades or qualifications. For example, a prestigious organisation may attract many high-quality applicants who all have the right degree qualification and high grades. In this situation the candidates may all be *eligible* for the role; what makes some stand out from the rest is that they may be more *suitable* for the role. Looking at their aptitudes, motivation and values to find a good fit with the company and the role could be a profitable way to differentiate between candidates.

There are several circumstances in which it may not be appropriate to use psychometrics. Typically, these are when the employer already knows more about an individual than a psychometric assessment is likely to tell them. Were this to be the case in a recruitment setting, it would only be fair to do this if all candidates underwent the same assessment procedures. That is to say, it would be unfair to test external candidates with psychometrics, but to rely on personal knowledge of an internal candidate.

Psychometrics are an excellent and efficient way to gather information about people unknown to an employer; however, if candidates already have work records at the organisation, psychometrics may be unnecessary. Here are a couple of fictional scenarios.

Choosing which of two interns to employ. If the interns have been doing a job very similar to the one on offer, their work performance may be a better indication of who to hire. However, if an external applicant needs to be considered, it would be fairer to assess all candidates using psychometric assessments, in order to treat all the candidates equally.

Choosing which of several individuals to make redundant. Again, the work records are likely to be a better source of information than psychometric assessments. However, if candidates are to be selected into *new roles*, psychometric assessments may be a fairer way to evaluate the potential to perform in unknown roles. Be aware that litigation has followed the use of psychometric tests in redundancy situations; it would be prudent to seek the advice of an occupational psychologist or the test publisher before using psychometrics for this purpose.

Will do

Assessing individuals for what they will do is largely to find out whether or not they are motivated to do a job. It may be that they are capable of performing the job ('can do'), but without the right motivation they could be uncooperative or unproductive.

Personality

Personality assessments are frequently in the form of a questionnaire. They are suitable for use in recruitment settings, and meta-analysis shows personality traits to be predictive of job performance (e.g. Ones, Dilchert, Viswevaran & Judge, 2007).

An example of a personality question is shown below.

In a room full of strangers, I quickly find a group of people and introduce myself.

1	2	3	4
Never	Rarely	Sometimes	Often

Normative/ipsative assessments   Some terminology for psychometric tests may be unfamiliar to those outside the field, in particular 'normative' and 'ipsative'. A normative example is shown above. An ipsative example follows.

Please indicate which of the following statements is most like you and which is least like you. Leave the remaining two statements blank.

	Most	Least
I am confident in groups.		
I like to plan well ahead.		
I am a compassionate person.		
I make quick decisions.		

In the normative example, respondents have a free hand to put high or low ratings against all the questions. In the ipsative example, the respondent's choices are limited: they cannot claim to be all things. As a result, ipsative questionnaires can help to show the relative preferences or tendencies of the test taker; they may also make faking a little harder as candidates cannot simply choose to elevate all their responses in a socially desirable manner.

A potential downside to ipsative tests is that if not enough concepts (for example personality traits) are being measured, a questionnaire taker's response options may be too constrained to answer properly. Some traits might start to become artificially negatively correlated with another. For example, if some options are more socially desirable (such as being sociable or emotionally stable), these are likely to be favoured more often than less socially desirable but possibly more honest responses. An ipsative questionnaire can therefore sometimes have bias built into the options.

Other assessments that may help estimate a candidate's 'will do' potential are less suited for recruitment, but may have an application in development activities. They are motivation questionnaires, interest inventories and career inventories.

Will fit in

A variety of instrument types can help to show whether or not an individual will fit with the culture or dynamics of a team or organisation. *Personality assessments* give an indication of a person's typical behaviour, which can indicate their likely fit at a company or team. *Situational Judgement Tests* can be designed to measure personality and behaviour by asking individuals to identify which of several actions they would be likely to take. (Asking them which is the *best* option assesses their intellectual capacity rather than their personality.) Other types of questionnaire that can be used to assess how well an individual will fit in include *culture fit questionnaires*, *values questionnaires* and *integrity tests*.

Some styles of questionnaire are general enough to cover all three categories of 'can do', 'will do', 'will fit in', but may only be suited to a person who is already in the role. For example, 360-degree questionnaires are completed by a range of people (boss, peers, direct reports, customers) who are in a position to rate a person's performance or behaviour because they have already seen it.

HOW DO YOU DECIDE WHICH PSYCHOMETRIC INSTRUMENT TO USE?

Before psychometric assessments are used in the workplace, it is vital to know what they are supposed to be assessing. In the case of recruitment (and some developmental uses), best practice is to conduct some form of job analysis. This is not a method in itself, as there are many ways to conduct job analysis; some of them are explained below. The aim of job analysis is to understand the nature of the job, its associated demands and the skills and knowledge necessary to good performance; typically it results in a job description and a person specification.

Methods of job analysis

The following methods are selected examples, not an exhaustive list, of how job analysis can be performed.

Critical incidents

The critical incident technique (CIT) was described by Flanagan in a 1954 article. During a critical incidents interview, job holders or their manager are asked to think of times when a highly significant event or a difficult or challenging incident has occurred at work. This technique can help to tease out the tasks, skills and personal qualities required for success in a given role.

Visionary interview

The visionary interview is typically an in-depth, structured discussion with senior managers. The aim is to understand what they see as the future priorities of the organisation and the role; this understanding can then be built into the job description and the person specification to try to future-proof the role.

Repertory Grid

The Repertory Grid is a method devised by Kelly (1955) for exploring an individual's understanding of various concepts. When applied to the occupational setting, it is typically conducted by asking an individual to think of ten or so people they know who have worked in a particular job. It is common to ask the individual to write the initials of these individuals down. The interviewer then selects three of these people at a time and asks the interviewee to say how two of the people are similar and how one is different. This leads to discussion of the quality that unites or divides these people, a name for the quality and a clear labelling of whether this is desirable or undesirable. Through repeating this process with many different combinations of threes, the interviewer is able to glean information about a variety of qualities likely to lead to successful performance in the role.

Competency sort

A competency sort exercise is typically a structured process using a standardised set of competencies provided by a test publisher or a consultancy. For example, 20 commonly used competencies may be printed on cards or displayed onscreen for someone who is knowledgeable about the job to rate. Managers or job incumbents might rate each competency for how important it is or how frequently it needs to be done. For more information about competency-based approaches, see Boyatzis (1982).

Example outputs from job analysis

Below are fictional examples of a job description, a person specification and competency selections, to show what might be created as a result of job analysis. Following these are illustrations of how these documents might link to psychometric assessments and their use.

Job description

Job title: Customer Service Adviser, financial services call centre
Reports to: Customer Service Team Leader
Staff: None

Job purpose and accountabilities:

- To be the principal point of contact between the customer and the online bank, delivering an effective telephone banking service to both personal and business customers.
- To contribute to the ongoing and developing excellence of the call centre.

The following tables are intentionally unnumbered and uncaptioned, as they represent things that an employer may include in a job description

Main accountability	Associated activities
Dealing effectively with customer enquiries	Handling customer enquiries effectively from start to finish, with minimal reference to team leaders. Following all relevant procedures and giving customers correct information. Meeting targets for call duration and productivity. Meeting service standards.
Dealing with complaints	Dealing effectively with customer complaints, referring to a team leader as and when necessary. Documenting complaints appropriately.
Identifying customer needs	Identifying the needs of customers and providing information on appropriate products and services.
Sales	Seeing sales opportunities and selling appropriate products and services. Meeting sales targets.
Administration	Keeping accurate records, with precise and efficient administration of all relevant paperwork and after-call documentation.
Maintaining expertise	Keeping up to date with knowledge of products and services so that customers receive consistent and accurate information.

Person specification (Customer Service Adviser)

	Essential	Desirable
Personal qualities	Friendly and helpful Calm under stress Prepared to work with others in a team	Self-confident; prepared to take the initiative when necessary Flexible Willing to learn People-focused
Motivation	Prepared to work hard Keen to 'get it right'	Committed to the organisation

(Continued)

	Essential	Desirable
Skills and abilities	Accurate; makes few errors Able to follow procedures accurately Able to combine information from different sources	Able to make quick, accurate estimates of numerical calculations
Qualifications	No specific qualifications needed	
Experience	Some experience of dealing with customers	Previous experience in a call centre or similar customer service environment
Other factors	Reliable timekeeper	

Note: © Copyright 2015 OPP Ltd. Reproduced from the Assessment Portfolio 'The Test User: Occupational Ability Programme' with the kind permission of the copyright holder. All further rights reserved.

From the above a list of competencies can be identified:

- customer focus
- commercial awareness
- drive for excellence
- continuous learning
- reliability
- coping with pressure
- flexibility.

A competency matrix showing which assessments could relate to each competency can then be created:

Competency	CV	Interview	Personality assessment	Numerical test	Integrity test
Customer focus		✓	✓		
Commercial awareness		✓		✓	
Drive for excellence		✓			✓
Continuous learning	✓	✓			
Coping with pressure		✓	✓		
Flexibility		✓	✓		
Reliability		✓	✓		✓

It is advisable to look for evidence from at least two sources of assessment, conducted by different assessors; this provides confirmation and may help to avoid bias from just one source or assessor.

This approach can be used both in recruitment settings and when assessing people for development programmes.

Assessment and development centres

As soon as more than one psychometric test is used, the process can be defined as an assessment or development centre; this is not a place, as the name implies, but a process. The aim of using multiple assessments is to control bias (as mentioned above) and to try to get a rounded view of an individual.

Typically all of the results are compiled in a 'wash-up session', also known as an 'integration meeting', where the assessors meet, often with the recruiting or line manager, to discuss all of the candidates. At this stage the results are often entered into a version of the competency matrix. Unfortunately it is at this stage that bias can return to the recruitment process; for example, the most powerful or influential person may fight to raise the ratings of their favourite candidate. Research over decades has shown that the more this process is automated, the more valid the results become, as mathematical calculations of the overall score are less affected by social bias (e.g. Hoffman et al., 2015, cited in CIPD Research Report 2015).

This replicates a job description as presented to potential applicants. It is intentionally not numbered or captioned

Competency	CV	Interview	Personality assessment	Numerical test	Integrity test	Overall score
Customer focus		5	4			4
Commercial awareness		3		3		3
Drive for excellence		2			3	3
Continuous learning	4	3				4
Coping with pressure		4	4			4
Flexibility		4	5			5
Reliability		3	3		3	3

EVALUATING THE TEST

When choosing a psychometric test, not only should you have a clear application and expected outcome in mind, but other qualities of the instrument need to be considered.

Ease of use

Administration methods: psychometric assessments can be administered through a variety of media. These include paper, standalone computers, online computers and mobile phones. Thankfully, research shows that all these forms of assessment give equivalent results for personality assessments (Bartram & Brown, 2004; Illingworth, Morelli, Scott & Boyd, 2014). This suggests that it does not matter which of these media candidates use – the results will be the same.

Scoring: scoring can be time-consuming and error-prone if done manually. Computer-, phone- and web-based scoring tends to be done automatically and is therefore quicker and less prone to error.

Applicant Tracking Systems (ATS): medium to larger employers may have their own computer-based HR systems, perhaps including an ATS, which enables the employer to easily manage and monitor a recruitment campaign, clearly following the progress of all candidates through the process. This means that the results of questionnaires or tests can be automatically combined with other information that a company collects during a recruitment campaign.

Off-the-shelf Applicant Tracking Systems (rather than ones configured specifically for a company) may be within budget for smaller employers.

Interpretation and feedback

Norm groups

A crucial quality of psychometric assessment is an appropriate comparison group against which to compare the results (also known as the norm group). A test provider should have already administered the instrument to a large number (for example 500+) of people from a sample representative of those likely to take the test. This means that any individual or group can be compared with the average results of a representative group. For example, norm groups could be specifically sampled from:

- an occupation (e.g. psychologists)
- an industry (e.g. finance)
- a particular age or life-stage (e.g. school leavers)
- a demographic group (e.g. according to gender or ethnicity)*
- people being assessed for a particular purpose (e.g., they are all job applicants)
- a nationally representative sample (e.g. to represent working-age people in the UK, with the same percentage of men and women and different ethnicities as is found in the population as a whole)
- a multinational group, in order to produce international norms.

* Note that in many countries using different minority or gender group norms in recruitment situations is illegal, under equality legislation. To treat the groups differently would risk discrimination against either the minority or majority group.

In some situations, using a highly specific norm group makes for best practice; this is particularly the case for aptitude tests. If a numerical test was administered to actuaries, but a secondary school comparison group was used, the results would most likely be unusable: the majority of the actuary candidates would bunch together at the high-performing end of the scale, with little differentiation between them. In this instance, a norm group specifically for actuaries, statisticians or mathematicians would be more suitable, as applicants within this level of numerical aptitude would then show a spread of scores across the scale.

Alternatively, if a school leaver receiving career guidance is completing a numerical aptitude test, it may be appropriate to compare them against at least two groups: (1) other school leavers, and (2) a group for the occupation in which they are interested.

Specific norm groups may, however, cause interpretation issues. As an example, a personality questionnaire is completed by a candidate for a management role and the results are compared with a norm group of managers; the results show the candidate to be less dominant than average. The interpretation could be that the manager may not stand their ground; however, when the same candidate's results are compared with a general population sample, the results show the candidate to be above average in their level of dominance. The everyday experience that others are likely to have of the candidate is that they are a dominant individual; however, the choice of norm group could distort the interpretation.

Other aspects of interpretation concern the manner in which the results are reported.

Reports

The results of psychometric assessments can be a simple set of scores (often called a profile), or an expert report consisting of many pages of textual interpretation compiled with the aid of a computer (which might be called a narrative report). These expert reports are frequently written by an experienced user of the instrument and are often based on prior use and research with the assessment. The advantage of this approach is that they are quicker and often cheaper than a hand-written report, and they will have consistent format, spelling and quality of presentation; the disadvantage is that they tend not to contain any personal observations from an assessor (unless there is a facility to add comments or data to the report).

Quality of the assessment

Before using a psychometric assessment, any user should be suitably convinced that it will work. In the language of psychometricians this means that the test is *valid*; that is, it measures what it says it measures, is relevant to the specific HR use, and is *reliable*, i.e., it will produce consistent results whenever it is used.

Test providers should produce manuals for each of their instruments which show different types of validity; if a test provider requires you to purchase the manual, it is entirely reasonable to ask for the reliability and validity information to be supplied to you without your having to make a purchase.

Validity

Below is a brief guide to the different types of validity that a test must demonstrate.

Criterion validity shows that the instrument measures something which is related to some other work competency, for example that the results of a verbal test are statistically correlated with performance in writing company communications. Without criterion validity (or a chance of establishing it by collecting data), there is little justification to use a psychometric test in an HR setting.

Construct validity shows that the instrument measures what it claims to; this is generally established by administering another assessment that measures a very similar concept alongside the test being evaluated and checking for agreement in the results.

Face validity is a different and more subjective type of validity. It concerns whether or not the assessment looks relevant to the application for which it is being used. Some very well-established and valid personality assessments include questions about a candidate's leisure interests. Although this can be highly relevant to assessing personality, some candidates may question its validity because of the seeming lack of face validity in the workplace.

Faith validity is a problematic form of validity. It is users' favouring of a psychometric instrument simply because they believe that is beneficial. This might be without evidence for such a view, or even despite evidence to the contrary. It may be based on positive anecdotal experience of the psychometric instrument. When HR professionals wish to introduce more scientifically grounded instruments into their processes, they may have a difficult, sensitive task to replace any psychometrics embedded in the organisation by more powerful individuals with a strong faith in them. This is where scientific arguments about validity and reliability can easily break down.

Consequential validity is concerned with the wider societal impact of the use of an assessment. This can include intended and unintended consequences, and so can be very hard to take into account. Adverse impact is an example of consequential validity: minority groups could be disadvantaged by the use of the test. As mentioned before, this does not necessarily make the test invalid; however, it may highlight a cause for concern that needs to be addressed in assessment design and use, and in wider society.

The test publisher may be able to provide research and case studies to help you to evaluate how valid the test is for your purpose.

Reliability

There are several kinds of reliability.

Internal consistency reliability is concerned with whether or not scales of the test include questions that are measuring a coherent trait or ability. For example, a scale measuring how socially confident someone is should not have a question about how much they like other people, as this is not closely enough related to the concept of social confidence. The level of coherence is measured by a statistic known as Cronbach's alpha (Cronbach, 1951).

A random relationship between questions (which might be called 'items' in a manual) would have an alpha coefficient of 0; questions which are identical would have a coefficient of 1. From George and Mallery (2003), a common rule of thumb for interpreting Cronbach's alpha (and the following types of reliability) is as follows:

Cronbach's alpha	Internal consistency
$α ≥ 0.9$	Excellent
$0.9 > α ≥ 0.8$	Good
$0.8 > α ≥ 0.7$	Acceptable
$0.7 > α ≥ 0.6$	Questionable
$0.6 > α ≥ 0.5$	Poor
$0.5 > α$	Unacceptable

Sometimes alpha coefficients are artificially high because the items lack any variety. This is not desirable; there should be some variety of content within a scale.

Test–retest reliability looks at the similarity of scores that individuals should expect if they take the questionnaire again after a pause.

Parallel versions of the test may exist; these are useful either to keep the content of an assessment from becoming over-exposed, or to retest a candidate if the first assessment seems questionable. The parallel versions should show a high level of reliability between the two. This is sometimes called 'alternate form reliability'.

Fairness

A test provider should provide evidence of the likely differences between different legally protected groups (e.g. concerning gender, disability, age and ethnicity). As far as possible, tests which produce unequal outcomes for different groups should be avoided. As discussed above, aptitude tests generally show higher levels of adverse impact than other psychometric instruments. Personality questionnaires and behavioural Situational Judgement Tests generally show lower levels of adverse impact than cognitive assessments (or cognitively loaded SJTs).

Discrimination on the basis of ethnicity, gender, sexual orientation, religion and disability are not only illegal in most circumstances, they are bad for a company's reputation and may prevent employers from selecting the best candidate, as bias may cause that candidate to be rejected.

The Americans with Disabilities Act (1990) and the UK Equality Act (2010) outline the protected groups and best-practice approaches.

Sources of information about specific psychometric assessments

To obtain more information about each psychometric assessment, you may contact the publisher, consult reviews of instruments provided by the British Psychological Society (https://ptc.bps.org.uk/), or in the UK seek the services of a registered occupational psychologist (an industrial or organisational psychologist in other territories).

NOTES

®MBTI, Myers–Briggs and Myers–Briggs Type Indicator are registered trade marks of the Myers & Briggs Foundation in the United States and other countries.

The 16PF® questionnaire (16 Personality Factors) is a registered trade mark of the Institute for Personality and Ability Testing, Inc. (IPAT Inc.), Champaign, Illinois.

FURTHER READING

CIPD (2015). A head for hiring: The behavioural science of recruitment and selection. Research Report. http://www.cipd.co.uk/hr-resources/research/head-hiring-behavioural-science-recruitment.aspx.

Cripps, B. & Spry, D. (2008). *Psychometric testing pocketbook*. Alresford: Management Pocketbooks.

Passmore, J. (2012). *Psychometrics in coaching: Using psychological and psychometric tools for development*. 2nd edn. London: Kogan Page.

Saville, P. & Hopton, T. (2014). *Psychometrics@Work*. Esher: Saville Consulting.

Smith, M. & Smith, P. (2005). *Testing people at work: Competencies in psychometric testing*. Oxford: BPS Blackwell.

REFERENCES

Americans with Disabilities Act of 1990 (ADA), *42 U.S.C.* Chapter 126.

Bartram, D. & Brown, A. (2004). Online testing: Mode of administration and the stability of OPQ32i scores. *International Journal of Selection and Assessment*, 12, 278–84.

Block, J. (1995). A contrarian view of the five-factor approach to personality description. *Psychological Bulletin*, 117, 187–215.

Boyatzis, R. E. (1982). *The competent manager: A model for effective performance*. London: Wiley.

Cattell, R. B., Cattell, A. K. & Cattell, H. E. P. (1993). Sixteen personality factor questionnaire, fifth edition. Champaign, IL: Institute for Personality and Ability Testing.

CIPD (2015). A head for hiring: The behavioural science of recruitment and selection. Research Report. http://www.cipd.co.uk/hr-resources/research/head-hiring-behavioural-science-recruitment.aspx.

Cook, M. & Cripps, B. (2005) *Psychological assessment in the workplace: A manager's guide*. Chichester: John Wiley & Sons. Published online 13 May 2008. doi: 10.1002/9780470713105.ch1.

Costa, P. & McCrae, R. (2008). The revised NEO personality inventory (NEO-PI-R). In G. Boyle, G. Matthews & D. Saklofske (eds.), *The SAGE handbook of personality theory and assessment. Volume 2: Personality measurement and testing*, pp. 179–99. London: SAGE Publications. doi: http://dx.doi.org/10.4135/9781849200479.n9.

Cronbach, L. J. (1951). Coefficient alpha and the internal structure of tests. *Psychometrika* 16(3), 297–334. doi: 10.1007/bf02310555.

Dickens, W. T. & Flynn, J. R. (2006) Black Americans reduce the racial IQ gap: Evidence from standardization samples. *Psychological Science*, 17, 913–20.

Equality Act (UK) (2010). The National Archives. http://www.legislation.gov.uk/ukpga/2010/15/contents. Accessed 2 October 2016.

George, D. & Mallery, P. (2003). *SPSS for Windows step by step: A simple guide and reference. 11.0 update* 4th edn. Boston, MA: Allyn & Bacon.

Flanagan, J. C. (1954). The critical incident technique. *Psychological Bulletin*, 51(4): 327–58.

Hausknecht, J. P., Day, D. V. & Thomas, S. C. (2004). Applicant reactions to selection procedures: An updated model and meta-analysis. *Personnel Psychology*, 57, 639–83.

Hough, L. M. (1992). The 'Big Five' personality variables–construct confusion: Description versus prediction. *Human Performance*, 5(1–2), 139–55.

Illingworth, A. J., Morelli, N. A., Scott, J. C. & Boyd, S. L. (2014). Internet-based, unproctored assessments on mobile and non-mobile devices: Usage, measurement equivalence, and outcomes. *Journal of Business and Psychology*, 30(2), 325–43.

Kelly, G. A. (1955). *The psychology of personal constructs*. New York: Norton.

Myers, I. B., McCaulley, M. H., Quenk, N. L. & Hammer, A. L. (1998). *MBTI® manual: A guide to the development and use of the Myers-Briggs Type Indicator®*. 3rd edn. Mountain View, CA: CPP.

Ones, D. S., Dilchert, S., Viswevaran, C. and Judge, T. A. (2007). In support of personality assessment in organizational settings. *Personnel Psychology*, 60(4), 995–1027.

Rivera, L. A. (2012) Hiring as cultural matching: The case of elite professional service firms. *American Sociological Review*, 77(6), 999–1022.

Robertson, I. T. & Smith, M. (2001) Personnel selection. *Journal of Occupational and Organizational Psychology*, 74(4), 441–72.

Rushton, J. P. & Jensen, A. R. (2005). Thirty years of research on race differences in cognitive ability. *Psychology, Public Policy, and Law*, 11(2), 235–94.

Saville, P., MacIver, R. & Kurz, R. (2009). Saville Consulting Wave® Professional Styles Handbook. *Saville Consulting Group*.

Smith, M. & Smith, P. (2005) *Testing people at work: Competencies in psychometric testing*. Oxford: BPS Blackwell.

Suzuki, L. & Aronson, J. (2005). The cultural malleability of intelligence and its impact on the racial/ethnic hierarchy. *Psychology, Public Policy, and Law*, 11(2), 320–7.

Verquer, M. L., Beehr, T. A. and Wagner, S. H. (2003). A meta-analysis of relations between person-organization fit and work attitudes. *Journal of Vocational Behaviour*, 63, 473–89.

Whetzel, D. L., McDaniel, M. A. & Nguyen, N. T. (2008). Subgroup differences in situational judgment test performance: A meta-analysis. *Human Performance*, 21(3), 291–309. doi: 10.1080/08959280802137820.

Woods, S.A., Hardy, C. & Guillaume, Y. R. F. (2011). Cognitive ability testing and adverse impact in selection: Meta-analytic evidence of reductions in Black–White differences in ability test scores over time. Paper presented at the 2011 BPS Division of Occupational Psychology Annual Conference, 12–14 January, Stratford-upon-Avon, UK.

8 Defining and Assessing Leadership Talent: A Multi-layered Approach

CAROLINE CURTIS

THE ENVIRONMENT WITHIN WHICH WE OPERATE

Banks and other financial services companies are operating in one of the fastest-moving environments around, experiencing unprecedented structural change and undergoing a once-in-a-generation shift – a real second big bang!

Across the financial services world, organisations are having to contend with increasing challenges, such as sophisticated cybercrime, a more demanding consumer, competition from inside and outside the industry, cultural change, ever-increasing regulatory scrutiny and a troubled economic outlook across most financial markets, including Europe, Asia and the Middle East. Many commentators talk about the end of banking as we know it.

This heralding of the end is nothing new though. More than 20 years ago, Bill Gates famously dismissed banks as dinosaurs that would soon be extinct in the modern marketplace. However, to channel Mark Twain, the reports of the death of banking are greatly exaggerated. Instead, observers of the industry will hear much about how the industry is adapting and responding, whether it's by mergers and acquisitions, tightening risk management processes, or leveraging new technology such as biometrics, mobile payments, social media and digital-only banks.

What we tend to hear less about is how the industry is investing in and evolving its leadership capability to meet the demands of this volatile, uncertain, complex and ambiguous (VUCA) business environment. However, as an HR Leader, I would agree with Warren Bennis (http://www.brainyquote.com/quotes/authors/w/warren_bennis.html) that 'Leadership is the capacity to translate vision into reality', and so we need to ensure that our leadership evolves in tandem with organisational developments.

In this chapter, we look at how Santander UK has risen to the leadership challenge and, more specifically, how it seeks to define and assess its leadership talent.

DEFINING A LEADERSHIP 'BLUEPRINT'

A business needs to understand what skills and personal attributes its leaders require in order to drive business and personal success, and it needs to be able to articulate this understanding to all concerned.

Establishing the 'blueprint'

In 2012, Santander was operating with a diverse range of HR 'instruments' which gave insights into the skills and behaviours required from its people (Figure 8.1). This set comprised:

- A set of six *corporate values* relevant to all of the Santander businesses across the world, focusing very much on the principles that the business valued, e.g. financial strength, commercial orientation and dynamism.
- A further four *UK values* – teamwork, innovation, commitment and efficiency – relevant to the UK market and ways of working.
- Ten *corporate competencies* providing an outline statement for skill sets such as collaboration, change agility and focus on results.
- Nine *UK competencies* outlined in a full multi-level competence framework developed previously for the UK business. Examples included business leadership, ethics and good governance, and client orientation, with detailed indicators for each competency.

While each 'instrument' provided insight into what leaders needed to 'do' and 'be', there was no one consolidated model aligned to the UK business environment or strategic direction. Hence, the time was ripe for a review of the leadership model in use.

The starting point was to understand the key challenges that the UK business was facing, in effect by looking at the VUCA environment and what this meant to the business in terms of impact on direction, strategy business approach and its resourcing requirements.

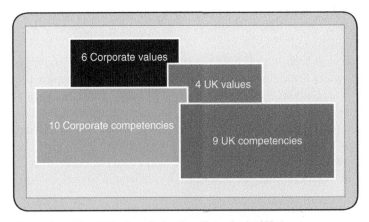

Figure 8.1   *The 2012 view of what 'excellence looked like'*

DEFINING AND ASSESSING LEADERSHIP TALENT 115

Sessions and facilitated discussions with Executive Committee members were held with a structure that asked:

- What are the *key challenges* that you believe your area and the organisation are facing now and in the future?
- What *skills and personal attributes* do your managers and leaders need to thrive in this environment and to meet their strategic objectives?
- How would you *rank and prioritise* these skills and attributes? Which need to be developed 'at point of entry' and which can we afford to develop 'in role'?

These sessions saw a wide range of views espoused, which was to be expected, as different Divisions were facing different challenges and so believed that specific skills or attributes were more relevant to them.

A series of challenges, reiterations, consolidations and considerations followed, resulting in what has now become known as the Executive Assessment Framework (EAF). Figure 8.2 shows the original EAF.

Behind this fairly simplistic articulation sat a further breakdown of competency or attribute areas (shown in Figure 8.3) and a full set of success indicators for each competency.

The development of the EAF meant that Santander UK had a leadership model that was completely aligned to the business direction and challenges and that was readily available for all stakeholders to use.

Evolving the EAF

We've touched on how quickly the financial services environment and market are moving, and a key challenge has been to constantly review the EAF so that it remains fit for purpose.

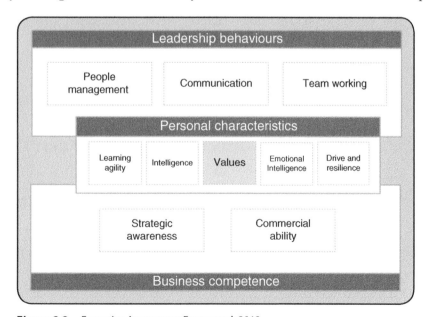

Figure 8.2 *Executive Assessment Framework 2012*

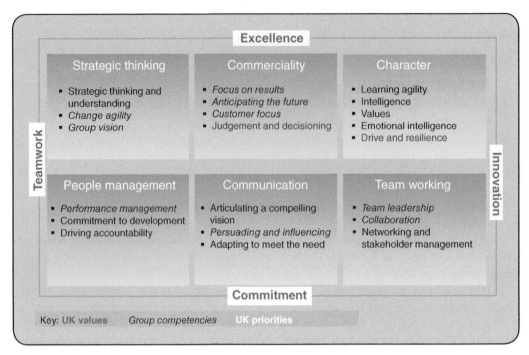

Figure 8.3 *Executive Assessment Framework 2012: further detail*

After two years' use, the framework has been updated to include new areas of competence that the business believes are vital for success. Figure 8.4 shows the updated model. This refreshed version sees the inclusion of leading cultural change (within the leadership behaviours domain), and of risk management, service orientation and technological awareness (within the business competence domain).

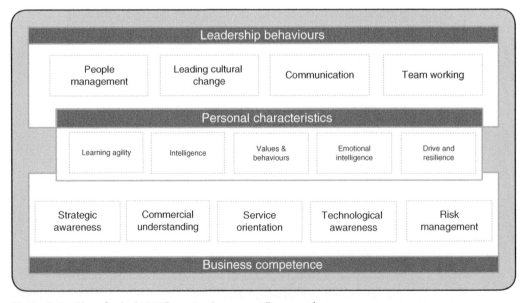

Figure 8.4 *The refreshed 2015 Executive Assessment Framework*

DEFINING POTENTIAL WITHIN SANTANDER

Understanding an individual's potential enables us to make the most of the talent within an organisation, balancing personal aspiration with business requirements.

The topic of 'potential' is one that is generally at the forefront of any talent manager's mind, especially as the much-vaunted 'War for Talent' has continued to rage unabated. As an industry, we continue to be fishing in a very small pool for the very best professionals, and this is exacerbated by the psychological contracts of a multi-generational workforce. No longer can we expect our management population to remain loyal to us without a strong development and career progression offering.

Thinking about potential has moved on greatly over the years, and Santander has continued to develop and evolve its model and assessment of this element.

The early years

Initial work with potential in 2007/8 focused on a very basic assessment, with little sophistication concerning the definition of what made up potential or how to evaluate or assess an individual. In relation to producing a talent rating, views centred on whether individuals had:

- *Low* potential – they were operating at the appropriate level;
- *Medium* potential – they had the capacity to move to a larger or more complex role one level higher; or
- *High* potential – they had the capacity to move up more than one level to a much larger or more complex role.

In these early days, no guidance was given on how a manager should be assessing these levels.

The subjective nature of the assessment led Santander to adopt guidelines concerning the make-up of potential. This evolution defined potential as being made up of three elements – aspiration, ability and commitment. This model, based on that developed by the Corporate Leadership Council and outlined in Figure 8.5, gave managers some key criteria to consider in coming to their view of an individual's potential.

Evolving the model

The majority of large organisations, and many smaller ones, invest in identifying their talent through the use of potential ratings, usually combined with performance appraisal levels. One of the best-known tools is the 9-box grid (see Figure 8.6), and this was the initial methodology used within Santander UK. Using the 9-box methodology, a view was reached about each management population and further talent interventions were assigned as appropriate.

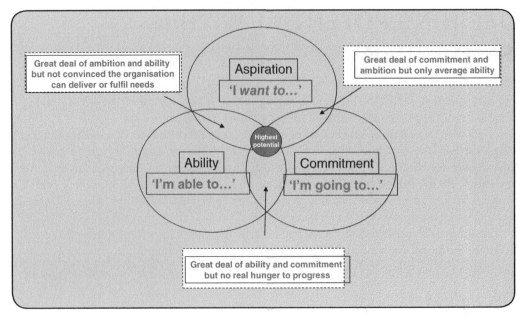

Figure 8.5 *The key aspects of potential*

At the same time, though, as the Executive Assessment Framework was being developed, work started on seeking to understand what really defined potential within Santander. Moving beyond the generic definitions, the Executive Talent team sought to develop a bespoke view that would be more sophisticated in terms of how it articulated what the drivers of potential were and differentiated the type and direction of potential. This in-depth work led to a new model of potential within the Santander UK operation, shown in Figure 8.7.

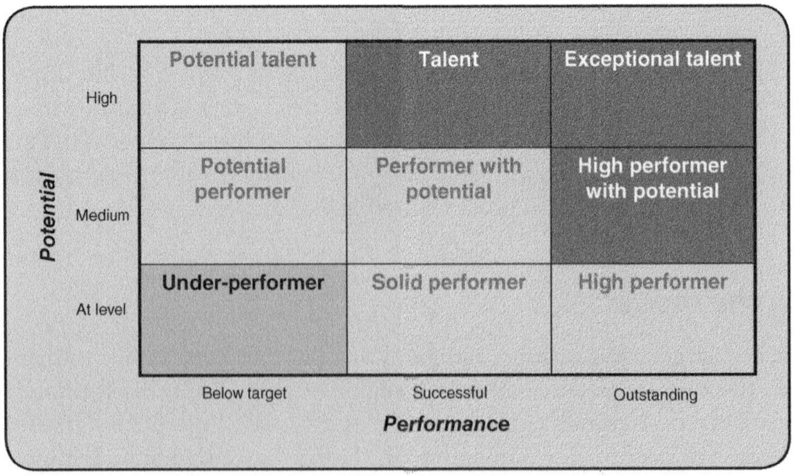

Figure 8.6 *The 9-box grid*

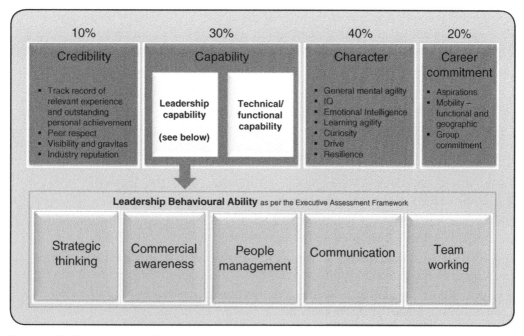

Figure 8.7 *The new model of potential*

IMPLEMENTING ROBUST LEADERSHIP ASSESSMENT

In assessing our people we need to ensure that we are assessing the right things, i.e. those that are critical to success, and that we assess them in the right way, a way that provides a strong user experience and that is valid and reliable.

Leadership assessment within Santander UK is undertaken for a wide range of reasons linked to Talent Management: to support executive selection, to enable benchmarking and also for purely developmental purposes such as to support coaching.

Establishing an organisation-wide assessment capability within Santander

In 2012 Santander UK sought to establish an organisation-wide Assessment Area of Expertise. The aim was to develop a centrally managed capability that enabled the business to use assessments more effectively and efficiently, adding value to the business, the individual under review and the HR business partners who were involved in the assessment.

The benefits of and case for a centralised capability were about being able to:

- work within a clear *framework*, understanding where assessment *adds value* and which are the best tools and methodologies to give the desired information;

- partner with selected *external providers* of psychometrics to develop reporting that meets Santander UK's specific needs, for example a match to our competence frameworks, branding;
- drive down *costs* through building in-house capability and leveraging volume discounts;
- *develop* our people through accrediting them to use specific psychometrics within their work; and
- ensure clear *governance* of the use of assessments and psychometrics.

The Area of Expertise (AoE) was established to meet the following objectives:

- to provide assessment *strategy*, *frameworks* and *tools* that enable Santander UK to optimise the value gained from investment in assessment;
- to *manage* assessment for executive and senior level roles and for transformation projects where *bespoke assessment* vehicles are required;
- to *advise*, *guide* and *support* HR, AoEs and the business to choose and implement appropriate assessment that improves decision making and development planning;
- to lead the *governance* of assessment across the business in order to drive up the quality and impact of the investment.

The initial work following the approval of the central capability was to understand the existing scope of assessment within the business and then to agree the most appropriate use in the future. Figure 8.8 shows the agreed scope of assessment within the UK business.

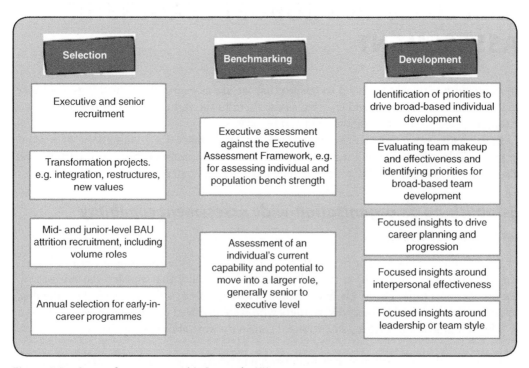

Figure 8.8 *Scope of assessment within Santander UK*

Once the scope of assessment had been understood and agreed, the priority was to agree a standard tool kit of psychometrics and other vehicles, such as Situational Judgement Tests and 360 tools. A particular focus was put on psychometrics because of the benefits and drawbacks associated with their use.

The role of psychometrics within Santander

The case for including psychometrics within the assessment tool kit was based on the premise that people have specific intellectual abilities and personality traits that can be measured and compared against others'. These relative scores can then be used to predict how individuals will perform in role or how well matched and motivated they will be in specific roles or areas of the business.

Selecting psychometric tools

An intensive programme of work (and self-discovery!) was undertaken to review and select a standard set of psychometrics. A variety of tools were reviewed: ability/aptitude tests, personality-type instruments and interest inventories; instruments were selected for review on the basis of either previous use or a strong industry reputation.

Specific criteria used to evaluate each tool included:

- **Test validity and reliability** Did the test have strong evidence of high validity and reliability? How well did the factors assessed match the Executive Assessment Framework or the specific ability that we wanted to assess?
- **Norms** What norms were available for the test and how well did these match the populations that we would ideally want to norm against?
- **Appropriateness** How appropriate was the tool (its operation, format and language) for the age, culture and language of users?
- **The user experience** Was the tool easy to access? What sort of platform would it run on? Were the look and feel modern and easy to navigate? Did the test have strong face validity?
- **Administration** How easy was it to set up testing? Was self-service or bureau support available? How quickly could reports be run and accessed? What options existed for own-branding? How flexible was reporting? For example, could a variety of reports be run from one user completion? What accreditation was required to administer, interpret and feedback the?
- **Economics** What was the cost of the tool in terms of training and accreditation, licences, self-service software or bureau costs, set-up and reporting? What benefit did we believe the insights would provide? Overall, did the benefit of the insights outweigh the cost of collecting the information?

The review of potential tools was completed initially on a desktop basis, reviewing reliability, validity, norms and match to requirements. Once these 'entry requirements' were met, each test was undertaken to establish the user and administration factors.

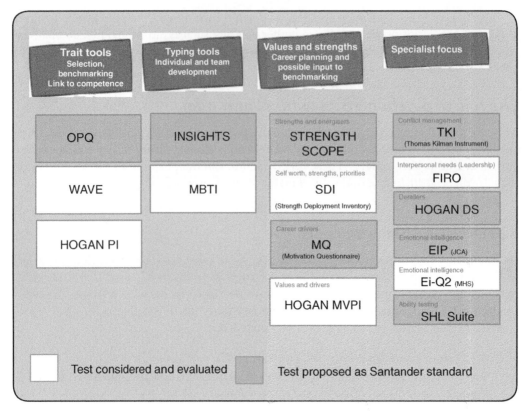

Figure 8.9 *The Santander psychometric tool kit*

The review resulted in a standard tool kit of psychometrics, not meant to be exclusive but outlining the tools that would be appropriate for the expected majority of assessment needs. Figure 8.9 shows the initial tool kit endorsed for use.

Principles of use for the psychometric tool kit

Initial work to establish the current use of psychometrics in the business had shown the degree to which these tools could elicit strong passions, either in favour of or against their use. Misinformation and misconceptions were evidenced and in response, a set of principles were developed around how psychometrics should be used.

- **Testing the right thing**   Users need to be clear about what is to be tested, that is, what are the traits or abilities that are essential to the job and that differentiate strong performance? For example, does the job holder need to be intellectually outstanding, or is it more important to make sure that they can lead in a democratic and consultative way? There needs to be a clear link between what is being tested and what the job requires for success.
- **Understand exactly what is being measured**   And don't confuse preference with ability! For example, the standard personality test OPQ measures a person's preference, not their competence in an area. Thus, they may prefer not to work with

data but may actually be very good at it. Or one person might really enjoy meeting new people and promoting their ideas, but it doesn't automatically follow that they're any better at it than someone who enjoys it less.

- **Don't take results as gospel** No matter how good the psychometrics, they are not infallible for a number of reasons. Candidates can 'fake good', and while some tools have a built-in check of the degree to which individuals answer in a socially desirable way, some don't. Additionally, false results can occur where there is a genuine lack of self-awareness.
- **Never make cut-off decisions solely on the basis of the test** Insights from psychometrics should inform and be used in conjunction with other assessment information. Use any discrepancies with other assessment information as a cue to explore for more information, rather than to form a final conclusion. Where psychometrics make up the primary evidence, ensure any judgements or insights are validated with the individual before being factored into assessment outputs.

Assessment for selection or benchmarking

When the central Area of Expertise has been set up and the standard assessment vehicles established, formal assessment for both selection and benchmarking purposes within the business takes place.

Benchmarking assessment is often used when an individual is looking to progress from a senior management level into executive management. The benchmarking can be done as part of the selection process, or, more usually, as part of career management, enabling the identification of 'readiness.'

- Does the individual have the technical or job-specific skills and experience to perform the role?
- Does the individual display the required leadership and personal attributes?

Assessment of job-specific skills runs along industry-standard lines, so here we concentrate on how Santander has developed its assessment of leadership and personal attributes.

The Executive Assessment Framework (EAF) has been instrumental in providing a solid basis for assessment, enabling us to have confidence that the assessment is valid, that it is measuring the right things. (The fact that the framework constantly evolves alongside business requirements means that we are looking to future-proof the model.) Having developed specific indicators of success for each element of the EAF, we have a clear benchmark to measure against. Figure 8.10 shows typical indicators that have been developed to support elements of the EAF. As with the overall framework, indicators will evolve and change according to the skills required by the business.

Assessing against the Executive Assessment Framework

Assessment against the EAF comprises a number of separate elements.

Knowledge	Maintains awareness of opportunities provided by new technology to address challenges or to enable new ways of working.
	Recognises the potential strategic application and commercial advantage of new technology landscapes
	Promotes the importance and benefits of understanding emerging technologies to the team and key stakeholders
Openness	Within their own sphere of influence, works to further organisational goals through the use of emerging technologies and products.
	Champions a constant focus on identifying improved ways of working and meeting business objectives
	Is challenging and innovative in their approach to reviewing current operations and identifying and proposing new and potentially better ways of doing things
	Demonstrates persistence and flexibility in progressing changes they believe in or that have been agreed

Figure 8.10 *Typical indicators for technology understanding*

Psychometrics   Individuals complete OPQ for general personality and EiP for emotional intelligence before their face-to-face assessment. These reports are analysed and elements for discussion are built into the structured interview. This enables the interviewer to validate any insights that are to be used in the final assessment report.

The psychometrics provide evidence across the full EAF but particularly against many of the personal attributes domain indicators, where it is more difficult to assess through other means. It is made clear to the individuals that there is no one preferred psychological profile; what the assessors are interested in is understanding where there may be potential springboards or barriers to success.

Line manager feedback   A number of the assessment areas cover both a generic and a Santander-specific element – a form of 'know' and 'do' distinction. For example, strategic, commercial and technology customer orientation all have this distinction. Input from the line manager, in the form of a structured questionnaire, enables us to gain insights into how the individual performs in the current role against specific indicators. In some cases, we find that the individual has generic knowledge but doesn't apply it on the job. This may be through a lack of opportunity or because they have not developed the Santander-specific contextual knowledge that will facilitate implementation. In other cases we find that the individual can do something in role but is unable to translate this learnt behaviour into a new and challenging situation. For example, they understand

Santander strategy but are unable to apply their strategic thinking ability effectively within the case study scenario.

Case study   A range of analytical, business-based case studies are used for assessment. These are bought-in materials and purposely set outside of Santander and financial services. Using proprietary material has a number of advantages, such as giving confidence that the material is set at the appropriate level and measures the correct abilities. Being set outside of Santander also ensures that we measure underlying ability, not learnt behaviour or Santander-specific knowledge. Case studies are completed at the face-to-face assessment event under exam conditions and take two hours. They are then marked internally and provide evidence against the business competence domain areas as well as learning agility and intellect.

Structured interview   The last element of assessment is a two-hour structured interview, primarily focusing on the leadership behaviours domain. The interview is also an opportunity to bring in any areas for discussion from the psychometrics. Where this is the case, the insights are presented and validated with the individual through discussion and requests for examples of where traits have been deployed.

The holistic assessment then results in a full assessment report outlining how the individual benchmarks against the EAF. Overall performance is rated against a five-point scale, with 'successful' set at the level of a fully competent executive leader.

Reports are initially reviewed with the line manager, to shed light on the extent to which the assessment reflects current reality, and then discussed in full with the individual. At this feedback session, there is also the opportunity for a full debrief of the two psychometrics.

Perceived benefits of the EAF assessment approach

This current multi-layered approach is seen as having benefits for both the organisation and the individual.

- The approach gives a much richer and more detailed view of the individual against a standardised benchmark. This enables comparison between candidates as well as against a specific leadership level. The assessment can be used to gauge readiness to progress as well as developmental progress.
- The focus on generic skills and attributes allows us to distinguish between job-specific skills and those required at a certain level of leadership, thereby supporting our aim to develop strong leaders able to perform effectively across a range of business areas.
- While the multi-layered approach is seen as challenging for the individual, it provides every opportunity for them to display just how very strong they are. The inclusion of

the external case study gives equal opportunity to those whose role may not include accountability for commercial or strategic elements.
- The inclusion of line manager feedback also provides additional intelligence, about the individual, about how well the line manager knows and assesses their own people, and also about how effective and representative the internal assessment is.

Bespoke assessment for selection or benchmarking

On an ad hoc basis, bespoke assessment vehicles, including assessment centres, are developed for use within the business. However, the same principles are adopted:

- a clear articulation of the skills or attributes required for success;
- the development or adoption of tests (personality or ability) that have a clear correlation with the skills required;
- a multi-layered approach, ideally with each competence area being tested twice and no exercise covering more than five key areas of competence.

Examples of these bespoke assessments include selection within the branch network and benchmarking within the contact centre middle manager population.

Assessment for development

A further key area for the use of assessment – primarily psychometrics – has been development, more specifically behavioural coaching, career counselling and coaching and leadership programme preparation.

Behavioural coaching

Coaching, especially for senior-level leaders, has a key role to play within Santander UK, enabling individuals to work on a one-to-one basis with a coach to make specific changes or to support particular career transitions.

In certain cases, the use of psychometrics is beneficial in providing insights into preferences and behavioural patterns. In this realm, real benefits have been seen from the use of psychometrics, such as HoganLead, with a focus on leadership derailment and the identification of potential dysfunctional interpersonal traits. Insights into emotional intelligence are also increasingly being used as it becomes more widely accepted that this intelligence 'type' can have as big an impact as general intelligence or intellect. On this front, positive feedback has been received about the use of the Emotional Intelligence Profile from JCA.

Career counselling and coaching

Santander puts a high emphasis on career development and has a commitment to at least annual career discussions of individuals' aspirations and career plans. This supplements the organisational development work undertaken in the area of succession planning.

Discovering and understanding strengths and work preferences is an effective catalyst to discussions about career options and effective transitions. Alongside generalist psychometrics

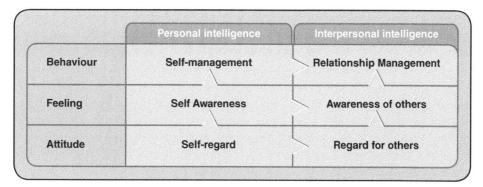

Figure 8.11 *Emotional Intelligence Profile model*

such as OPQ, the more focused StrengthScope tool (Strengths Partnership Ltd) has provided additional insights by reporting on

- an individual's standout strengths,
- the unintended consequences that may arise when strengths go into overdrive,
- the extent to which an individual can productively apply their strengths at work, and
- how visible their strengths are to others.

Leadership programme preparation

2015 saw Santander introduce a new leadership programme aimed at key successors for executive and board-level roles. The programme, Leadership Excellence in Action Programme (LEAP), is an innovative combination of academic input, Santander-contextual input, self-awareness and self-development. Combined with real-world problem solving and action set learning, the programme has brought together a wide range of development areas in support of the overall Executive Assessment Framework.

As part of the programme preparation, individuals complete the Emotional Intelligence Profile to gain insights into their own perception of their emotional intelligence as outlined in Figure 8.11. These insights are then built upon as part of the self-development section of the programme.

Gaining benefit from the use of psychometrics in development

There is a real emphasis on understanding return on investment (or return on expectation) in the use of psychometrics as part of assessment. Santander is committed to bringing out the best in its leaders, and this means investing time and money in development solutions such as learning, mentoring and coaching. The use of psychometrics gives us insightful and objective information with which to start discussions and planning concerning the focus of development and the most appropriate vehicles.

The return, though, only comes where action follows on from the completion and feedback of the psychometric report. Our learning is that for psychometrics to be effective and to show a return the following need to be in place:

- A clear understanding up front of *why* the psychometric is being used; for example, what 'problem' needs to be resolved or what opportunity needs to be leveraged?

- Timely and skilled *feedback* of the report and insights. As per best practice, face-to-face feedback, discussion and challenge can ensure that key elements of learning are recognised, strengths leveraged and risks mitigated.
- A drive for *action*. Especially in a developmental context, the driver of action needs to be the individual whose development is in focus. There is a temptation to receive the feedback and then just file the report, noting the traits that were known and at times dismissing those that were either a surprise or not in line with self-perception. Without strong challenge and encouragement, psychometrics can become an expensive exercise in self-reflection with no real return. Ensuring that relevant points are built into coaching and development plans will optimise the return on investment.

CONCLUSIONS

All HR and talent managers are under increasing pressure to justify the investment that is made across the talent management cycle, whether that's in selection, talent identification, development or talent deployment. They increasingly need to show the value that they add by enabling the business to meet its strategic imperatives while minimising and mitigating business risks.

For Santander's Executive Talent Team, a real value-add is the work that has been outlined on providing models, solutions and practices for what excellence looks like (performance and potential) along with expertise in the assessment that underpins these models.

This focus on assessment frameworks and solutions (which constantly evolve) provides what Bob Johansen termed the 'VUCA Prime' response; it enables the business to meet some of the challenges of the VUCA world by supporting the business to meet

Volatility *with* Vision
Uncertainty *with* Understanding
Complexity *with* Clarity
Ambiguity *with* Agility.

9 Psychometrics: The Evaluation and Development of Team Performance

STEPHEN BENTON

INTRODUCTION

This chapter will examine the strengths and the weaknesses of teams and team working, with a view to exploring the attributes of high- and low-quality performance, which may result from the interaction of individual differences, as identified by psychometrics. The well-documented global increase in the volatility of organisational life has resulted in a step change in competitiveness (Lawrence, 2013; Luttwak, 1999). Hence, an explanation of the type of competitive environment within which organisations operate may help an understanding of just what it is that can make teams such a valuable organisational resource. This organisational context highlights the importance of a team's functional diversity, its evaluation and integration, as a prime determinant of its productivity. Psychometric tools are used extensively in an attempt to support individuals and teams working with these differences of style or personality in order to deliver that special 'added value' claimed to characterise the effective utilisation of personality difference within teamwork. Psychometrics can play a deciding role in building personal and interpersonal competence in teams in order to promote and support working with behavioural diversity.

THE ORGANISATIONAL CONTEXT

Organisations are challenged to compete in a global economy that is fiercely competitive, one which has been characterised by authors such as Luttwak (1999) as 'turbo-capitalism'. Luttwak argues that immense and dynamic market forces have been released by deregulation and the adoption of free market 'fundamentalism'. He argues that the retreat of governments from the market place has undermined a moderating influence between national economic policies, social and cultural values and volatile business priorities. Moreover, the finance, production and marketing pressures emanating from turbo-capitalism have resulted in direct and escalating competitiveness in every aspect of organisational performance. These organisational conditions, combined with continuing market and organisational volatility, point to the strong likelihood that pressure on individuals' performance and organisations' competitiveness will continue to increase and make them prone to extremes of opportunity and threat.

In this highly competitive environment, organisations have acknowledged that it is not only the type, depth and quality of the skills base that are valued, but also an ability to work effectively and creatively within teams, through cycles of intense and diverse demands (Luftans, Vogelgesang & Lester, 2006).

Under these conditions sustained competitiveness requires an operational capacity that maintains fitness for stability as well as fitness for generating and then maximising opportunities. Accordingly, it is argued that this changing business paradigm has intensified fundamental ingredients of uncertainty (both inter-organisational and interpersonal), which in turn prompts widespread and escalating volatility within working environments. This convergence of pressures has been described as a 'VUCA' environment, a term that denotes increasingly **v**olatility, in **u**ncertain, **c**omplex and **a**mbiguous organisational environments (Lawrence, 2013).

In response to such environments organisations have identified the central need to collect information within a format that maintains and exploits the information's complexity. An effective team has the capacity to provide cognitive complexity, motivational drives and focus, diverse perspectives and emotional robustness when dealing with complex and uncertain information and diagnoses. Utilising such talent requires a degree of devolved responsibility with associated development and support for behaviours that, in dealing with uncertain outcomes, are often diverse and explorative. All of this needs to occur within 'real-time' organisational environments, which, as Maravelas (2005) argues, have become more 'terrifying and less predictable'. In response, as organisations restructure, refocus and rethink they have tended towards the creation of flatter hierarchies and employed a highly diverse, empowered workforce (De Dreu & Gelfand, 2008), with an associated reliance on teams.

During these intense times a team may be prone to failing interpersonal coherence as differences in thinking, emotional and behavioural styles and range can trigger defensive, as well as directly damaging, behaviours. The aim of team psychometrics is to provide a team with a shared 'framework' from which to diagnose what is working well or not well, so that the team can then work through differences of styles in, for example, conflict handling, communication, listening styles or, in general terms, personality.

TEAM CONTEXT

A working definition of a team should reflect the central importance of collaboration in pursuit of an outcome for which all the team members are accountable. Moreover, effective teams are able to actively benefit from sources of 'difference' within the team, as they can promote diversity of perspective, analysis and solution.

Various models describe how a team should organise itself. In broad terms teams require a working structure, which includes clarity of leadership, purpose, and responsibilities. This structure would be supported by the processes within the team shaped by established team roles and individuals' personal and professional skills.

Highly effective teams consistently display a number of core behaviours, which are taken to indicate a high-functioning team, one that is efficient, cognitively and emotionally robust and able to create high-quality outcomes, under varying degrees and types of pressure. Such a team works together, unified in the overarching goal and associated purposes while committed to delivery of personal and shared tasks. Of equal importance are the behavioural qualities of active support, participation and respect (Peltokorpi & Hasu, 2014). Here team members are able to work with a diversity of interpersonal styles in a constructive manner, while maintaining a focus on task goals and team outcomes. The team's organisational working environment is every bit as volatile as that created for the organisation by global business pressures. The relationships between team members can fracture, leading to the generation of interpersonally damaging and organisationally costly behaviours.

Unsurprisingly, the internal operations of teams have attracted extensive attention. Various research and professional reports have provided a stark profile of unwanted team behaviours, those which emerge when the pressure on team members causes preferred communication and coping styles to break down (Acas, 2014, p. 3). These behaviours emerge in five broad areas within which quality will decline – decision making, conflict handling, interpersonal communication, information exchange and person competence – with an overall negative impact on team coherence. Typically, a team's, as well as the team members', focus will become obscured by personal issues and behaviours, which undermine the quality of information to be shared and the manner in which it should be shared. Behaviours associated with this decline include deliberate withholding of information, hostility to increased variety of perspectives and ideas, stereotyping, emotional outbursts, social loafing and unresolved conflict. These behaviours prompt consequences in the team of missing delivery deadlines, poor ideation, compromise rather than innovation, and mediocre commitment and follow-through. The organisational consequences can present as missed targets, slow responsiveness to market opportunities and threats, poor risk assessments, and low staff motivation and engagement.

However, the competitive advantage that teams can potentially deliver for an organisation, from a synthesis of differences, is huge. For example, the expertise, experience, ideation, productive errors, reflection and mutual support that organisations are able to utilise are all ingredients of an effective team. Such teams are argued to provide organisations with resilience of both thought and action (Ricci & Wiese, 2011; Tjosvold, 1990). Hence, when the pressures for competitiveness are global in scale, it is not surprising that it is to teams that organisations have turned in the search for that competitive edge (Glassop, 2002).

Accordingly, various team models and related psychometric applications, designed to guide the understanding, management and development of team qualities, have become a fundamental component of team development practice.

TEAM DEVELOPMENT: THE PSYCHOMETRIC CONTEXT

Teams may be created by organisations for a variety of reasons with a wide range of specific outcomes or objectives in mind, but teams are viewed as having fundamental properties, comprising an intrinsic motive volatility, common to most teams. Importantly, it is the power of various team models to identify and clarify these underlying dynamics which has prompted much behavioural and psychometric development.

An example of a team model that has created effective operational terms of reference, across generations, is Tuckman's four-stage model (Tuckman, 1965), later expanded into a five-stage model (Tuckman & Jensen, 1977). The original four stages are named Forming, Storming, Norming and Performing. The fifth is Adjourning.

Stage 1: Forming

Teams start by identifying what the nature of the team task is, attending to practical constraints such as the time available and the need to timetable team meetings, and rigorously considering just what kinds of expertise and physical resources will be necessary for the team's success. Roles and responsibilities will at least be initialled and at this stage communications between members are largely uncontested, as are the relationships. In practice the allocation of roles and responsibilities is unlikely to fully meet the task and interpersonal demands which will emerge, with better definition, as the team progresses. However, there exist a number of psychometric approaches which have been designed to facilitate the use of individual differences in a manner that supports particular team roles. For example, the Team Focus Managing Team Roles Indicator (MTR-i™) is used as a platform for preparing individuals to understand the link between personality-based preferences and Jungian psychological types in the context of team behaviour. Although based on the Jungian typology, the *MTR-i* is fundamentally a team roles model, shown with Jungian overlap in the list below (Team Focus, n.d.). It identifies what kind of contribution is being made to the team and 'complements the MBTI [Myers–Briggs Type Indicator; see Figure 9.2] by enabling a comparison between preferences and roles being performed' (Team Technology, 2015).

- **Curator** (ISTJ, ISFJ) questions and collects ideas that help to clarify; focuses on the immediate priority and approaches tasks in a thoughtful, reflective way.
- **Sculptor** (ESTP, ESFP) seeks action, is keen to get things done and remains practical while focusing on getting tangible results.
- **Innovator** (INFJ, INTJ) is ideas-oriented and seeks to create something different and original; can be seen as either a vague dreamer or a focused visionary.
- **Explorer** (ENFP, ENTP) seeks variety and experimentation; introduces the new and the unusual, challenges the status quo and acts as an agent of change.
- **Scientist** (ISTP, INTP) creates intellectual understanding using sharp logic and builds grand theories or mental maps but may not always find them easy to communicate.
- **Conductor** (ESTJ, ENTJ) reduces ambiguity by bringing structure, organisation and plans to get the job done.
- **Campaigner** (ISFP, INFP) focuses on a core purpose with real meaning and value; looks beyond the immediate and commits to a cause with passion.
- **Coach** (ESFJ, ENFJ) focuses on creating a harmonious atmosphere; avoids conflict and helps others to contribute by encouraging and supporting.

The instrument seeks to provide a common language – one that allows people to explore their own and each other's actual team contribution rather than simply focusing on formal roles, status or personality stereotype. The instrument works with the view that personality affects a person's role and that the role in turn impacts on the personality. However, in teams the roles needed are clearly linked with performance and situational demands. Identifying individual differences and preferences between people and organising people into useful 'roles' unites these differences in support of the team's endeavours. Without this 'role' framework the differences (especially under pressure) may subvert the team's unity and aims. Hence the interplay of skills, personality and the individual's preferred role needs to be planned if it is to add to a team's capacity to perform well.

Clearly, the creation of a common language for the intensely personal and subjective processes which differentiate individuals in terms of style, attitude, temperament and personality offers the potential for shared insight and improved communications. Moreover, in practical terms, awareness of the potential for building a balanced and comprehensive mix of role-based behaviours within a team can highlight developmental opportunities.

Stage 2: Storming

As team tasks are undertaken, team members develop opinions about aspects of other members, for example their attitudes, communication styles and behaviour. These impressions and views are generated by the quality of interactions and it is likely that the team will experience expression of disagreement, discontent and conflict. There may even be challenges to the leader's authority, either directly or indirectly or both. Before the team can move onto the next stage of development, these conflicting views and clashes of personality need to be resolved. Consequently, it is the case that some teams fail to move on to the next level of performance, which should be achieved within the subsequent stage. Various psychometric applications have been devised to address these challenges. It is the recognition of such underlying properties which can lay the ground for focused personal and team development, which aligns with the team dynamic. For example, the Fundamental Interpersonal Relations Orientation (FIRO®)team assessment toolshows the links between core interpersonal needs and the five stages of the Tuckman model.

To achieve high performance, team members need to operate with mutual respect and trust and a sound basis of proven working relationships. This instrument offers a framework from which to help people understand their interpersonal needs and how such needs play an important role in their communication style and behaviour. Failure to develop appropriate resolution behaviours can seriously impede a team's development to stage 3; in fact Tuckman and Jensen (1977) denote this stage one of 'catharsis'. The FIRO instrument can target this need, identifying the drivers underlying the behaviours that shape relationships for individuals and teams.

Stage 3: Norming

Individuals will have worked through their disagreements and earned a degree of mutual respect, possibly based on a pragmatic assessment of others' overall worth or value to the team. Differences will have been acknowledged and addressed constructively. Valuing differences prompts a degree of resolution of differences and is taken to promote strong relationships, tested and strengthened by the differences rather than the differences being resented. Individuals and relationships which survive these clashes are characterised by a deeper degree of mutual commitment. This stage is associated with collaborative conflict resolution and problem solving, and a shared responsibility for delivery of personal and team tasks. The psychometric identification and management of different preferred conflict styles has provided individuals and teams with a practical approach to coping with and managing potentially damaging interpersonal conflict. For example, the Thomas–Kilmann Conflict Mode Instrument (TKI) (Thomas & Kilmann, 1974) assesses an individual's preferred behaviour when in a conflict situation. This tool describes conflict-handing behaviour or style in terms of two dimensions: assertiveness and cooperativeness. An individual who inclines towards 'assertiveness' stresses the outcome and its value or importance to them, while one who values 'cooperativeness' is interested in and committed to acknowledging and supporting a shared outcome, of value to all parties. Active choice of style is correlated with individuals' personality and level of skill (for example negotiation skills). The choice is also responsive to expectations, which may be associated with perceived roles (their own and others'), status, and cultural values and norms. The situation or context is made up of these interactive 'situations'. The instrument proposes that five styles are the most likely; they are shown in Figure 9.1.

This instrument is among the most popular available for addressing interpersonal conflict. As part of the training and development for individuals and teams it provides a framework from which to diagnose and manage your own and others' behaviour, based

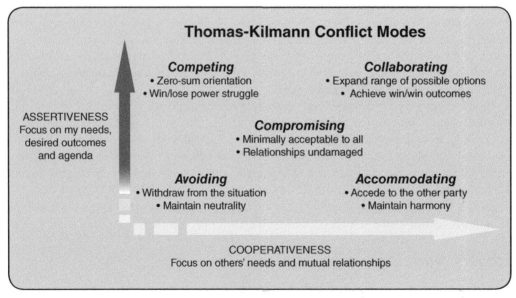

Figure 9.1 *The two primary axes of assertiveness and cooperativeness*
Source: http://www.edbatista.com/2007/01/conflict_modes_.html.

on identification of styles at work and the types of differences presenting. Rather than individuals relying on habitual responses to conflict, the instrument highlights alternative styles or strategies which reflect, it is argued, the primary dimensions (axes) along which conflict may be evaluated. The negative consequences of failed conflict resolution are frequently the product of escalating and poorly handled disagreement. This approach claims to offer a method for increasing team members' coping capacity during conflict while reducing their anxiety and defensive behaviours by creating effective personal strategies that actively engage with their judgement of their assertiveness (e.g. their degree of task focus) and cooperativeness (e.g. their preference for interpersonal communication) during conflict.

Stage 4: Performing

As the team consolidates – in practical behavioural terms – issues of norms and team roles, the cognitive and emotional processes converge so that the functional commonality of the team roles and agreed protocols underpin the goals common to every team members' understanding of their personal and team purpose. At this stage the team should be characterised by highly motivated, well-informed and engaged individuals, all aligned with the team outcomes and able to cope and work with differences. According to the model, this stage is likely to display high-quality information exchange, analysis, decision making and outcome focus. In brief, such a team will display what is described as 'empowerment'. It is arguable that at this stage the team environment will be able to promote, encourage and consolidate innovative ideas, actions and solutions. The multidimensional nature of applied creativity, namely innovation, and psychometric developments are moving swiftly into this prime area of team and organisational aspiration and need. An example of a psychometric application in this area is the OPP Innovation Pi. Getting the best mix of differences to work well together is a key aspect of teams; getting them to work towards applied innovation is likely to be driving team development even harder during this phase of global turbo-economics. Arguably, measures of innovation style could provide an early indication to the organisation of how to facilitate innovation in teams.

The Innovation Pi instrument measures five key areas: motivation to change, challenging behaviour, adaptation, consistency of work styles, and a 'faking' scale, social desirability. From these it creates a profile of preferred behaviours which are argued to prompt and maintain innovative thinking and action. The output, in the form of a report, provides a basis for identifying an individual's innovation style from among 'change agent', 'consolidator' and 'catalyst', three approaches central to applied innovation within organisations.

Stage 5: Adjourning

Tuckman's fifth stage, Adjourning, takes a perspective of the team that goes beyond the team purpose that drove the first four stages and concerns what happens when the team has come to the end of its time. If the team process has included a successful resolution of the challenges in the preceding stages the probability is high that individuals will leave the team with a strong sense of achievement and confidence. However, individuals vary in how they cope with this stage. If the members of the team have formed close working relationships, with intense periods of interdependence, self-esteem and sense of security may be threatened. Indeed, most members of high-performing teams describe being able to work intensely yet collaboratively as enjoyable, satisfying and stimulating. It could be that individuals experience a sense of loss, as a very successful team may represent the highest point of their performance and participation (Aldag & Kuzuhara, 2015).

PSYCHOMETRICS AND PERSONALITY

The study and evaluation of the type and qualities associated with intra-team communication and interpersonal behaviour has consistently placed 'personality' at the centre of team thinking and development. There are many examples of psychometric applications directed at teams. Popular Jungian-based team applications include the Myers–Briggs Type Indicator (MBTI) and Insights Discovery. Factor-based (Big Five) instruments are available and include SHL's OPQ32 and Lumina Learning's Spark psychometric, which is based on the Big Five but informed by Jungian precepts.

TYPOLOGY AND TEAMS

Currently, the most widely cited and used psychometric in this field is the MBTI, although it is noted that other highly successful psychometric developments have expanded into this area of organisational learning and development. In broad terms these typological applications are frequently derived, in varying degrees, from Jung's psychodynamic model of personality (Jung, 1923; Sharp, 1987). According to Jung, human functioning and personality are the product of intra-psychological opposites, interacting to shape how a person tends to experience and interact with the world.

> Based on his observations, Jung concluded that differences in behavior result from individuals' inborn tendencies to use their minds in different ways. As people act on these tendencies, they develop predictable patterns of behavior. Jung's psychological type theory defines eight different patterns, or types, and gives an explanation of how type develops. (Myers, 1998)

Jung's theory highlights the influence of internal subjective processes and how they interact with external focused information collection and processing. He identified eight different patterns for how we carry out these mental activities. These patterns are comprised of attitudes and functions, which are combined in pairs of opposites, as shown in Table 9.1. Jung described these eight combinations as the basis for understanding why people seem habitually to prefer one pattern over another. Jung's eight types form the basis of the MBTI

Table 9.1 *Jungian attitudes and functions and typical preferences*

Attitude	Function	Typical team preferences
Extraverted	Sensing	**Outward focus.** Actively and directly engaged with the objective world. Focus on gathering factual data and sensory experiences. Setting specific targets and criteria for evaluation.
Introverted	Sensing	**Inward focus.** Reflective focus on subjective sensory experiences and stored information. Questioning and analysing.
Extraverted	Intuition	**Outward and active.** Open to new possibilities and meanings, stimulated by new patterns encountered in the objective world. Challenging the process and established thinking.
Introverted	Intuition	**Inward and reflective.** Focus on subjective processes, accessing and developing symbols, meanings and patterns that are reflected from the unconscious. Creative use of potential links and patterns. Clarifying and consolidating.
Extraverted	Feeling	**Outward and active.** Focus on construction of order based on engaging with others. Stimulation of ideas and motivating.
Introverted	Feeling	**Inward and reflective.** Focus on the subjective world of deeply felt values. Evaluation of phenomena through the lens of personal values. Important to give and win support.
Extraverted	Thinking	**Outward and active.** Focus on building logical structure for information organisation and subsequent making of decisions.
Introverted	Thinking	**Inward and reflective.** Focus on the subjective world of reason, seeking for understanding through extracting logical principles from experience or phenomena.

16 types, created by Katharine Briggs and her daughter Isabel Briggs Myers and summarised in Figure 9.2.

The Myers–Briggs Type Inventory and teams

Teams require diversity in order to function at the highest level and to avoid falling into comfortable or damaged modes of operation. This diversity is the product of individual differences; for the MBTI, this means utilising a diversity of team behaviours made available through the interaction of different personalities. The sheer variation of behaviours expressed through this diversity can overwhelm individuals' and a team's coping. For example, as a team moves from storming to norming, differences about how to structure a solution, and then to represent an idea or perhaps redefine an issue, can create toxic relations and failure. The MBTI's framework is an elaboration of the basic Jungian model, with the addition of a judging and perceiving function, shown in Figure 9.2. The MBTI claims to be a simple method of helping people to register fundamental preferences in behavioural areas which also map onto areas of team performance and development.

ISTJ Introverted Sensing with Thinking	ISFJ Introverted Sensing with Feeling	INFJ Introverted iNtuition with Feeling	INTJ Introverted iNtuition with Thinking
ISTP Introverted Thinking with Sensing	ISFP Introverted Feeling with Sensing	INFP Introverted Feeling with iNtuition	INTP Introverted Thinking with iNtuition
ESTP Extraverted Sensing with Thinking	ESFP Extraverted Sensing with Feeling	ENFP Extraverted iNtuition with Feeling	ENTP Extraverted iNtuition with Thinking
ESTJ Extraverted Thinking with Sensing	ESFJ Extraverted Feeling with Sensing	ENFJ Extraverted Feeling with iNtuition	ENTJ Extraverted Thinking with iNtuition

Figure 9.2 *The 16 MBTI types*
Source: Team Technology: http://www.teamtechnology.co.uk/myers-briggs/myers-briggs.htm

Myers–Briggs personality types

An MBTI analysis of team members before the team formation provides a summary of the team's personality profile, likely strengths and challenges. For example, an individual's likely style or form of contribution to the team can be outlined, as can their associated problem-solving process, needs and style. Indications of the likely response to conflict and associated irritants, from the interaction of different styles, can afford time for training and preparation. However, the MBTI is also used as a team diagnostic where communications between team members may already be strained, if not fractured. The overall aim is to offer a framework, one that prompts a common understanding and helps individuals to identify others' needs and preferences in such a way that the quality or substance of the message or intent is not distorted by the style of communication. Instead of giving rise to clashes, personality differences are turned into part of the team's body of knowledge, where, once recognised, personality differences can be respected, which will clear the way forward. For example, introverted, sensing types may be challenged when team-working with extraverted, intuitive types, and vice versa. Introverted, sensing individuals tend to distrust intuition when problem-solving, are inclined to base their solutions on data and facts, and use concrete methods to find answers, while 'extraverted, intuitive types may be more inclined to rely on abstract theories and consider future possibilities rather than just the task at hand' (Shorr, 2012).

In short, the sources of complex, and often unrealised, sources of miscommunication can be acknowledged, and narrow habitual forms of communication can be broadened to accommodate and work with different styles of communication.

LUMINA LEARNING: SPARK PSYCHOMETRIC

The Lumina Spark system was created in 2009 by Stewart Desson, CEO of Lumina Learning®. The declared intention of this psychometric is to demonstrate the utility of expanding the Big Five model by measuring each end of the scale separately. In this system respondents do not face a 'forced choice' on a question item; this permits high scores in one area without forcing low scores in another. Participants can therefore register qualities at opposite ends of a polarity. Spark measures the individual's traits on a continuum using a Likert scale. This method acknowledges that people differ in the *quantity* of a quality they possess, and also allows for individuals' claiming qualities at both ends of a polarity. Indeed, this latter capacity is a key element of the instrument, in that it enables individuals to recognise their own opposing personality traits as paradoxes and so to utilise them.

According to Lumina, their research has found an underlying Big Five structure to personality and identified useful attributes by measuring both polarities, of each factor, independently. The consequence of this approach is that each polarity now generates different and independent attributes, which within the model are responsible for the type and location of 24 qualities. Moreover, the approach applies the Jungian perspective of 'opposites', which is applied to form an integrated model and instrument.

Lumina Spark is designed to accommodate apparent contradictions in a subject's personality. For instance, introversion may co-exist with a significant contribution from extraversion; hence a subject may record high scores in two opposing qualities. For example, a respondent may record high scores for both 'collaborative' and 'competitive'. This approach has produced a structure characterised by several classifications of increasing specificity. This multi-level structure comprises:

- four coloured **archetypes** (Table 9.2) underpinned by
- eight more detailed **aspects** (Table 9.3), which are in turn made up of
- 24 specific **qualities** (Table 9.4).

The eight more detailed **aspects** are also categorised by colour but with a level of overlap. For example, the 'extraverted' aspect includes elements of both yellow and red.

Table 9.2 *Archetypes, colour-coded*

Archetype	Colour
Inspiring	Yellow
Commanding	Red
Empowering	Green
Conscientious	Blue

Table 9.3 *The eight aspects*

Aspect	Colour
People-focused	Green
Outcome-focused	Red
Inspiration-driven	Green/yellow
Discipline-driven	Red/blue
Big-picture thinking	Yellow
Down to earth	Blue
Extraverted	Yellow/red
Introverted	Blue/green

The 24 **qualities** are arranged in twelve pairs of contrasting attributes. A quality can have contributions from more than one colour.

Lumina Learning claims that, being based on their latest Big Five research and certain elements of the Jungian lens, the Spark psychometric is able to measure an individual's 'three personas' at the quality level. These personas represent three different yet related modes available to the personality; they are named underlying, everyday and overextended. The

Table 9.4 *24 qualities, in contrasting pairs*

Qualities (in contrasting pairs)	
Intimate	Takes charge
Accommodating	Tough
Collaborative	Competitive
Empathetic	Logical
Adaptable	Purposeful
Flexible	Structured
Spontaneous	Reliable
Conceptual	Practical
Imaginative	Evidence-based
Radical	Cautious
Sociable	Observing
Demonstrative	Measured

personas reflect a person's personality across different situations. The following scenarios use the quality 'Imaginative' as an example to illustrate the effects of the different modes.

The underlying persona is the person at their most relaxed and natural, and is the persona most likely to be displayed in private. A person in 'underlying' mode believes that they 'enjoy being the source of innovative ideas'.

The everyday persona is the one a person uses in public, and is the one most often seen by other people. The everyday persona believes that they 'have a lot of creative ideas'.

The overextended persona indicates the subject's personality when under stress or confronted with unexpected situations. In this case, the person 'can get lost in their imagination and ignore the facts'.

TEAMS AND THE LUMINA SPARK MANDALA

The example of a Lumina Spark Mandala shown in Figure 9.3 has captured a tendency towards the Conscientious Blue archetype (Down to earth), while also registering a strong element of the apparent paradox of the Inspiring Yellow archetype (Big-picture thinking).

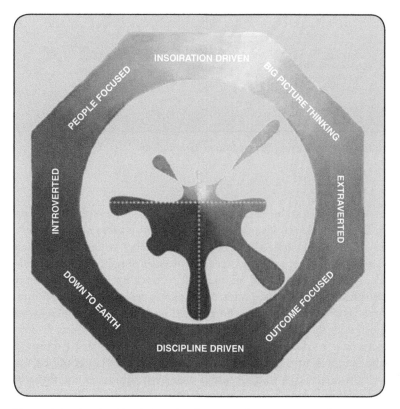

Figure 9.3 *Lumina Mandala registering a paradox: opposing tendencies are shown as 'Blue' and 'Yellow'*

142 PSYCHOMETRIC TESTING: CRITICAL PERSPECTIVES

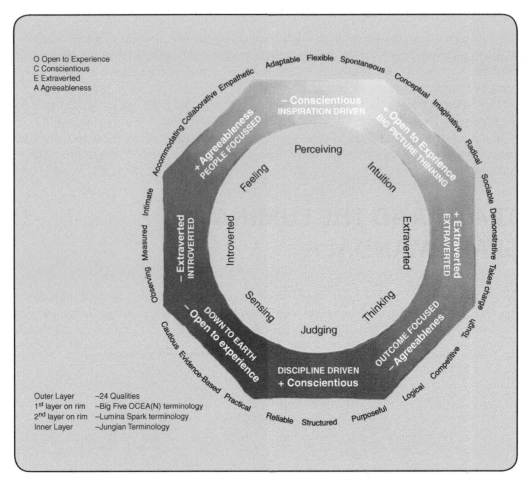

Figure 9.4 *Twenty-four qualities positioned around the mandala*

The mandalas are designed to be easily comparable with others' mandalas, creating a common language based on shared visuals. In this way team leaders and members can quickly gain a 'picture' of their own and others' personality profiles which allows the identification of potential areas of conflict, synergy, strength or commonality. The mandalas also allow graphical and direct comparison of individuals' personality 'splash', highlighting overlap as well as opposites in individuals' preferred thinking, feeling and behavioural styles. The 'Splash' signature is directly related to the 24 qualities, and these qualities would be recognised and adjusted as they manifest within each of the three persona modes. Figure 9.4 shows the positioning, of the Lumina qualities around the mandala's circumference.

These qualities represent the full range of 'contributions' that could be made available to the team as individuals learn to understand their own paradoxes and those of others. For a team format, the team members' scores are plotted onto a single team mandala which allows an overview of team strengths and challenges in addition to mapping out routes to effective communications and performance.

The Lumina Spark model clearly draws on the empiricism of the Big Five approach, but at the same time it can be viewed through a Jungian lens. The inclusion of scales of introversion and extraversion and the Jungian lens invites limited comparisons with Jungian applications, such as the MBTI®.

CONCLUSION

Psychometrics have contributed, or arguably led the way, towards improving organisational and personal effectiveness for decades. However, it may be observed that, given the current immense global pressure on organisational competitiveness, it is the coming decade that will see a spike in need and demand. As organisations drive towards increasing their talent base, human innovativeness and teams' productivity, it is likely to be the successful development of this diverse human factor that will prove decisive in determining organisational success or failure. It may well be that organisations increasingly turn to psychometrics to provide a source of commonality and a basis for shared communication as a route towards maximising productive behavioural diversity.

REFERENCES

Acas (2014). Managing conflict at work. June. London: Acas. http://www.acas.org.uk/media/pdf/i/d/Managing-conflict-at-work-advisory-booklet.pdf. Accessed 4 October 2016.

Aldag, R. & Kuzuhara, L. (2015). *Creating high performance teams: Applied strategies and tools for managers and team members*. Abingdon: Routledge.

De Dreu, K. W. & Gelfand, M. J. (2008). *The psychology of conflict and conflict management in organizations*. Abingdon: Lawrence Erlbaum Associates.

Glassop, L. I. (2002). The organizational benefits of teams. *Human Relations*, 55(2), 225–49

Jung, C. G. (1923). *Psychological types: or, The psychology of individuation*. London: Routledge & Kegan Paul.

Lawrence, K. (2013). Developing leaders in a VUCA environment. UNC Kenan-Flagler Business School. http://www.growbold.com/2013/developing-leaders-in-a-vuca-environment_UNC.2013.pdf. Accessed 4 October 2016.

Luttwak, E. (1999) *Turbo-capitalism: Winners and losers in the global economy*. New York: HarperCollins.

Maravelas, A. (2005). *How to reduce workplace conflict and stress*. Franklin Lakes, NJ: Career Press.

Myers, I. B. (1998). *Introduction to type*. Sunnyvale, CA: CPP.

Peltokorpi, V. & Hasu, M. (2014) How participative safety matters more in team innovation as team size increases. *Journal of Business and Psychology*, 29(1), 37–45.

Ricci, R. & Wiese, C. (2011). *The collaboration imperative: Executive strategies for unlocking your organization's true potential*. San Jose, CA: Cisco Systems.

Sharp, D. (1987). *Personality types: Jung's model of typology*. Toronto: Inner City Books.

Shorr, K. (2012). Using the Myers-Briggs Type Indicator to improve teamwork. *Human Resources*, 20 December. http://b2binsights.com/using-the-myers-briggs-type-indicator-to-improve-teamwork/. Accessed 4 October 2016.

Team Focus (n.d.). Management Team Roles Indicator (MTR-i™). http://www.teamfocus.co.uk/user_files/file/Management%20Team%20Roles%20Indicator%20_MTRI_.pdf. Accessed 30 October 2016.

Team Technology (n.d.). Belbin®, MTR-i™ and MBTI®. http://www.teamtechnology.co.uk/belbin.html. Accessed November 2015.

Thomas, K. W. & Kilmann, R. H. (1974). *Thomas–Kilmann Conflict Mode Instrument*. Mountain View, CA: CPP.

Tjosvold, D. (1990) *Team organization: An enduring competitive advantage*. Wiley Series in Industrial and Organizational Psychology. Chichester: Wiley-Blackwell.

Tuckman, B. W. (1965) Developmental sequence in small groups. *Psychological Bulletin*, 63(6), 384–99.

Tuckman, B. W. & Jensen, M. C. (1977). Stages of small-group development revisited. *Group & Organization Studies*, 2(4), 419–27.

10 Psychometrics in Sport: The Good, the Bad and the Ugly

DAVE COLLINS AND ANDREW CRUICKSHANK

INTRODUCTION

Reflective perhaps of the greater overlap/interaction with organisational psychology, there is an increasing use of psychometrics in sport. Some of these applications are doubtless of great value and provide an additional and useful tool for the practitioner's armoury. Others are less positive, however; issues of theoretical base, ecological validity and application to identification and selection are of particular concern. Other measures, the 'ugly' of the title, take apparently well-founded ideas from other environments and uncritically transfer them to sport, trading on the original's reputation and the apparent simplicity and power of the questionnaire approach. In this chapter, we consider examples of all three, offering some guidelines for effective practice in both the development and the application of psychometrics in sport.

Psychometrics, or at least the use of metrics to measure psychological aspects that are (presumed) pertinent to performance, has a rich history in sport. Arguably, this peaked in the 1970s and early 1980s, when 'sport personology' (Morgan, 1978) played a substantial role in the lexicon and armoury of sports psychologists, especially in the US and the UK. As we will demonstrate throughout this chapter, however, this widely touted promise tended to evaporate, because of a variety of important 'learn from history' lessons. For example, take the Athlete Motivation Inventory (AMI) of Tutko, Lyon and Ogilvie (1969) which, at its peak, was widely used in professional sports in the US as a part of the talent identification and recruitment from college process, most notably in the National Football League (NFL). Interestingly, as far as we are aware this instrument was tightly controlled by the authors. Subjects completed the measure, which was then sent away for scoring. We are not even sure that the instrument had passed peer review, or that subjects got to see their profiles. Unsurprisingly, the AMI disappeared from use, perhaps as a result of these issues, perhaps even as a result of one of the players' strikes which were happening around then. In any case, in our understanding, the AMI, or more properly its (mis)use, would be firmly placed in our Ugly category.

Returning to our main point, and irrespective of the use or misuse of psychometrics, there seemed to be an increasing disenchantment with the personology approach in the latter stages of the twentieth century. A lot of this seemed to come down to growing recognition of the different scales on which the developers and deliverers were working. Indeed, as one personality researcher observed at a specific Sport Personality Conference in 1975, 'we have been fishing for minnows with nets designed for whales … we cannot complain about the paucity of the catch!' (Collins, personal recollection).

More recently, however, psychometrics in sport has enjoyed a renaissance. The combination of tighter links and cross-over between sport and organisational psychology, coupled with the increase in the number of institutes of sport and the associated systemisation of support services, has led to increased interest, usage and application. We will argue, however, that unfortunately this return has not been universally positive; much of the previously recognised limits and baggage of psychometrics is still prevalent. In fairness, barring weaknesses in design or the underpinning science (some of which we will also touch on in this chapter), by far the biggest issue with psychometrics in sport relates to misapplication. We will leave it to other authors to consider the extent to which this is a problem across domains. For this chapter, however, we will present good and not so good features of usage, design and underpinning science in three categories, as indicated by the chapter title. Interestingly, several instruments will make an appearance in more than one category, supporting our contention that optimally relevant and impactful tools must tick all boxes relating to theoretical base, ecological validity and appropriate application. To be clear, the psychometrics that we discuss should be considered exemplars; we certainly don't attempt to evaluate and classify all or even most of the psychometrics that are available to those operating in sport. Rather, we discuss tools that are representative of the typically good, bad or ugly features across the whole field, at least as we see it.

There is one other important criterion which needs to be applied when establishing the worth of an instrument: that is, the purpose it is being used for. In this regard, we would distinguish between two extremes of usage, namely research and performance support. Using the classification proposed by Collins and Kamin (2012), the former can encompass mainstream psychology that uses sport as a laboratory and the evolution of sport-specific theories (psychology *through* sport and *of* sport, respectively). The latter can be seen as the use of psychology to support performance (psychology *for* sport). We would suggest that the two are relatively distinct, but that confusion of purpose can call the use of psychometrics into question when tools designed for one purpose are used for another.

THE GOOD: EXEMPLARS OF POSITIVE CONTRIBUTIONS FROM SOUND SCIENCE

It is certainly better to see an instrument applied in an environment for which it has been designed. Thus, while we will leave aspects of effective *statistical* design to other authors in this volume, we would highlight the combination of ecological issues and underpinning science as being particularly important for sport. Somewhat immodestly (clearly a personality trait!), we would highlight one of our own instruments as a positive exemplar. The Talent

Development Environment Questionnaire (TDEQ) (Martindale et al., 2010) was specifically designed for the accurate and evidence-grounded evaluation of environment quality for the development of athletes. Therefore, a number of careful steps ensured that factors were built on a systematic review of the extant literature (Martindale, Collins & Daubney, 2005) and on solicitation of the perspectives of talent development (TD) coaches (Martindale, Collins & Abraham, 2007) and athletes (Martindale & Mortimer, 2011). The use of a Discriminant Function Analysis (Martindale, Collins, Douglas & Whike, 2013) to show that the instrument effectively did what it was designed to do (discriminate between good and poor talent development environments (TDEs)) was a final step. In short, from inception to presentation on the 'open market', the instrument was designed for a specific purpose, population and environment, with all necessary statistical guidelines followed against these criteria. We would suggest that this is good practice, especially when instruments are designed for specific purposes, be this research or application.

This same specificity trend is apparent in the work of Tynke Toering and colleagues (e.g. Toering, Elferink-Gemser, Jordet & Visscher, 2009). Their self-regulation questionnaire has been designed specifically for use in football and cleverly includes items designed specifically against the behaviours and environments typically encountered by their target populations. Built carefully through qualitative study (cf. Martindale and colleagues' work mentioned earlier), the constructs were subsequently refined through further qualitative work (Toering et al., 2011).

In our opinion, this process of bespoke design provides for optimum discriminatory power when the instrument is applied. Thus, for example, an application on senior premiership and championship footballers (Toering & Jordet, 2015) accounted for around 40 per cent of the variance in their teams' final season placements in the league table: an impressive outcome for any instrument in a complex multi-faceted challenge like professional football, but particularly so for a tool focused on psychological constructs.

As a different exemplar of good practice, we suggest that the application guidelines offered with the Insights Discovery instrument (Benton, van Erkom Schurink & Desson, 2008) are worthy of note. Although we are far less happy with the theoretical grounding of this instrument, as the next section shows, its application credentials are strong, a characteristic that is being reflected by its increasingly common use in sport across the UK. As one positive example, the feedback from this instrument often includes (in our experience) general advice, based on clear behavioural actions, on how the recipient (on the basis of his or her profile) can expect to enhance, limit, promote or inhibit communication with other styles. As an adjunct to the descriptive feedback and categorisation provided (that is, one's personality is mainly *fiery red*, *sunshine yellow*, *earth green* or *cool blue*), this translation into specific and developable behaviours provides a significant addition to the interpretation and application of the provided profile: in short, the instrument's applied purpose is fulfilled and brought to life by such practical advice, offered in non-technical language and situated in the business-like interactions for which it was designed. Of course, and aligning with our criticisms offered later, the extent to which these descriptions are valid and functional for sport is debatable. But, being fair, this sort of information represents good practice and enhances the application of the instrument, *in the environment for which it was designed*. So, when business-focused instruments are used for business purposes (including *business* purposes in sport), and accurate indicative feedback is provided to expand on typology, we see this as good practice.

THE BAD: EXEMPLARS OF QUESTIONABLE THEORETICAL BASE, DESIGN OR USAGE

Having considered the Good elements of psychometrics in sport, we now consider more questionable examples. Specifically, this section on the Bad revolves around issues of both theoretical and applied foundation. Taking theoretical issues first, we focus on the case of a previously dominant force in personality-related psychometrics in sport and its heir: the Myers–Briggs Types Indicator (MBTI) and Insights Discovery.

Both the MBTI and Insights are built on Carl Jung's seminal thinking on the typology of personality. At the broadest level, Jung theorised that people can be classified as one of eight mutually exclusive types. These types are a mix of one psychological 'function' (*sensation, intuition, thinking, feeling*) and a modifying 'attitude' (*extraversion* or *introversion*). Unlike trait-based approaches, where components of personality run along continua, Jung's types are dichotomies: people are, for example, *either* extravert *or* introvert (being slightly one way or the other is not possible). Based on Jung's approach, but embellishing it with another opposing pair (*judging–perceiving*) that extended the number of possible types to 16, the MBTI categorises people so that they can be directed to the 'right' role or career and then managed 'correctly' when there. To provide such definitive answers, the MBTI 'forces' people to choose between two extremes in each item of the questionnaire. In fact, the developers added a procedure to make sure that scores at the centre of the scales weren't possible (Myers, McCaulley, Quenk & Hammer, 1998) – a particularly impressive example of downright bad science! Unsurprisingly, the MBTI has therefore come in for criticism for a black-and-white approach to an inherently shades-of-grey topic. Indeed, the theoretical failings of the MBTI (and in effect of Jung's typology) have been demonstrated by incongruent descriptive statistics (scores coalescing around the middle of scales), correlations among the four dimensions, and poor test–retest reliability (Pittenger, 2005). In sum, it has been argued that the MBTI (1) measures elements of personality but not necessarily those identified by Jung, (2) creates differences where none may practically exist (i.e., between individuals who fall just either side of the centre of a scale) and (3) fails to provide a consistent measure of what Jung deemed to be consistent constructs (Pittenger, 2005). Whether these issues stem from Jung's typology – which was based on observation rather than empirical evaluation – or from Myers and Briggs's interpretation, this clearly isn't a great list of accolades.

It is notable that, perhaps as a result of (or by adjusting for) these issues, Insights has argued that Jung's types don't represent distinct personalities but rather a set of *preferences*. More specifically, its developers have stressed Jung's view that reducing people to *pure types* was impossible (Beauchamp, MacLachlan & Lothian, 2005). Importantly, this point is consistent with multiple sources about Jung's beliefs (McGuire & Hull, 1987). The constructs of Insights (*fiery red, sunshine yellow, earth green* and *cool blue*) are therefore deemed to *embody* rather than directly reflect Jung's typology (a position that has enabled the numerous benefits listed in our 'Good' section). Unfortunately, there is a sizeable and damaging 'however': while sensitivity to the 'it depends' nature of personality has helped Insights to achieve high levels of popularity, it appears to have done so by distorting its theoretical base. More specifically, it fails to sufficiently discriminate between Jung's wider views on personality (that everyone is fundamentally different) and those on his actual typology (that there are eight types of people), a problem that is compounded by the developers' glossing over the theoretical issues faced by the MBTI (see Beauchamp et al., 2005). As a result, contradictions across the tool's aims and outputs prevail.

Indeed, while Insights emphasises Jung's awareness that people are different and capable of a full range of behaviours, Jung also asserted that 'an understanding of typology may act as a compass for psychological orientation', or more specifically that 'its *purpose* is to provide a critical psychology which will make a *methodological investigation* and presentation of the *empirical material* possible. First and foremost it is a critical tool *for the research worker*, who needs *definite* points of view and guidelines if he is to *reduce* the chaotic profusion of individual experiences to any kind of order' (Jung, cited in Beauchamp et al., 2005; emphasis added). Hence, Insights has been created as a *flexible* tool for chiefly *applied* purposes with *individuals* from a theory that was created to provide a *rigid* account of personality for chiefly *research* purposes with *groups*. By both using *and going beyond* the goals of Jung's typology, Insights may offer more than the MBTI but ultimately suffers the same limitations.

So, although Insights may be built on the idea that individuals have *preferences*, it still *classes* people as (a cleverly marketed) 'cool blue', 'earth green', 'sunshine yellow' and 'fiery red'. So while facilitators may stress that each profile depicts one's *preferences*, tasks such as standing on the Insights Wheel or having a block of your colour placed on your desk send an altogether different, more clear-cut, more Jungian typology message; especially for those who want 'I'm an X, they're a Y' answers. On this basis, we remain unsurprised by reports from various colleagues that Insights profiling has led to people to being put in boxes ('he's a red and always will be!'), to self-handicapping ('I'm cool blue and can't be fiery red in this situation') or social loafing ('earth greens will handle that'), to the complexity being sucked out of case conferences ('she's very blue'), and to a difference in the nature of essential critical debate (people dodging criticism for not doing a job that doesn't fit their preference). Of course, proponents of Insights will argue that the point is being missed, and to a large extent we agree. However, proceeding with a focus on preferences *and* typology makes the pitfalls of 'psychosocial shorthand' virtually inescapable. Of course, some may also argue that Insights is still a better answer than the MBTI; again, we completely agree. However, it isn't *the* answer, or the quality of answer, that many seem to suggest.

In short, if the theory doesn't quite cut it then there is a need to change or develop the theory, not to paper over the cracks by adjusting the measure. To be clear, it is the attempt of Insights to soften Jung's types or bend them towards *preferences*, and thus to selectively deviate from the theory on which it is based in way that leads to inherent contradictions ('you can be what you want to be .... but you're still a [colour]'), that has led us to place this tool also in our Bad section.

Building on this issue of what a measure can and can't say, we conclude this section with an example that emphasises the importance of face validity in psychometrics. Intending to provide a comprehensive assessment of perceived organisational stressors in sport, Arnold, Fletcher and Daniels (2013) have developed the Organisational Stressor Indicator for Sport Performers (OSI-SP). Clearly of potential value to scholars and practitioners alike – given the increasing structure, regulation and organisation of sport – the OSI-SP appears, however, to have exaggerated the role and reach of sport organisations. For example, consider the difference between items that seem clearly related to sport organisations (e.g., 'the organization of the competitions that I perform in'; 'the funding allocations in my sport'; 'the accommodation used for training or competitions') and those whose organisational genesis seem rather ambiguous (e.g., 'my teammates' attitudes'; 'the shared beliefs of my teammates'; 'my coach's personality'; 'injuries'; 'the spectators that watch me perform'), something that isn't helped by the authors not providing the final version of the psychometric in the paper describing its development. On closer inspection, this apparent ambiguity was perhaps driven by the fact that the final five subscales of the OSI-SP started out as 31 independent subcategories of organisational stressors, as previously identified in Arnold and Fletcher (2012). Interestingly, the research team identified as a benefit of this more parsimonious, five-factor account that it would be less time-consuming in future research studies (and later emphasised the value of the measure for supporting future experiments and hypothetical interventions), suggesting that this tool was primarily developed for research purposes. In any case, and regardless of the environment targeted for application or the final number of subscales, it is difficult to see how the OSI-SP can distinguish, for example, between injury-based stress that is organisationally driven (the selection policies of the organisation make me over-train) and injury-based stress in someone who does extra sessions of their own volition at home. Of course, that these are potential stressors can't be denied, but whether these are *organisational* stressors, we suggest, certainly can.

To delve deeper into the reasons for this poor face validity, organisational stress was originally – and aptly – defined as 'an ongoing transaction between an individual and the environmental demands associated *primarily and directly* with the organization within which he or she is operating' (Fletcher, Hanton & Mellalieu, 2006, p. 329; emphasis added). Arnold et al. (2013), however, also based their development of the OSI-SP on a taxonomy developed by the same research team, which classed as organisational stressors 'any environmental demands that were considered to be primarily associated with the organization ... *but often related in some secondary sense with competitive or personal aspects of performers' lives*' (Arnold & Fletcher, 2012, p. 402; emphasis added). Additionally, clues come from the expert panel that rated the relevance of each item, as well as from the question they were posed. Regarding the latter, this panel were asked, 'Does this question potentially relate to the sport organization environment?' (Arnold et al., p. 184). First, the use of 'potentially' rather than 'directly' and 'sport organisation environment' rather than 'sport organisation' alone raises additional questions; indeed, almost *any* stressor could be classed as organisational according to this question as long as it is experienced when one attends organised activities. The expert panel itself consisted of 28 academics, performers and sport psychologists. While we clearly can't comment on the orientation and quality of the applied practitioners, the fact that this group had an average of 3.19 years of experience with a standard deviation of 4.68 raises eyebrows, as does the 'expert' academic with one month's experience. Also, 13 of the 15 performers on this panel competed at club, county or university/college level and only two at international level with apparently no professional athletes, despite the importance of this group for the ecological validity of an organisational stress instrument. Indeed, the limited inclusion of those operating at the top end of sport, where organisational factors are invariably more prevalent and magnified than, and just generally different to, those at lower levels, is a further issue, especially for a psychometric that claims to be 'comprehensive' and able to 'assess organizational stressors across different groups of sport performers' (Arnold et al., p. 192). Finally, it should be noted that two of the factors contain only two items – surely an issue for the psychometric properties of the instrument.

Significantly, all of the issues listed here are limiters for both studies with and application of the OSI-SP. Certainly, whether focused on psychology *of*, *through* or *for* sport, all of these paths need to accurately reflect the real world if they are to say anything meaningful about it or the people in it. Currently, the OSI-SP guides scholars and practitioners towards an organisational interpretation of what may possibly be very non-organisational stressors. It also perpetuates, rather problematically in our view, the uncritical push for more organisational psychology in performance psychology matters.

THE UGLY: MEASURES WHICH REALLY SHOULDN'T BE USED IN THIS WAY, OR PERHAPS AT ALL

To turn to the final part of our trilogy, there also exist a number of measures in sport that we would class as 'ugly'. Once again, the roots of our view relate to issues of ecological validity, design and application. As our first example, we call on Chellardurai and Saleh's (1980) Leadership Scale for Sport (LSS), a tool created to assess and build on Chelladurai's (1980) Multidimensional Model of Leadership. In this model, Chelladurai argued that leaders are effective when they act in a way that matches the preferences of their followers and the needs of a given situation. In its first phase of development, Chelladurai and Saleh's (1978) LSS was made up of items from organisation-based measures of leadership; they asked 160 physical education students at a Canadian university to specify the extent to which they felt that their coach should use a range of different behaviours, in other words, to indicate their preferred leader behaviours. As a result of this procedure, five factors were identified, labelled Training, Democratic Behaviour, Autocratic Behaviour, Social Support and Rewarding Behaviour. Although some questionable statistical procedures (by today's standards) were used in the development, Chelladurai and Saleh quickly realised that some core features of coaching were missing, and so items were added to fill the gaps on training and social support-related behaviour, a recovery process that was perhaps unsurprising given that the original items were transferred from other instruments mainly developed for mainstream (non-sport) organisations. As highlighted in other chapters, and earlier in ours, failing to generate a large and specific pool of items that cover all aspects of the focal concept from the off is a notable psychometric faux pas.

In the second phase, the revised LSS was administered by Chelladurai and Saleh (1980) to a second sample of physical education students (who were asked how they would prefer a leader to act in their favourite sport) and male varsity athletes (who were asked how they would prefer a leader to act, plus how their leader actually did act for the sport that they currently competed in). Of course, this mix of subjects and questions is another issue. Furthermore, the five factors of the LSS (now labelled Training and Instruction, Democratic Behaviour, Autocratic Behaviour, Social Support and Positive Feedback) accounted for only 39 to 55 per cent of the variance in the data, with developers acknowledging that these low levels were perhaps due to shortcomings in the number and nature of the original pool of items. Despite this issue, Chelladurai and Saleh persisted, stressing the validity of their measure through the emergence of a similar factor structure across both 1978 and 1980 samples. This result was, of course, relevant and informative to the data presented. However, as the LSS was developed through male and female physical education students then all male, university athletes, the tool was, by design, applicable to a narrow (and rather messy) mix of individuals. Unfortunately, this point was not acknowledged by Chelladurai and Saleh (1980); in fact, the developers proposed, without any delimitation, that the LSS could measure the appropriateness and effectiveness of leadership behaviour – full stop. We would suggest that, unfortunately, Chelladurai and Saleh developed a measure for widespread use that was composed of factors which apparently couldn't account for most of the data it solicited.

As well as being a rather ugly measure, the LSS has been used and interpreted in rather ugly ways. For example, despite acknowledging that the internal consistency of the autocratic behaviour scale was consistently low in previous studies, as well as being part of a problematic factorial structure, Hampson and Jowett (2014) justified its inclusion in their work on British footballers (who played at university, regional, national or international level) for reasons of 'completeness' (p. 456). Additionally, there are serious questions over scholars' continued use of the LSS given inherent problems with the current relevance (and appropriateness) of many of the tool's items. Take, for example, items asking participants to rate the extent to which they preferred or felt that their coach was prone to 'give specific instructions to each athlete as to what he should do in every situation' (Training and Instruction), 'express appreciation when an athlete performs well' (Positive Feedback), 'let athletes work at their own speed' (Democratic Behaviour), and perhaps most questionably, 'do personal favours to the athletes, express affection s/he feels for his/her athletes, invite athletes to his/her home' (Social Support), all of which, in today's climate, may be seen as at least questionable.

Of course, as the LSS was designed to measure participants' preferences or perceptions of their leader's behaviour, some may argue that *if* these items are not relevant then they can simply be scored as *never* preferred or perceived. This is completely fair. However, the resultant scores always carry the risk of making some rather ugly assumptions. For instance, Fletcher and Roberts (2013) reported that female netball players felt that their female coaches demonstrated low levels of social support, a finding that aligned with prior studies using female athletes (Chelladurai, 1993; Riemer & Toon, 2001). Picking up on the rationale provided by Riemer and Toon, Fletcher and Roberts suggested that, rather than problems with the relevance of items in the LSS, a possible reason for the low level of perceived social support was that responses to some items (e.g., 'invites athletes home') could have been shaped by homophobia! Making similarly questionable assumptions, Sherman, Fuller and Speed (2000) then Surujlal and Dhurup (2012) considered that their participants' low preference for social support was perhaps due to these athletes' not being reliant on the moral and personal support of their coach as physical conditioning, practice, competition and rehabilitation from injury leaves little time to focus on or use social support. Contrary to much other research (and the real world), others have suggested that social support might also not be an important element of dance teaching (Rafferty & Wyon, 2006). In sum, although well intentioned, the LSS has had its day.

The issues of ecological validity highlighted above are also apparent in other approaches. For example, and unfortunately in our view, sport is increasingly 'blessed' with a variety of what might be described as psychophysical metrics: in short, an attempt to blend movement attributes with trait personality characteristics. The idea is certainly not new; indeed, Sheldon's original work on anthropometry (Sheldon, 1954) included a significant personality dimension. Termed 'constitutional psychology', the idea was that different body types (endo-, meso- or ectomorph) possessed a trend towards certain styles of behaviour (respectively the 'barrel of fun', adventurous and assertive, and intense and withdrawn). The idea was even extended to suggest physically based criminal types – largely mesomorphic and thus rather bad news for physical sports. Indeed, with somewhat less causative inference, the ideas persist even more recently (Genovese, 2008). The premise of this work seems to us to be extremely psychosocially mediated, however, and thus would surely be subject to change over time and across cultures. Thereby hangs the weakness, and our classification of these approaches, however purportedly rigorous, as 'ugly'. In simple terms, whatever is observed is unlikely to hold the generic capacity which is surely the selling point of the psychometric approach; rather, it represents a psychosocially specific perception. Fortunately for us, the authors (we both display a mesomorphic tendency, however well disguised), the criminal relationships seem to have been quashed (Hartl, Monnelly & Elderkin, 1982).

So, with these many caveats, we provide two exemplars of the psychophysical approach to sport psychometrics: up first is the 'Approche Action Type' or AAT, which is avowedly based on such a link between personality measures and fundamental elements of movement. As Barel (2004) states, this measure is based on 'a strong correlation between the Jungian functions [i.e. those that also underpin the MBTI and Insights] and the motor preferences of individuals (preferred muscular chains, underlying bone structure and the head-spine-pelvis dynamics of Noguchi's Seïtai)'. It may be that we are just too ignorant to understand this, but it seems worrying that physical treatment (in this case osteopathy) might be based on such underexplored – but presented as strong – links, especially when causative factors other than physiological ones are being described. As ever, the most important issue is exactly how the instrument is used. Application as a part of a comprehensive screening and diagnosis process may be innocuous, especially if the user is suitably qualified and experienced and applies an appropriate 'weighting' to the information yielded by the instrument when it is triangulated with other data sources. Unfortunately, however, in our experience the influence of such instruments can quickly stray into selection and direction territory. Certainly, this matches business use of psychometrics. Personally, however, we would much rather see such tools used for formative purposes than as a summative tool.

Another, somewhat similar, example of rather esoteric practice is provided by Ekman's Facial Action Coding System (FACS). This approach has a long history and is supported by some prestigious research (e.g. Ekman & Friesen, 1969; Ekman, Sorenson & Friesen, 1969), providing users with a tool with which thoughts and attitudes may be evaluated through observable changes in appearance. Its use as a selection tool for athletes seems to have a rather less robust base, however. Once again, therefore, the potential for the inflation of a potentially effective formative tool to a summative selection instrument is apparent. Although press coverage has been positive, there are certainly some dissenting voices (see Randall, 2014). For our purposes, it is the somewhat unsubstantiated 'new' use that places it in our 'Ugly' category.

It is worth considering the pressures for ever more accurate and powerful selection tools. The US drafting system, UK Premiership Football Academies and all elements of Talent Identification are built on this foundation. The evidence for the use of psychometrics in this sporting role is far from robust. For example, Rasmus Ankersen (2012) cites the case of Dan Merino and Terry Bradshaw, two extremely successful American Football players, who 'achieved' two of the lowest scores ever on the Wonderlic Intelligence Test, the psychometric which was, at that time, the preferred test for aptitude in quarterbacks.

As Ankersen observed, the test was clearly testing for *a* talent (purportedly cognitive skill and decision making) but was it the *right* talent – that is, the talent to play in arguably the most demanding position on the pitch? In short, and once again, the ecological validity of any test is paramount in the sports setting, and must be the primary concern of the user. Otherwise, the risk of ugly applications, such as that of the Wonderlic Intelligence Test for quarterback selection, will continue as the inevitable next wave of psychometrics approaches.

CONCLUDING COMMENTS

In a context of increasing interaction between sport and organisational psychology, and more and more organisation of sport itself, the scale on which psychometrics are used and perceived to deliver impact has grown. Importantly, these instruments can be of undoubted value for those measuring, interpreting and acting on psychological aspects, especially when they hit all the markers of ecological validity, suitable theoretical base, rigorous development, and relevant application and interpretation in the target environment. However, such tools seem to be the exception rather than the norm; many suffer from the limits highlighted in our 'bad' and 'ugly' sections as being related to development and, in particular, application. This being so, we hope that the combination of our messages on what helps to make tools 'good' and these ongoing lessons helps to support instruments that are theoretically, statistically and ecologically sound.

REFERENCES

Ankersen, R. (2012). *The gold mine effect: Crack the secrets of high performance*. London: Icon Books.

Arnold, R. & Fletcher, D. (2012). A research synthesis and taxonomic classification of the organizational stressors encountered by sport performers. *Journal of Sport & Exercise Psychology*, 34, 397–429.

Arnold, R., Fletcher, D. & Daniels, K. (2013). Development and validation of the organizational stressor indicator for sport performers (OSI-SP). *Journal of Sport & Exercise Psychology*, 35, 180–96.

Barel, P. (2004). L'approche Action Types en Ostéopathie. *ApoStill, la revue de l'Académie d'Ostéopathie de France*, 24–5, 41–8. http://academie-osteopathie.fr/publications/apostill/article/view/108. Accessed 13 June 2009.

Beauchamp, M. R., MacLachlan, A. & Lothian, A. M. (2005). Communication within sport teams: Jungian preferences and group dynamics. *Sport Psychologist*, 19, 203–20.

Benton, S., van Erkom Schurink, C. & Desson, S. (2008). An overview of the development, validity and reliability of the English version 3.0 of the Insights Discovery Evaluator. University of Westminster Business Psychology Centre.

Chelladurai, P. (1980). Leadership in sport organizations. *Canadian Journal of Applied Sport Sciences*, 5, 226–31.

Chelladurai, P. (1993). Leadership. In R. N. Singer, M. Murphy & K. L. Tennant (eds.), *Handbook of Research on Sport Psychology* (pp. 647–71). New York: Macmillan.

Chelladurai, P. & Saleh, S. D. (1978). Preferred leadership in sports. *Canadian Journal of Applied Sports Sciences*, 3, 85–92.

Chelladurai, P. & Saleh, S. D. (1980). Dimensions of leader behaviour in sports: development of a leadership scale. *Journal of Sport Psychology*, 2, 34–45.

Collins, D. & Kamin, S. (2012). The performance coach. In S. Murphy (ed.), *Handbook of sport and performance psychology* (pp. 692–706). Oxford: Oxford University Press.

Ekman, P. & Friesen, W. V. (1969). The repertoire of nonverbal behavior: Categories, origins, usage, and coding. *Semiotica*, 1(1), 49–98.

Ekman, P., Sorenson, E. R. & Friesen, W. V. (1969). Pan-cultural elements in facial display of emotions. *Science*, 164, 86–8.

Fletcher, D., Hanton, S. & Mellalieu, S. D. (2006). An organizational stress review: Conceptual and theoretical issues in competitive sport. In S. Hanton & S. D. Mellalieu (eds.), *Literature reviews in sport psychology* (pp. 321–73). Hauppauge, NY: Nova Science Publishers.

Fletcher, R. B. & Roberts, M. H. (2013). Longitudinal stability of the Leadership Scale for Sports. *Measurement in Physical Education & Exercise Science*, 17, 89–104.

Genovese, J. E. C. (2008). Physique correlates with reproductive success in an archival sample of delinquent youth. *Evolutionary Psychology*, 6(3), 369–85.

Hampson, R. & Jowett, S. (2014). Effects of coach leadership and coach–athlete relationship on collective efficacy. *Scandinavian Journal of Medicine & Science in Sport*, 24, 454–60.

Hartl, E. M., Monnelly, E. P. & Elderkin, R. D. (1982). *Physique and Delinquent Behavior: A Thirty-Year Follow-up of William H. Sheldon's Varieties of Delinquent Youth*. New York: Academic Press.

Martindale, R. J. J., Collins, D. & Abraham, A. (2007). Effective talent development: The elite coach perspective within UK sport. *Journal of Applied Sports Psychology*, 19(2), 187–206.

Martindale, R. J. J., Collins, D., Douglas, C. & Whike, A. (2013). Examining the ecological validity of the Talent Development Environment Questionnaire. *Journal of Sports Sciences*, 31(1), 41–7.

Martindale, R. J. J., Collins, D., Wang, J., McNeill, M., Lee, S. K., Sproule, J. & Westbury, T. (2010). Development of the Talent Development Environment Questionnaire for sports. *Journal of Sport Sciences*, 28(11), 1209–21.

Martindale, R. J. J. & Mortimer, P. W. (2011). Talent development environments: Key considerations for effective practice. In D. Collins, A. Button & H. Richards (eds.), *Performance psychology: A practitioner's guide* (pp. 65–84). Edinburgh: Churchill Livingstone.

McGuire, W. & Hull, R. F. C. (1987). *C.G. Jung speaking: Interviews and encounters*. Princeton, NJ: Princeton University Press.

Morgan, W. P. (1978). Sport personology: The credulous-skeptical argument in perspective. In W. F. Straub (ed.), *Sport psychology: An analysis of athlete behavior* (pp. 218–27). Ithaca, NY: Mouvement Publications.

Myers, I. B., McCaulley, M. H., Quenk, N. L. & Hammer, A. L. (1998). *Manual: A guide to the development and use of the Myers–Briggs Type Indicator*. Palo Alto, CA: Consulting Psychologists Press.

Pittenger, D. J. (2005). Cautionary comments regarding the Myers–Briggs Type Indicator. *Consulting Psychology Journal: Practice and Research*, 57(3), 210–21.

Rafferty, S. & Wyon, M. (2006). Leadership behaviour in dance: Application of the leadership scale for sports to dance technique teaching. *Journal of Dance Medicine & Science*, 10(1–2), 6–13.

Randall, K. (2014). Teams turn to a face reader, looking for that winning smile. *New York Times*, 25 December. http://www.nytimes.com/2014/12/26/sports/nba-bucks-looking-for-an-edge-hire-expert-in-face-time.html?_r=0. Accessed 13 January 2015.

Riemer, H. A. & Toon, K. (2001). Leadership and satisfaction in tennis: Examination of congruence, gender, and ability. *Research Quarterly for Exercise and Sport*, 72, 243–56.

Sheldon, W. H. (1954). *Atlas of men: A guide for somatotyping the adult male at all ages*. New York: Harper.

Surujlal, I. & Dhurup, M. (2012). Athlete preference of coach's leadership style. *African Journal for Physical, Health Education, Recreation and Dance*, 18, 111–21.

Toering, T., Elferink-Gemser, M., Jordet, G., Jorna, C., Pepping, G.-J. & Visscher, C. (2011). Self-regulation of practice behavior among elite youth soccer players: An exploratory observation study. *Journal of Applied Sport Psychology*, 23(1), 110–28.

Toering, T. T., Elferink-Gemser, M. T., Jordet, G. & Visscher, C. (2009). Self-regulation and performance level of elite and non-elite youth soccer players. *Journal of Sports Sciences*, 27, 1509–17.

Toering, T. & Jordet, G. (2015). Self-control in professional soccer players. *Journal of Applied Sport Psychology*, 27(3), 335–50. Advance online publication doi: 10.1080/10413200.2015.1010047.

Tutko, T. A., Lyon, L. P. & Ogilvie, B. C. (1969). *Athletic Motivation Inventory*. San Jose, CA: Institute for the Study of Athletic Motivation.

11 Using Psychometrics to Make Management Selection Decisions: A Practitioner Journey

Hugh McCredie

THE STARTING POINT: THE WAY THINGS WERE

An anecdote from the start of my career as an assessor may serve to illustrate the generally tacit nature of selection 50 years ago. The principal method of assessment was the 'interview' and I was rushed into my first series of candidate encounters at extremely short notice. 'What do I do?', I asked of my more experienced colleague. He paused momentarily, then replied 'If in doubt, chuck them out!' The same colleague later claimed that he had rarely, if ever, made a selection error. This worried me until a few years later I was presented with evidence (Morgan, 1973) to suggest that confident selectors were rarely the most competent. It was in such circumstances that I began my search for a better way to assess candidates.

EARLY ASSESSMENT MODELS AND THEIR SCOPE FOR PSYCHOMETRICS

It soon became apparent that there are two key aspects to making a selection decision, or, more usually, a selection recommendation, if you are the HR adviser and not the ultimate decision maker. The first aspect concerned the nature of the data that was collected; the second was how this was used in arriving at the decision or recommendation. The conventional wisdom of the time was to focus on retrieving biographical data, following a chronological route which terminated with the most recent events. Having completed this invariably tedious process, the next task was to interpret the data against some form of template. Arguably, in a high-volume recruitment programme, the latter could have been an empirically derived customised template. However, in the absence of this there were two generic templates available.

The better known of the two templates was *The Seven-Point Plan* (Rodger, 1952), which sought to apply the biographical data obtained from the interview to answer the following questions:

1. Physical make-up: Has he any defects of health or physique that may be of occupational importance? How agreeable are his appearance, his bearing and his speech?
2. Attainments: What type of education has he had? How well has he done educationally? What occupational training and experience has he had already? How well has he done occupationally?
3. General intelligence: How much general intelligence can he display? How much general intelligence does he ordinarily display?
4. Special aptitudes: Has he any marked mechanical aptitude? manual dexterity? facility in the use of words? or figures? talent for drawing? or music?
5. Interests: To what extent are his interests intellectual? practical–constructional? physically active? social? artistic?
6. Disposition: How acceptable does he make himself to other people? Does he influence others? Is he steady and dependable? Is he self-reliant?
7. Circumstances: What are his domestic circumstances? What do the other members of the family do for a living? Are there any special openings available for him?

While being a step in the right direction, the Seven-Point Plan raised a number of issues. The inclusion of points 1, Physical make-up, and 7, Circumstances, are, at best, questionable in the light of current discrimination law. Also, inductive leaps are required to bridge from raw biographical data to some of the judgements demanded, for example: How much general intelligence does he ordinarily display? How acceptable does he make himself to other people? Finally, the Plan lacked behavioural anchors which would facilitate the comparison of the individual with the requirements of the role under review. The last objection was met by a second generic British assessment template, the Five-Fold Grading System (Munro Fraser, 1954).

Interestingly, from the perspective of this volume, points 3, 4 and 5 (General intelligence, Special aptitudes and Interests) would all have benefited from psychometrics. The (now defunct) National Institute of Industrial Psychology (NIIP), with which Rodger was associated, developed and distributed highly reputable intelligence and aptitude tests, albeit intended for lower-level occupations. In fact, Rawling (Rodger & Rawling, 1985) did sterling work in 'operationalising' and referencing aspects of the Plan to a range of available psychometrics (16PF, Eysenck Personality Inventory, Edwards Personality Preference Schedule, Gordon Personal Profile, FIRO and MBTI). However, by this time, best practice was moving away from broad biographical themes towards the assessment of specific requisite competencies.

A UNIQUE OPPORTUNITY

In 1981, I accepted an offer to manage the assessment and development of constituent business unit directors in a substantial, FTSE 250, heavy-industry conglomerate. At peak, the business units totalled around 50 and the incumbents, across 18 years of association, exceeded 600. The attraction of the offer was the opportunity to explore the nature of some core management roles (managing director, sales/marketing directors, operations directors and finance directors), the attributes of the role occupants and the qualities which correlated with overall effectiveness.

From the start, I used 16PF Form A (Cattell, Eber & Tatsuoka, 1970), the pre-eminent personality psychometric of its day. Initially, this served as an adjunct to a biographical interview which focused heavily on achievements in recent roles. As far as can be generalised about this pre-empirical stage, personality data was used in an intuitive manner but with reference to published profiles (e.g. Cattell et al., 1970, pp. 171–82; Harston & Mottram, 1976) approximating to the role for which assessment was taking place and in the light of known or probable risk factors. Harston and Mottram had collected 16PF Form A primary scale scores from 603 respondents attending general management courses at Henley Management College, with means for 12 role subsets, including sales, marketing, production and finance.

THE GENESIS OF COMPETENCIES

In the meantime, following the publication of the seminal monograph *The Competent Manager* (Boyatzis, 1982), there developed increasing interest in assessing specific skill competencies rather than drawing inferences from biographical details. Boyatzis collected interview data relating to managers' handling of critical incidents. His subsequent analysis of the data revealed the following generic list of competencies which differentiated poor-, average- and superior-performing managers:

Accurate self-assessment
Conceptualisation
Concern with close relationships
Concern with impact
Developing others
Diagnostic use of concepts
Efficiency orientation
Logical thought
Managing group processes
Perceptual objectivity
Positive regard
Proactivity
Self-confidence
Self-control
Spontaneity
Stamina and adaptability
Use of oral presentations
Use of socialised power
Use of unilateral power

Boyatzis also explored whether a variety of personal characteristics differentiated levels of managerial performance. These included activity inhibition, learning style, social motives (achievement, affiliation, power), self-definition and stage of adaptation. He also found occasional connections between these characteristics and specific competencies and made the more general assertion that this general class of phenomenon underpinned the development of competencies at the behavioural or skill level. The personal characteristics featured in *The Competent Manager* did not readily equate with instruments from mainstream psychometrics. This was left to Boyatzis's associates the Spencers (1993), who we will encounter at a later stage.

THE IN-HOUSE STUDY

Although the potential of *The Competent Manager* was exciting, Boyatzis did not leave his readers with a readily usable selection tool. In the circumstances, I resolved to use another published managerial competency framework (Wellin, 1984) as a basis for my own empirical research. The framework included 16 competencies, each with a definition and three behavioural markers. To construct a survey amenable to busy line managers, the single, most readily observable marker for each competency was selected, as shown in Table 11.1.

Table 11.1 *Generic managerial competencies used in the research*

Dimension	High-scoring statement *The person most likely to …*
Problem analysis	… consider facts from a number of sources before coming to a conclusion
Detail	… want to know the detailed aspects of any issue
Judgement	… give clear reasons for making decisions
Flexibility	… incorporate other people's ideas or suggestions
Initiative	… put forward ideas, suggestions and proposals for tackling an issue
Risk-taking	… take a calculated gamble to achieve an objective
Tenacity	… achieve objectives within the agreed time scale
Listening	… listen to and take account of others' points of view
Persuasiveness	… get positive responses from others
Leadership	… develop unity and purpose in a group
Delegation	… involve colleagues and subordinates when making decisions
Planning and organising	… get things done and meet deadlines

Dimension	High-scoring statement *The person most likely to ...*
Management control	... know if something in his or her operation is going wrong and do something about it
Written communication	... produce written work in a language or style suited to the occasion
	The person least likely to...
Decisiveness	... sit on the fence or defer decisions unnecessarily
Stress tolerance	... give in when opposition or difficulties appear

Respondents were asked to identify up to nine director-level colleagues and subordinates with whose work they were familiar and write their names on cards. They were then requested to select the colleague who displayed a behaviour most like the high-scoring statement and the one who reflected it the least and give them a rating of five and one, respectively. The remaining cards were placed in order between these two poles and then rated between one and five. This procedure was followed for each competency and for a rating of overall effectiveness.

The survey was launched on a series of in-house residential courses for business unit managing directors, and subsequently extended to higher levels in the organisation. In all, 42 senior directors rated 219 colleagues and subordinates. All unit directors attending the course were also requested to complete a 16PF Form A questionnaire, so that the final data set consisted of 178 subjects for whom there were both personality data and competency/overall effectiveness ratings.

MORE SYSTEMATIC USE OF PSYCHOMETRICS

At the beginning of the 1990s, two events occurred which facilitated the more systematic use of the 16PF Form A in management selection. First, Bartram (1992) published normative data for approximately 1,800 UK managerial applicants. Secondly, I had accumulated sufficient in-house data, from the same psychometric, to use it arithmetically, as recommended by Meehl (1954). Cattell et al. (1970, p. 141) offered a statistic to compare patterns of individual candidates' scores with the norm for a group. This was termed the Profile Similarity Co-efficient (PSC). Mean profiles were calculated for the entire data set and for each of the four role subsets, and the PSC was calculated, by means of a computer programme, for each respondent against mean role profiles, that is, for the whole sample, managing directors, sales/marketing directors, operations directors and finance directors. It was discovered that the PSC statistic correctly predicted overall managerial effectiveness, in the role then occupied, in approximately two-thirds of cases (McCredie, 1993). Collection of 16PF Form A data from selected candidates continued until the late 1990s. Subsequently, comparative second-order (Big Five) means for my own and Bartram's data were published (McCredie,

2010). This data will be revealed shortly. We shall note the surprisingly high degree of correspondence, which suggests the legitimacy of the notion of a generic managerial personality.

DEVELOPMENTS IN THE USE OF COMPETENCIES: CLOSER TIES WITH PSYCHOMETRICS

In the meantime, Spencer and Spencer (1993) had gone some way towards streamlining and operationalising Boyatzis's model for use in selection. They started by asserting the relationship of personal characteristics to performance via skill/behavioural competencies in what they termed the Causal Flow Model. Of particular interest to this survey is that they suggested some mainstream psychometrics for assessing the personal characteristics. These measures included 16PF for the domains of self-control, achievement orientation, impact and influence, directiveness, and team leadership, without indicating which specific traits were implicated. The Watson–Glaser Critical Reasoning test was recommended for the conceptual thinking domain.

IN-HOUSE DEVELOPMENTS IN PSYCHOMETRIC USAGE

As the in-house personality data accumulated, an attempt was made to improve the link between personality scores and managerial performance. To this end, 16PF Form A primary scale profiles were calculated for high, medium and low performers in each of the small and medium-sized enterprise (SME) director roles. A computer programme was then commissioned to find the closest matches between the personality profile of recruitment candidates and the performance category means for the different roles. These matches were reported as performance potentials. For example, the printout on an operations director candidate might be as shown in Table 11.2. The split potential ratings (e.g. Medium/high) arose when a candidate's profile equally matched two performance means for a role. When a candidate's score equally matched the means for all three performance levels, the printout recorded 'No discrimination'.

Table 11.2 *A specimen candidate performance potential report*

Role	Performance potential
Managing director/general manager, manufacturing businesses	Medium
Managing director/general manager, distribution businesses	Medium/high
Sales/marketing director	Medium
Operations director	Medium/high
Finance director	Medium/low

Table 11.3 Concurrent validity of performance potential predictions

Role	Correctly predicted (%)	Under-predicted (%)	Over-predicted (%)	No discrimination (%)
Manufacturing unit MD	44	7	0	49
Distribution unit MD	88	6	6	0
Sales/marketing director	96	4	0	0
Operations director	94	0	0	6
Finance director	98	2	0	0
Total	83	4	1	13

A concurrent validation of this reporting facility revealed the accuracy of potentiality predictions, as shown in Table 11.3. A split prediction was recorded as correctly predicted if a respondent achieved either of the predicted categories. The 83 per cent success rate was an improvement over the two-thirds prediction success achieved by the use of the Profile Similarity Coefficient. However, both were concurrent validations based on respondents already selected and in post. This is generally regarded as less demanding than true predictive validation based on predictions made *before* selection (Bartram, 2004).

FURTHER DEVELOPMENTS IN PSYCHOMETRICS

The rise of the Big Five

Returning to the wider scene, two important movements were abroad in the 1990s. First was the rise to prominence of the Big Five (or Five-Factor Model) of personality. This movement stemmed from a re-analysis of Cattell's work by a succession of researchers (Fiske, 1949; Goldberg, 1981; Norman, 1963; Tupes & Christal, 1992). Using constrained orthogonal methods of factor analysis, these successive investigations repeatedly yielded five underlying factors rather than the 16 'source traits' discovered by Cattell's – arguably idiosyncratic – oblique method of factor extraction. The factors extracted by Tupes and Christal, in order of variance explained, were:

Factor I: Surgency (or Extraversion)

Factor II: Agreeableness

Factor III: Dependability, the main components of which were orderliness, responsibility, conscientiousness, perseverance and conventionality (now typically labelled Conscientiousness)

Factor IV: Emotional stability

Factor V: Culture, the least clear of the five factors (now frequently called Openness).

On the basis of this research Costa and McCrae developed the NEO series of personality measures which were initially inspired by Eysenck's P-E-N (Psychoticism, Extraversion, Neuroticism) model (Eysenck, 1952). Costa and McCrae (1992) published *The Revised NEO Personality Inventory (NEO-PI-R)*. This measured five domains of personality: Neuroticism (low stability), Extraversion, Openness, Agreeableness and Conscientiousness together with six 'facets' for each domain. NEO became the pre-eminent dedicated Big Five measure and its use by published personality researchers did much to promote the Big Five model amongst psychometric users. In fairness, Cattell (1946) had factor-analysed his 16 trait scores and discovered five higher-order factors which bore some resemblance to the Big Five model. Later, he labelled these Anxiety, Extraversion, Subduedness, Tender mindedness and Superego strength.

THE EMERGING USE OF META-ANALYSIS

The second important development of this era was the meta-analysis of psychometric data. In 1968, Mischel had launched a major attack on personality psychometrics. He suggested that the reported small and inconsistent correlations between personality traits and overt behaviour were due to the neglect of intervening situational variables and that the very concept of stable personality traits predicting behaviour across diverse situations was flawed. Schmidt, Hunter and Urry (1976) countered this assertion by demonstrating that the inconsistent criterion correlations were due to the small size of the data sets, which inhibited the emergence of statistically significant correlations. Schmidt and associates obtained substantial and stable results by combining data from a range of studies and applying corrections for the unreliability of criterion measures and range restriction of the test scores. Using this work as a basis, Robertson and Smith (2001) reported correlations of r 0.51 for cognitive tests and an estimated r 0.40 for personality tests with job performance. Hunter and Hunter (1984) had found a marginally higher cognitive correlation, r 0.58, with professional-managerial job performance.

EXPLORING THE IN-HOUSE DATA AND ITS WIDER RELEVANCE: (1) RELATIONSHIPS BETWEEN PSYCHOMETRIC FACTORS AND COMPETENCIES

In 2001, I started research on a PhD thesis entitled 'The essence and varieties of managerial competence' at UMIST, supervised by Dr Mike Smith (McCredie, 2004). Essentially, this empirically tested the Spencer and Spencer (1993) causal flow model linking personal characteristics to performance via skill competencies. It used the in-house data collected between 1981 and 1998, mentioned above. Concurrently with this study, Bartram and associates at the test publishers SHL Ltd were undertaking a meta-analytical investigation involving relationships amongst similar constructs. The two studies were complementary and Professor Bartram was appointed as external examiner for the current author's thesis. We shall explore the SHL study first.

A parallel study: The emergence of the Great Eight competencies and their psychometric correlates

Kurz and Bartram (2002, pp. 232–3) outlined a competency framework consisting of:

- 110 component competencies ... derived from extensive content analysis of both academic and practice-based competency models
- 20 middle-level dimensions ... derived from analyses of generic and client-specific competency models
- The 'Big Eight' (later Great Eight) competencies emerging from factor analysis.

It was postulated that each of the Great Eight competencies was related to a broad psychometric factor (see Table 11.4). This hypothesised model was generally supported (Bartram 2004, 2005) using data from tests in the OPQ (Occupational Personality Questionnaire) series, although the effect sizes were small, averaging only r 0.16 (uncorrected). Also, since nPow and nAch were measured by combinations of lower-order traits it is difficult to generalise beyond the OPQ measures. Of these two, need for power is less problematic and

Table 11.4 *The Great Eight competencies and their psychometric correlates*

Great Eight competencies	Psychometric correlates
Leading/deciding	Need for power (nPow)
Supporting/co-operating	Agreeableness
Interacting/presenting	Extraversion
Analysing/interpreting	g
Creating/conceptualising	Openness
Organising/executing	Conscientiousness
Adapting/coping	Neuroticism (–)
Enterprising/performing	Need for achievement (nAch)

Table 11.5 *Clustering of competencies*

Results-orientation	Interpersonal	Intellectual	Adaptability
Initiative	Listening	Written communication	Risk-taking
Tenacity	Persuasiveness	Detail	
Planning	Leadership	Problem analysis	
Control	Delegation	Judgement	
Decisiveness	Flexibility		
Stress tolerance			

is probably a blend of extraversion as the main component and low agreeableness as the secondary element (see, for example, Hofstee, de Raad & Goldberg, 1992, p. 149). nAch is more ambivalent; Bartram (2005) found small correlations with extraversion and low agreeableness for this factor also, but it might be expected to relate to the achievement facet of the Achievement-striving facet of conscientiousness in NEO PI-R.

The in-house study: Four competency clusters

Kurz and Bartram (2002) suggested that SHL's eight competency factors provided a parsimonious account of the 12 Supra-Competencies identified by Dulewicz (1989). McCredie (2004, 2010) grouped the 16 competencies from the in-house study under four commonly used (e.g. Dulewicz, 1994) cluster headings. Following a closer examination of their intercorrelations, the competencies were regrouped for a later report (McCredie, 2012), shown in Table 11.5.

McCredie found that the 16PF Form A proxy for *g*, 'source trait' Factor B and three of the instrument's Big Five proxies correlated with ratings in each of the competency clusters, as in Table 11.6. For example, the IQ proxy scores correlated with all four competencies in the

Table 11.6 *Significant correlations between psychometric factors and competency clusters*

Factor	Best predicted competency cluster	Significant correlations	Mean r_s	Effect size
g	Intellectual	4/4	0.34	Moderate
Neuroticism (−)	Interpersonal	4/5	0.22	Small
Agreeableness (−)	Results-orientation	5/6	0.19	Small
Extraversion	Adaptability	1/1	0.23	Small

intellectual cluster. The mean for the significant correlations, calculated by Spearman's rank correlation method, was 0.34, denoting a moderate effect size according to the Cohen (1988) descriptors. We shall say more about the relationship between the 16PF Form A constructs and those of dedicated Big Five measures later.

Thus, both Bartram (2005), using OPQ variants, and McCredie (2004, 2010, 2012), using 16PF Form A, have found modest relationships between broad personality dimensions and broad competency measures. This would seem to support the first premise on which the Spencer and Spencer (1993) Causal Flow Model is based. We shall determine later whether or not measures of personality and cognition add value to overall performance measures or whether these are fully mediated by competency ratings, which is implicit in that model.

EXPLORING THE IN-HOUSE DATA AND ITS WIDER RELEVANCE: (2) IS THERE A GENERIC PSYCHOMETRIC PROFILE FOR MANAGERS AND ARE THERE GENERIC PSYCHOMETRIC PREDICTORS OF MANAGERIAL PERFORMANCE?

We leave the relationships between psychometrics and competencies for the time being in order to explore (1) whether there is a generic managerial personality profile, and (2) if so, whether this is predictive of managerial effectiveness.

A generic psychometric profile for managers?

For the first of these tasks, we shall draw upon three sources. The first two (Bartram, 1992; McCredie, 2004, 2010) are based on second-order factors derived from 16PF Form A primary scales. The third is a unique small study of high-profile international chief executive officers (Peterson, Smith, Martorana & Owens, 2003).

Bartram's (1992) study involved 1796 candidates for managerial roles whose applications were processed by recruitment consultants. McCredie (2004, 2010) reported derived scores from 445 business unit directors actually in roles for which they had been selected, their seniors and staff executives of equivalent rank. McCredie's primary scale scores had been corrected for 'faking good' and 'faking bad' (IPAT, 1979), while Bartram's had not. Peterson et al. (2003) had psychologists assess 17 high-profile CEOs against the 100 descriptors in the California Adult Q-Set (CAQ) (Block, 1978). Assessments were based on archival sources (published biographies, interviews, etc.), and scores on the five factors of personality were computed using McCrae, Costa and Busch's (1986) factor loadings for the CAQ.

Table 11.7 *Comparison of factor percentile ranks from three studies*

Factor	Mean percentile ranks		
	UK management candidates (N = 1796)	UK unit directors (N = 445)	US CEOs (N = 17)
g	81	85	unknown
Extraversion	86	85	82
Neuroticism	12	27	27
Conscientiousness	73	70	50
Agreeableness	11	25	22
Openness	54	26	38

Summary data from the three studies is given below. The lower percentile rank for neuroticism in the case of the UK management applicants can be explained by the fact that while both 16PF data sets were self-reports, Bartram (1992) had not applied the correction for faking and the scales loading on this factor were notoriously prone to faking good. The CEO data was not, of course, from self-reports. Allowing for this, there is a very close correspondence amongst the mean percentile ranking for three data sets in respect of g, extraversion and neuroticism (Table 11.7). These factor means indicate that the typical manager is intelligent, extraverted and stable.

We can also infer that managers share a moderate level of conscientiousness and are low on agreeableness. The latter is unsurprising, given that we have shown that low agreeableness closely relates to the results-orientation cluster of competencies. It is thought that the differences in the openness scores can be accounted for by (1) the gender make-up of the samples and (2) variations in the requirement to deal with novelty. Both of these could explain the lower score for the business unit directors; more than 95 per cent of these respondents were male and they were generally operating in traditional heavy industry. In contrast, around 20 per cent of the managerial applicants were female. A principal primary scale loading on 16PF Form A openness is labelled 'tender-minded' and the difference in average male/female scores for this factor is greater than for any of the other 16 scales (Saville, 1972, p. 15). While the CEOs were all male, they headed brand-leading organisations.

McCredie (2013) found very few significant differences between the overall managerial profile and those for the four functional roles: sales/marketing directors were more extraverted and finance directors were less extraverted, operations directors were even less open-minded and finance directors had higher g scores. These variations were nuances, because the means for all roles were still clearly on the extraverted, low-openness and intelligent side of the normal distribution for these factors.

Generic psychometric predictors of managerial performance?

Having established that *g* correlates with overall managerial effectiveness, meta-analytical evidence for specific Big Five factors predicting manager performance is scant. There are two key studies, Barrick, Mount and Judge (2001) and Hurtz and Donovan (2000). Both found a correlation with extraversion. Barrick et al., the larger study, also found conscientiousness to be a contributor. Hurz and Donovan, who included only dedicated Big Five measures, found stability or low neuroticism to be a factor.

McCredie (2004, 2010) correlated 16PF Form A, Factor B and the second order Big Five proxies with (1) ratings of overall effectiveness and (2) highest job size achieved as measured by the Hay Job Evaluation method (Table 11.8).

It is thought that the smaller than expected correlation for *g* was a reflection of the brevity of the measure (13 items) and its verbal saturation; Eysenck (1998[1947]) found that extraverts did better at non-verbal tests and introverts did best with verbal items. The non-significant correlation of extraversion with overall effectiveness is believed to be due to range restriction because nearly all of those sampled were extraverts. Low neuroticism and low agreeableness correlated with both performance measures. Conscientiousness did not correlate with either criterion; Witt, Burke, Barrick and Mount (2002) noted that 'Highly conscientious workers who lack interpersonal sensitivity [i.e., they have low agreeableness] may be ineffective particularly in jobs requiring co-operative interchange with others'. Such a requirement is a key factor in managerial roles (see, for example, Stewart, 1988). Openness may be a role-contingent factor and it is interesting that more senior respondents were less closed-minded even in this traditional sector of industry.

Once again, differences amongst the roles were minimal: the most effective operations directors had lower neuroticism and lower agreeableness scores, the most effective finance

Table 11.8 *Predictive strength of psychometric factors*

	Strength of prediction for:			
	Overall effectiveness (N = 178)		Job size (N = 391)	
Factor	r	Effect size	r	Effect size
g	0.35**	Moderate	0.09^{NS}	Not significant
Extraversion	0.11^{NS}	Not significant	0.14*	Small
Agreeableness (–)	0.34**	Moderate	0.19*	Small
Conscientiousness	0.09^{NS}	Not significant	0.01^{NS}	Not significant
Neuroticism (–)	0.47***	Moderate	0.10^{NS}	Not significant
Openness	0.13^{NS}	Not significant	0.12*	Small
All factors	0.56**	**Large**	0.29*	**Small**

Note: ** = $p<0.01$; * = $p<0.05$; NS = not significant.

directors scored higher for extraversion. With regard to personal characteristics, holders of the different core managerial roles have much more in common than is distinctive between them.

Additionally, certain combinations of personality scores have been found to link with behavioural dysfunctionalities which can cause problems in managerial contexts (Costa & McCrae,1990; Moscoso & Salgado, 2004). In particular, a combination of high extraversion and low agreeableness may predict combative or provocative behaviour, and low agreeableness with low conscientiousness may indicate a lack of consideration for others or unruliness.

USING PSYCHOMETRICS TO PREDICT PERFORMANCE

Based on the foregoing evidence, McCredie (e.g. 2010, p. 45) developed the guidelines for using personality tests in selection shown in Table 11.9.

Kahneman (2012), at that time psychology's only living Nobel laureate, strongly advocated the use of algorithms or formulas over intuition in complex decision making. He drew heavily on Meehl (1954) and claimed that in 200+ studies following that publication, 60 per cent showed significantly better accuracy for simple algorithms, while in no case was expert judgement superior. He also pointed out that statistical rules were less expensive to apply.

Table 11.9 *Guidelines for using personality tests in management selection*

Factor	Guidelines
General mental ability	Look for at least 75th percentile and as high as possible.
Extraversion	Look for at least 25th percentile and as high as possible.
	For those scoring between the 25th and 75th percentiles, check the narrowband facets of extraversion to ensure that none are likely to be problematic with the particular role in question.
Neuroticism	Look for below 60th percentile and as low as possible.
Conscientiousness	Look for around 50th percentile.
	For those with lower scores, check whether dependability has been a problem in the past.
	For those with higher scores, check whether inflexibility has been a problem in the past.
Agreeableness	Look for 25th percentile and lower scores.
Openness	Depends on organisational factors. Look for around 50th percentile in top management appointments. Be wary of scores reflecting lack of either necessary adaptability (extremely low) or common sense (extremely high).

Table 11.10 *A suggested psychometrics scoring algorithm for management selection*

Factor	Sten Percentile	1 1st	2 4th	3 10th	4 23rd	5 40th	6 60th	7 77th	8 90th	9 96th	10 99th
g		High risk (0)						1	1	2	2
E		High/med risk (0)		1	1	1	1	1	1	1	1
N		2	2	2	2	1	High risk (0)				
O		Medium risk (0)		1	1	1	Medium risk (0)				
A		2	2	2	2	2	High/med risk (0)				
C		Medium risk (0)		1	1	1	Medium risk (0)				

Encouraged by Kahneman's advocacy, and drawing from his findings discussed above, McCredie (2014) developed the algorithm shown in Table 11.10.

Recommended application of the algorithm is as follows:

1. Discount candidates scoring in a high-risk zone but be prepared to check the risk against alternative measures.

2. Be very cautious with the high/medium risks and cautious with the medium risks relative to the demands of the role.

3. Wherever possible, check whether a combination of upper-decile extraversion and lower-decile agreeableness has led to a reputation for combative or provocative behaviour, or lower-decile agreeableness combined with lower-decile conscientiousness has left a reputation for inconsiderate or unruly behaviour.

4. Total the values achieved against the factors and favour the highest-scoring candidate.

A Chi-squared test (n = 178, $p < 0.04$) of total profile scores against ratings of overall effectiveness revealed the results in Table 11.11.

Table 11.11 *Psychometric profile scores and performance probabilities*

Profile score	Probability
1–3	2–1 chance of selecting low vs high performer
4–6	3–1 chance of average or high performer
7–9	4–1 chance of selecting high vs low performer

CAN PSYCHOMETRICS ADD VALUE IN MANAGEMENT SELECTION?

We have seen above that the combined psychometric factors can have a large effect (R 0.56). However, McCredie (2004, 2010 Appendix H) discovered that no significant value was added, by either 16PF Form A primary scales or their Big Five proxies, to the variation in overall effectiveness explained by the combination of competency ratings on their own. Thus, the premise of the causal flow model, that competency ratings mediate the relationship between personality characteristics and managerial performance, is supported. Potentially, therefore, good quality within-role ratings render psychometric data redundant as a predictor of managerial effectiveness. However, in the real world, we rarely have access to such unbiased personal competency ratings based on long-term observation of candidates at work. This is generally true of candidates currently outside of the organisation and is particularly the case with new graduates who probably have no managerial track record. Accordingly, we are at best forced to use off-job simulations in assessment centres, which make a lower average contribution to predicting overall effectiveness than do either general mental ability measures or personality questionnaires (Robertson & Smith, 2001). In such circumstances added value will almost certainly be gained by combining all available measures to predict future effectiveness.

REFERENCES

Barrick, M. R., Mount, M. K. & Judge, T. A. (2001). Personality and performance at the beginning of the new millennium: What do we know and where do we go next? *International Journal of Selection and Assessment*, 9, 9–30.

Bartram, D. (1992). The personality of UK managers: 16PF norms for short-listed applicants. *Journal of Occupational and Organizational Psychology*, 65, 159–72.

Bartram, D. (2004). Predicting the Great Eight competencies: Meta-analysis and moderator effects. *BPS Occupational Psychology Conference 2004 Book of proceedings and compendium of abstracts*, pp. 45–9. British Psychological Society.

Bartram, D. (2005). The Great Eight competencies: A criterion-centric approach to validation. *Journal of Applied Psychology*, 90(6), 1185–1203.

Block, J. (1978). The Q-sort method. Palo Alto, CA: Consulting Psychologists Press.

Boyatzis, R. E. (1982). *The Competent Manager*. New York: Wiley.

Cattell, R. B. (1946). *The description and measurement of personality*. New York: World Books.

Cattell, R. B., Eber, H. W. & Tatsuoka, M. M. (1970). *The handbook for the Sixteen Personality Factor Questionnaire*. Champaign, IL: Institute for Personality and Ability Testing,.

Cohen, J (1988). *Statistical power analysis for the behavioural sciences*. Hillsdale, NJ: Erlbaum.

Costa, P. T. & McCrae, R. R. (1990). Personality disorders and the five-factor model of personality. *Journal of Personality Disorders*, 4, 362–71.

Costa, P. T., Jr. & McCrae, R. R. (1992). *Revised NEO Personality Inventory (NEO-PI-R) and NEO Five-Factor Inventory (NEO-FFI) professional manual*. Odessa, FL: Psychological Assessment Resources.

Dulewicz, S. V. (1989). Assessment centres as the route to competence. *Personnel Management*, 21(9), 56–9.

Dulewicz, S. V. (1994). Personal competences, personality and responsibilities of middle managers. *Journal of Competency*, 1(3), 20–9.

Eysenck, H. J. (1998[1947]). *Dimensions of personality*. New Brunswick, NJ: Transaction Publishers.

Eysenck, H. J. (1952). *The scientific study of personality*. London: Routledge & Kegan Paul.

Fiske, D. W. (1949). Consistency of the factorial structures of personality ratings from different sources. *Journal of Abnormal and Social Psychology*, 44, 329–44.

Goldberg, L. R. (1981). Language and individual differences: The search for universals in personality lexicons. In L. Wheeler (ed.), *Review of personality and social psychology* (vol. 2, pp. 141–65). Beverly Hills, CA: Sage.

Harston, W. R. & Mottram, R. D. (1976). *Personality profiles of managers: A study of occupational differences*. Cambridge: Industrial Training Research Unit.

Hofstee, W. K. B., de Raad, B. & Goldberg, L. R. (1992). Integration of the Big Five and circumplex approaches to trait structure. *Journal of Personality and Social Psychology*, 63(1), 146–63.

Hunter, J. E. & Hunter, R. F. (1984). Validity and utility of alternative predictors of job performance. *Psychological Bulletin*, 96, 72–98.

Hurtz, G. M. & Donovan, J. J. (2000). Personality and job performance: The Big Five revisited. *Journal of Applied Psychology*, 85, 869–79.

IPAT (1979). *Key for validity scales, 16PF, Form A, 1967–68 edition only*. Champaign, IL: Institute for Personality and Ability Testing.

Kahneman, D. (2012). *Thinking, fast and slow*. London: Penguin.

Kurz, R. & Bartram, D. (2002). Competency and individual performance: Modeling the world of work. In I. T. Robertson, M. Callinan & D. Bartram (eds), *Organizational effectiveness: The role of psychology* (pp. 227–55). Chichester: Wiley.

McCredie, H. (1993). High volume, low budget 16PF. *16PF Newsletter*, 4.

McCredie, H. A. (2004). The essence and varieties of management competence. PhD thesis, University of Manchester.

McCredie, H. (2010). *Selecting and developing better managers*. London: Lulu Enterprises.

McCredie, H. (2012). Relating personality, competencies and managerial performance. *Assessment & Development Matters*, 4(3), 6–8.

McCredie, H. (2013). Managerial differences? *Assessment & Development Matters*, 5(1), 6–8.

McCredie, H. (2014). Towards a generic algorithm for selecting managers. *Assessment & Development Matters*, 6(1), 11–13.

McCrae, R. R., Costa, P. T. J. & Busch, C. M. (1986). Evaluating the comprehensiveness in personality systems: The California Q-Set and the five-factor model. *Journal of Personality*, 54, 430–46.

Meehl, P. E. (1954). *Clinical versus statistical prediction: A theoretical analysis and a review of the evidence*. Minneapolis: University of Minnesota.

Mischel, W. (1968). *Personality and assessment*. London: Wiley.

Munro Fraser, J. (1954). *A handbook of employment interviewing*. London: Macdonald and Evans.

Morgan, T. (1973). Recent insights into the selection interview. *Personnel Review*, 2(1), 4–13.

Moscoso, S. & Salgado, J. F. (2004). 'Dark side' personality styles as predictors of task, contextual, and job performance. *International Journal of Selection of Assessment*, 12, 356–62.

Norman, W. T. (1963), Toward an adequate taxonomy of personality attributes: Replicated factor structure in peer nomination personality ratings. *Journal of Abnormal and Social Psychology*, 66(6), 574–83.

Peterson, R. S., Smith, D. B., Martorana, P. V. & Owens, P. D. (2003). The impact of chief executive officer personality on top management team dynamics: One mechanism by which leadership affects organisational performance. *Journal of Applied Psychology,* 88(5), 795–808.

Robertson, I. T. & Smith, M. (2001). Personnel selection. *Journal of Occupational and Organisational Psychology,* 74, 441–72.

Rodger, A. (1952). *The Seven-Point Plan.* London: National Institute of Industrial Psychology.

Rodger, A. & Rawling, K. (1985). *New Perspectives Fifty Years On: The Seven Point Plan.* Windsor: NFER-Nelson.

Saville, P. (1972). *The National Adult Standardisation of 16 Personality Factor Questionnaire (16PF).* London: NFER.

Schmidt, F. L., Hunter, J. E. & Urry, V. W (1976). Statistical power in criterion-related validation studies, *Journal of Applied Psychology,* 61(4), 473–85.

Spencer, L. M. & Spencer, S. M. (1993). *Competence at work: Models for superior performance.* New York: Wiley.

Stewart, R. (1988). *Managers and their jobs* (2nd edn). London: Macmillan.

Tupes, E. C. & Christal, R. E. (1992). Recurrent personality factors based on trait ratings. *Journal of Personality,* 60, 225–51. (Reprinted from USAF ASD Tech. Rep. No. 61–97, 1961, Lackland Air Force Base, TX: U.S. Air Force.)

Wellin, M. (1984). *Behaviour technology: A new approach to managing people at work.* Aldershot: Gower.

Witt, L. A., Burke, L. A., Barrick, M. R. and Mount, M. K. (2002). The interactive effects of conscientiousness and agreeableness on job performance. *Journal of Applied Psychology,* 87(1), 164–9.

12 Psychometrics in Clinical Settings

HAMILTON FAIRFAX

INTRODUCTION

Psychometrics, be it for personal use, organisational demands, the results of relevant research or audits, has a constant and valued presence in my clinical practice as a counselling psychologist. I have spent the last 15 years employed in clinical practice and latterly also in a managerial position in Adult Mental Health Secondary Care services in the National Health Service (NHS) in the United Kingdom. Institutions such as the NHS have increasingly adopted the policies of 'evidence-based practice' (EBP), which put simply requires the practitioner to be able to demonstrate that the treatment they offer is justifiable according to the national recognised accumulation of research evidence.

Evaluating 'what we do and if and how it works' has always been of integral interest to psychologists, who often use the term 'scientist practitioner' to describe themselves. Jones and Mehr (2007) describe scientist practitioners as 'trained professional psychologists [who] should be knowledgeable in both research and clinical practice. Emphasis should be placed on the successful integration of science and practice, where the relationship between the two variables is carefully considered. ... [T]here are three vital assumptions of the scientist-practitioner model. The first assumption is that professionals with knowledge and skills related to research will facilitate effective psychological services. The second assumption identified research as imperative to the development of a scientific database. Last, ... direct involvement in clinical practice by researchers will result in studies on important social issues' (p. 766). The use of psychometric assessments which are designed to provide an objective measure of a psychological phenomenon are central tools in the application of the scientist practitioner model.

Following the Boulder Conference in 1949 at the University of Colorado, the scientist practitioner has been a dominant model in Western psychology training for over 60 years; with its strong basis in empirical science methodology, it has a significant impact on shaping what is considered 'good psychological research' (Benjamin and Baker, 2000). The development of the scientist practitioner identity helps to satisfy the historical need for psychology to be seen as a valid 'science' within the more ineffable clinical realities confronting therapists when they meet with clients (Barrett, 2003). As a result, positivistic methodologies that attempt to 'prove' hypothesis are privileged and have become the standard by which research findings are evaluated and supported (Barrett, 2003; Mitchell, 1997). There are, however, a number of difficulties with this position, namely the generalisability of both the method and the results to real-world practice (Albee, 2000; Fairfax, 2008).

This chapter will develop these themes further, exploring how psychometric assessments and their results impact upon everyday clinical practice. It will also use psychometrics to explore the relationship between organisational and managerial pressures, political and theoretical concerns such as EBP, and individual clinicians' desire to evaluate their practice. The utilities of psychometrics, and its contribution or otherwise to clinical practice and as an instrument for clinical research, will be discussed. Finally, the contribution of psychometrics to the identity and role of the psychologist both as a professional and as a practitioner in an increasingly competitive environment will be discussed.

PSYCHOMETRIC ASSESSMENTS AND CLINICAL PRACTICE

This section will consider general uses of psychometrics in clinical practice, then more individualistic uses of tests. The discussion is based on two central questions.

What is it we are doing and are we making a difference?

One principal use of psychometrics clinically is to establish if a particular diagnosis, problem or attribute is present in an individual at a given time. The second main aim is to establish to what degree the person has the quality being tested. As has been explored in previous chapters this judgement is based on empirical qualities of validity (does the test do what it sets out to do?) and reliability (can it be counted on to produce similar results when re-used). By establishing a measure of whether someone has the quality being tested for and the degree to which they have it using a tool that is recognised as being able to do both, one can test, for example, whether the treatment one offers has made a difference by repeating it at the end of the intervention.

On the surface this would seem an entirely reasonable process. However, these aims are based on significant assumptions. First, it is presumed that the disorder or quality being tested is able to be quantified. If, for example, one is assessing a diagnosis such as personality disorder, there are a number of things to consider. For example, is the psychometric used based on the description in the Diagnostic and Statistical Manual (DSM-V) or the International Classification of Diseases (ICD-10)? Does the measure claim to capture all of the criteria on which the diagnosis is based or just a selection? Is the clinician aware of the theoretical issues underlying the test being used and do they agree with them? For example, the Millon Multiaxial Clinical Inventory (MCMI-III) is the second most widely used test of personality disorder (Millon, Millon, Davis & Grossman, 2009), but it doesn't measure all the diagnoses of personality disorder in DSM-V. It is based on a conception of personality disorder that is more dimensional than categorical (Boyle, Matthews & Saklofske, 2008). This is important in considering how the results may be used and who the information may be communicated to. It is easy to control for this in the context of a research trial but less so in everyday practice when any professional and personal perspectives are involved in an individual's care.

There is also a fundamental assumption that any psychological quality, disorder or attribute is a discrete entity that has a fully shared understanding amongst those who deal with it.

Unlike gold, for example, which can be expected to conform to predictive chemical analysis to confirm its identity, a psychological term such as schizophrenia, despite its ubiquity, is a far more disparate concept, with many researchers agreeing that it may not even exist (Henderson & Malhi, 2014). As Barrett (2003) summarised it, 'The problem that faces psychology is that the variables that are of most interest to investigators are latent or unobservable. That is, they do not exist as physical objects or material, which can be manipulated in order to determine the empirical relations that may hold between amounts of an object (like the length of wooden rods for example). Psychological variables such as intelligence, motivation, personality, self-esteem, anger, religiosity, beliefs etc. do not "exist" except as inferred constructs' (p. 428).

There is therefore a significant problem in being able to state, on the basis of psychometric information, that someone has a psychological difficulty. Furthermore, if one were able to do this with confidence there would be no guarantee that others being informed of the results shared the same understanding of the concept measure. Even when individual test items are statistically investigated it is not possible to conclude that agreement on, for example, 87 per cent of items, means that measures support the same underlying concept. Even if a measure were to be supported by different measures there is the danger of what Kuhn (1997) calls incommensurability. This argues that when new theories develop from existing ideas, the central meaning of the old theory can often change, as can the exploratory process surrounding it.

This difficulty is compounded when different psychometric assessments that purport to measure the same concept produce different results, finding more or less of the quality being tested, or even disagreeing on whether it is present at all. Psychometricians attempt to control this by producing statistics for their instrument's reliability, such as correlations between measures. However, a significantly strong correlation of inter-reliability could be interpreted more as support of a 'proof of concept' than as necessarily saying something new about the person. By this I mean that two tests that correlate with each other in relation to a concept such as depression may only be able to support the first test's original definition of depression. A bias in the measurement could arise if a particular viewpoint is generally supported by selecting similar tests in the standardisation process. This is a distinct possibility if tests are developed through a restrictive process of inter-measure reliability. For example, selections of measures identified by a given organisation or culture as 'evidence-based' could arguably only be producing self-justifying and self-perpetuating results, which through the principle of incommensurability could become far removed from the subject they originally intended to explore. Furthermore, the extent to which measures differ from each other could cause conceptual questions and clinical ramifications for the person being treated.

There is therefore a basic criticism of psychology's comfort in the generation of a number, and the idea that may provide a 'proof' which could legitimise the assumptions of the context that produced the number. Michell (1997) refers to psychometrics as 'pathological science', and central to this criticism is what is seen as the erroneous belief that numbers based on an independent relational system can prove facts about another radically different empirical system. The aspiration of psychology to produce numerical support for theory and practice has been described as a flawed attempt to be taken seriously by other established pure science disciplines that are based on the Western positivist tradition, which can have significant implications when applied to real-world practice (Barrett, 2003; Molenaar, 2006).

Stepped mental health care in the UK for example led to the development of Improving Access to Psychological Therapies (IAPT) services. IAPT identifies a clear pathway for treating depression, which increases the length and intensity of 'evidence-based' psychological interventions according to the severity of the condition, starting with the least intensive intervention. This is a sensible way to design a service, but it ignores several issues. First, the diagnostics and severity criteria that discriminate the step intervention required involve, amongst other things, a consideration of an individual's performance on the Patient Health Questionnaire (PHQ-9). This is also the main way of measuring the success of an intervention for depression, and it is completed by the client at each session. However, the PHQ-9 consists of only nine questions to assess depression, which cover the more demonstrable symptoms but, interestingly, not suicidality (Blacker, 2009). This is, therefore, a limited, individualistic and symptom-based way of measuring a complex difficulty such as depression. The PHQ-9 is derived from a larger measure, the Primary Care Evaluation of Mental Disorders (PRIME-MD) developed by Spitzer, Kroenke and Williams (1999). The PRIME-MD was funded by the pharmaceutical company Pfizer. This highlights issues of context and applicability. How much internal consistency and predictive value has the PHQ-9 lost in the process of being abstracted from the PRIME-MD? Is it an issue that it is based on a conception of depression from nearly two decades ago? Is there a possible bias in test selection, due to funding from a company that may be inclined to medicalise psychological difficulties in order to increase its profits?

What theory and practice inform clinicians' use of psychometrics?

EBP is arguably ignoring a much greater body of historical psychotherapeutic research in the effectiveness of therapies (Cooper, M., 2008; Norcross, 2002). This concluded that there is little difference between the different therapeutic approaches, locating the ingredients of successful therapeutic outcomes in intra-therapeutic process (such as the quality of the therapeutic alliance) and extra-therapeutic qualities (the engagement and motivation of the client), referred to as 'common factors' (Messer and Wampold, 2002). The accumulation of research supporting this finding has been so great that it has led to the identification of the 'Dodo bird verdict' (Luborsky et al., 2002; Wampold et al., 1997), which contends that all therapies are of equal value as the technical differences of each model are consistently found to be of minor relevance to the success of the intervention. This finding needs to be interpreted carefully as, for some conditions, there is much stronger evidence that specific techniques are integral to success, for example the use of exposure and response prevention (E-RP) in obsessive compulsive disorder (OCD) (Abramowitz, 2006).

However, even in these circumstances, what is defined as a 'successful outcome' needs to be explored; is it merely relief from specific symptoms or behaviours as opposed to general well-being? Is the change permanent or temporary (Western, Novotny & Thompson-Brenner, 2004)? Moreover, the use of a psychological technique does not necessarily support the therapeutic approach it is based on. Is the mechanism of change in E-RP principally behavioural, cognitive, neurological, all of the above, or something different? Psychometric assessment can tell us that something may be less present than it was, but without more substantive research it cannot be used to validate a particular theory. At heart, therefore, by rejecting or devaluing the substantial body of research produced by other methodologies (many of which support a general conclusion as in the case of the Dodo Bird verdict), EBP may be criticised for making a Type 1 error by claiming that interventions are different when in fact they are not.

It is important to acknowledge that this does not call for a rejection of psychometric assessments – far from it. What appears clear from outcome research is that opinion and psychological knowledge are best served by research that involves mixed methodology to capture as much detail as possible that could be helpful. It is important therefore to consider the wider process behind why clinicians choose psychometrics, and more importantly how they apply it to their practice.

Clinical use of psychometrics

Anecdotally, when one speaks to clinicians about which psychometrics they choose to use, it is usually the ones they have become most familiar with, either when training, on clinical placements, or at the point of specialising in a particular model. They are aware of the most well-known tests and use these if appropriate, but tend to gravitate towards what they are familiar with. What is more interesting is *how* clinicians use them.

In my experience most psychologists do not decide their intervention or formulation purely on the basis of psychometric assessments. Instead they use them to inform their practice. This is not to diminish the importance they may place on being able to show a lower score on a Beck Depression Inventory (BDI-II) for example, but points to a more thoughtful use. For example, in treatments of Post-Traumatic Stress Disorder (PTSD) clinicians often use the Impact of Events Scale Revised (IES-R), a well-known measure that describes symptoms of flashbacks, avoidance and hyperarousal. In practice the IES-R is often used collaboratively with the clients, repeated at regular intervals during the intervention and shared with the client to support changes and identify areas where there may still be difficulties. However, the IES-R is used alongside an existing therapeutic process, the clinical judgement of the therapist and the perceptions of the client. It is the combination of all these and not a simple numeric result that determines the therapeutic outcome. It would be questionable to simply discharge a client without further consideration when their outcome scores had significantly reduced, if their reported mental and social health had declined.

The need therefore is for a wider perspective informed by clinical experience, client opinion and psychometric results, which all increase with the complexity of the difficulties the individual reports. Most clients in secondary care, step 4 services, have multiple, co-morbid psychological difficulties and social, financial and accommodation issues. Even if a main issue is identified for a psychological intervention, it will inevitably be affected by the context of other difficulties and therefore cannot progress in either course or manifestation the same way as a more straightforward presentation. Attempts to measure and predict a varied and qualitatively different process using the same styles of measurement are evidently erroneous. Yet this is what EBP implementation seeks to do.

This suggests a clear distinction between the use of psychometrics in clinical practice and in the empirically based research model. Clinically, psychometrics is best understood as a contribution to holistic formulation, while research tends to be more outcome-based. This is a dimensional conceptualisation as opposed to a mutually exclusive position, but the two can be in greater opposition the more an individual or organisation locates itself at one or the other pole. As previously suggested, while both positions can share the same language, what they imply and describe can be qualitatively very different.

If psychologists and psychological therapists are using psychometrics in this more integrated, reflective way, that calls into question the traditional scientist practitioner model; its claims are perhaps better seen as informative or even aspirational than as 'evidence'.

Positivistic bias

The above difficulties highlight a more overarching problem with psychometrics which I call a *positivistic bias*. Put simply this is the underlying tendency of psychology to identify psychological knowledge and 'best practice' with whatever conforms best to a positivistic theory of science, namely the experimental method of observation, hypothesis generation, test and re-test. It is through this Western system that clinical interventions, theoretical developments and professional practice have to be demonstrated and seem as 'valid', 'effective' or 'useful', and despite increasing globalisation this encultured perspective remains the most dominant narrative. Faucher et al. (2002) argue that all scientific theory is inseparable from cultural and sociological ingredients and that it is not possible to identify a 'pure' or removed concept that is separate from the specific cultural context and the individual circumstances of each mind that is forming them.

The dominance of EBP in Western care services is an obvious example of the positivistic bias. Although a detailed discussion of this matter is outside the current remit, a basic outline is provided for illustrative purposes. In the UK, mental health EBP is based on the findings of the National Institute for Health and Care Excellence (NICE). This is an organisation which collates high-quality research evidence in specific areas of physical and mental health, reviewed by a panel of experts in the particular field, to recommend the best evidence-based clinical practice for each condition. Its guidelines are regularly reviewed and updated.

In many ways NICE can be lauded for providing a helpful resource. The problem occurs when one questions how this research is gathered and collated, what is meant by 'high-quality research', and how services and organisations such as the NHS or private insurance companies use the information. NICE grades research from A to GPP (the lowest form of evidence, recommended good practice based on expert consensus only). The randomised control trial (RCT) is identified as the best level of evidence: an 'A'-level intervention requires at least one RCT. Leaving aside the relegation of identified experts to the bottom of the evidential source table, and despite criticism of the RCT as methodology (Hammersly, 2013; Williams, 2010), its pre-eminence illustrates the positivistic bias. Whereas RCTs may have an arguably more natural use in medical interventions and medication, the main measurement of change in mental health is psychometrics. As previously suggested, there are fundamental problems in using psychometrics in this way. Secondly, if one investigates the guidelines in more detail a central problem with bias emerges, particularly in research selection, funding and publication (Attia, 2005; Cooper, Hedges and Begg, 1994; Hammersly, 2013).

RCTs are expensive and labour-intensive activities. Therefore, while it is understandable that funding will be carefully considered, that consideration is within the context of the Western positivistic environment. Grants will therefore prioritise research that is based on empirical experimentation. Critiques of NICE highlight the fact that in many cases the research used to guide recommended practice is not generalisable, as the cohorts used in RCTs are often so strictly selected that they do not represent the average mental health client

(Duncan & Miller, 2006; Mollon, 2009). As will be discussed in the following section, this has particular relevance to the organisational pressures that lie behind the use and selection of psychometrics by the clinicians.

THE ORGANISATIONAL IMPACT OF PSYCHOMETRICS

In identifying the positivistic bias, I am not denying the usefulness of EBP; after all, I am guilty of being comforted by the generation of a number that indicates something is going well. The call instead is for a replacement of this theoretical hegemony with one that is more balanced and is based on professional concern, not personal anxiety. To put it simply, I am worried, fearful and angered about how psychological research can be used to affect the quality and effectiveness of mental health services. This is not to reject NICE, but to argue that its outcomes should be understood properly and implemented appropriately. I feel it would not be possible to do the latter without an equally powerful counter-narrative to EBP, such as practice-based evidence (PBE) which investigates such questions as 'what actually works in practice' more accurately. Psychometrics has its place, but once again it is how it is used and reported that is central.

In the NHS it is common for all clients to complete a standardised set of measures regardless of presentation or current emotional or physical difficulties. A psychometric measure used frequently throughout the UK is the Clinical Outcomes Routine Evaluation (CORE). This is a 34-item measure that provides an indication of an individual's well-being, function, severity of problems and current risk. This is helpful information, and the CORE is a measure that has undergone rigorous evaluation (Barkham et al., 2001). The CORE can produce individual item scores and overall scores to grade the individual's difficulty from Severe to Sub-clinical, which can be compared with clinical and non-clinical populations. There is substantial research that indicates psychological therapies, in particular CBT for depression and anxiety, can improve individuals' performances on the measure. However, it does not necessarily follow that the CORE should be given to all users of mental health services regardless of severity, particularly as most of the research – though certainly not all – that supports the effectiveness of the CORE is on primary care or selected secondary care populations (Barkham, Gilbert, Connell, Marshall & Twigg, 2005).

These concerns are increased when organisations place value on such scores, and base commissioning and service decisions on them away from the clinical context. Increasingly, such decisions by NHS and private health care providers are made by individuals who are either not familiar with the specifications of services or not sufficiently trained clinically or methodologically to understand the information they are provided with. Instead they are under pressure to ensure services are economically viable; the attraction of a number that purports to measure improvement is obvious. It is possible to manage mental health services in a way that would not be permissible in banking, the military or food production. One risks accusations of arrogance or pomposity if one's critique of a management decision is based on the manager's lack of awareness or training. A strange and unintended consequence of EBP is that it provides a heuristic for the uninformed to speak with authority in a way in which many of us would not speak to a mechanic just because we had read a car manual. Stating that something is 'evidence-based', whether or not the person knows much about the area being discussed, is often seen as sufficient. It is dangerous to base policy and the survival of clinical services on this level of insight.

In outlining this position I do not want to demonise managers or create an equally unhelpful heuristics. Many are well informed, with good clinical experience, but their roles have increasingly alienated them from the realities of practice. Demand and the pressure to be more effective can diminish flexibility and creative thinking, leading to a reliance on quick information such as numbers and 'evidence'. I speak from personal experience and am aware that these pressures only increase with more responsibilities.

CONCLUSION

This chapter has attempted to highlight the current tension in psychometrics in clinical practice. A number of fundamental limitations require that it and its results are used with caution, more sensitively and from a fully informed perspective. This is not, however, to reject psychometrics. It can be helpful to both clients and clinicians, and an important way to help the profession develop and understand itself. Instead it has been argued that its place in clinical practice should be properly understood and that psychological practitioners have gradually lost their governance. Psychometrics is best understood as part of the clinician's ongoing formulation that is collaboratively developed with the client. To abstract them from this context is to lose the exploratory contributions of clinical skills, wider systemic understandings and the richness of the phenomenological realities, reducing them purely to an anonymous number. As Guttman (1991) suggested, 'Those who firmly believe that rigorous science must consist largely of mathematics and statistics have something to unlearn. Such a belief implies the emasculation of the basic substantive nature of science. Mathematics is content-less, and hence not in itself empirical science. … [R]igorous treatment of content or subject matter is needed before some mathematics can be thought of as a possibly useful (but limited) partner for empirical science' (Guttman, 1991, p. 42).

It has also been argued that exploring the use of psychometrics forces psychologists to re-evaluate the underlying theories and training that govern research and practice. It may be that psychology felt the need to survive by replicating an approved methodological tradition, but is this still relevant for today's vibrant, multicultural and confident profession? A strength of psychology is that it is a constantly questioning, growing and adopting profession. Nowhere is it more so than in clinical practice, where the vagaries of concepts such as diagnosis are confronted on a daily basis. Perhaps what is needed is for psychology to take back tools such as psychometrics, and reinvigorate them with newer knowledge and with the confidence that positivism can take us only so far. Psychological research increasingly supports mixed methods: clinical practice and therapeutic pluralism (Chwalisz, 2003; Cooper, 2008; Stricker, 2002). Both acknowledge that many different ways of increasing understanding are required but that the ultimate skill lies in being able to apply these in a way that increases the possibly of helping.

REFERENCES

Abramowitz, J. S. (2006). The psychological treatment of obsessive-compulsive disorder. *Canadian Journal of Psychiatry*, 51, 407–16.

Albee, George W. (2000). The Boulder Model's fatal flaw. *American Psychologist*, 55(2), 247–8.

Attia, A. (2005). Bias in RCTs: Confounders, selection bias and allocation concealment. *Middle East Fertility Society Journal*, 10, 258–61.

Barkham M., Gilbert, N., Connell, J., Marshall, C. & Twigg, E. (2005). Suitability and utility of the CORE–OM and CORE–A for assessing severity of presenting problems in psychological therapy services based in primary and secondary care settings. *British Journal of Psychiatry*, 186(3), 239–46.

Barkham, M., Margison, F., Leach, C., Lucock, M., Mellor-Clark, J., Evans, C. et al. (2001). Service profiling and outcomes benchmarking using the CORE–OM: toward practice-based evidence in the psychological therapies. *Journal of Consulting and Clinical Psychology*, 69(2), 184–96.

Barrett, P. T. (2003). Beyond psychometrics: Measurement, non-quantitative structure, and applied numerics. *Journal of Managerial Psychology*, 3(18), 421–39.

Benjamin, L. T. & Baker, D. B. (eds) (2000). History of psychology: The Boulder Conference. *American Psychologist*, 55, 233–54.

Blacker, D. (2009). Psychiatric rating scales. In B. J. Sadock, V. A. Sadock & P. Ruiz (eds), *Kaplan & Sadock's comprehensive textbook of psychiatry* (9th edn, pp. 1032–58). London: Wolters Kluwer Health/Lippincott Williams & Wilkins..

Boyle, G. J., Matthews, G. & Saklofske. D. H. (eds) (2008). *Sage handbook of personality theory and assessment. Volume 2: Personality theory and assessment*. Los Angeles, CA: SAGE.

Chwalisz, K. (2003). Evidence-based practice: A framework for twenty-first-century scientist-practitioner training. *Counseling Psychologist*, 31, 497–528.

Cooper, H., Hedges, L. V. & Begg, C. B. (1994). Publication bias. In H. Cooper & L. V. Hedges (eds), *The handbook of research synthesis* (pp. 399–409). New York: Russell Sage Foundation.

Cooper, M. (2008). *Essential research findings in counselling and psychotherapy: The facts are friendly*. London: Sage.

Duncan, B. & Miller, S. (2006). Treatment manuals do not improve outcomes. In J. Norcross, L. Beutler & R. Levant (eds), *Evidence-based practices in mental health* (pp. 140–8). Washington, DC: American Psychological Association.

Fairfax, H. (2008). 'CBT or not CBT', is that really the question? Re-considering the evidence base: The contribution of process research. *Counselling Psychology Review*, 23(4), 27–37.

Faucher, L., Mallon, R., Nazer, D., Nichols, S., Ruby, A., Stich, S. & Weinberg, J. (2002). The baby in the labcoat: Why child development is an inadequate model for understanding the development of science. In P. Carruthers, S. Stich & M. Siegal (eds.), *The cognitive basis of science* (pp. 335–62). Cambridge: Cambridge University Press.

Guttman, L. (1991). *Chapters from an Unfinished Textbook on Facet Theory*. Jerusalem: Hebrew University Press.

Hammersly, M. (2013). *The myth of research-based policy and practice*. London: SAGE.

Henderson, S. & Malhi, G. S. (2014). Swan song for schizophrenia? *Australian & New Zealand Journal of Psychiatry*, 48, 302–5.

Jones, J. L. & Mehr, S. L. (2007). Foundations and assumptions of the scientist-practitioner model. *American Behavioral Scientist*, 50(6), 766–71.

Kuhn, T. S. (1997). *The structure of scientific revolutions*. Chicago: Chicago University Press.

Luborsky, L., Rosenthal, R., Diguer, L., Andrusyna, T. P., Berman, J. S., Levitt, J. T. et al. (2002). The Dodo Bird verdict is alive and well – mostly. *Clinical Psychology Science and Practice*, 9(1), 2–12.

Messer, S. B. & Wampold, B. E. (2002). Let's face facts: Common factors are more potent than specific therapy ingredients. *Clinical Psychology: Science and Practice*, 9(1), 21–5.

Michell, J. (1997). Quantitative science and the definition of measurement in psychology. *British Journal of Psychology*, 88, 355–83.

Millon, T., Millon, C., Davis, R. & Grossman, S. (2009). *MCMI-III Manual* (4th edn). Minneapolis, MN: Pearson Education.

Molenaar, P. C. M. (2006). Can psychology be a quantitative science, or is Kant right after all? In L. Smith and J. Voneche (eds), *Norms in Human Development* (pp. 211–9). Cambridge: Cambridge University Press.

Mollon, P. (2009). The NICE guidelines are misleading, unscientific, and potentially impede good psychological care and help. *Psychodynamic Practice*, 15, 9–24.

Norcross, J. C. (2002). *Psychotherapy relations that work: Therapist contributions and responsiveness to patients*. Oxford: Oxford University Press.

Spitzer, R. L., Kroenke, K. & Williams, J. B. (1999). Validation and utility of a self-report version of PRIME-MD: The PHQ primary care study. *JAMA*, 10, 1737–44.

Stricker, G. (2002) What is a scientist-practitioner anyway? *Journal of Clinical Psychology*, 58, 277–83.

Wampold, B. E., Mondin, G. W., Moody, M., Stich, F., Benson, K. & Ahn, H. (1997). A Meta-analysis of outcome studies comparing bona fide psychotherapies: Empirically, 'All must have prizes'. *Psychological Bulletin*, 122, 203–15.

Westen, D., Novotny, C. M. & Thompson-Brenner, H. 2004. The empirical status of empirically supported psychotherapies. *APA Psychological Bulletin*, 130, 631–63.

Williams, B. A. (2010). Perils of evidence-based medicine. *Perspectives on Biology and Medicine*, 53, 106–20.

Part III Best-Practice Considerations

13 The Use and Misuse of Psychometrics in Clinical Settings

SUSAN VAN SCOYOC

This chapter raises the philosophical and ethical dilemmas which inevitably arise from being in clinical practice and in particular from using psychometrics with a potentially vulnerable population within a clinical setting. Before I come to the use of psychometrics I will discuss the widespread use of diagnosis in order to explore how this medical construction is inextricably linked with the use of psychometrics. I will discuss why this should be borne in the mind of any clinician considering the use of psychometrics as part of an assessment or treatment process. I will then explore a collaborative approach to the use of psychometrics in clinical settings and why this approach might be considered the gold standard approach to assessment and treatment planning. All of my shared thoughts and observations arise out of my own practice experience.

ARE DIAGNOSTIC CATEGORIES SOCIAL CONSTRUCTIONS?

In my view, any discussion of psychometric use has to be preceded by a discussion of the use of diagnosis in clinical settings. For most people who seek assistance within the mental health system a diagnosis is *required* in order to obtain treatment. People are usually assessed and then coded within a medical system which chooses to categorise people into a diagnostic category. Mental distress is conceptualised in the same way as medical illness and physical injury. The most widely used diagnostic systems are the International Classification of Diseases-10 (ICD-10) and the Diagnostic and Statistical Manual version 5 (DSM-5). Each presents a list of the symptoms required for a diagnosis of a particular disorder. Such symptoms are presented as components of a distinct disorder, akin to what one might expect in the diagnosis of physical illness.

This approach to the categorisation of human suffering has been criticised extensively. Gergen, Hoffman and Anderson (1996) have suggested that diagnosis is more to satisfy the psychologist than the client. Gergen, Hoffman and Anderson do not hold back when stating:

> Diagnostic systems give a sense of legitimacy, confidence, and predictability both to the professional and to the client. In both psychotherapy and the broader culture, a diagnosis

implies that the object of inquiry and the method of inquiry are based on stable assumptions like those in the biomedical realm. It operates as a professional code that has the function of gathering, analyzing, and ordering waiting-to-be-discovered data. As similarities and patterns are found, problems are then fitted into a deficit-based system of categories. In a larger sense, this framework is based on the assumption that language is representational and can accurately depict 'reality'. (Gergen, Hoffman & Anderson, 2006, p. 104)

More recently, David Pilgrim has written extensively on the underlying difficulties of such a diagnostic model (Pilgrim, 2007, 2009). Major points of criticism are the ontological and epistemological assumptions that mental abnormality simply exists 'out there', awaiting verification during an assessment by the expert psychologist, and that these categories of mental abnormality are inherently pathological in nature rather than variations on 'normal'. Such assumptions, argues Pilgrim, imply and justify a further assumption that professionals have a resulting 'duty of care' and 'right to treat', even when the person identified as having the disorder objects to treatment.

The history of the ICD and the DSM adds fuel to this debate. When the DSM-I was published in 1952, it featured descriptions of 106 disorders, referred to at the time as *reactions* of the personality to psychological, social and biological factors. In 1980 the DSM-III changed from the original psychodynamic perspective to that of empiricism, and this resulted in 265 research-based diagnostic categories. Since 1980 each new edition of the DSM has increased the number of formal diagnoses by approximately ten per cent. Depending upon one's view, this is evidence of the social construction of diagnostic categories or our improving ability to identify previously unrecognised disorders.

It is important for the clinician to hold in mind such philosophical consideration of the meaning of diagnosis and its uses over human history. It was explored extensively by Foucault (2013) in his classic work *History of Madness*. Careful consideration of these issues assists in deciding what might be in the best interests of the client, avoiding the dogmatism which can come from strict adherence to a medically based formal diagnostic model. It assists in assessment of whether the distress described by the client is caused more by economic or social hardship than by a disorder of the psyche. Such philosophical awareness also assists in decision making regarding psychometric use. But it raises its own dilemmas. For example, how do we, as clinicians, act in the best interests of our clients when we are aware of the debates regarding the classification of mental distress as 'illness'?

One attempt to counter this dilemma has encouraged psychologists to use formulation rather than the medically conceptualised use of diagnosis. Strawbridge goes as far as stating, 'Formulation is a key element of psychological practice, and one that is often seen as distinguishing a psychological from a medical approach to distress' (Strawbridge, 2010). Formulation is described as 'a concept that organizes, explains, or makes clinical sense out of large amounts of data and influences the treatment decisions' (Lazare, 1976, p. 97). It is hypothesis-driven, should be continually revised, and allows for a fluidity of thinking which avoids the concreteness of a fixed diagnosis which has a tendency to resist being revised. The formulation approach allows for the consideration of hidden materials that are not apparent to the client or the clinician (because they have not yet been discovered) but are held in mind as present and future possibilities. In my practice, it is this search for as yet unidentified and hidden information which encourages me to use psychometric testing. My intention is to integrate science-based practice with a focus upon the shared, collaborative understanding

I have with my client. As a practitioner, I also often have to provide a diagnosis in order to enable my client to have access to certain 'treatments' for a 'mental illness'. A refusal to provide a diagnosis can result in my client having no access to otherwise available support. These are the dilemmas faced by psychologists in practice even before they consider the use of psychometric measures in their assessment and ongoing evaluation of a client.

How might providing a diagnosis assist with treatment in clinical settings?

As stated previously, the provision of a formal diagnosis within mental health settings is usually the *required* first step towards access to treatment. For example, an individual who has not been formally assessed and diagnosed with depression is unlikely to be able to access ongoing psychological and psychiatric services. Without a formal assessment and diagnosis of a learning disability an individual with a learning disability will not have access to support within the community. Access to services and funding for treatment, whether within the NHS or via medical insurance, is often what is being sought by the client, so diagnosis, to all intents and purposes, provides the access which would otherwise be denied in a system which at present has a medically based way of seeing 'disorders'.

IMPROVING THE RELIABILITY OF ASSESSMENT AND DIAGNOSIS

Indeed, as a scientist practitioner I am aware research has indicated that where particular symptoms are *required* to be observed by clinicians, making diagnostic decisions has increased agreement between clinicians when they are making a formal diagnosis (American Psychiatric Association, 1994, p. xi; Spitzer, Endicott & Robins, 1978). This is the strongest evidence-based argument for the use of standardised assessment methods, including psychometrics, as a contribution to standardised methods of determining diagnosis. Research evidence shows that use of formal diagnostic categories allows clinicians, even those from different professional groups or training backgrounds, to communicate with each other using a common language and understanding of diagnosis, which in turn benefits their clients.

Research studies have already indicated the imprecision and unreliability of traditional clinic interviews. Such unreliability and lack of correlation between the subjective (if clinically experienced) judgement of psychologists and psychiatrists can result in confusion for the client and confuse the selection of the most appropriate treatment plan. Structured interviews have been shown to provide a far higher level of reliability and correlation between professionals (Miller, 2001). A high level of reliability and correlation between professionals benefits clients as it allows the selection of an evidence-based treatment plan. Indeed, guidelines on the selection of evidence-based treatments, such as *What Works for Whom?* (Roth & Fonagy, 2005) or the National Institute for Health and Care Excellence guidelines (NICE, 2016), have an underlying assumption of carefully completed assessment and formally made diagnosis using accepted, agreed criteria. In turn, the monitoring and appraisal of outcomes, and thus the perceived measure of the success of any particular treatment approach, are part of this rather circular process of validation; that is, we confirm diagnosis by using psychometric measures and the psychometric measures confirm the usefulness of both the diagnosis and the treatment provided.

The use of psychometrics adds further to this sense of the reliability of and correlation between professional judgements by allowing the rapid yet in-depth exploration of presenting difficulties. Most interestingly, the use of psychometrics has the advantage of exploring issues the psychologist may not be able to observe directly and which the client has not presented for assessment even though they are significant for an understanding of the bigger picture.

In my own practice I use a three-stage model of assessment for the purpose of diagnosis, as well as clinical formulation and treatment planning. Such a three-stage assessment, using free-flowing narrative, a semi-structured interview (for identifying specific difficulties, symptoms and matching categories required for a diagnosis) and psychometric measures might be described as the 'gold standard' method of clinical assessment. This three-stage process allows the integration of evidence-based practice with working with the client, so that both the individual, as the client, and I, as the clinician, are working together, learning as we proceed along the path of diagnosis, treatment and recovery. Three-stage assessment has long been recognised as particularly important in the context of psychological assessments in the court arena (Scott & Sembi, 2002), where reliability is paramount.

Free-flowing narrative

Although not the focus of this chapter, the importance of hearing the client's own description of their life, their current difficulties and their own understanding of what is happening cannot be overemphasised. There is always a danger in using psychometrics as one part of an assessment of the clinician losing sight of the human being before them. There is a danger of becoming increasingly focused upon having the client complete the test in order to 'discover' the results, believing these represent the client more accurately than the client themselves. Listening to and sharing the understandings is the essential first step to any assessment in which the clinician and the client work together to form a shared, agreed understanding of the presenting issues, even when the client is attempting to present themselves in a pleasing or a negative light.

Semi-structured interviews

The second stage of the three-stage assessment process in clinical practice is the semi-structured interview, if it is appropriate. Semi-structured interviews are used as a means of standardising the questions used in an initial therapeutic or diagnostic assessment. The aim of the interview is to standardise the information gathered and the way in which that information is considered. It explores the issues or symptoms in a way that assists the making of decisions on the classification or categorisation of disorders. Commonly used semi-structured interview methods include: the Structured Clinical Interview for DSM-5 (SCID-5) (First, 2014); the Clinician-Administered PTSD Scale (CAPS) originally developed by Turner & Lee (Turner & Lee, 1998) and now replaced by CAPS-5 (Weathers, Marx, Friedman & Schnurr, 2014); and the Hare Psychopathy Checklist – Revised (PCL-R) (Hare, 2003), often used in clinical forensic settings.

Research has shown that the use of such semi-structured and structured interviews gives better reliability of data collection and between raters regarding diagnostic decisions than free-flowing narrative and clinician 'experience' (Falloon et al., 2005; Miller et al., 2001; Miller, 2001; Miller, 2002). Considered carefully, this finding is not surprising. The semi-structured interview questions are created using the currently existing diagnostic criteria 'checklists', which assist in preventing pertinent information from being overlooked. However, such highly structured questions may also prevent the gathering of information which falls outside the usual 'diagnostic criteria'. Hence the importance of the free narrative as the first stage of the assessment, when the clinician uses their training and experience to listen carefully for issues relevant to classification and, most importantly, to the client themselves.

Tests used in clinical practice

The third and final stage of a thorough assessment comprises psychometric tests, but only where appropriate. The fact that the use of a psychometric test is routine, or simply available, in one's practice setting is not a sufficient reason to choose it. Thought must be given to whether the client's personal history, ethnicity, culture and educational opportunity (amongst other things) match the population on which the proposed test was standardised. Without such consideration the client's psychometric results are likely to misrepresent their true condition and thus any clinical decisions made are likely to be flawed. For example, a mood measure such as the Beck Depression Inventory, standardised on Western European or North American populations, is unlikely to be appropriate for a Chinese male who has only recently arrived in the West. Understanding of mood, of the acceptable expression of emotion and of the recognition of the need of the individual self rather than the collective community varies in different cultures. The use of any psychometric measure through the agency of an interpreter must also raise a high degree of concern as to whether the answers obtained reflect the true answers of the client, and whether the results have any meaning because of translation difficulties as well as cultural difficulties. The clinician must take care to include the *crucial* but often neglected step of carefully selecting the most appropriate test measure for their client. For the selection of *any* test measure the practitioner should consider a number of key questions:

1. Does the client match the norm population on which the test was developed?
2. Is the client able to engage in the test process directly or do they need assistance?
3. To what extent will this assistance influence possible responses to questions, making them less reliable?
4. Might the possible results of the test cause harm to the client rather than assist?

While it is beyond the remit of this chapter to describe and review all the test measures used within clinical practice, I consider a number of widely used measures for adults along with concerns about their use. Assessments of children, older adults and other special populations such as those in forensic settings require their own specialist measures.

Measures of affect (mood state)

In mental health services the most widely used psychometrics are self-report measures of affect, questionnaires which ask the client to rate how they have been feeling during the past two weeks. These measures give an indication of emotional state (rather than a long-lasting trait) and the two-week period is chosen so that the questions used correlate closely to the requirements of a diagnosis from DSM. Such measures are developed and validated within clinical populations in order to determine cut-off scores that indicate the likelihood of the presence of particular mood states which are likely to be problematic and likely to respond to treatment. Widely used measures of mood include the Beck Depression Inventory-II, the Beck Anxiety Inventory-II, the Generalised Anxiety Disorder-7, the Patient Health Questionnaire-9 and the Clinical Outcomes Routine Evaluation (CORE).

These measures of affect are frequently used to track the client's current mood state and thus to evaluate the effectiveness of treatment as it progresses within therapeutic treatment settings. In the UK one of the most widely used measures of psychological state is CORE, usually used to measure distress or symptoms and then provide reliable outcome measures (CORE-OM) (Barkham et al., 1998). (Detailed information on this is available from www.coreims.co.uk.) However, while CORE is a widely used means of measuring mood state, progress of therapy and outcomes within the NHS there is widespread criticism of how it has been implemented. Even those involved in the development of such measures have expressed concern. Chris Evans (2013) describes the weekly use of a self-report outcome measure as 'power steering for psychotherapy' and suggests, rather like Gergen et al. speaking of diagnosis, that it is 'merely an anxiety-reducing device' for the clinician. He also considers that the outcome measures may distract attention from the other, rich levels of communication available within the therapeutic relationship, using what might be described as qualitative rather than quantitative information. Other criticisms of the use of self-report mood measures as a means of case management have been: of their use to pre-screen clients in order to decide who receives treatment (how can we be sure who actually completed the mood measure form?); of the reliability of such measures when the client is likely to wish to please the therapist; and of the reliability of such measures when the therapist is under scrutiny for payment by results and the assumption may be made that no 'improvement' in scores means the therapist is not working hard enough.

Ability assessments

Measures of ability are used to compare an individual with others in the same age range. They are described as measures of maximum performance, as they are designed to take the client through tasks arranged in order of difficulty until they are no longer able to complete them correctly. Ability measures are used to assess intelligence and memory as well as achievement in areas such as reading, writing and mathematical ability. The most widely used ability and achievement scales are the Wechsler Scales, but in the UK the Ravens Progressive Matrices and the British Ability Scales are also widely used.

Within clinical practice the usual reason for measuring ability is that it is suspected the client suffers from a learning disability, a particular learning difficulty or a neuropsychological difficulty. For the assessment of a learning disability the British Psychological Society have published guidelines (British Psychological Society, 2000) which emphasise the importance of considering adaptive, social functioning alongside intellectual functioning. The inclusion of adaptive social functioning encourages the consideration of how the client copes on a day-to-day basis with the demands of their daily environment. Measures of adaptive behaviour include the Adaptive Behaviour Assessment System (ABAS-3) and the Vineland

Adaptive Behaviour Scales (Vineland-II). As always the clinician has many ethical issues to consider, such as the educational, social and economic influences on an individual's cognitive test results, their daily life and the potential impact on the client of being recognised as learning-disabled.

Neuropsychology

Neuropsychological assessment is regarded as a highly specialist area of psychological assessment, although in practice many applied psychologists do use neuropsychological skills. Neuropsychological measures such as the Repeatable Battery for the Assessment of Neuropsychological Status Update (RBANS™ Update), the Delis–Kaplan Executive Function System (D–KEFS), the California Verbal Learning Test (CVLT-II) are widely used in addition to the usual ability and achievement measures. Often such neuropsychological assessment can provide a more in-depth, detailed interpretation of presenting difficulties which may have resulted from brain injury or illness. Commonly neuropsychological results are considered in terms of domains (such as language ability, visual-spatial ability, impulse control, emotional lability) rather than individual test score results, allowing a clearer picture to be presented of the client being assessed. However, there has been some criticism of the usefulness of many neuropsychological assessments in that the results are often not made available to fellow professionals or, perhaps most importantly, to the client, in a useful, meaningful manner. It is argued by Tad Gorske and others that neuropsychology needs to move towards a humanistic, collaborative method of assessment and feedback to make its true contribution (Gorske, 2008; Gorske & Smith, 2008).

Personality assessments (trait)

Personality measures are probably the least used measures within general clinical practice, and yet they can provide rich materials with which to work collaboratively in a therapeutic setting. Commonly used personality measures are the Myers–Briggs Type Indicator (MBTI), the Millon Clinical Multiaxial Inventory-III (MCMI-III) (version IV is now available, which relates to the requirements of DSM-5), the NEO Personality Inventory Revised (NEO PI-R), the Personality Assessment Inventory (PAI) and the Minnesota Multiphasic Personality Inventory-2 (MMPI-2). Discussion with the client of the results and their meaning should be a core part of any collaborative assessment. The MBTI, the Millon and the NEO PI-R are probably the most client-friendly, and therefore the most supportive of collaborative working. The in-depth information available from personality tests can be used to confirm what the client already knows about themselves, but also to reveal to the client information previously unavailable to them about how others might interpret their attitudes and behaviours. This may help provide an insight into, for example, present relationship conflicts which are part of their presenting difficulties and so become the focus of therapy.

The usual cautions apply to personality tests regarding the matching of the client to the population upon which the test was developed and normed. In particular, the clinician should consider cultural and social issues which may influence how someone's personality is measured against the dominant cultural norms. Psychologists must consider the evidence base for the personality tests. There is strong criticism of older tests such as the MBTI and the MMPI, in particular for their early lack of a science base and for not being based upon the Big Five personality theory (Furnham, 1996; Lewin, 1984; McCrae and Costa, 1989). It is generally accepted that there is strong theoretical and research support for those personality tests based upon the Big Five personality theory. This suggests that clinicians should prefer the use of the Big Five based measures to that of older, less evidence-based measures.

WEIGHING THE INFORMATION

Most test manuals contain the following standard warning:

> The interpretive information contained in this report should be viewed as only one source of hypotheses about the individual being evaluated. No decisions should be based solely on the information contained in this report. This material should be integrated with all other sources of information in reaching professional decisions about this individual.

This is a vital reminder to all clinicians not to prioritise test results over information gained from the client, from other sources of information and from the semi-structured interview. The clinician's training and experience are important in assisting them to weigh all the information as a whole before drawing any conclusions to assist with diagnosis, formulation or both. In my experience the collaborative approach to assessment and feedback encourages this weighing of information and allows the client to feel fully participant in the process even if the clinician and the client agree to disagree on some matters. This collaborative working is counter to the other warning placed at the beginning of most psychometric reports:

> This report is confidential and intended for use by qualified professionals only. It should not be released to the individual being evaluated.

CONCLUSIONS

I have written previously, 'The basis of any psychometric assessment is the measure of individual difference. Each individual is viewed as unique and from this comes the conclusion that each individual has a combination of abilities and traits which, if described accurately, would describe this uniqueness' (Van Scoyoc, 2010, p. 613). The clinician is seeking to understand and then work therapeutically with a unique individual who has sought assistance. The use of tests can help with this process only when the client feels the tests are a useful tool that they too can benefit from, rather than something that is being 'done to' them. American psychologists such as Stephen E. Finn and Constance T. Fischer have pioneered an approach to psychometric assessment within therapeutic practice which emphasises the humanistic, collaborative way of working (Finn, Fischer & Handler, 2012). Such an approach encourages both the clinician and the client to make the best of their clinical encounters and avoids the loss of the human being seeking therapeutic help to a simplistic diagnostic label. This approach to the use of psychometric measures within a clinical setting should be our goal even when we feel pressured within the workplace to forget the unique human being before us.

REFERENCES

American Psychiatric Association (1994). *Diagnostic criteria from DSM-IV*. Washington, DC: American Psychiatric Association.

Barkham, M., Evans, C., Margison, F., Mcgrath, G., Mellor-Clark, J., Milne, D. & Connell, J. (1998). The rationale for developing and implementing core outcome batteries for routine use in service settings and psychotherapy outcome research. *Journal of Mental Health*, 7(1), 35–47.

British Psychological Society (2000). *Learning disability: Definitions and contexts*. Leicester: British Psychological Society.

Evans, C. (2013). The danger of trading measures but not meeting distressed minds: 'Outcome' measurement in MH and psychological therapies. Paper presented at the Medical Psychotherapy Faculty Annual Residential Meeting: A joint conference of the Royal College of Psychiatrists and the Royal College of General Practitioners, Stratford-upon-Avon, 17–19 April. http://www.psyctc.org/talks/2013/20130417_RCPsych_Faculty_talk.pdf. Accessed 15 October 2016.

Falloon, I. R. H., Mizuno, M., Murakami, M., Roncone, R., Unoka, Z., Harangozo, J. et al. (2005). Structured assessment of current mental state in clinical practice: An international study of the reliability and validity of the Current Psychiatric State interview, CPS-50. *Acta Psychiatrica Scandinavica*, 111(1), 44–50.

First, M. B. (2014). *Structured Clinical Interview for DSM-5 (SCID-5) Research Version*. Washington, DC: American Psychiatric Association.

Finn, S. E., Fischer, C. T. & Handler, L. (2012). *Collaborative/therapeutic assessment: A casebook and guide*. Hoboken, NJ: John Wiley & Sons.

Foucault, M. (2013). *History of madness* (trans. J. Murphy & J. Khalfa). London: Routledge.

Furnham, A. (1996). The big five versus the big four: The relationship between the Myers–Briggs Type Indicator (MBTI) and NEO-PI five factor model of personality. *Personality and Individual Differences*, 21(2), 303–7.

Gergen, K. J., Hoffman, L. & Anderson, H. (1996). Is diagnosis a disaster? A constructionist trialogue. In F. W. Kaslow (ed.), *Handbook of relational diagnosis and dysfunctional family patterns* (pp. 102–18). Chichester: Wiley.

Gorske, T. T. (2008). Therapeutic neuropsychological assessment: A humanistic model and case example. *Journal of Humanistic Psychology*, 48(3), 320–39.

Gorske, T. T. & Smith, S. R. (2008). *Collaborative therapeutic neuropsychological assessment*. New York: Springer.

Hare, R. D. (2003). *Hare Psychopathy Checklist – Revised* (2nd edn). Toronto: Multi-Health Systems.

Lazare, A. (1976). The psychiatric examination in the walk-in clinic: Hypothesis generation and hypothesis testing. *Archives of General Psychiatry*, 33(1), 96–102.

Lewin, M. (1984). Psychology measures femininity and masculinity: From '13 gay men' to the instrumental-expressive distinction. In M. Lewin (ed.), *In the shadow of the past: Psychology portrays the sexes: A social and intellectual history* (pp. 179–204). New York: Columbia University Press.

McCrae, R. R., & Costa, P. T., Jr (1989). Reinterpreting the Myers–Briggs Type Indicator from the perspective of the five-factor model of personality. *Journal of Personality*, 57(1), 17–40.

Miller, P. R. (2001). Inpatient diagnostic assessments: 2. Interrater reliability and outcomes of structured vs. unstructured interviews. *Psychiatry Research*, 105(3), 265–71.

Miller, P. R. (2002). Inpatient diagnostic assessments: 3. Causes and effects of diagnostic imprecision. *Psychiatry Research*, 111(2), 191–7.

Miller, P. R., Dasher, R., Collins, R., Griffiths, P. & Brown, F. (2001). Inpatient diagnostic assessments: 1. Accuracy of structured vs. unstructured interviews. *Psychiatry Research*, 105(3), 255–64.

NICE (2016). 'Find guidance.' https://www.nice.org.uk/guidance/conditions-and-diseases/mental-health-and-behavioural-conditions.

Pilgrim, D. (2007). The survival of psychiatric diagnosis. *Social Science and Medicine*, 65(3), 536–44.

Pilgrim, D. (2009). Abnormal psychology: Unresolved ontological and epistemological contestation. *History and Philosophy of Psychology*, 10(2), 11–21.

Roth, A. & Fonagy, P. (2005). *What Works for Whom? A Critical Review of Psychotherapy Research* (2nd edn). New York: Guilford Press.

Scott, M. J. & Sembi, S. (2002). Unreliable assessment in civil litigation. *The Psychologist*, 15(2), 80–1.

Spitzer, R. L., Endicott, J. & Robins, E. (1978). Research diagnostic criteria: Rationale and reliability. *Archives of General Psychiatry*, 35(6), 773–82.

Strawbridge, S. (2010). Prologue: Telling stories. In S. Corrie & D. Lane (eds), *Constructing stories, telling tales: A guide to formulation in applied psychology* (pp. i–xxx). London: Karnac.

Turner, S. & Lee, D. (1998). *Measures in post traumatic stress disorder: A practitioner's guide*. Windsor: NFER-Nelson.

Van Scoyoc, S. (2010). The collaborative use of psychometric assessment. In S. Strawbridge, R. Woolfe, B. Douglas & W. Dryden (eds), *Handbook of counselling psychology* (3rd edn, pp. 611–29). London: SAGE Publications.

Weathers, F. W., Marx, B. P., Friedman, M. J. & Schnurr, P. P. (2014). Posttraumatic stress disorder in DSM-5: New criteria, new measures, and implications for assessment. *Psychological Injury and Law*, 7(2), 93–107.

14 Measuring the Dark Side
Adrian Furnham

INTRODUCTION

It is uncertain whether he was the first to coin the term, but it was Robert Hogan who made the concept of 'the dark side' popular in the psychometric community. With his initial suite of three instruments he talked about measuring the 'bright' side (normal personality functioning), the 'dark' side (the personality disorders) and the 'in' side (motives and values).

It is due to that brilliant insight of Robert and Joyce Hogan in the 1990s that it has become possible to describe, explain and predict a good deal of management derailment in terms of the psychiatric personality disorders conceptual system. Further, by developing a measure called the Hogan Developmental Survey (HDS) they made research in this area possible. There are, however, other measures, like the Dark Triad.

The dark side has come to be known as a marker of derailment at work. Over the last 20 years there has been a growing interest in leadership derailment. The spectacular fall from grace of a number of executives, particularly in the banking sector, has made selectors interested in trying to detect those that might derail.

THE PERSONALITY DISORDERS

Psychologists are interested in personality traits, psychiatrists in personality disorders. Psychologists interested in personality have made great strides in describing, taxonomising and explaining the mechanisms and processes in normal personality functioning. Psychiatrists also talk about personality functioning. They talk about personality disorders that are typified by early onset (recognisable in children and adolescents), pervasive effects (on all aspects of life) and with relatively poor prognosis (that is, they are difficult to cure).

Both argue that the personality factors relate to *cognitive, affective and social aspects of functioning*. It is where a person's behaviour deviates markedly from the expectations of the individual's culture that the disorder is manifested. The psychiatric manual is very clear that 'odd behaviour' is not simply an expression of habits, customs, religious or political values professed or shown by a people of particular cultural origin.

Over the years psychiatrists have made great strides in clarifying and specifying diagnostic criteria and these can be found in the various editions of the *Diagnostic and Statistical Manual of Mental Disorders* (DSM). The criteria have changed over the years and the manual is now in its fifth edition. Some disorders have 'disappeared', like 'passive aggressive'.

Psychiatrists and psychologists share some simple assumptions with respect to personality. Both argue for the *stability* of personality. The DSM criteria talk of 'enduring pattern', 'inflexible and pervasive', 'stable and of long duration'. The DSM manuals note that personality orders all have an onset no later than early adulthood. Moreover, there are some gender differences: thus the anti-social disorder is more likely to be diagnosed in men while the borderline, histrionic and dependent personalities are more likely to be found in women.

The manuals are at pains to point out that some of the personality disorders look like other disorders: anxiety, mood, psychotic, substance-related, etc., but have unique features. The essence of the argument is that 'Personality Disorders must be distinguished from personality traits that do not reach the threshold for a Personality Disorder. Personality traits are diagnosed as a Personality Disorder only when they are inflexible, maladaptive, and persisting and cause significant functional impairment or subjective distress' (American Psychiatric Association, 2014, p. 633).

One of the most important ways to differentiate personal style from personality disorder is flexibility. There are lots of difficult people at work but relatively few whose rigid, maladaptive behaviours mean they continually have disruptive, troubled lives. It is their *inflexible, repetitive, poor stress-coping responses* that are marks of disorder.

Personality disorders influence the *sense of self* – the way people think and feel about themselves and how other people see them. The disorders often powerfully influence *interpersonal relations at work*. They reveal themselves in how people 'complete tasks, take and/or give orders, make decisions, plan, handle external and internal demands, take or give criticism, obey rules, take and delegate responsibility, and co-operate with people' (Oldham & Morris, 1991, p. 24). The anti-social, obsessive, compulsive, passive-aggressive and dependent types are particularly problematic in the work place.

People with personality disorders have difficulty expressing and understanding emotions. It is the intensity with which they express them and their variability that makes them odd. More importantly, they often have serious problems with self-control.

Many other researchers have been influenced by the usefulness of the DSM classification of the personality disorders. In order to explain and describe these disorders, other writers have changed the names to make them easier to interpret to a wider audience. Table 14.1 shows the labels given by different authors.

Table 14.1 *Different labels for the personality disorders*

DSM-IV personality disorder	Hogan & Hogan (1997)	Oldham & Morris (1991)	Miller (2008)	Dotlich & Cairo (2003)	Moscoso & Salgado (2004)
Borderline	Excitable	Mercurial	Reactors	Volatility	Ambivalent
Paranoid	Sceptical	Vigilant	Vigilantes	Habitual	Suspicious
Avoidant	Cautious	Sensitive	Shrinkers	Excessive caution	Shy
Schizoid	Reserved	Solitary	Oddballs	Aloof	Lone
Passive-aggressive	Leisurely	Leisurely	Spoilers	Passive resistance	Pessimistic

DSM-IV personality disorder	Hogan & Hogan (1997)	Oldham & Morris (1991)	Miller (2008)	Dotlich & Cairo (2003)	Moscoso & Salgado (2004)
Narcissistic	Bold	Self-confident	Preeners	Arrogance	Egocentric
Anti-social	Mischievous	Adventurous	Predators	Mischievous	Risky
Histrionic	Colourful	Dramatic	Emoters	Melodramatic	Cheerful
Schizotypal	Imaginative	Idiosyncratic	Creativity and vision	Eccentric	Eccentric
Obsessive-compulsive	Diligent	Conscientious	Detailers	Perfectionistic	Reliable
Dependent	Dutiful	Devoted	Clingers	Eager to please	Submitted

There is a higher-order threefold classification based on both theory and research (Table 14.2). This makes things a little easier as one can concentrate on three rather than ten to 13 disorders.

Table 14.2 *The higher-order classification of the personality disorders*

DSM	Horney	Hogan
Cluster A (odd disorders)	**Moving away from people**	**Moving away from people**
Paranoid personality disorder: characterised by a pattern of irrational suspicion and mistrust of others, interpreting motivations as malevolent	The need for **self-sufficiency** and independence; while most desire some autonomy, the neurotic may simply wish to discard other individuals entirely	Excitable Moody and hard to please; intense but short-lived enthusiasm for people, projects or things Sceptical Cynical, distrustful and doubting others' intentions
Schizoid personality disorder: lack of interest and detachment from social relationships, apathy and restricted emotional expression	The need for **perfection**; while many are driven to perfect their lives in the form of well-being, the neurotic may display a fear of being even slightly flawed	Cautious Reluctant to take risks for fear of being rejected or negatively evaluated Reserved Aloof, detached and uncommunicative; lacking interest in or awareness of the feelings of others
Schizotypal personality disorder: a pattern of extreme discomfort interacting socially, distorted cognitions and perceptions	Lastly, the need to **restrict life practices** to within narrow borders, to live as inconspicuous a life as possible	Leisurely Independent; ignoring people's requests and becoming irritated or argumentative if they persist

(Continued)

Table 14.2 *Continued*

DSM	Horney	Hogan
Cluster B (dramatic, emotional or erratic disorders) **Anti-social personality disorder:** a pervasive pattern of disregard for and violation of the rights of others, lack of empathy, bloated self-image, manipulative and impulsive behaviour **Borderline personality disorder:** pervasive pattern of instability in relationships, self-image, identity, behaviour and affects often leading to self-harm and impulsivity **Histrionic personality disorder:** pervasive pattern of attention-seeking behaviour and excessive emotions **Narcissistic personality disorder:** a pervasive pattern of grandiosity, need for admiration, and a lack of empathy	**Moving against people** The need for **power**; the ability to bend wills and achieve control over others – while most persons seek strength, the neurotic may be desperate for it The need to **exploit others**, to get the better of them, to become manipulative, fostering the belief that people are there simply to be used The need for **social recognition**, prestige and limelight The need for **personal admiration** for both inner and outer qualities – to be valued The need for **personal achievement**; though virtually all persons wish to achieve, like No. 3, the neurotic may be desperate for achievement	**Moving against people** Bold Unusually self-confident; feelings of grandiosity and entitlement; overvaluation of one's capabilities Mischievous Enjoying risk taking and testing the limits; needing excitement; manipulative, deceitful, cunning and exploitative Colourful Expressive, animated and dramatic; wanting to be noticed and needing to be the centre of attention Imaginative Acting and thinking in creative and sometimes odd or unusual ways
Cluster C (anxious or fearful disorders) **Avoidant personality disorder:** pervasive feelings of social inhibition and inadequacy, extreme sensitivity to negative evaluation **Dependent personality disorder:** pervasive psychological need to be cared for by other people **Obsessive-compulsive personality disorder (not the same as obsessive-compulsive disorder):** characterised by rigid conformity to rules, perfectionism and control	**Moving towards people** The need for **affection and approval**; pleasing others and being liked by them. The need for **a partner**, one whom they can love and who will solve all problems	**Moving towards people** Diligent Meticulous, precise and perfectionistic; inflexible about rules and procedures; critical of others Dutiful Eager to please and reliant on others for support and guidance; reluctant to take independent action or to go against popular opinion

MEASURING THE PERSONALITY DISORDERS

There has been much debate concerning the definition, conceptualisation, occurrence and assessment of the personality disorders. The greatest change in the way PDs were described occurred in the move from DSM-IV (American Psychiatric Association, 2000) to DSM-5 (American Psychiatric Association, 2014), proposing dimensional alternatives for the DSM-IV categorical diagnoses (Widiger, Livesley & Clark, 2009). On the other hand, there is a great deal of activity developing and validating new instruments like the Personality Inventory for DSM-5 (PID-5) (Krueger, Derringer, Markon, Watson & Skodol, 2012). This new trait model, the diagnosis and assessment of categorical PDs, is primarily advocated in the official nomenclature of the American Psychiatric Association.

Whereas clinical psychologists have been treating patients with one or more PDs and co-occurring pathology, industrial and organisational psychologists have been running career development programmes to coach people on how to deal with the dark sides of their personality. A common need for all these professional groups is well-designed and psychometrically sound assessment instruments. In addition, they need criteria to choose among the different instruments currently available.

In a critical and comprehensive review Furnham, Milner, Akhtar and De Fruyt (2014) attempted a systematic review of current PD measures together with a decision tree to choose among them (see Figure 14.1). They noted that over the years a large number of

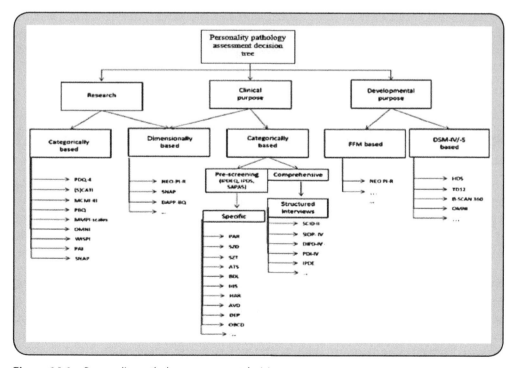

Figure 14.1 *Personality pathology assessment decision tree*

measures have been devised for research and practice. They also pointed out that the available PD measures differed on at least four major characteristics.

First, some instruments attempt to be comprehensive and measure *all* of the PDs currently (or previously) thought to exist. Some describe disorders that others discount, but the usual number is around 10–15 disorders. However, some instruments set out simply to measure *one* very specific disorder.

Second, there seem to be four common methods to assess the PDs: structured diagnostic interviews, rating instruments for clinicians, self-report questionnaires and other-report questionnaires (Friedman, Oltmanns & Turkheimer, 2007). Thus, two use observer data (clinician, family) and two use self-report data approaches to measurement. By far the most common methods, however, are questionnaires and structured interviews.

Third, some measures are about subtypes of the PD in the sense that they are multidimensional measures that yield scores on different, but related, facets of the disorder. For example, some measures and theorists may distinguish between grandiose and vulnerable, or communal and agentic Narcissistic PD (NPD) (Gebauer, Sedikides, Verplanken & Maio, 2012). Most measures, however, mimic DSM-5 categorical criteria and are not about the distinctions among subtypes of a specific PD.

Fourth, PD measures have been developed for essentially five target groups of users. The first group comprises clinicians attempting a reliable and valid diagnosis of a PD. The second is a related group, namely academic researchers who may be testing theories of the aetiology or prognosis of a PD after treatment. Industrial and organisational psychologists form a third professional group interested in evaluating aberrant personality and subclinical forms of personality pathology in the context of personnel selection or career coaching and development. Finally, there are two other groups, namely 'lay people' who may be interested in self-diagnosis, and relatives of those with a specific PD requiring information about its symptoms and prognosis.

In the review Furnham et al. (2014) documented 22 measures (interview and questionnaire) of all the PDs as well as some designed to measure the specific disorders. Interestingly, these tests differed considerably for each disorder. For instance, there are seven for Borderline, none for Avoidant and nine for Narcissistic.

There continues to be an interest in, and development of, instruments in this area.

THE HOGAN DEVELOPMENT SURVEY (HDS)

Perhaps the most widely used measure for the dark side is the HDS. The HDS contains 168 true/false items that assess dysfunctional interpersonal themes. These dysfunctional dispositions reflect one's distorted beliefs about others that emerge when one encounters stress or stops considering how one's actions affect others. Over time, these dispositions may become associated with one, affect one's reputation and impede job performance and career success.

The HDS is not a medical or clinical assessment. It does not measure personality disorders, which are manifestations of mental disorder. Instead, the HDS assesses self-defeating expressions of normal personality. The DSM-5 (American Psychiatric Association, 2014, p. 647) makes this same distinction between behavioural traits and disorders – self-defeating behaviours, such as those predicted by the HDS, come and go depending on the context. In contrast, personality disorders are enduring and pervasive across contexts.

The HDS is now extensively used in organisational research and practice to measure dysfunctional personality in the 'normal population' (Furnham, 2006, 2008; Furnham & Crump, 2005; Hogan & Hogan, 1997). Its aim is partly to help selectors, executive coaches, management development consultants and individuals diagnose how they typically react under work stress. It has the advantages of being psychometrically valid, of measuring all the personality disorder categories in DSM-IV and of being appropriate for a 'normal' population.

The HDS focuses only on the core construct of each disorder from a dimensional perspective (Hogan & Hogan, 2001, p. 41). It has been cross-validated with the MMPI personality disorder scales. Correlations (n = 140) range from 0.45 for Mischievous to 0.67 for Excitable (Hogan & Hogan, 2001). Fico, Hogan and Hogan (2000) report coefficient alphas between 0.50 and 0.70 with an average of 0.64 and test–retest reliabilities (n = 60) over a three-month interval ranging from 0.50 to 0.80, with an average of 0.68. There were no mean-level differences between sexes, racial/ethnic groups, or younger versus older persons (Hogan & Hogan, 2001) though Furnham and Trickey (2011) did find evidence of sex differences. Various relatively small-scale studies have used the HDS and have shown it to be a robust, reliable and valid instrument (De Fruyt et al., 2009; Furnham, 2006; Furnham & Crump, 2005; Khoo & Burch, 2008; Rolland & De Fruyt, 2003).

The latest advance of the HDS is to develop facets for each of the scales. This will inevitably lead to a finer-grained analysis of the different concepts and a better understanding of how the process works. Table 14.3 shows these facets.

Table 14.3 *Subscale names, definitions and sample items*

HDS Subscale	Definition	Sample Item
Excitable: Volatile	Moody, often angered or annoyed, easily upset and hard to soothe.	I can get angry quickly.
Excitable: Easily disappointed	Initial passion for people and projects, who inevitably disappoint, and passion then turns to rejection.	Few people have met my expectations.
Excitable: No direction	Lacking few well-defined beliefs or interests, but with regrets about past behavior.	Sometimes I am not sure what I really believe.
Skeptical: Cynical	Prone to doubt others' intentions and assume they have bad ulterior motives.	When someone does me a favor, I wonder what he/she wants.
Skeptical: Mistrusting	Generalized mistrust of people and institutions; being alert for signs of perceived mistreatment.	People who are in charge will take advantage of you if you let them.
Skeptical: Grudges	Holding grudges and being unwilling to forgive real or perceived wrongs.	There are some people I will never forgive.

(Continued)

Table 14.3 *Continued*

HDS Subscale	Definition	Sample Item
Cautious: Avoidant	Avoiding new people and situations to avoid imagined potential embarrassment.	I feel awkward around strangers.
Cautious: Fearful	Afraid of being criticized for making mistakes and being reluctant to act independently or make decisions.	People sometimes think I am timid.
Cautious: Unassertive	Unwilling to act assertively and therefore prone to being overlooked or ignored.	People tell me I'm not assertive enough.
Reserved: Introverted	Valuing one's private time and preferring to work alone.	I consider myself a loner.
Reserved: Unsocial	Keeping others at a distance, limiting close relationships, and being generally detached.	I prefer to keep people at a distance.
Reserved: Tough	Indifferent to the feelings and problems of others, focused on tasks rather than people.	Other people's problems don't concern me.
Leisurely: Passive aggressive	Overtly pleasant and compliant but privately resentful and subversive regarding requests for improved performance.	I sometimes put off doing things for people I don't like.
Leisurely: Unappreciated	Believing that one's talents and contributions are ignored; perceiving inequities in assigned workloads.	People at work expect me to do everything.
Leisurely: Irritated	Privately but easily irritated by interruptions, requests, or work-related suggestions.	It irritates me to be interrupted when I am working on something.
Bold: Entitled	Feeling that one has special gifts and accomplishments and, consequently, deserves special treatment.	I would never take a job that is beneath me.
Bold: Overconfidence	Unusually confident in one's abilities; belief that one will succeed at anything one chooses to undertake.	I do many things better than almost everyone I know.
Bold: Fantasized talent	Believing that one has unusual talents and gifts and that one has been born for greatness.	I was born to do great things.

HDS Subscale	Definition	Sample Item
Mischievous: Risky	Prone to taking risks and testing limits; deliberately bending or breaking inconvenient rules.	I try things that other people think are too risky.
Mischievous: Impulsive	Tending to act impulsively without considering the long-term consequences of one's actions.	I often do things on the spur of the moment.
Mischievous: Manipulative	Machiavellian tendencies – using charm to manipulate others and feeling no remorse about doing so.	When I want to get my way, I know how to 'turn on the charm.'
Colorful: Public confidence	Expecting others to find one's public performances fascinating and not knowing when to be quiet.	In a group, I am often the center of attention.
Colorful: Distractible	Easily distracted, minimal focus, needing constant stimulation, confusing activity with productivity.	I like to have several things going on at the same time.
Colorful: Self-display	Wanting to be the center of attention and using dramatic costumes and gestures to attract attention to oneself.	I sometimes dress so as to stand out from the crowd.
Imaginative: Eccentric	Expressing unusual views that can be either creative or merely strange; tendency to be absorbed in these ideas.	People describe me as unconventional.
Imaginative: Special sensitivity	Believing that one has special abilities to see things others don't and understand things others can't.	I sometimes feel I have special talents and abilities.
Imaginative: Creative thinking	Believing that one is unusually creative; easily bored and confident in one's imaginative problem-solving ability.	Many of my ideas are ahead of their time.
Diligent: Standards	Having exceptionally high standards of performance for oneself and others.	I have high standards for my performance at work.
Diligent: Perfectionistic	Perfectionistic about the quality of work products and obsessed with the details of their completion.	I tend to be a perfectionist about my work.

(Continued)

Table 14.3 *Continued*

HDS Subscale	Definition	Sample Item
Diligent: Organized	Meticulous and inflexible about schedules, timing, and rules and procedures.	I am fussy about schedules and timing.
Dutiful: Indecisive	Overly reliant on others for advice and reluctant to make decisions or act independently.	On important issues, I dislike making decisions on my own.
Dutiful: Ingratiating	Excessively eager to please one's superiors, telling them what they want to hear, and never contradicting them.	There is nothing wrong with flattering your boss.
Dutiful: Conforming	Taking pride in supporting one's superiors and following their orders regardless of one's personal opinion.	I take pride in being a good follower.

THE DARK TRIAD

There is a relatively new area of research into a concept called the 'Dark Triad', which is an individual differences construct proposed by Paulhus and Williams (2002). Since that publication there has been an asymptotic rise in papers, and most of an issue of the journal *Personality and Individual Differences* in 2014, dedicated to it.

Paulhus and Williams (2002) proposed a psychologically coherent triad construct of previously studied unique constructs, namely Narcissism, Machiavellianism and Psychopathy at their subclinical or 'normal' level of functioning. This is in essence the combination of well-known measures and is therefore not an example of the 'jingle-jangle' fallacy.

Of these three constructs Machiavellianism is the only one that is traditionally seen not as a clinical syndrome (i.e., a personality disorder), but rather as a 'normal' personality belief dimension or personal philosophy characterised by cynical, manipulative, expedient and self-interested (rather than principled) behaviour and by cold affect. A measure was derived from a selection of statements from Machiavelli's books and from experimental and correlational work by Christie and Geis (1970) called the Mach-IV inventory.

Narcissism and Psychopathy are constructs traditionally seen as clinical in nature, though there are measures of both at the subclinical level (Hogan & Hogan, 1997). Specifically, they are usually thought of in *DSM IV-TR* as personality disorders. 'Normal' Narcissism was originally operationalised by Raskin and Hall (1979). It is characterised by a grandiose sense of self-worth, entitlement, dominance and superiority. Frequently the construct is measured using the Narcissistic Personality Inventory (NPI) (Raskin & Hall, 1979), though sometimes it is measured using the NPI (Raskin & Terry, 1988), as well as the NPI-16 (Ames, Rose, Anderson & Cameron, 2006).

In the Dark Triad literature psychopathy has been noted as the most 'dangerous' of the three (Paulhus, Williams & Harms, 2001). Subclinical psychopathy manifests itself mainly by high levels of impulsivity and thrill-seeking behaviour along with low levels of empathy and anxiety. The Self-Report Psychopathy (SRP) scale has, at its core, the same four-factor solution as the Psychopathy Check List (Hare, 1991), which is the 'gold standard' for the measurement of psychopathy. It has been validated by Forth, Brown, Hart and Hare (1996) as useful in the assessment of non-forensic samples. The SRP is not the only measurement of subclinical psychopathy used in the Dark Triad research.

The central questions for this new research area are both theoretical and psychometric. The first concerns the conceptual and empirical coherence of the triad as well as evidence for the psychological processes that underlie the Dark Triad. Related to this is the explanation for the aetiology and the Dark Triad. The second question concerns the measurement of the triad, namely the psychometric properties of any instruments used as well as correlates of these measures. Inevitably, the most important psychometric questions are the construct, incremental and predictive validity of measures of the Dark Triad over other measures as well as their individual parts.

At the core of the Dark Triad of personality is a negative relation to the Big Five personality trait Agreeableness (Jonason, Li & Teicher, 2010; Miller et al., 2010; Paulhus & Williams, 2002; Paulhus, Williams & Harms, 2001; Williams, Nathanson & Paulhus, 2010). Individuals who are agreeable in nature are interested in social harmony, while those who are disagreeable manifest characteristics that are anti-social, which is how this personality trait relates to the Dark Triad constructs. All of these sub-facets have been shown to have negative relations to Anti-social Personality Disorder and Narcissism at the clinical level (Widiger, Trull, Clarkin, Sanderson & Costa, 2002). Those scoring low on Agreeableness are described as demanding, clever, flirtatious, charming, shrewd, autocratic; selfish; stubborn, demanding, headstrong, impatient, intolerant, outspoken, hard-hearted; clever, assertive, argumentative, self-confident, aggressive, idealistic; and unstable. This offensive nature helps explain how Machiavellians are able to have a cold affect and be manipulative; narcissists can exude superiority and entitlement; and psychopaths can be unempathetic – all of which are distasteful to more pro-social members of society.

When considering the sub-facets of Agreeableness – trust, straightforwardness, altruism, compliance, modesty and tender-mindedness – and their relationship to anti-social personality disorder and narcissism, two factors emerge as having low scores for both. These defining features are altruism and tender-mindedness. Those that score low on the altruism subscale are somewhat more self-centred and reluctant to get involved in the problems of others, while those that score low on the tender-mindedness subscale are more hard-headed and less moved by appeals to pity and consider themselves realists who make rational decisions based on cold logic.

In the literature pertaining exclusively to the Dark Triad, a substantial number of tests have been implemented in the measurement of the constructs individually or collectively. Of the three constructs, Machiavellianism has only been measured by two different tests: the Mach-IV inventory (Christie & Geis, 1970) and an 18-item adaptation of the Mach-IV inventory (Henning & Six, 2008). Narcissism has been measured using three separate measures: the Narcissistic Personality Inventory (NPI) (Raskin & Hall, 1979; Raskin & Terry, 1988), the Narcissistic Personality Inventory (NPI-16) (Ames, Rose, Anderson & Cameron, 2006), and a modified German version of the Narcissistic Personality Inventory (NPI-d) (von Collani, 2008).

Researches have used a varied mix of measures to assess psychopathy. These measures include the Psychoticism subscale of the Eysenck Personality Questionnaire (PEN) (Eysenck

& Eysenck, 1985), the Self-Report Psychopathy scale II (Hare, 1985), the Self-Report Psychopathy scale III (SRP-III) (Hare, 1985), the Levenson Self-Report Psychopathy Scale (LSRP) (Levenson, Keihl & Fitzpatrick, 1995), the Primary Psychopathy (Levenson, Keihl & Fitzpatrick, 1995), the Psychopathic Personality Inventory (PPI) (Lilienfeld & Andrews, 1996), the Self-Report Psychopathy scale II (SRP II) (Forth et al. 1996), the Self-Report Psychopathy Scale-III (Williams, Nathanson & Paulhus, 2003), the Youth Psychopathic traits Inventory (YPI) (Andershed, Hodgins & Tengström, 2007), the full 60-item SRP-II, and the Self-Report Psychopathy Scale-III (SRP III-R12).

Thus not all studies are strictly comparable, given that they are using different measures. This makes the whole research agenda more complicated. However, there has been, as one may expect, an attempt to devise a new brief measure. Thus Jonason and Webster (2010) have developed and validated the Dirty Dozen, which is a 12-item, three-factor measure that may take the field forward. It is clear that there is now a tremendous interest in the Dark Triad in many different areas of psychology.

Most researchers of individual differences feel obliged to describe their measures in Five Factor space. One personality trait, namely neuroticism, seems weakly (negatively) related to the triad. Next, the correlations are rather different for the three measures: Extraversion is most consistently the trait most highly correlated with Narcissism, whereas for Machiavellianism it is most often Disagreeableness along with low Conscientiousness. The correlations for Psychopathy, too, implicate Disagreeableness as the major Big Five correlate and also low Conscientiousness.

To dismiss the Dark Triad as simply low Agreeableness is not warranted, though it is clear why the correlations are highest for that trait. A Dark Triad person seems to be predominantly disagreeable, low on conscientiousness, stable, extravert. This is confirmed by the excellent work by Widiger, Costa and McCrae (2001), who plotted the Big Five facet scores against the personality disorders. Thus they noted that five of the six Agreeableness and three of the six Conscientiousness facets were associated with Psychopathy. Narcissism was more complicated: they suggested that four of the Neuroticism, one Extraversion and two Conscientiousness dimensions related to NPD. Neither was at all related to Openness facets.

It seems that the attempt to understand the Big Five in factor space would really benefit from having a very large sample complete more than one of each of the Dark Triad measures, as well as the long version NEO-PI-R with the facet scores. What is required is both evidence of convergence and perhaps more discriminant validity of the Dark Triad.

CONCLUSION

Overall it appears that psychologists have developed a greater interest and expertise in psychometrics and measurement than psychiatrists have. While the latter have developed reliable and comprehensive interview schedules, the former have spent a great deal of time on self-report measures. However, it appears that the rapprochement between these disciplines, at least in terms of the personality disorders, has been very good for practitioners and there are now a number of instruments to choose from.

Inevitably, as Furnham et al. (2014) have shown, there are many tests that attempt to measure various dark-side variables like psychopathy. Some are much better constructed and validated than others. As manuals (DSM) and systems get revised certain dark-side factors receive more attention than others. The psychiatrists seem particularly interested in Borderline Personality Disorder (Furnham et al., 2015), while the psychologists have become more interested in Anti-Social, Narcissistic and Schizotypal Personality Disorders.

As noted at the beginning of the chapter, it was the Hogans who pioneered this work and also did all the necessary psychometric work to support their increasingly popular measure, the HDS. With all the interest in, and scandals surrounding, leadership derailment, it has become the most popular instrument for assessors, coaches and selectors who hope to avoid derailment.

REFERENCES

American Psychiatric Association (2000). *Diagnostic and statistical manual of mental disorders* (4th edn, text revision). Washington, DC: Author.

American Psychiatric Association (2014). *Diagnostic and statistical manual of mental disorders* (5th. edn). Washington, DC: Author.

Ames, R., Rose, D., Anderson, P. & Cameron, P. (2006). The NPI-16 as a short measure of narcissism. *Journal of Research in Personality*. 40, 440–50.

Andershed, H., Hodgins, S. & Tengström, A. (2007). Convergent validity of the Youth Psychopathic Traits Inventory (YPI): Association with the Psychopathy Checklist: Youth Version (PCL:YV). *Assessment*, 14(2), 144–54.

Christie, R. & Geis, F. L. (1970). *Studies in Machiavellianism*. New York: Academic Press.

De Fruyt, F., De Clercq, B., Miller, J., Rolland, J.-P., Jung, S.-C., Taris, R., Furnham, A. & Van Hiel, A. (2009). Assessing personality at risk in personnel selection and development. *European Journal of Personality*, 23, 51–69.

Dotlich, D. & Cairo, P. (2003). *Why CEOs fail*. New York: Jossey-Bass.

Eysenck, H. J. & Eysenck, M. W. (1985). Personality and individual differences. New York: Plenum Press.

Fico, J., Hogan, R. & Hogan, J. (2000). *Interpersonal compass manual and interpretation guide*. Tulsa, OK: Hogan Assessment System.

Forth, A. E., Brown, S. L., Hart, S. D. & Hare, R. D. (1996). The assessment of psychopathy in male and female noncriminals: Reliability and validity. *Personality and Individual Differences*, 20, 531–43.

Friedman, J. N. W., Oltmanns, T. F. & Turkheimer, E. (2007). Interpersonal perception and personality disorders. *Journal of Research in Personality*, 41, 667–88.

Furnham, A. (2006). Personality disorders and intelligence. *Journal of Individual Differences*, 27, 42–5.

Furnham, A. (2008). *Personality and intelligence at work*. London: Routledge.

Furnham, A. & Crump, J. (2005). Personality traits, types and disorders. *European Journal of Personality*, 19, 167–84.

Furnham, A., Lee, V. & Kolzeev, V. (2015). Mental health literacy and borderline personality disorder (BPD): What do the public 'make' of those with BPD? *Social Psychiatry and Psychiatric Epidemiology*, 50(2), 317–24.

Furnham, A., Milner, R., Akhtar, R. & De Fruyt, F. (2014). A review of the measures designed to assess DSM-5 personality disorders. *Psychology*, 5, 1646–86.

Furnham, A. & Trickey, G. (2011). Sex differences in the dark side traits. *Personality and Individual Differences*, 50(4), 517–22.

Gebauer, J. E., Sedikides, C., Verplanken, B. & Maio, G. R. (2012). Communal narcissism. *Journal of Personality and Social Psychology*, 5, 854–78.

Hare, R. D. (1985). Comparison of procedures for the assessment of psychopathy. *Journal of Consulting and Clinical Psychology*, 53, 7–16.

Hare, R. D. (1991). *The Hare Psychopathy Checklist – Revised*. North Tonawanda, NY: Multi-Health Systems.

Henning, H. & Six, B. (2008). Machiavellismus [Machiavellianism]. In A. Glöckner-Rist (ed.), *Zusammenstellung sozialwissenschaftlicher Items und Skalen* [Compilation of social science items and scales] (ZIS) Version 12.00. Bonn: GESIS.

Hogan, R. & Hogan, J. (1997). *Hogan Development Survey Manual*. Tulsa, OK: Hogan Assessments.

Hogan, R. & Hogan, J. (2001). Assessing leadership: A view from the dark side. *International Journal of Selection and Assessment*, 9, 40–51.

Jonason, P. K., Li, N. P. & Teicher, E. A. (2010). Who is James Bond? The Dark Triad as an agentic social style. *Individual Differences Research*, 8(2), 111–20.

Jonason, P. K. & Webster, G. D. (2010). The dirty dozen: A concise measure of the dark triad. *Psychological Assessment*, 22(2), 420–32.

Khoo, H. & Burch, G. (2008). The 'dark side' of leadership personality and transformational leadership. *Personality and Individual Differences*, 44(1), 86–97.

Krueger, R. F., Derringer, J., Markon, K. E., Watson, D. & Skodol, A. E. (2012). Initial construction of a maladaptive personality trait model and inventory for DSM-5. *Psychological Medicine*, 42(9), 1879–90.

Levenson, M. R., Keihl, K. A. & Fitzpatrick, C. M. (1995). Assessing psychopathic attributes in a noninstitutionalized population. *Journal of Personality and Social Psychology*, 68, 151–8.

Lilienfeld, S. O. & Andrews, B. P. (1996). Development and preliminary validation of a self-report measure of psychopathic personality traits in noncriminal populations. *Journal of Personality Assessment*, 66, 488–524.

Miller, J. D., Dir, A., Gentile, B., Wilson, L., Pryor, L. R. & Campbell, W. K. (2010). Searching for a vulnerable dark triad: Comparing Factor 2 psychopathy, vulnerable narcissism, and borderline personality disorder. *Journal of Personality*, 78(5), 1529–64.

Miller, L. (2008). *From Difficult to Disturbed*. New York: Amacom.

Moscoso, S. & Salgado, J. (2004) 'Dark side' personality styles as predictors of task, contextual, and job performance. *International Journal of Selection and Assessment*, 12(4), 356–62.

Oldham, J. & Morris, L. (1991). *Personality self-portrait*. New York: Bantam.

Paulus, D. L. & Williams, K. M. (2002). The Dark Triad of personality: Narcissism, Machiavellianism, and psychopathy. *Journal of Research in Personality*, 36, 556–63.

Paulhus, D. L., Williams, K. & Harms, P. (2001). Shedding Light on the Dark Triad of Personality: Narcissism, Machiavellianism, and psychopathy. Presented at the 2001 Society for Personality and Social Psychology Convention, San Antonio.

Raskin, R. & Hall, C. S. (1979) A Narcissistic Personality Inventory. *Psychological Reports*, 45(2), 590.

Raskin, R. N. & Terry, H. (1988). A principal components analysis of the Narcissistic Personality Inventory and further evidence of its construct validity. *Journal of Personality and Social Psychology*, 54, 890–902.

Rolland, J. P. & De Fruyt (2003). The validity of FFM personality dimensions and maladaptive traits to predict negative affects at work: A six-month prospective study in a military sample. *European Journal of Personality*, 17, 101–21.

von Collani, G. (2008). Modifizierte deutsche Versionen des Narcissistic Personality Inventory (NPI-d) [Modified German version of the Narcissistic Personality Inventory (NPI-d)]. In A. Glöckner-Rist (ed.), *Zusammenstellung sozialwissenschaftlicher Items und Skalen* [Compilation of social science items and scales] (ZIS) Version 12.00. Bonn: GESIS.

Widiger, T. A., Costa, P. T. & McCrae, R. R. (2001). Proposal for Axis II: Diagnostic personality disorders using the five-factor model. In P. T. Costa and T. E. Widiger (eds), *Personality disorders and the five factor model of personality* (2nd edn, pp. 432–56). New York: Oxford University Press.

Widiger, T. A., Livesley, W. J. & Clark, L. A. (2009). An integrative dimensional classification of personality disorder. *Psychological Assessment*, 21(3), 243–55.

Widiger, T. A., Trull, T. J., Clarkin, J. F., Sanderson, C. & Costa, P. T., Jr (2002). A description of the DSM-IV personality disorders with the five-factor model of personality? In P. T. Costa, Jr & T. A. Widiger (eds), *Personality disorders and the five-factor model of personality* (pp. 89–99). Washington, DC: American Psychological Association.

Williams, K. M., Nathanson, C. & Paulhus, D. L. (2010). Identifying and profiling scholastic cheaters: Their personality, cognitive ability, and motivation. *Journal of Experimental Psychology: Applied*, 16(3), 293–307.

15 Projective Measures and Occupational Assessment
Christopher Ridgeway

INTRODUCTION

Projective measures in the field of psychometric testing are normally referred to as idiographic in contrast to psychometric tests, which are usually called nomothetic. An idiographic measure is focused on the individualistic characteristics of the subject, those unique personality attributes or qualities within the person. This is very different to the psychometric test, which is concerned with the commonalities between an individual and their comparator group. (See Chapter 2 in this volume by Barry Cripps for an exploration of the differences between the idiographic and nomothetic approaches.)

The *stimuli* that the subjects respond to are also very different. For a nomothetic measure the stimuli are structured, whereas an idiographic test has unstructured stimuli. Typically, a nomothetic test will have stimulus items such as written questions. An idiographic stimulus will normally be quite different – an ink blot or an uncertain picture, perhaps.

The derivation of a nomothetic test is usually via statistical analysis, normally factor analysis. That of an idiographic measure is via use, practice and impressions of utility.

There would be little else to consider about projective measures if the criticisms of Eysenck (1957) were accepted. Eysenck considered that projective measures did not have the required reliability or validity to be used in occupational assessment. For Eysenck the only possible use for the projective measure was in the clinical setting.

Perhaps a riposte to the Eysenck critique is that of Allport (1937) who held the view that nomothetic tests were limited because they do not 'explore' the 'interesting' individual qualities of a person. Perhaps Allport provides a good reason to explore the projective's use in the occupational world.

THEORIES RELATING TO PROJECTIVE MEASURES

An analysis of the theoretical bases of projective measures was provided by Murstein (1963), whose conclusion was that assessees would project their 'inner' thoughts and feelings onto the stimuli because, as Freud had said in 1911 (Freud, 1958), those thoughts and feelings which were painful would be repressed and so would not be made overt; therefore the projective stimulus requires an object which is not obviously directive in order to make the covert unconscious open to exposure and interpretation.

The basis of the projective might be inferred from the development of the measure. A projective test is devised to measure global aspects of personality and personality dynamics after the psychodynamic tradition.

An example is the generation of the Thematic Apperception Test (TAT). Murray (1938) describes its development. He led a team of psychoanalysts (Freudian and Jungian), anthropologists and clinical psychologists who were seeking to identify the causes of human behaviour. The team concluded that a significant determinant was the individual's unconscious thoughts and feelings, and so they needed to develop means of measuring this determinant. The measure they developed was the TAT.

The participant's response, since it cannot be attributed to the stimulus itself, is believed to reflect the individual's basic personality make-up. The initial use was in the occupational sector. TAT was one of the measures or tests used in the selection of applicants for the OSS (Office of Strategic Service, now the CIA). Its use for CIA operative selection is a pointer to the predicted future use of projective measures, for roles that are rapidly changing, difficult to predict and complex. An uncertain occupational world is the place where selection might be made, in part, on the basis of the 'Core' unconscious individual. Cases in which the relationships of the psychometrically measured qualities cannot be related to future job dimensions may well be the ones where projective instruments will be used.

THE USE OF PROJECTIVE MEASURES SINCE THE 1960s

In the 1960s the world of occupational psychology, or industrial psychology as it was then called, was small. Psychological tests could only be used by psychologists, statistics had major limitations because of computers' low speed and capacity, few tests were available, and of those that were most were US-normed. The number of UK-normed tests was very limited. The only widely used personality test was the Eysenck Personality Questionnaire. The most used US tests were the Minnesota Multiphasic Personality Inventory (MMPI) and the Edwards Personal Preference Schedule (Edwards, 1953). There were other tests, from the National Institute for Industrial Psychology (NIIP), but they were underexposed because of limited marketing.

The use of projective measures was, even in the 1960s, mainly limited to the clinical domain, although some occupational use, perhaps as a result of the limited number of alternative psychometric tests, existed. Some clinicians working in industry used the measures, and there was (limited) use by industrial psychologists. Some selection of shop floor employees was undertaken using projectives, but research and evaluation were not published. An example from my personal experience was the selection of electrical wiring staff.

Comments made at industrial psychology meetings from 1960 to 1970 suggested that projective use was fairly frequent.

The use of projectives was probably greater in the USA than in the UK. The Sentence Completion method, which can be considered when the item involves objects such as 'My mother was …', 'I have dreams that …', shows that projectives were relatively widely used.

Given that the projective method is based on Jung's (1910) word association technique, it is suggested that the latter is probably projective in form, so it may also be why it was relatively widely used. Users had probably received some education in psychoanalysis and may well have been introduced to projectives at university.

The Brook Reaction Test (Heim & Watts, 1969) was used for the assessment of interests. Interestingly, the test is presented by verbal stimulus. Eighty stimulus words are presented on tape and respondents have to provide a response within 12 seconds. This is very similar to an orally presented sentence completion test except that in the latter case the required response time is five seconds. The response time in both cases is designed to reduce the possibility of cognitive filtering.

The method has been little used, but Kline (1969) found that it was at least as reliable as interest inventories, so it is suggested that it may have current use possibilities.

It would be expected that Rorschach and the TAT, which have poor face validity in occupational assessment, would have had little use in occupational settings. Personal experience in the 1960s suggests that this may not have been the case. Observations were made of ink blots being used in the selection of factory shop floor workers and sales personnel.

INTERNATIONAL COMPARISONS OF THE USE OF PROJECTIVES

Experience of consulting in Europe, Africa, the Far East and the USA from 1980 onward gave me an impressionistic view of how projectives were used in different countries.

Use in mainland Europe was significantly higher than that in the UK. Indeed, some psychologists and consultants in mainland Europe expressed surprise that our assessment processes did not include them. Mainland Europeans appeared to believe that the 'professional' skill of the assessor was in the interpretation of projective responses. Perhaps this response could also explain their use of graphology. Similar responses were common in Southern Africa and parts of the Far East. The USA appeared more akin to the UK. The US psychologists seemed to have a similar projective usage to the UK ones.

Piotrowski, Keller and Ogawa (1993) assert that the use of projectives in the US, the Netherlands, Japan and Hong Kong was higher than previous reports had suggested. They found that projectives were being used for the assessment of intelligence, interests and personality. This study states that the measures being used were Bender Gestalt, Draw-a-Person, Sentence Completion, House–Tree–Person, Rorschach and TAT. The authors assert that the continued and growing use of projectives in these countries was a result of the problems with psychometrically based questionnaires. It is asserted, by the authors, that the translation of questions did not meet the 'District' languages of the 'Local' assessees but the 'Local' assessors could give stimuli in local dialect and also understand dialect responses.

Projectives continue to be used in many countries, including the UK, in consumer research and consultancy.

Dichter (1964) promoted the concept of 'plugging into subconscious desires' in the use of projectives in advertising research. Boddy (2004) confirms, as does Steinman (2009), that projectives are regularly and frequently used in advertising and marketing, because it is believed that only they can reveal the 'key' unconscious feelings and drives that are the focus of these activities. Steinman provides an example of how projectives were used to evoke the 'unconscious' images associated with instant coffee.

Soley (2010) makes a direct link between psychoanalytic concepts, achievement motivation and product marketing. The projective used in this case was Jungian word association.

It is suggested that if the occupational psychological community were more aware of the research and practice in consumer psychology which use projectives, they could be motivated to add it to their resources in selection, development and organisation development.

THE RELIABILITY AND VALIDITY OF PROJECTIVE MEASURES

There are no published reliability or validity studies of many projective measures. However, it is suggested that the ambiguity of the ink blots might elicit evidence about the individual which might not be elicited by the – possibly cognitively filtered – information obtained from questionnaires. It could be hypothesised that assessees are significantly less likely to fake a good response when they cannot conceive what a good response would be. Where a candidate is unaware of what a good response is, it is suggested that they may make overt characteristics that they may consider negative.

I have used sentence completion for over 40 years because, intuitively, it seems to provide useful information about an individual that other methods do not. This might suggest that it has wider use than is revealed in the literature. Secondly, it does not have the disadvantage of lack of face validity that other projectives can have, suggesting that it may have wider use than reported in journal articles. The fact that I have taught the method to a significant number of others gives weight to the belief that it could be widely used.

A possible conclusion is that projectives are more widely used in occupational assessment than is reported, because: they are normally used in conjunction with other assessment methods; they are often used for very senior selection decisions; and they are often used for selecting for relatively unique jobs, and in the armed forces for restricted- information roles.

Classic reliability and validity statistics would be considered by many projective users to be of little importance. The information from a projective is regarded as specific to the individual (that is, it is ipsative), so it is considered unique and therefore comparison to groups and others is of little significance.

STIMULUS MATERIAL FOR PROJECTIVE MEASURES

Sentence completion

The stimulus can be written or oral. As an oral stimulus tends to generate a faster response it can be considered to be less likely to produce a fake response.

Drawings

The House, Tree, Person test (Buck, 1970) requires the assessee to draw an orally stimulated object. For example, they are asked to 'draw a tree'.

Solid objects

Lowenfeld's (1954) Mosaic Test requires wooden shapes to be made into objects.

Auditory stimulus

Bean (1965) requires assessees to provide an 'interpretation' of a variety of sounds.

AN ESTIMATION OF THE AMOUNT OF USE OF PROJECTIVES

There are a number of surveys of the use of projectives. Most record that the use outside the clinical field has been falling since the 1950s; they also show that those with the highest use are the Rorschach, the TAT and its variants, and the Sentence Completion and its variants (Piotrowski et al., 1997).

The following descriptions of these measures give an overview. It is suggested that, because projective measures are very different in appearance, presentation and transparency, it is probably only by observing an 'expert' assessor that their usage can be judged.

The Rorschach

The test is presented as 10 cards bearing ink blots; five are in shades of grey, five are coloured. Participants are asked, 'What do they look like?', and then asked to explain their responses. Currently most scoring is undertaken via the Exner system. This is a computerised coding scheme which provides a measure of coping style. It also assesses resources and, from the Allison (1988) additions, intellectual performance and inhibitions. Additionally, some 'intuitive' assessment via the responses to the blackness and whiteness of the images can provide evidence on depression and desolation.

Wiener-Levy and Exner (1981) report inter-rater reliability of .85 and a test–retest reliability of .85. Allison (1988) attempts to validate Wiener-Levy and Exner's findings, but only produces confusion as they conflict with the validation of Howard (1989).

The Rorschach is still used, if only by a limited number of occupational assessors, but is difficult to evaluate for validity or reliability.

The Thematic Apperception Test (TAT) (Murray, 1938)

The TAT presents 31 cards which show drawings of people – individuals and groups – in a variety of situations. Assessees are asked to say what they believe the people on the cards are thinking and feeling.

Karon (1981) suggests that the TAT has value because it seeks to assess aspects of personality that are outside those assessed by conventional psychometric tests. It argues that the low inter-scorer reliability generally found is not important, because the scorers are assessing different personality characteristics.

Validity is difficult to assess as users tend to state that the validity depends on the interpretive skill, perhaps based on intuition, of the interpreter. To occupational assessees, the cards can seem 'old-fashioned'. They are therefore often considered to have low face validity.

The previous comments suggest that the TAT would not be recommended for use in occupational assessment. However, there could be a case for their use where the assessee has a high degree of concern about the assessment. Participants lack trust and may well try to fake. The ambiguity of the TAT may provide a more open response, but it still requires interpretation. Perhaps if it is used to confirm the results of other forms of assessment, such as interview, workplace reports, 360-degree assessment – that is, as an adjunct – TAT could be useful.

Maybe the cards could be updated to have higher face validity, or perhaps they could be replaced with computer-generated images which have a specific relationship to the job role the assessment is for. For example, for a finance role the images could be set in a bank.

For those who continue to believe that the unconscious can, at times of great pressure or stress, be a dominant determinant of behaviour and therefore a factor it is necessary to assess, the Blacky Pictures test (Blum, 1945) could be a means of accessing the unconscious.

The stimuli are 11 cartoons of a family of dogs. The assessee is asked to tell the story of what is happening and then describe how each character feels. The cards were designed to assess the psychoanalytic concepts of oral eroticism, oral sadism, anal sadism, oedipal intensity, masturbation guilt, castration anxiety or penis envy, positive identification, sibling rivalry, guilt feelings, positive ego ideal and love objects. Occupational assessment, it is suggested, would not require these traits, except, perhaps, ego ideal. However, if the cards were redesigned to assess occupational 'themes' they could provide a useful stimulus for career discussions, team evaluation, etc.

Perhaps the Defence Mechanism Test (DMT) (Kragh, 1985; Kragh & Smith, 1970) is a more useful instrument? The DMT is an adaption of the TAT. The stimuli are two cards. One portrays a heroic figure, the other a threatening figure. The authors claim that the traumatic events of the assessee's life will be reflected in their descriptions of what they think and feel about the figures. The responses are scored for repression, denial, reaction formation, and identification with the hero as an aggressor.

It is suggested that the measure could be used if an occupational assessor considers that some personal characteristic that has emerged in interview requires further exploration. If the assessment is for a high-pressure/stress role then maybe the DMT could provide useful information.

SOME CONCLUDING OBSERVATIONS

There has been, over the past 50 years, a marked decline in the use of projective measures in occupational psychology. This decline is, it is suggested, a result of: the elimination of the teaching of psychoanalysis at undergraduate level; a reduction in marketing expenditure on psychometric instruments; a reduction of the time spent on assessment; and an increased belief that individual characteristics, particularly those that are not overt, are of little interest.

In classic reliability and validity terms, many projectives are judged to be unreliable and invalid. For many psychologists educated and trained in the past few decades, the relative ease of use of computer-presented, -scored and -interpreted psychometric questionnaires will ensure that they do not try projectives. Maybe the limited number of projective users should market their positive characteristics. Responses to projectives, it is suggested, are less easy to fake than those to questionnaires which an assessee may well have completed previously and which they may have had feedback on. It is suggested that projectives may be able to assess personal characteristics which, because they are 'unconscious', questionnaires do not access in the same way. It is further suggested that in the uncertain commercial future environment these 'Core' unconscious motives, anxieties, etc. could be crucial to staff success.

Perhaps the projective which has the greatest possibility of resurgence is the Sentence Completion, administered orally. The following guidelines should be followed: ensure that the stems are job-related; retain the stems with the possibility of generating 'unconscious response'; consider the measure for global or multicultural positions where the stems can elicit responses relating to candidates' empathy with other cultures.

It is suggested that occupational psychologists who are unfamiliar with the work of colleagues in marketing and advertising should read about their uses of projectives.

Projectives are not extinct; they are waiting to be rediscovered by a new generation, who may well find exciting new ways to use them in future practice.

REFERENCES

Allison, J., Blatt, S. J. & Zimet, C. N. (1988). *The interpretation of psychological tests*. Washington, D.C.: Hemisphere.

Allport, G. W. (1937). *Personality: A psychological interpretation*. New York: Henry Holt & Co.

Bean, K. L. (1965). The sound-apperception tests: Origin, purpose, standardization, scoring and use. *Journal of Psychology*, 59, 371–412.

Blum, G. S. (1945). A study of the psychoanalytic theory of psychosexual development. *Genetic Psychology Monographs*, 39, 3–99.

Boddy, C. R. (2004). Projective techniques in business research: Are they useful? Curtin University Graduate School of Business school, Perth.

Dichter, E. (1964). *Handbook of consumer motivations*. New York: McGraw-Hill.

Edwards, A. L. (1953). *Manual for the Edwards Personal Preference Schedule*. New York: Psychological Corporation.

Eysenck, H. J. (1957). *Sense and nonsense in psychology*. Harmondsworth: Penguin.

Freud. S. (1958). Psycho-analytic notes on an autobiographical account of a case of paranoia (dementia paranoides) (1911). In *The standard edition of the complete psychological works of Sigmund Freud* (trans. J. Strachey) (vol. 12, pp. 9–82). London: Hogarth Press.

Heim, A. W. & Watts, K. P. (1969). The Brook reaction test of interest. *British Journal of Psychology*, 57, 171–85.

Howard, J. C. (1989). The Rorschach Test: Standardization and contemporary developments. *In* S. Wetzler & M. M. Katz (eds), *Contemporary approaches to psychological assessment* (pp. 127–53). New York: Brunner/Mazel.

Jung, C. G. (1910). The association method. *American Journal of Psychology*, 31, 219–69.

Karon, B. P. (1981). The thematic apperception test. In A. I. Rabin (ed.), *Projective techniques in personality assessment* (2nd edn, pp. 85–120). New York: Springer.

Kline, P. (1969). The reliability of the Brook Reaction Test. *British Journal of Social and Clinical Psychology*, 9, 42–5.

Kragh, U. (1985) *Defense Mechanism Test manual*. Stockholm: Persona.

Kragh, U. & Smith G. S. (eds) (1970). *Percept-Genetic Analysis*. Lund: Gleerup.

Lowenfeld, M. (1954). *The Lowenfeld Mosaic Test*. London: Newman Neame.

Murray, H. A. (1938). *Explorations in personality*. Oxford: Oxford University Press.

Murstein, B. I. (1963). *Theory and research in projective techniques, emphasizing the TAT*. New York: Wiley.

Piotrowski, C., Keller, J. W. & Ogawa, T. (1993). Projective techniques: An international perspective. *Psychological Reports*, 72(1), 179–82.

Soley, L. (2010). Projective techniques in US marketing and management research: The influence of *The Achievement Motive*. *Qualitative Market Research*, 13(4), 334–53.

Steinman, R. B. (2009). Projective techniques in consumer research. *International Bulletin of Business Administration*, 5, 37–45.

Wiener-Levy, D. & Exner, J. E. (1981). The Rorschach Comprehensive System: An overview. In P. McReynolds (ed.), *Advances in psychological assessment* (vol. 5, pp. 236–93). San Francisco, CA: Jossey-Bass.

16 Testing Across Cultures: Translation, Adaptation and Indigenous Test Development

LINA DAOUK-ÖYRY AND PIA ZEINOUN

THE APPLICATION OF PSYCHOLOGICAL TESTING ACROSS THE GLOBE

Psychometric tests are a common denominator across different fields in psychology, including, but not limited to, industrial/organisational, educational/school, clinical, neuropsychological, forensic, cross-cultural and quantitative psychology. They are quite appealing, for researchers and practitioners alike, because they are relatively easy to use, they are standardised, their reliability and validity are typically established before use, and there is strong evidence supporting their validity across fields. For instance, psychometric tests are widely used as a method of assessment for employee selection and development, educational placement decisions, clinical and neuropsychological diagnoses and interpretations about brain and behaviour, and comparative research across the globe (Robertson & Smith, 2001; Ryan, McFarland, Baron & Page, 1999).

Globalisation, however, is continuing to change assessment dynamics, making the test usage increasingly complicated. Researchers and practitioners from many fields across the globe are venturing into test development, or transferring existing tests developed for a particular language, usually a Western language and culture, to another language and culture (Brown, Green & Lauder, 2001). These tests are then used to make high-stakes decisions about individuals around the world, using constructs and norms developed in Western countries. In some cases, they are used to make cross-country comparisons between constructs (e.g., prevalence of clinical syndromes), before establishing that the constructs, scores and items are in fact equivalent before comparison. In such a global economy, it is essential to have common grounds according to which individuals from different cultural backgrounds can be compared (Daouk, Rust & McDowall, 2005), and guidelines that regulate the cross-cultural application of tests have become increasingly important (e.g., the International Test Commission (ITC), the European Federation of Psychologists' Associations (EFPA)).

THE CHALLENGES OF DEVELOPING AND USING PSYCHOMETRICS FOR OTHER LANGUAGES AND CULTURES

The use of multilingual versions of the same instrument is indeed growing with the popularity of tests (Hambleton, 2005). However, validity and reliability, the most important criteria that distinguish psychometric tests from other methods of assessment, are not easily transferable from the original to the multilingual versions of tests (Geisinger, 1994). First, the new-language version of the test needs to be valid in the target culture group for test takers from that culture to be meaningfully compared. This is called *construct equivalence* between the two tests, in which each language version of the test is assessing the same construct within each culture. However, this does not guarantee that scores can be compared between cultures. That is, if there is construct equivalence between two language versions of a test that measures extraversion, then we can be confident that each of the tests is measuring this construct. However, the scores of an individual who took the test in one language cannot be compared to the scores of another person who took another language version. Another level of equivalence in cross-cultural or comparative research, in any field, is achieved when the two language versions enable the scores of test takers from two different cultures to be compared. This is called *measurement unit equivalence* or *scalar equivalence* (see van de Vijver, 1998 for a full review). Table 16.1 describes the types of comparison that could be achieved with the different levels of equivalence.

Poor test translation is the most common source of lack of validity of translated tests (Hambleton, 2005). However, equivalence (or lack of it) between multilingual versions of a test relates to a number of complex questions beyond a good adaptation (van de Vijver & Hambleton, 1996). First, does the construct exist in the target culture? Even if it does exist, is it defined and manifested in the same way in both cultures? So, are the questions in the multilingual version measuring the same construct as the questions in the original test? Below we discuss three sources of bias that have a direct effect on equivalence between multilingual versions of tests.

Table 16.1 *Types of comparison achievable with different levels of equivalence*

Construct equivalence	Measurement unit equivalence	Scalar equivalence	Possible comparison
Yes	No	No	Within cultures only
Yes	Yes	No	Within cultures and indirectly between cultures
Yes	Yes	Yes	Within cultures and directly between cultures

ITEM BIAS

Although there are multiple reasons for item bias, in this section we will focus on test adaption and the item bias it might create between multiple language versions of the same test. Translation theories that focus on the accuracy of information presented in a language it was not originally written in, have shifted tremendously in their focus since their development. The earlier focus was mainly on the grammatical syntax of sentences and maintaining this balance in the new language. However, the cultural aspect soon began to gain more attention. That meant a shift from direct translation of words towards translation of paragraphs as a whole. This helps transfer meaningful context across languages. That is, the complexity of each sentence on its own is reduced by the context of the material it belongs to. In psychometrics and personality testing specifically, it is difficult to rely on the context to achieve equivalence in meaning, as the sentences that make up a questionnaire are independent of each other in the way they are presented. Each group of items is designed to measure a certain personality trait. These items are typically randomly mixed with other items measuring other traits. Therefore, items are listed somewhat out of context, unless the translator has knowledge about which items belong to which scale. Knowledge of psychology becomes necessary for understanding the meaning of the scales and the underlying constructs they measure. Additionally, in psychometric testing, the psychological effect that a sentence or word conjures in test takers is an integral part of achieving equivalence in translation. *Meaning* and *style* are crucial to all types of translations, but in the context of testing across languages and cultures, maintaining the same *psychological effect* between the multilingual versions is essential for achieving equivalence between them.

As a result, the term 'test translation' has frequently been replaced by the more accurate term 'test adaptation'. Although sometimes used interchangeably with 'test translation' to refer to the construction of tests that require cultural and linguistic sensitivity, test adaptation encompasses broader issues that are fundamental to the production of comparable versions across cultures, namely linguistic, cultural and psychological equivalence (Casillas & Robbins, 2005).

Source 1: Linguistic bias

This type of bias can result from mistranslation, inappropriate use of wording, or even mistakes in the translation of idioms and the use of colloquialisms (van de Vijver & Jeanrie, 2004). In an example by Hambleton (1996), the question 'Where is a bird with webbed feet most likely to live?' proved to function differently with a Swedish sample than with most other European samples. The term 'webbed feet' was translated to 'swimming feet' in Swedish, which rendered the item easier in the Swedish version than the English one. Therefore members of one group (Swedish), with the same overall ability on the test as their counterparts in the other group (English), were more likely to answer this question correctly. However, this likelihood is due to an anomaly in the item rather than a difference in ability between the groups. Mistranslations challenge the *linguistic equivalence* between multilingual versions of tests, by threatening the attainment of the same literal and connotative meaning on an item (van de Vijver & Jeanrie, 2004). Although linguistic equivalence is important, it is not sufficient for comparability of items.

Source 2: Psychological bias

This type of bias relates to situations in which the psychological impact of the item is not the same in the two or more target cultures (see Cheung, F. M., 2004a). The psychological function the item serves, especially in personality testing, affects the way it is viewed by test takers. The differential psychological effect can arise even when the translation is accurate and linguistic equivalence is achieved. For example, emotions could have different intensity across cultures, which make respondents in different cultures exhibit stronger or weaker psychological reactions towards an item (Marsella et al. 2000). This source of item bias challenges the *psychological equivalence* between items, that is, the equivalence of the psychological effect the item has in the different language versions. Items should therefore be adapted in a way that ensures that the different versions of the same item serve the same psychological function in each language.

Source 3: Conceptual bias

Conceptual bias, also referred to as cultural bias, is another source of item bias that relates to the relevance of the item content to the target culture (for example see Byrne & Watkins, 2003; Hambleton, Merenda & Spielberger, 2005; van de Vijver & Hambleton, 1996; van de Vijver & Tanzer, 1997). That is, the concepts covered by a certain item need to be meaningful in the target culture. This source of bias is also independent of the quality of the translation. Cheung (2004a) provides an example from the MMPI-2 that illustrates this source of bias. The item 'I used to like to play hopscotch and jump rope', even if well translated, will present a problem in cultures where hopscotch and jump rope are not common as children's games. Therefore content should also be adapted to be culturally appropriate in order to avoid creating bias. This source of bias challenges the *conceptual equivalence* between multilingual items (Cheung, F. M., 2004a; Jeanrie & Bertrand, 1999). Conceptual equivalence accounts for the suitability of the situations and information contained in each item and also for the equivalence in calibration, such as using metric versus imperial units (Jeanrie & Bertrand, 1999).

Methods for monitoring adaptation

The traditional back translation

There are several methods for assessing the quality of a translation. One is back translation (Brislin, 1980), in which a test is first translated from the original language to the target language, then translated back to the original language by another, independent translator. The traditional back-translation method (Brislin, 1980) has been widely used in the area of cross-cultural assessment (Daouk et al., 2005; Geisinger, 1994; Hambleton, 1993; van de Vijver & Hambleton, 1996; van de Vijver & Tanzer, 2004). Typically, close similarity between the original version and the back-translated one suggests a good translation. However, a close match between the versions could be the result of a word-for-word translation, which often leads to nonsensical sentences in the target language. For example, if the idiom 'everything is coming together' is translated literally into Arabic, the same sentence can be replicated in English during the back translation. However, the idiom 'everything is coming together' in English implies that a situation is working out well in every way. Whereas in Arabic, the literal translation of this item implies that everything bad is happening at the same time. Hambleton (1993) highlighted additional criticisms of this judgement technique:

1. Naturally, the back-translation technique leads to an assessment of the quality of the translation that uses the original language only, and therefore biases may arise. A word with two (or more) meanings in the target language may translate into the same word in the original language. Thus, comparing the back-translated version with the original might lead to a mistaken assumption that the translated version is appropriate. For example, the word 'sense' has several meanings, including 'the meaning or gist of something', 'sound practical intelligence', 'feeling or perception produced through the organs' and many more (Cambridge Dictionary, 2007, s.v. 'sense', n.). A sentence 'Something makes sense' could be mistranslated as 'Something makes feeling' in the target language, but be back-translated as 'Something makes sense', thus hiding the mistranslation.

2. Problems may also arise from a discrepancy between the translation skills of the forward and back translators. For example, the back translator may recognise a mistake in the translation to the TL, but correct it in the back translation. This can lead to sentences that are unnatural or misleading in the TL, yet perfectly fine in the back-translated language.

In summary, the back translation procedure on its own is directed towards reaching the linguistic equivalence of items without taking into account the cultural aspects of the target culture. ITC guideline D.1 clearly states that

> Test developers/publishers should insure that the adaptation process takes full account of linguistic and cultural differences among the populations for whom adapted versions of the test or instrument are intended. (International Test Commission, 2010)

That is, when an instrument is adapted from one language to another, not only the literal meaning of items should be preserved but also the connotative one (Hambleton, 2001). Back-translation alone – even if adequately executed – does not ensure the production of an appropriately adapted target version (Brislin, Lonner & Thorndike, 1973; Hambleton, 1993). Conversely, this method is still widely used but is agreed to be effective only when used as part of a sequential process of test adaptation or as a supplement to forward translation (Geisinger, 1994; Hambleton & Patsula, 1999).

The bilingual judges technique

The use of bilingual judges/translators to check the quality of the translation has been suggested as an alternative or additional method to back translation (Geisinger, 1994; Hambleton, 1994; Sireci, 2005). Using this technique, two or more judges/translators directly compare the original and translated versions. Therefore, the bilinguals base their judgements on the parallel versions in both languages, so there is less risk of the back translator correcting the forward translator's mistakes. Hambleton (1993) also draws attention to pitfalls associated with this method when it is used on its own:

1. It may be difficult to find judges/translators who are equally proficient in both languages.
2. Unlike examinees who will be taking the test later, bilinguals make use of insightful guessing when trying to understand the meaning of a translated item, because they know it is a translated version and because they have access to the original version.
3. Bilingual translators might not understand the item in the same way as monolinguals who will be taking the translated test in the future.

New directions

The complexity of achieving equivalence between multilingual versions of tests is an obvious challenge facing practitioners and academics alike. Single-method approaches to test adaptation may not be well suited to achieving linguistic, cultural and psychological equivalence between versions. Therefore, a combination of techniques, though more cumbersome, is essential for increasing the accuracy of the adaptation and minimising the chances of having malfunctioning items after field testing. Daouk-Öyry and McDowall (2013) propose a multi-step process of test adaptation that provides a good example of how different methods can be used to improve test adaptation. In this process, the authors rely on both techniques – back translation and the bilingual judges method – in a sequential manner, in order to provide a solid monitoring tool for test adaptations.

Although test translation or adaptation is the main source of lack of validity in multilingual versions of tests, there are other problems that may lead to lack of equivalence between tests. In the next section, we will shed light on method bias and construct bias as two additional sources that could lead to lack of equivalence between multilingual versions of tests.

METHOD BIAS

If the test developers adopted a thorough approach to adapting the psychometric tool and reaching linguistic, cultural and psychological equivalence, this is a prerequisite but not an assurance that the multilingual versions are truly equivalent and their results can be compared across cultures. Method bias is another type of bias that could present an obstacle to tests reaching equivalence (van de Vijver, 1998; van de Vijver & Hambleton, 1996; van de Vijver & Poortinga, 1997, 2005). Method bias is related not to the conceptual development of the questionnaire but to the instrument itself, the data collection process, or the characteristics of the sample.

Instrument bias

Instrument bias is associated with characteristics that can affect candidates' scores but that relate to the measurement tool rather than to the characteristic being measured. An example of such characteristics could be familiarity with the response format or the style of responding, or even with the purpose of taking the tests.

Source 1: Familiarity with the response format

Psychometrics tests differ in the response format they employ (such as the Likert scale, multiple-choice pictorial items, or open-ended questions). However, certain cultures may be more familiar with one type of response format than others. In some countries, for example, questionnaires are only filled out for governmental or legal purposes (Fife-Schaw, 2006). People in these countries are different from their European counterparts, who are used to taking questionnaires for scientific research. The type of answer format that the instrument relies on potentially leads to method bias.

Source 2: Response style

In line with the previous point, there is evidence that supports the existence of cultural differences in the style of responding to psychometric tests (Cheung, G. W. & Rensvold, 2002; Hui & Triandis, 1989; van de Vijver, 1998 in van de Vijver & Poortinga, 2005). For example, Extreme Response Style (ERS) is the tendency to endorse extreme answer options rather than middle ones. On a personality questionnaire with a Likert scale from 1 to 5, for example, participants who belong to groups high on ERS are likely to systematically endorse responses 1 and 5 and avoid the middle ones. Low ERS participants are likely to cluster around the middle (2, 3 and 4), whereas no ERS participants' scores are likely to be spread on all the scale. The presence of ERS, whether high or low, suggests that responses have different meanings to different groups (Cheung, G. W. & Rensvold, 2002), making the results incomparable between them. Another example is Acquiescence Response Style (ARS), whereby one group consistently scores higher or lower than (an)other group(s). Taking the example of the personality test above, a group with high ARS is likely to agree or disagree with an item more than other groups, which makes it uniformly different from them, either higher or lower. The uniformity of this response style makes comparison between groups possible, but indirect. That is, if a group consistently scores higher than another, then the difference between them is systematic and can therefore be adjusted for.

Source 3: Purpose and motivation

Perhaps another type of instrument bias relates to the purpose and the question format of specific questionnaires. Schmit and Ryan (1993) investigated the differences in factor structure on the NEO-FFI between job applicants and college students. They found that the data from the student sample fitted the NEO-FFI model better than data from job applicants. They also labelled one of the factors from the job applicants' data as 'ideal-employee' factor because it combined all the desirable work-related personality characteristics. This suggests that the reason for filling out the instrument has an impact on participants' scores.

Administration bias

Administration bias is associated with environmental or communicational differences in administering the tests that affect the scores of the comparison groups differently. The following are few examples of administration bias.

Source 1: Test instructions

Tests usually come with a set of standardised instructions to be read during test administration, and also recommendations on best practice in administration settings. Any instructions made by the test administrator that do not follow these recommendations can potentially bias test takers' responses either negatively or positively and result in error (Rust & Golombok, 1999). Fair comparison between candidates relies on an equal treatment of all participants, and the ITC guidelines (International Test Commission, 2005) on computer-based testing clearly state that the valid and reliable interpretation of scores assumes that the test has been administered in a standardised way. Receiving the same instructions about taking the test in a relatively similar environment is one way of ensuring this equality in treatment.

Source 2: Technology experience (in computer-based testing)

Although administration bias can have an effect on participants' score, it generally has small consequences for equivalence between multilingual versions of tests. An exception to this is the case where the instructions given to the two groups are significantly different. However, the most severe forms of administration bias result from computer-based testing and people's experience with the Internet and the use of computers. Some countries have limited access to the Internet and computers, which can affect participants' performance on computer-based tests. A culture group that has a slower Internet connection in its country is likely to spend more time taking the test than another group using a faster connection, and consequently their performance might be affected by fatigue or stress or boredom.

Sample bias

Sample bias is a potentially dangerous type of bias, because it does not necessarily affect the equivalence between multilingual versions, but may affect the validity of the inferences that test users make from them. Sample bias is directly associated with specific characteristic of the sample, such as age, gender and education level and their consistency across the comparison groups.

Source 1: Sample convenience and snowballing

When collecting data to make inferences about the general population, it is important to collect it from a sample representative of the one it is being generalised to. There are two systematic methods of sampling that maximise the likelihood of a sample resembling the general population: random sampling and matching (Pelham, 1999; van de Vijver, 1998). Random sampling consists of randomly selecting participants from the overall population, whereas matching consists of matching participants in two groups on some specific criterion, such as age or educational level. However, many researchers tend to rely on samples of convenience and snowballing techniques as the most convenient sources of data. Samples of convenience are direct contacts of the researcher, such as friends, family, co-workers and so on, and the snowballing technique relies on using the sample of convenience to recruit future participants. This method of sampling has strong implications for generalisability and also for cross-cultural comparisons (McCrae & Costa, 2003).

Source 2: Digital divide

Collecting data electronically could also produce another example of sample bias if it results in favouring a subgroup of the general population that has access to computers. As an example, according to the International Telecommunication Union statistics (2005), in Lebanon the average PC penetration per 100 inhabitants was 11.45%. The number of Internet users was estimated to be 2,152,950 by the end of 2012, which means that 48% of the population did not have Internet access by that year, creating a sort of digital divide in the country. Access to computers could therefore be considered limited, especially when compared with accessibility in countries such as the United Kingdom (62.88%). Additionally, Lebanon ranked 167th on the Net Index, leaving only 26 countries with slower download speeds around the globe. Restricted access to the Internet and computers (administration bias) therefore limits the participation of certain percentages of the population in research (sample bias). It is likely that people who have access to a computer and the Internet are systematically different from those who do not have access to them in terms of socio-economic status, education, etc.

Source 3: Self-selection bias

Pelham (1999) argues that 'people who choose to answer surveys are systematically different from people who choose not to do so' (p. 88). As a hypothetical example, let us consider that a group of researchers at a university are interested in measuring students' attitudes to exams. They hand out surveys to all 5000 students at the university and receive 1000 back. The analysis shows that students believe exam questions are too difficult and do not reflect the material learnt in classrooms. Although a sample of 1000 is large, it might not be a representative one. For one, students who respond to these surveys are likely to be those who failed their exams and have found an opportunity to relieve their frustration. The 4000 students who do not take part in the survey create sample bias by choosing not to participate.

Construct bias

Now if we consider that the test has been adapted well, and administered systematically while taking into consideration the possible pitfalls, there is still another potential threat to reaching equivalence: construct bias. Such a bias occurs when constructs being measured are not equivalent between given cultures (Byrne & Watkins, 2003). Construct bias can arise from two main sources, differential construct manifestation and construct under-representation.

Source 1: Differential construct manifestation

First, construct bias could result from the fact that the construct, although it exists in both cultures, is defined and exhibited differently in each (Byrne & Watkins, 2003; van de Vijver, 1998; van de Vijver & Hambleton, 1996; van de Vijver & Leung, 1997; van de Vijver & Poortinga, 1997; van de Vijver & Tanzer, 1997). To illustrate the concept of *differential construct manifestation*, we will consider the example of depression. Differences in the symptoms of depression between Eastern and Western cultures are a good example of this concept. Although for a number of years depression was thought to exist only in advanced industrialised societies (American Psychiatric Association, 2000), extensive research in this field revealed that this psychological disorder does exist in pre-industrialised societies as well (Sulaiman, Bhugra & de Silva, 2001a, 2001b). However, it emerged that its existence in the latter societies was masked by the use of Western diagnostic tools and procedures. Depression as described in the DSM-IV-TR is usually experienced through a feeling of guilt and sadness. But in some cultures it is experienced and expressed through physiological symptoms, such as headaches and nerves in Latino and Middle Eastern cultures, and tiredness and imbalance in Asian cultures (American Psychiatric Association, 2000). In such cases, translating or adapting a test into another culture is not enough to secure construct equivalence. Further evidence through indigenous research would be needed to define the construct and its manifestation in the 'less studied' culture.

Source 2: Construct under-representation

This source of construct bias is characterised by insufficient sampling of the behaviours that explain the construct (Messick, 1995). This is parallel to the concept of *content validity* in classical test theory, which assumes that the test measuring a certain construct should be fully representative of this construct (Kline, 1993). *Construct under-representation* is an anomaly related to the original instrument because it does not cover all the essential dimensions and facets that define the construct (Messick, 1995). Generally, for constructs to be under-represented, either the original test is too short to make valid deductions from or the items are too badly written to tap into the construct it is claiming to measure (Downing, 2002). In line with the previous source of construct bias, if the construct and its manifestations have not been fully investigated in the target culture, the items of the original language version may not be inclusive of all the behaviours that define the construct in the target culture.

CONCLUSION

In a globalised world, researchers and practitioners are increasingly interested in comparing results in their country with those obtained in other countries. Even within the same country there are subgroups that vary in terms of ethnic, cultural and linguistic background, and test developers need to take that variety into consideration if fairness and accuracy in assessment are their ultimate aims. A good translation of a test cannot guarantee the reproduction of an appropriate and metrically equivalent version of a test. Test adaptation is the norm today and the onus is on test developers to make sure that all necessary measures have been taken to produce a linguistically, psychologically and culturally equivalent version of the test.

REFERENCES

American Psychiatric Association (2000). *Diagnostic and statistical manual of mental disorders* (4th edn). Washington, DC: American Psychiatric Association.

Brislin, R. W. (1980). Translation and content analysis of oral and written material. In H. C. Triandis & J. W. Berry (eds), *Handbook of cross-cultural psychology* (vol. 1, pp. 349–444). Boston, MA: Allyn & Bacon.

Brislin, R. W., Lonner, W. J. & Thorndike, R. M. (1973). *Cross-cultural research methods*. New York: John Wiley & Sons.

Brown, P., Green, A. & Lauder, H. (2001). *High skills: Globalization, competitiveness, and skill formation*. Oxford: Oxford University Press.

Byrne, B. M. & Watkins, D. (2003). The issue of measurement invariance revisited. *Journal of Cross-Cultural Psychology*, 34(2), 155–75.

Cambridge Dictionary (2007). Cambridge: Cambridge University Press.

Casillas, A. & Robbins, S. B. (2005). Test adaptation and cross-cultural assessment from a business perspective: Issues and recommendations. *International Journal of Testing*, 5(1), 5–21.

Cheung, F. M. (2004a). Use of Western and indigenously developed personality tests in Asia. *Applied Psychology*, 53(2), 173–91.

Cheung, F. M. (2004b). Translation East and West. Paper presented at the 28th International Congress of Psychology (ICP), Beijing, July.

Cheung, G. W. & Rensvold, R. B. (2002). Evaluating goodness-of-fit indexes for testing measurement invariance. *Structural Equation Modeling*, 9(2), 233–55.

Daouk-Öyry, L. & McDowall, A. (2013). Using cognitive interviewing for the semantic enhancement of multilingual versions of personality questionnaires. *Journal of Personality Assessment*, 95(4), 407–16.

Daouk, L., Rust, J. & McDowall, A. (2005). Testing across languages and cultures: Challenges for the development and administration of tests in the internet era. *Selection and Development Review*, 21(4), 11.

Downing, S. M. (2002). Threats to the validity of locally developed multiple-choice tests in medical education: Construct-irrelevant variance and construct underrepresentation. *Advances in Health Sciences Education*, 7(3), 235–41.

Fife-Schaw, C. (2006). Levels of measurement. In G. M. Breakwell, S. Hammond, C. Fife-Schaw & J. A. Smith (eds), *Research methods in psychology* (3rd edn, pp. 50–63). London: Sage.

Geisinger, K. F. (1994). Cross-cultural normative assessment: Translation and adaptation issues influencing the normative interpretation of assessment instruments. *Psychological Assessment*, 6(4), 304–12.

Hambleton, R. K. (1993). Translating achievement tests for use in cross-national studies. *European Journal of Psychological Assessment*, 9, 57–68.

Hambleton, R. K. (1994). Guidelines for adapting educational and psychological tests: A progress report. *European Journal of Psychological Assessment*, 10, 229–44.

Hambleton, R. K. (1996). Guidelines for adapting educational and psychological tests. Paper presented at the Annual Meeting of the National Council on Measurement in Education, New York, 9–11 April.

Hambleton, R. K. (2001). The next generation of the ITC Test Translation and Adaptation Guidelines. *European Journal of Psychological Assessment*, 17(3), 164–72.

Hambleton, R. K. (2005). Issues, designs, and technical guidelines for adapting tests into multiple languages and cultures. In R. K. Hambleton, P. F. Merenda & C. Spielberger (eds.), *Adapting educational and psychological tests for cross-cultural assessment* (pp. 3–38). Mahwah, NJ: Lawrence Erlbaum Associates.

Hambleton, R. K., Merenda, P. & Spielberger, C. (2005). *Adapting educational and psychological tests for cross-cultural assessment*. Mahwah, NJ: Lawrence Erlbaum Associates.

Hambleton, R. K. & Patsula, L. (1999). Increasing the validity of adapted tests: Myths to be avoided and guidelines for improving test adaptation practices. *Association of Test Publishers*, 1(1), 1–13.

Hui, C. H. & Triandis, H. C. (1989). Effects of culture and response format on extreme response style. *Journal of Cross-Cultural Psychology*, 20(3), 296–309.

International Telecommunication Union (2005). *The Internet of Things*. Internet Report. Geneva: International Telecommunication Union.

International Test Commission (2005). International guidelines on computer-based and internet delivered testing. http://www.intestcom.org/guidelines.

International Test Commission (2010). International test commission guidelines for translating and adapting tests. http://www.intestcom.org. Accessed 18 October 2016.

Jeanrie, C. & Bertrand, R. (1999). Translating tests with the International Test Commission's guidelines: Keeping validity in mind. *European Journal of Psychological Assessment*, 15(3), 277–83.

Kline, P. (1993). *Personality: The psychometric view*. London: Routledge.

Marsella, A. J., Dubanoski, J., Hamada, W. C. & Morse, H. (2000). The measurement of personality across cultures: Historical, conceptual, and methodological issues and considerations. *American Behavioral Scientist*, 44(1), 41–62.

McCrae, R. R. & Costa, P. T. (2003). *Personality in adulthood: A five-factor theory perspective*. New York: Guilford Press.

Messick, S. (1995). Standards of validity and the validity of standards in performance assessment. *Educational Measurement: Issues and Practice*, 14, 5–8.

Pelham, B. W. (1999). *Conducting research in psychology: Measuring the weight of smoke*. Pacific Grove, CA: Brooks/Cole.

Robertson, I. T. & Smith, M. (2001). Personnel selection. *Journal of Occupational and Organizational Psychology*, 74(4), 441–72.

Rust, J. & Golombok, S. (1999). *Modern psychometrics: The science of psychological assessment*. London: Routledge.

Ryan, A., McFarland, L., Baron, H. & Page, R. (1999). An international look at selection practices: Nation and culture as explanations for variability in practice. *Personnel Psychology*, 52(2), 359–92.

Schmit, M. J. & Ryan, A. M. (1993). The Big Five in personnel selection: Factor structure in applicant and nonapplicant populations. *Journal of Applied Psychology*, 78(6), 966–74.

Sireci, S. G. (2005). Using bilinguals to evaluate the comparability of different language versions of a test. In R. K. Hambleton, P. Merenda & C. Spielberger (eds.), *Adapting educational and psychological tests for cross-cultural assessment* (pp. 117–38). Mahwah, NJ: Lawrence Erlbaum Associates.

Sulaiman, S. O., Bhugra, D. & de Silva, P. (2001a). Perceptions of depression in a community sample in Dubai. *Transcultural Psychiatry*, 38(2), 201–18.

Sulaiman, S. O., Bhugra, D. & de Silva, P. (2001b). The development of a culturally sensitive symptom checklist for depression in Dubai. *Transcultural Psychiatry*, 38(2), 219–29.

van de Vijver, F. J. R. (1998). Towards a theory of bias and equivalence. *ZUMA-Nachrichten Spezial*, 3, 41–65.

van de Vijver, F. J. R. & Hambleton, R. K. (1996). Translating tests. *European Psychologist*, 1(2), 89–99.

van de Vijver, F. J. R. & Jeanrie, C. (2004). Assessing structural and metric equivalence: A case study. Paper presented at the 28th International Congress of Psychology (ICP), Beijing, July.

van de Vijver, F. J. R. & Leung, K. (1997). *Methods and data analysis for cross-cultural research.* Cross-Cultural Psychology Series 1. London: Sage.

van de Vijver, F. J. R. & Poortinga, Y. H. (1997). Towards an integrated analysis of bias in cross-cultural assessment. *European Journal of Psychological Assessment*, 13(1), 29–37.

van de Vijver, F. J. R. & Poortinga, Y. H. (2005). Conceptual and methodological issues in adapting tests. In R. K. Hambleton, P. F. Merenda & C. D. Spielberger (eds.), *Adapting educational and psychological tests for cross-cultural assessment* (pp. 39–63). Mahwah, NJ: Lawrence Erlbaum Associates.

van de Vijver, F. J. R. & Tanzer, N. (1997). Bias and equivalence in cross-cultural assessment. *European Review of Applied Psychology*, 47(4), 263–79.

van de Vijver, F. J. R. & Tanzer, N. K. (2004). Bias and equivalence in cross-cultural assessment: An overview. *European Review of Applied Psychology*, 54(2), 119–35.

17 Personality Testing in the Workplace: Can Internet Business Disruption Erode the Influence of Psychology Ethics?

Earon Kavanagh

INTRODUCTION

In this chapter I employ my training in psychology and business to address the threat of Internet business disruption to the ethics-informed field of occupational testing. While the central theme is competition, the forces of competition in the testing industry are explored through the conflicting discourses of psychology and its ethics, and business and its practices of utilisation in marketing; these are interwoven with the Internet's power to disrupt markets and whole industries. Three decades of psychologists' examinations of DISC-based personality tests are explored and the conclusion is reached that these instruments operate as 'grey market', defined as existing outside of the intended and established standards of psychological testing.

While from a business competition perspective the above is not a bad thing, it does pose problems from a psychological perspective, and from a competitive analysis perspective it poses threats to the psychological testing establishment and creates confusion in public perception of psychological testing. My conclusion is that it is the responsibility of the psychological establishment to declare and educate the public on what is psychology and what isn't psychology in occupational testing, and recommendations are made on that basis.

The Internet has created new challenges in how personality tests can be screened for quality and delivered to the market. In this chapter the current market is defined as the space of interaction between the test taker and the test. Traditionally that space was occupied by the interaction of the test taker, the test and the credentialed test practitioner. Kline (2000) argued that this was essential for reliability. Currently, some personality tests for occupational use can be taken on the Internet directly, without interaction or preparation with a qualified test practitioner. While the results of a study by Arthur, Glaze, Villado and Taylor (2009) suggested that the use of unproctored Internet testing does not threaten to elevate levels of response distortion in personality testing, the Internet, by its ability to disrupt and distribute technology, leadership, identity and discourse (Holmes, Hosking & Grieco, 2002), has increased the opportunity to market personality tests of questionable reliability and validity. The Internet was seen as having significant potential for emerging discourses that could contribute to social change, and improve relations in organisational life (Hosking, 2002; Kavanagh, 2002); and yet in 2015 much of what we see online is seemingly about face validity and commercial interests. Nevertheless, multiple perspectives and discourses do co-exist on the web, and many are interwoven with commercial interests.

THE STRUCTURE OF THIS CHAPTER

I begin this exploration by identifying two conflicting discourses in the testing field, the discourse of psychology and the discourse of business, and their interplay with economics. After a brief introduction to the various uses of occupational testing I argue that the discourse of business sometimes creates grey markets, in which products are distributed through channels not intended by their manufacturers. I provide cases to show that grey markets exist in Internet business, and existed before the Internet, including psychological testing. I then introduce the competitive nature of DISC-based tests and follow with case examples of how disruption destabilises established business practices and strong positions in an industry. (DISC and its variations are popular personality tests marketed on the Internet.) I follow this with a discussion of the substitution strategy in competitive analysis and potential disruptions in the testing industry. I then discuss DISC's high attention to face validity, its history, and DISC theory. Shifting into the importance of real validity, I discuss Paltiel's (1986) examination of validity in DISC-based instruments. This is followed by an introduction to later reviews of DISC tests by the BPS and the Buros Institute for Mental Measurements. I then provide a short discussion on testing and competition. In my conclusion and recommendations I examine DISC's competitive strategy, including its grey market approach, and make recommendations for what the occupational testing industry can do in response to increased Internet disruption from grey market strategies that work outside of the standards for occupational personality tests.

TWO CONFLICTING DISCOURSES INHERENT IN OCCUPATIONAL TESTING

The Internet entered a period of widespread public use in 1995 (Bartram, 2006). In personality testing 'the web', as it is known, brought together two fields that operate from different discourses: the field of psychological practice and the field of business. Discourses comprise statements that construct objects, and speakers who mobilise different levels of power and those same objects to accomplish their goals (Parker, 1992). In personality testing, the newest Internet objects include do-it-yourself personality inventories and superb inventories such as the Saville Wave (https://www.savilleconsulting.com/). The discourse of psychology provides certain rights to practitioners, but those rights come with prescribed rules and limitations for practice. Business, on the other hand, is generally not a regulated profession. The discourse of business leans towards self-serving statements celebrating the 'visions' of corporate leaders, new products, promises, possibilities and success. It is generally embedded in marketing drive. Both discourses can also be seen as harbours in which multiple smaller discourses operate and mobilise power.

While Chartered Psychologists who have a consulting practice are generally 'in business', their business activity is guided by the ethical rules of psychological practice, which includes the public good and attention to doing no harm. The managerial economics of business decision making states that management's primary goal is to 'maximize the value of the firm' through increased profit, whereas public-interest decisions (and therefore psychological practices) are informed by analysis of costs and benefits to stakeholders (Samuelson & Marks, 2012). Thus, in the practice of psychology, maximising the value of the firm is not the primary goal. Private-practice psychologists will appreciate the irony of this, in that a practice's sustainability requires profitability, and so successful psychologists must balance the discourses of business and psychology.

USES FOR PERSONALITY TESTING IN THE WORKPLACE

Personality tests are used in various workplace contexts, often with other tools such as bio-data, interviewing and coaching. The other tools used (e.g., coaching, interviewing) and the type of personality test depend on the context (Cripps & Spry, 2008). The general contexts are as follows.

- Selection
- Promotion
- Individual personal development
- Team development
- Redundancy/outplacement
- Career guidance
- Counselling

On the surface, selection is perhaps the most important from an employer's perspective, because of the need to make performance predictions that are correct. But ultimately all of these areas are important and create an integrated system that supports employee productivity from the beginning of a career to retirement. There are many personality tests that can be used, all of which have good reliability and validity. Some are factor-based while others are based on a norm group. Most measure personality traits, while others measure personality type, which has limited utility. The important thing is to investigate the reliability and validity of each test with independent institutions whose expertise in reviewing such tests is recognised.

HOW THE DISCOURSE OF BUSINESS CREATES GREY MARKETS

> A grey market is the trade of a commodity through distribution channels which, while legal, are unofficial, unauthorized, or unintended by the original manufacturer.
>
> Wikipedia

A grey market emerges out of competition when a commodity or product is manipulated and sold outside of normal distribution channels. Grey market operators play by their own standards rather than generally accepted standards in an industry. For example, selling tests to unqualified test users allows the unqualified to enter the testing industry and compete without adequate training and with a low barrier to entry. In the short term this can provide increased profits for the test publisher, but eventually it floods the market with competitors, and increases rivalry while decreasing profit capability. But, of equal importance in testing, this scenario increases risk to the public, and the potential for lawsuits and damaging the reputation of the industry. The nature of supply and demand is that customers are always attracted to a better deal, and buyers have power, but they need to be fully informed to make wise decisions. It's not in the overall interests of grey market operators in any industry to provide such information, even if they had access to it. The most common disruption strategy in the age of the Internet is substitution and low prices rather than differentiation, high-value products, and high-quality service combined with a higher price.

Some time ago, through Internet grey markets, one could buy expensive video cameras at reduced prices. However, manufacturers such as Panasonic refused to honour warranties for products purchased in the grey market. Once this information circulated in the prosumer filmmaking community there was a reduction in grey market purchases. The risk was just too high to warrant them. Grey markets have also emerged in the international testing domain, and it is my belief that professionals need to keep addressing this trend before the Internet makes it unmanageable.

Two decades ago an emerging grey market was spotted in Canada and quickly responded to. In 1994 the Canadian Psychological Association (CPA) recommended that the standardised three levels of tests (levels A, B and C) should be supplemented with descriptions of the training required to access each level (Simner, 1994). This was the result of an examination carried out by the CPA in relation to one publisher who had mislabelled tests: a CPA member had written a letter of concern that this publisher was selling Level B tests as Level A, which required lower qualifications to administer and interpret. The CPA also recommended that the responsibilities assumed by test users should be clearly defined and that first-time test purchasers should have to disclose their qualifications to be able to purchase and use tests. The CPA further recommended that test publishers should be encouraged to insert into their catalogues a clear statement about who may purchase their tests, and that firms that followed these prescriptions should receive some sort of recognition. Test publishers often work around such recommendations by 'certification' schemes in the use of specific tests.

Over the years, the British Psychological Society has implemented standards for test use and a Register of Qualifications in Test Use, and begun a programme of test reviews using a five-star rating system. These reviews can be purchased by BPS members, Register members, or members of the public. The BPS knew that a problem had developed with unqualified test users and questionable test publishers (Paltiel, 1986), and had instituted a programme to set standards and qualify practitioners in educational testing, occupational testing, and now forensic testing (British Psychological Society, 2015). However, some British psychologists have expressed concern that the BPS reviews are currently 'benign' and need to be more rigorous.

THE COMPETITIVE ATTRACTION OF DISC-BASED PERSONALITY TESTS

DISC-based tests seem to be vigorously marketed on the Internet, for example on LinkedIn. The marketing is so effective that DISC and some other products appear to be ever present in the business testing area. Yet psychologists trained in psychometrics frequently express concern about such tests (Conoley & Castillo, 2005; Munro, 2011). Upon first glance DISC-based personality tests are an interesting phenomenon. They are often recommended by persons other than trained psychologists; they are reasonably inexpensive to purchase and can be administered without a proctor. There is at least one book written about using DISC for increasing leadership capabilities (Sugerman, Scullard & Wilhelm, 2011). However, one rarely finds independent third-party reviews of DISC online, or peer-reviewed articles on it in the psychology literature.

There are many websites that distribute DISC-related products. At one website I can get a free DISC personality test (https://discpersonalitytesting.com/). The test takes between five and ten minutes to complete and promises the test taker a better understanding of why they communicate in a particular style, insights into how they can improve, and that the results will allow them to:

- Immediately improve interpersonal communications
- Connect with co-workers more effectively
- Understand what [they] need to do to be more successful in [their] interactions with others.

Who would not want to get this kind of outcome at no charge? The DISC agents appear to be using a value-added approach, which means they are giving something away, and that will probably lead the potential customer to purchase more. This is generally seen as a good business strategy, and similar competitive strategies are employed by large companies such as SHL, which offers free services and information through its Test Preparation and Career Centre (see SHL, n.d.; also Bartram, 2006, p. 19). But the DISC personality testing website sends another business signal about the current state of testing: immediate results for little investment via the Internet mean potential disruption to the testing industry. One way in which industry disruption can occur is through large-scale dissemination of tests with questionable reliability or validity. Amazon has disrupted the book industry and other industries by using this technology strategy.

SUBSTITUTION AND DISRUPTION IN BUSINESS AND PSYCHOLOGY

In MBA courses on business strategy one common competitive strategy is known as *substitution*. Substitution occurred in the yoga wear industry once Lululemon Athletica, Inc. experienced high success with its body-shaping fabrics and fashions. Others quickly entered the industry with products that looked similar but sold for less; some even opened stores down the street from Lululemon retailers. Eventually Lululemon could not hold its differentiated position in the industry it pioneered, and its stock value began to drop, leading its founder and chairman to resign.

Another example of substitution is coaching, which started as a substitution for counselling psychology. Counselling helps people cope with common problems that occur in the life, marital or career cycle rather than with mental illness, which is considered 'clinical' or psychiatric. Substitution strategies aim to siphon off a share of the industry profits with a cheaper replacement product that claims to get the same or a better result but is not born of the same classification. It's even better to enter an industry with a substitute product that costs little. Psychologists understand, for example, that a counsellor credential takes years of study and cost to achieve, whereas a coaching credential takes roughly 120 hours of training and some testing of skill. Coaching creates a low entry barrier into the helping industry and in some cases coaches charge higher than counselling rates. The word 'coaching' as a behavioural change methodology first appeared in the psychological literature with Dr Murray Bowen's cultivation of techniques to 'coach' parents on their behaviour, emotions and ability to observe their emotions in a family system (1978, pp. 235–46), but most non-psychologist coaches are unaware of this. Life coaches, in competing in the market with their substitution strategy, often misrepresent what counsellors do, preferring to position them as dealing with the past, while coaches allege that they deal with the present and the desired future.

We have also witnessed this kind of disruptive substitution with Amazon publishing, thanks to the Internet. The publisher as vetting agent has been removed and virtually anyone can become an author in as little as one week; there are many books on Amazon about how to achieve this. Substitution with low price value results in a glut of inferior products in the market, but the theory is that the market determines that the best products succeed. Thus, new customised 'bottom feeder' strategies emerge to compete in selling one's book on Amazon, including giving large quantities away for free. This can create many competitive problems for the existing industry, which has to find ways to compete with the glut of inferior products. To start, it is very difficult to compete.

Potential disruption challenges for testing

All one needs to enter the Internet-based testing industry is a computer, a server, coding skills and a cool-sounding theory of personality or behaviour. Moreover, if authorities are not able to force certain test publishers to follow standards, such as those established by the International Test Commission (Oakland, 2006), the perceived value of testing could decrease and the industry could suffer.

Internet-based testing allows the elimination of a third-party adviser who normally controls who takes the test and the test conditions, and ensures conformity to good practice (Bartram, 2006, p. 29). Removing the test supervisor can result in a drop in reliability, as well as lowering the test price. There are many important actions taken by supervisors that ensure the reliability and, ultimately, the validity of the test. Bartram (p. 31) states that, depending on the kind of test being taken, these responsibilities include the following:

- Test taker identity authentication
- Establishing rapport and a stress-free climate
- Ensuring instructions are carried out as per standards
- Addressing problems or unexpected conditions before the test session
- Validation of the test results
- Ensuring the test results are what they appear to be and are based solely on the test taker's input without aid
- Ensuring secure filing/storage of the test results
- Feedback to the test taker from a qualified person
- Report writing for the client or referring third party, if necessary.

From Bartram's perspective we learn that attention should be paid to the whole test-taking process, or, as he puts it, the design of the whole process. The late Paul Kline (2000) also expressed concern over this and placed particular emphasis on the importance of the supervisor for reliability, and ultimately validity and utility.

DISC: A QUEST FOR FACE VALIDITY

The DISC blog at the above website discusses such topics as the history of the DISC model, how understanding others is an important skill for effective communication, the four DISC types, the DISC behavioural blends, how to set up an account, and more. Blogs are commonly associated nowadays with a business trend known as 'thought leadership', which creates the sense that the writers have done some research, are informed, and are at the leading edge of the market. However, this is not always the case, and there is an abundance of Internet-based articles which have low value. For evidence just examine the multitude of human resource advice articles on LinkedIn. Most of these articles are personal opinions with no reference to empirical research or related bodies of literature, and appear to target the uninformed layperson.

The blog also links the DISC theory to the late 'Harvard psychologist' Dr William Marston. Thus far we can ascertain that this website provides a simple way to experience a free DISC analysis, coupled with a section to add what psychometrics professionals call 'face validity'. This term is explained by the psychologist Paul Kline, who was a leading voice in psychometrics.

> Face validity. This refers to the appearance of a test. If it looks valid it has face validity. Unfortunately, with personality tests, there is no necessary connection between face validity and true validity. Indeed, the only demand that tests have some degree of face validity is that without it subjects may not cooperate in the testing. (Kline, 1993, p. 13)

Kline also believed in the importance of the credentialed expert working as a go-between with the test taker, administering the test and providing feedback and a report. This, in traditional practice, added reliability, because the practitioner followed prescribed formats in both administration and feedback on the test. The new era of Internet testing allowed test purveyors using the substitute strategy to remove the practitioner from the equation. The result is that face validity in such contexts is little more than marketing copy. For the public there is only one real way to establish the presence of true validity and reliability. To be fair, I did perform university library searches on the validity and reliability of DISC, and will address the results later. In the next section I will discuss the history of DISC, its theory, and Marston himself.

DISC-BASED TESTS AND THEIR ORIGINS

There are several instruments that claim William Marston's D-I-S-C framework as their theoretical foundations. These include DISC, Discus, the Personal Profile System, Insights Discovery, Personal Profile Analysis, Personal Development Analysis, Predictive Index, Style Analysis, and the Strategic Assessment System. The following information on DISC-based personality instruments is from a white paper by UK Chartered Occupational Psychologist Andrew Munro (2011).

DISC-based personality test facts

- Originally designed in the 1950s
- Completed by around 10 million persons per year
- Used in recruitment, development, coaching and team building
- Many variations from a variety of publishers
- Hundreds of thousands of consultants, trainers and coaches accredited in its use
- Originally USA-based, now global, available in many languages
- Internet-based, inexpensive, and easy to access
- Just take the test online and view your results without needing a third party to explain them.

The DISC-based value proposition

- Promises to 'create an alignment between employees' drive and organizational goals'
- Claims it 'possesses 85% plus validity'
- Claims it 'is 91% predictable in classifying people into superior performer or inferior performer categories'
- More recently repositions itself within neuroscience, brain functioning or hormonal patterns.

THE DISC THEORY FOUNDATION

DISC-based instruments are based on William Marston's four-dimensional theory of human behaviour. Munro writes that this is now hard-wired into many different personality tests, many of which are listed above.

Who was William Marston?

William Marston (1883–1947), born in the USA, was a psychologist, a lawyer, and the inventor of the 'lie detector'. He married his research assistant, and then took a student as a simultaneous second wife. He had four children, two with each wife, and, allegedly, they all lived together as one big, happy family.

Marston's personality theory

In 1928 Marston published *Emotions of Normal People*, identified by Munro (2011) as a sprawling and almost unreadable mess. Typical of the utterances in Marston's writing are statements such as 'all phasic motor impulses are compelled to combine with, or to conflict with, the tonic motor impulses continuously discharging in a pattern which may be called … our natural reflex equilibrium' (p. 87). Munro called the book a brave if flawed attempt to synthesise developments in physiology with the results of Marston's own lie detector research and, importantly, his personal views of human nature, gender differences and social interaction.

Munro writes that Marston's ideas were dismissed by professional peers, who saw him as an intellectual charlatan, and his ideas as 'a mix of unabashed hucksterism, earnest utopianism, insightful criticism, and calculated subterfuge', and the FBI in an official report suggested he was a phony and crackpot (p. 3). Despite his rejection by professional peers, some, such as Walter Clarke in the 1940s, began to take an interest in Marston's ideas as a potential basis for personality analysis. In the early 1970s John Geier at the University of Minnesota acquired the copyright to Marston's work and developed the Personal Profile System (PPS), which can be seen as the first of many instruments associated with Marston's theory.

Marston proposed that in human behaviour there are four emotional responses against two axes, of attention (passive or active) and environment (favourable or antagonistic). This theory was invented long before Selye (1974) divided work-related stress into eustress (positive and motivating) and distress (negative and risk-causing). Marston's four DISC responses are:

- Dominance: activity in an antagonistic environment (work, and stress situations)
- Inducement: activity in a favourable environment (non-work and no stress)
- Submissive: passivity in a favourable environment (non-work and no stress)
- Compliance: passivity in an antagonistic environment (work, and stress situations).

We can ascertain from the above that Marston's theory yielded a broad-brush approach to human behaviour.

- **Dominance** reflects the need to overcome and 'conquer'.
- **Inducement** reflects the need to persuade and motivate.

- **Submissive** reflects the need to support and be of service.
- **Compliance** reflects the need to avoid trouble and to be correct.

Paltiel (1986) and colleagues acquired seven personality inventories claiming to measure these four personality categories. Paltiel reports that while the trait names are not always the same the descriptions remain identical. It should be noted, for example, that the Discus publisher has not followed the original Marston DISC trait vocabulary, electing instead to shift the language.

TRUE VALIDITY REQUIRES MOVING BEYOND FACE VALIDITY

Kline (1993, p. 13) made another comment on the irony of face validity, leading us to believe that a strong level of face validity could lead to undesired outcomes based on test-taker perceptions: 'However, if a test is truly face valid, it may lead to distortion, especially in selection. Candidates for the armed services would be unlikely to admit to physical fears, for example.' If we accept Kline's view, it is easy to understand that face validity sets up perceptions that produce less than wonderful results in certain circumstances. There is no half-way with validity. The test must have true validity, be improved, or be discarded.

Validity is generally measured in two ways, and face validity isn't one of them. We must begin by asking if the test is a useful measure of the psychological characteristic it is attempting to assess (Paltiel, 1986). As Kline (2000) argues, we are seeking the psychological meaning of the scales. This question has two parts. First, is the test reliable? Second, is the test valid? Reliability tells us to what degree a person's score on a test is affected by factors extraneous to it, such as a practitioner not following the same administration procedure for all test takers, or complex computer screen directions confusing the test taker. Validity informs us about the relevance of inferences drawn from the test scores. There are statistical techniques for determining the internal consistency reliability of scale items, and ways to determine validity through correlation as well as ways to determine predictive validity; these will not be discussed here.

Once the test developer establishes that the test is truly valid, the test must be held up to public scrutiny. This is best done through independent societal institutions that place economic and ethical value on balancing costs and benefits rather than the business primary goal to 'maximize the value of the firm'. One example of this is when Raymark, Schmitt and Guion (1997) included a large number of psychologists from multiple universities in their research and then turned over the resulting instrument to academics and psychometrics professionals for further testing and research. These institutions can include groups of universities and psychological societies such as the BPS or the APA, as well as the Buros Institute. By doing the above the test developers are increasing validity through multiple raters, and in effect adhering to the psychological ethics discourse of benefiting the public and doing no harm. Until the test is held up to public scrutiny by independent experts it will always appear suspect. If a test is submitted for review and gets a poor score, the test developer knows what has to be done to improve it.

The above information can only be assured through 'independent third parties' who have nothing to gain from recommending the test. This is known in psychology as the absence of any dual relationship or conflict of interest. If an institution recommended a terrible test it would lose credibility as an institution. Persons must also be wary of test developers employing 'independent' consultants or 'psychologists' who confirm the reliability and validity of tests. Such independence can only be had from a distance with no dual relationship or conflict of interest.

PALTIEL'S REVIEW OF THE DISC-BASED APPROACHES

Some decades ago (1986) Paltiel acquired seven DISC-based tests, and examined two in depth: the Thomas International Personal Profile Analysis (PPA) and the Personality Profile System (PPS). In his examination of the PPA test user qualification courses, which he described as 'one and two day courses', Paltiel stated that the courses 'do not have psychometric content'. This contrasted significantly with the BPS standards, which at that time required a five-day basic course on psychometric testing, followed by another five days on the specific test. Paltiel further reported that validity was described in the Thomas PPA courses as '"how good a respondent considers his/her own result". … If the customer likes the analysis, which is often the case, he/she is sold on the concept. With a one-day course (and the option of "advanced user status") the customer becomes a "fully trained" test-user' (Paltiel, 1986, p. 3).

The biggest challenge seemed to be in Marston's theoretical construct, and its application in a reliable and valid manner. Paltiel stated that the items used to measure Marston's four D-I-S-C dimensions are not independent and that the PPA hypothesis for measuring different characteristics was 'fairly implausible'. Paltiel concluded that there was little evidence to suggest 'that either the PPA or the PPS can provide the detailed analysis of personality which the authors claim of their system' (p. 6).

But let's be fair, and provide room for development. Paltiel carried out his examination in 1986, almost 30 years ago. Surely DISC-based personality tests have further developed since then. Seeking to find out if psychologists had changed their opinions on DISC-based tests, I carried out searches at the BPS and Buros online test review databases for reviews of the following tests: DISC, Discus, the Personal Profile System, Insights Discovery, Personal Profile Analysis, Personal Development Analysis, Predictive Index, Style Analysis, and the Strategic Assessment System. The date of this search was 14 January 2015. The results are below.

OTHER FINDINGS ON DISC-BASED TESTS

Personal profile system

The following comments from the Buros Institute for Mental Measurements review address the PPS, which is listed in the report as sold by Performax Systems International, Inc. It is reviewed by McGinnis (1989).

A serious concern with this instrument is its lack of reported research. While the authors state the instrument shows good reliability and validity, they provide the user with virtually no data to support these claims.

The manual refers to a study of 300 Minnesota dentists using the system, but neglects to provide the reader with statistical specifics. The manual also refers to studies involving 'hundreds of thousands of people' but does not provide specific results or references, stating that these studies 'are not widely available' or 'cannot be included in this packet because of their confidential nature'…

While the theory behind this instrument holds promise in increasing individuals' awareness of their behavioral styles with environmental conditions, the clear lack of data to support this instrument should preclude its use.

One of the concluding comments in this review was that 'such vague and incomplete information regarding the construct or convergent validities of the Personal Profile is unacceptable'.

Later findings for Personal Profile Analysis

In the UK, test reviews conducted by the British Psychology Society also express concerns, noting for PPA, 'considerable caution, therefore, is required when interpreting the evidence presented in the technical documentation concerning the psychometric properties of the PPA' (Robertson & Hodgkinson, 2002, p. 211).

Findings for Insights Discovery

And in the case of Insights Discovery, an instrument that has its origins in both DISC and MBTI, the BPS reviewers wrote that 'it is difficult to uncover relevant information about the development of the instrument and about consequent studies that support the psychometric properties of the instrument' (Munro, 2011).

Findings for DISC Classic

The following comments from the Buros Institute for Mental Measurements review address the DISC Classic and is listed in the report as sold by Inscape Publishers. It is reviewed by Conoley and Castillo (2005).

> The DISC measure is designed for layperson use. Each participant receives a self-explanatory test booklet that contains a self-scoring chart and self-interpretation table. The facilitator's manual (which suffices for the test manual) describes the history of the Marston Model, the development of the measure, the psychometric data, and the interpretation guidelines ….
>
> A user of the DISC should be cautious. The reliability data for the items appear to be moderate at best. The use of test-retest reliability is recommended to the publishers if they wish to examine the reliability of the profiles. Additionally, there are no studies that specify what the DISC predicts. The validity of the instrument is also questionable. Given the current reliability and validity information, it appears that the DISC is limited to Caucasian professionals … to white collar professionals such as executives and management.

The developers claim that the DISC has broad applicability within most organizations. However this statement should be taken with caution. The developers list a variety of ways in which the DISC can be helpful in areas such as communication skill development and conflict resolution. However, many of the statements are beyond the demonstrated applicability of the instrument.

The presentation and organization of the assessment does make it easy for the untrained administrator.

The DISC Classic is an easy-to-use, well-organized self-assessment of behavior responses to work environments. On the surface level, it appears that the instrument is useful in personal or professional development. However, the test suffers from questionable reliability and unknown validity. The measure is also remiss in its lack of reliability and validity for diverse ethnic/racial populations and professional occupations. Therefore, the use of the DISC is not recommended.

COMPETITION AND PERSONALITY TESTING

Competition is an industry condition which is continually in flux. The five competitive forces outlined by the Harvard model (Porter, 2011) start with the established industry rivals; the four remaining competitive forces are customers, suppliers, the threat of potential entrants, and substitute products. The forces of competition can be intense, benign, or somewhere in between. The referenced articles by Munro (2011) and Paltiel (1986) are indicators that DISC-based tests have been around for decades, and are part of the established rivalry, although they might be marching to the discourse of business rather than to the discourse of psychology. When juxtaposed with the ethics and long tradition of psychological testing this fact renders the tests grey market outliers, operating outside of practice standards.

With the Internet capabilities speeding rapidly, through smartphones, iPads, Facebook, Twitter and Hootsuite the rivalry will undoubtedly increase. The Internet model for business is rapidly including the notion of 'engage and share'. Any product can now be promoted and 'liked' on Facebook, which is a new form of marketing in which the marketers cleverly get the public to carry out their marketing. The Internet technology also makes it easy for new entrants into the market. The more intense the competition gets, the less profit is to be had. Less rivalry usually means less intense competition and more room for the competitors to be profitable. All of the above forces are happening simultaneously, so one thing that mainstream testing should do is to keep the grey area at bay and design strategies so that the grey area players get less share of the market. The ethical characteristics of the grey market and their implications for consumers also need to be taken into account.

CONCLUSION AND RECOMMENDATIONS

There is a common theme in the three decades of reviews of DISC-based instruments. The reviews addressed here occurred in 1986, 1989, 2002, 2005 and later. The common theme is that these products do not seem to be improving over time with respect to accepted standards for occupational personality tests.

DISC's substitute strategy as approach to competition

What can be determined from the Paltiel, BPS and Buros reviews of DISC-based tests is that their approach to competition is one of substitution of reliable and valid tests with inferior products, but the claim is generally that their products will do what real tests are designed to do in occupational contexts, and do it for less in a user-friendly manner.

DISC's low barrier to market entry

The substitute competitive strategy also adopts a low barrier to market entry by using methods used in multi-level marketing and previous versions of the life insurance industry:

1. Test users are cultivated with little training.
2. The test is made easy for lay people to understand.
3. Lay persons can then become test users and market the product.
4. Perceived expertise can be had with little investment.

Grey market

The grey market is created by DISC-based test publishers, and others, seemingly by not following or adhering to accepted test standards in the design and distribution of their products and the training of their test users.

Internet disruption of the industry

It's conceivable that the Internet will only increase sales of such grey market products (there are others as well), because they are highly marketed and shared using the 'engage and share' approach that is favoured, for example, in online social media. DISC can be found in fan groups on Facebook as well. The low barrier to entry makes this highly workable.

What can the testing industry do?

The testing industry can learn a lesson from the American post-secondary education system and the proliferation of Internet-marketed degree and diploma mills after 1995. The mills were always around, but they multiplied after the masses went online. Fortunately, the degree and diploma mills met with significant resistance, but new mills pop up every month on the Web. A wave of resistance occurred, from consumers as well as educational allies. Websites such as www.degreeinfo.com and alt.distance.education sought to advise consumers on which the real accredited institutions were and which were the diploma and degree mills. Eventually state governments began to adopt new regulations to force out the degree and diploma mills and close the loopholes that allowed them to exist. In occupational testing, the challenge for both consumers and ill-informed HR professionals is how to look through the cracks in the grey market plaster of face validity to see what's really going on behind that wall.

This can be done by the following means:

- Ongoing education of the public, with particular emphasis on HR societies, the universities, and counselling and psychology groups.
- Lower costs on quality products for test users (lower the barrier to market entry)
- Raising awareness of the three test-reviewing institutions (BPS, APA, Buros).
- Establishing regulations and enforcing them if possible (despite any objections from supporters of free market enterprise). This probably means creating a lobbying effort to governments, which can be long and costly.
- Accessible and affordable liability insurance programmes for accredited test users.
- Creating categories for tests: for example, accredited, engaged in a five-year development process, and unaccredited.
- Limiting the period of time for tests to achieve a reasonable state of reliability and validity.

To conclude, there is nothing illegal about what I propose are grey market personality tests. What makes them grey market is that they are not psychology and not psychometric, and this is evidenced by their not adhering to sound standards of psychology in test development and practice. The evidence on the above tests over the past three decades speaks for itself. The discourse of business is known to use anything it can find in the marketing interest of 'maximizing the value of the firm'. This, as some say in sports, is 'fair ball'. Business interests will link all kinds of services and products with the words 'psychology', 'psychometrics' or 'psychologist' to create a good marketing impression (face validity). In the spirit of competition the onus is on real psychological practitioners and associations to declare what is psychology and what isn't psychology. The field of psychology owes this service to the public and to organisations that wish to improve productivity with the help of real psychological instruments.

REFERENCES

Arthur, W., Jr., Glaze, R. M., Villado, A. J. & Taylor, J. E. (2009). Unproctored Internet-based tests of cognitive ability and personality: Magnitude of cheating and response distortion. *Industrial and Organizational Psychology*, 2, 39–45.

Bartram, D. (2006). Testing on the internet: Issues, challenges and opportunities in the field of occupational assessment. In D. Bartram & R. Hambleton (eds.), *Computer-based testing and the Internet: Issues and advances* (pp. 13–37). Chichester: John Wiley and Sons.

Bowen, M. (1978). *Family therapy in clinical practice*. Oxford: Rowman and Littlefield.

British Psychological Society (n.d.). Psychological testing: A new approach. http://www.bps.org.uk/psychological-testing-new-approach. Accessed 16 February 2015.

Conoley, C. & Castillo, L. (2005). A review of the DiSC Classic. In R. A. Spies & B. S. Plake (eds.), *The sixteenth mental measurements yearbook* (pp. 312–14). Lincoln, NE: Buros Institute of Mental Measurements.

Cripps, B. and Spry, D. (2008). *Psychometric testing pocketbook*. Alresford: Management Pocketbooks.

Holmes, L., Hosking, D. M. & Grieco, M. (2002). *Organising in the information age: Distributed technology, distributed leadership, distributed identity, distributed discourse*. Aldershot: Ashgate.

Hosking, D. M. (2002). E-communications and relational constructionism: Distributed action, distributed leadership and ecological possibilities. In L. Holmes, D. M. Hosking & M. Grieco (eds.) *Organising in the information age: Distributed technology, distributed leadership, distributed identity, distributed discourse* (pp. 27–44). Aldershot: Ashgate.

Kavanagh, E. (2002). Epilogue: A juxtaposition of virtual discourse communities and organizational life. In L. Holmes, D. M. Hosking & M. Grieco (eds.), *Organising in the information age: Distributed technology, distributed leadership, distributed identity, distributed discourse*. Aldershot: Ashgate.

Kline, P. (1993). *Personality: The psychometric view*. London: Routledge.

Kline, P. (2000). *Handbook of psychological testing* (2nd edn). London: Routledge.

Marston, W. (1928). *Emotions of normal people*. London: Kegan Paul, Trench, Trubner & Co.

McGinnis, E. (1989). Review of the Personal Profile System. In J. C. Conoley & J. J. Kramer (eds.), *The tenth mental measurements yearbook*. Lincoln, NE: Buros Institute of Mental Measurements.

Munro, A. (2011). DISC based personality assessment: History and current status, and the fascinating life of William Marston. White paper. http://www.amazureconsulting.com/wp-content/uploads/2016/07/DISCPastAndPresentAndWilliamMarston.pdf.

Oakland, T. (2006). The International Test Commission and its role in advancing measurement practices and international guidelines. In D. Bartram & R. Hambleton (eds.), *Computer-based testing and the Internet: Issues and advances* (pp. 1–12). Chichester: John Wiley and Sons.

Paltiel, L. (1986). Self-appraisal personality inventories. *Guidance and Assessment Review*, 2(3), 3–6.

Parker, I. (1992). *Discourse dynamics*. London: Routledge.

Porter, M. (2011). The five competitive forces that shape strategy. In *HBR's 10 must reads on strategy* (pp. 39–76). Boston, MA: Harvard Business School Publishing.

Raymark, P., Schmitt, M. & Guion, R. (1997). Identifying potentially useful personality constructs for employee selection. *Personnel psychology*, 50, 723–36.

Robertson, S. & Hodgkinson, G. P. (2002). Review of the Personal Profile Analysis (PPA). British Psychological Society.

Samuelson, W. F. & Marks, S. G. (2012). *Managerial economics* (7th edn). New York: John Wiley and Sons.

Selye, Hans (1974). *Stress without distress*. Philadelphia, PA: J.B. Lippincott.

SHL (n.d.). Take practice tests to familiarise yourself with the online testing experience. Test preparation and career centre. http://www.shldirect.com/en/practice-tests/. Accessed 19 October 2016.

Simner, M. L. (1994). Recommendations by the Canadian Psychological Association for improving the North American safeguards that help protect the public against test misuse. Canadian Psychological Association. http://www.cpa.ca/cpasite/UserFiles/Documents/publications/TestMisuse.pdf.

Sugerman, J., Scullard, M. & Wilhelm, E. (2011). *The 8 dimensions of leadership: DiSC strategies for becoming a better leader*. San Francisco, CA: Berrett–Koehler Publishers.

Wikipedia (n.d.). Grey market. http://en.wikipedia.org/wiki/Grey_market. Accessed 19 January 2015.

18 A Practitioner's Viewpoint: Limitations and Assumptions Implicit in Assessment

JAY ROSEVEARE

This chapter sounds a cautionary note to practitioners about their use of psychometrics. It is a warning, first, to be aware of the limitations of psychometric tools and, second, to allow for the different viewpoints inherent in an assessment situation.

My own viewpoint is that of an occupational psychologist who has a reasonably good understanding of psychometrics but focuses on leadership coaching and career development. Since 1993, I have taken a series of psychological, then psychometric, qualifications in parallel with running a consultancy advising people, usually one to one, on careers and leadership.

Since 2001, I have made a point of attending at least one psychometric course a year, partly to refresh and reinforce my understanding of the key tenets of testing in general. This continuous and contiguous development of theory and practice has informed the reservations I am about to express about the way in which psychometrics are seen and used in practice.

I will focus in turn on three components of the assessment process – the practitioner, the instrument, and the client – and how each can adversely impact or even negate the usefulness of the exercise. A frequent issue for consultants in this field is the identity of 'the client'. Is this our employer or is it the individual with whom we are working? For clarity, where the distinction appears relevant I will throughout this chapter refer to the latter as the 'candidate', even where it is not in a selection situation.

My over-arching concern is the extent to which assumptions underlying each of these components in any given situation are adequately allowed for – or in many cases even recognised to exist.

THE INSTRUMENT

It is worth briefly recapping how psychometric measurement evolved. The first real recognition of individual differences was made by Francis Galton (1822–1911), who focused on physical measurements. The earliest measurement of mental prowess was by Alfred Binet

(1857–1911), who set out to identify which French children he felt were not worth schooling. The concept of each individual having an Intelligence Quotient ('IQ') emerged, but the extent to which the measure assessed purely school-based skills was not generally recognised for some time and the term is still frequently misused to suggest a measure of more generalised intelligence. The assessment process was comprehensive but slow, and was refined into the Stanford–Binet measure and used to evaluate conscripts during the First World War. The crudity of this measure became apparent and by the Second World War a more sophisticated approach had emerged.

For this, Charles Spearman (1863–1945) employed factor analysis, a statistical method of grouping items according to the degree of similarity in response patterns across a given sample. The result was his 1923 concept of general intelligence ('g'), which was not itself measurable but which was manifested in five different ways, each of which *could* be assessed. The five were:

1. Fluid intelligence – inference, induction, closure;
2. Crystallised intelligence – verbal, numerical, mechanical, social skills;
3. Visualisation – spatial orientation;
4. Retrieval capacity – fluency, association;
5. Cognitive speed – speed of performance.

The same factor analysis technique was applied to personality by Raymond Cattell (1905–98), who was a student of Spearman's. As a former chemist, he set out to produce a Table of Elements for personality and reduced the nearly 18,000 words Gordon Allport (1897–1967) had identified in the English language that were used for personal characteristics to just 16 factors. This resulted in Cattell's 16PF test in the late 1940s, which has since gone through a number of manifestations. By further application of factor analysis this was later reduced (Tupes and Christal 1961) to produce the Five Factor Model ('FFM') or 'Big 5', which comprised:

1. Neuroticism – Stability;
2. Extraversion – Introversion;
3. Openness to ideas – Conformity;
4. Agreeableness – Tough-mindedness;
5. Conscientious – Flexible.

Wars have prompted two other approaches to personality research and generated now well-established personality tests. A theory-based approach was chosen by Katharine Cook Briggs and her daughter Isabel Briggs Myers when America entered the Second World War. The two of them set out to find a way of helping women entering the workforce for the first time to identify what sort of jobs would suit them. They developed the personality theories of Karl Jung (1875–1961) into what became known as the Myers–Briggs Type Indicator (MBTI).

During the Korean War, a more bottom-up approach was adopted to improve team effectiveness in the US Navy by Will Schutz (1925–2002). This resulted in the FIRO

(Fundamental Interpersonal Relationship Orientation) model and assessment tools. In a peace-time commercial environment a third, hybrid, approach appears to have been adopted by Peter Saville to develop the Occupational Personality Questionnaire (OPQ) by looking for items that correlated with what his target market saw as key qualities for success in organisations.

One inevitable consequence of the employment of correlations and factor analysis is concern about trait breadth. Looking just for strong correlations can result in items which are effectively paraphrases with no underlying quality. Factor analysis software like SPSS, on the other hand, affords the opportunity to specify parameters which include the number of factors to be obtained and the degree of correlation acceptable. The analyst will therefore tend to make assumptions and decisions which essentially dictate the shape of the final model or instrument.

A crude analogy might be a belief that by specifying the size of the mesh in a sieve we can effectively control the quantity of material that is filtered out.

Essentially subjective decisions along these lines, though with differing raw data, have progressively reduced Allport's 18,000 words in the early twentieth century to Cattell's sixteen Personality Factors in the late 1940s, to Tupes and Christal's 1961 Five Factor Model, to Eysenck's 1991 three traits theory and finally to one General Factor of Personality (Rushton, Bons & Hur, 2008). It is therefore important to know the basis on which a model or instrument has been formulated, the assumptions implicit in its development and the population used to collect supporting data.

Knowing the composition of the test population is important for several reasons. Quite apart from the fact that many of the less used tests are based on results obtained from a relatively small number of psychology students pressed into service during their degrees, the relevance of any one set of test results to your client's situation can be substantially undermined if the candidate is compared to a group of people who are obviously different from him or her in age, upbringing, education, nationality, cultural identity, industry exposure, or other factors likely to influences their views and life experience.

While responsible test publishers constantly monitor results and periodically update their items and norms where necessary, some data sets are very old and may include references and terminology now less well understood. In much the same way, the pace of technological advancements we are seeing today is adding words and phrases to the language all the time and may already be rendering recently written items obsolete.

In the field of intelligence testing, too, there have been developments since the 1920s. What has become known as the 'Flynn Effect' was identified by James Flynn in 1982. He found that, even allowing for the changes in the tests themselves, the average IQ in the developed world increased at the rate of 10 points per generation between 1918 and 1950. After 1950, however, there had been no improvement in scholastic areas, while problem-solving scores had improved at the rate of 20% per generation. Flynn himself attributed this to the success of a drive to educate the entire population, since the IQ test is designed primarily to assess the success of school learning. He felt that by the early 1950s this had largely been achieved, however, and education systems began to focus on more abstract challenges (Appleyard, 1999), which would have had the effect of improving problem-solving.

It had thus become clear that IQ (one definition of which is 'that which distinguishes those who perform well across a representative range of work activities from those who perform less well') was not on its own an adequate measure of an individual. IQ tests are usually a mix of visual puzzles, verbal-reasoning questions and elementary arithmetic. Despite attempts to avoid it, they tend to be culture-specific.

'Intelligence', however, is even harder to define and has attracted a number of subordinate descriptors, of which 'emotional intelligence' is but one, albeit currently the most commonly heard. Once a broader view of the person was taken it became clear that not only should a number of scales be used, but different skills, abilities and cultures called for different tests and testing methods. Inevitably, not all such tests lent themselves to the statistical methods being developed or met the crystallising requirements for a 'psychometric'. One consequence of this was the emergence of a strongly defended 'qualitative' school of testing in opposition to the statistically driven quantitative school.

Nowadays, a psychological assessment or technique is generally held to fall into one of the following categories:

1. Cognitive ability tests;
2. Personality assessments (objective, projective and behavioural);
3. Interest inventories;
4. Motivational questionnaires (values, drivers, etc.).

There are several reasons and perspectives for the assessment of an individual, so component elements vary. In selection, while the predictive validity of techniques continues to be questioned, the underlying matching process is relatively unchanged, but recruiters now tend to talk in terms of 'competencies', 'situational judgement inventories' and 'assessment centres'.

David McClelland's paper 'Testing for competence rather than for intelligence (McClelland, 1973) suggested using measures which reflected more directly the work to be done. In most cases, jobs could be adequately defined from a limited number of commonly occurring 'competencies' (clusters of relevant skills and attributes).

Competency frameworks emerged in the 1980s (Boyatzis, 1982) and have become increasingly behaviourist in tone, reminiscent of the Management by Objectives techniques of the same era. As competencies can be selected and defined by the employer – who may break them down further by specifying positive and negative indicative behaviours – a formidable number now exist. In much the same way as abilities and personality traits were simplified, SHL claim to have reduced competencies to what they call the 'Great Eight'. These are:

1. Leading and deciding;
2. Supporting and co-operating;
3. Interacting and presenting;
4. Analysing and interpreting;
5. Creating and conceptualising;
6. Organising and executing;
7. Adapting and coping;
8. Enterprising and performing.

THE PRACTITIONER

For a practitioner tasked with assessing one or more individuals, therefore, there are probably thousands of questionnaires and other selection and assessment tools to choose from, many of which can justifiably claim to have psychometric properties. From the preceding brief outline of how the various models and tools evolved it should be clear that they do not do the same thing, have not been formulated along similar lines or with the same level of skill and knowledge, and may not even have established exactly what is being measured.

Most people in this position are likely to fall back on instruments on which they have been trained. As the interpretation and feeding back of results calls for understanding of the underlying concepts this is sensible, but may carry a risk of over-simplification. To a man with a hammer everything looks like a nail; excessive attachment to any specific model of personality or intellect, or to a limited range of instruments, is likely to reduce or even negate the usefulness of an assessment to the client.

To the question of which instruments to use, one well-established British coach and counsellor who, like many, is a non-psychologist, states his position clearly. 'Because these models are so numerous, and, frankly, because I am relatively inexperienced in using so many of them, I have not highlighted their use' (McLeod 2003, p. 192). Another, this time an American psychologist, encourages the development of what he describes as 'homemade instruments' (Peltier, 2001, p. 7). Coaching and careers guidance literature tends to emphasise some form of 360-degree feedback in conjunction with interviews and possibly simulations.

The assessment centre answer is to establish triangulation: every quality sought should be assessed in two, preferably three, different ways. While this is laudable in theory, in practice the attendant increase in time and costs and the impact on the attention span of all concerned are likely to limit the number of qualities which can reasonably be assessed in this way.

The application of each of even SHL's 'Great Eight' competencies depends on the situation, so one solution is to take trouble to establish a standardised and hopefully convincing context. Situational judgement theory recognises that behaviour is the result of the interplay between the situation and the individual's personality, and so tests set out to replicate typical workplace situations. The ability of the candidate to react authentically to such artificial situations must be debatable, as must be the reliability of outcomes.

While it is desirable for the selection process to reflect as accurately as possible the requirements of the post to be filled, this can become over-complicated, as a University of East London assessment centre (Lyons, 1997) for head teachers demonstrates. It comprised:

1. Verbal, numeric reasoning tests;
2. OPQ (including feedback);
3. In basket exercise;
4. Decision-making exercise;
5. Written presentation;
6. Verbal presentation;
7. Leaderless group exercise;

8. Problem-solving exercise;
9. Structured interview;
10. Career development interview.

This level of complexity is particularly extravagant if one accepts the view that the composition of such centres is more likely to identify present ability than it is to indicate potential.

A further complication is that computerisation and the internet have led to online testing. While this saves time and is much more convenient for both the practitioner and the candidate, it removes the ability to standardise the conditions under which a test is taken or even to be sure that the test has been completed by the applicants themselves, alone and unaided.

With computerisation has come the ability to standardise reports. While this saves the practitioner time and goes some way to reassuring conscientious test publishers that the various elements of the test are covered, it does not necessarily mean the recipient understands the implications or contextualises the findings appropriately. This may be either because the report has been designed for a different audience or purpose, or because the language used is not appropriate for the actual recipient. I can think of at least one publisher whose standard reports needed editing before they were sent on to a client. While this person had English as a native tongue, living abroad had introduced subtle – and sometimes not so subtle – differences in how the language was used. This had the potential to be misunderstood and to upset the candidate unnecessarily and unintentionally. This underlined for me the need for a practitioner to understand the tool and to ensure the comprehension of the candidate by feeding back personally and being able to answer any questions that might arise.

The extent to which our language is idiosyncratic and nuanced is often under-rated. The fact that Gordon Allport found some 18,000 words to express what Raymond Cattell reduced to 16 factors is indicative, but does not allow for the fact that the same word may be used to mean different things in the same conversation.

In my own research, the approach I chose to establish values and clarify meanings with my participants was to use Personal Construct Psychology (Kelly, 1955) to establish a contrast pole. This required the participant to identify a word or phrase which described a complete absence of the value in question. The deeper understanding which resulted from interviews which typically lasted three hours and addressed key aspects of each participant's life made it clear that common words like 'control' and 'autonomy' tend to have highly context-specific meanings. Selection of very different contrast poles emphasised the extent to which users intend common words and expressions to convey very different messages.

The contrast to 'control' for example, was variously described as 'no ability to change anything', 'responsibility without authority, undermined', 'a dreary little cog in a machine', 'uncertainty', 'failing', and 'out of my depth' – subtly different implications. To underline the subtlety and complexity, to be 'a cog in a machine' was seen by one participant as a good thing implying essential even if 'backroom' involvement, and by another as a bad thing implying invisibility and insignificance.

Most practitioners will tend to operate with a combination of instruments and techniques that works for them and which they have found appropriate for their particular area of specialisation. This may not always be possible. A complication I have come across more than once is that the client organisation specifies the use of a different tool, usually because someone senior has been trained on it or, often, has been on the receiving end and liked what had been fed back to him or her. A second reason to vary instruments may arise from a peculiarity of the specific assignment. A third is the possibility of bias in the instrument.

For no particular reason that I am aware of, most of my clients are British residents with English as their first language and are over 30 years old. Where this is not the case or where there is any reason to suspect that the validity of instruments may be impacted by cultural or other differences, the possibility of bias in the instruments needs to be considered. For example, I already use the Watson Glaser Critical Thinking Appraisal (WGCTA) and the Rust Advanced Numerical Reasoning Appraisal (RANRA), but several of my clients have found them dishearteningly difficult and I had to look for lower-level instruments with more face validity. While I sometimes rely on the 15 questions that make up the 'Reasoning' (Scale B) factor in the 16PF5, as it correlates reasonably well with accepted ability measures and significantly with similar scales in other personality instruments, it has been suggested there may be problems there, too (Cattell & Schuerger, 2003).

While no bias was detected in the 16PF5 between the genders or between those over and under 40 years of age, differences were found between whites on the one hand and blacks and Hispanics on the other (Cattell & Schuerger, 2003). An alternative might be Raven's Advanced Progressive Matrices (RAPM), which set out to assess 'ability to forge new, largely non-verbal insights' (Raven, 1994) and therefore 'ability to draw meaning out of confusion, i.e. "eductive" ability' (Brady, 2000). In one public sector recruitment programme, however, even the supposedly non-verbal RAPM seemed to favour white applicants over non-whites (Brady, Bacon &Ryves, 2000).

Other areas may have specific vulnerabilities. Practitioners working with women clients are, for example, cautioned against the Self-Directed Search and Kuder Occupational Interest Survey on the basis of an alleged gender bias, while, in another area, validity of the widely used Strong Interest Inventory with African Americans is questioned (Subich & Billingsley, 1995).

In a time of increasing sensitivity and litigiousness it is therefore wise to check whether there are any obvious causes for concern about bias.

My 2001 resolution to attend a psychometric CPD event annually had the incidental effect of gaining a qualification in a number of personality instruments. The first two were, almost inevitably, the 16PF and the Myers–Briggs Type Indicator (MBTI). For some time these were the only two I used, as between them they gave a useful spread. MBTI is forced-choice same-scale (so not ipsative) with extensive user-friendly documentation written in positive terms. This has the advantage of making a superficial grasp of the terminology easy to obtain, facilitating discussion in groups, but renders it liable to the accusation of 'putting people in boxes' unless it is fed back properly and the 'best fit' process thoroughly assimilated.

In contrast, the 16PF is a more complex trait instrument that provides more nuanced information to the user but calls for far greater interpretation skills, although the quality of the take-away materials has improved since OPP bought the distribution rights to the instrument (Cattell, 2007). An unkind analogy might be that the MBTI is painting by numbers whereas the 16PF provides the practitioner with a blank canvas and a palette of 16 colours to mix, but I often use both with the same client. The MBTI gives the client something to take home and think about and gives us a common language while the 16PF offers the potential for deeper understanding. OPP came to a similar conclusion when they asked some 700 UK managers and professionals to complete both the MBTI and the 16PF5. OPP consultants found the reports so complementary that they suggested the two instruments should be fed back together.

Other instruments add new dimensions to understanding. The FIRO Element B adds a state measure and was until recently the only instrument to explore what the client actually *wanted* out of relationships and life, and it contrasts that with what was perceived by the client as actuality. This contrast, and a comparison between this state measure and a supposedly more stable type measure such as the MBTI, might suggest a current stressful situation. FIRO can also help select an effective team, which is the function for which it was originally designed by Will Schutz.

Contextual factors often dictate the design and selection of personality instruments, too. Hogan instruments are designed specifically for use in working environments, although the apparent irrelevance of some of the items to the commercial world can sometimes make feeding back to a somewhat cynical executive seem an uphill struggle. In this context it is worth noting that performance correlates with cognitive ability rather than personality, although a glib analogy might be that cognitive ability provides horsepower whereas personality can be a lubricant – or not!

A series of revelations about dubious behaviour by prominent financial and political figures worldwide created considerable interest in identifying aspects of the personality that are potential 'derailers'. One option is the 21-item Peters Delusions Inventory (PDI), but this has a clinical flavour; the main instrument associated with derailment is the Hogan Development Survey (HDS) which focuses on the so-called 'dark side' of the personality. While the concept of over-used strengths is implicit in reports from other personality instruments, the HDS makes this very explicit. In consequence, this may require skilful feedback if the client is to learn from the experience. Curiously, given that the avowed focus of the Hogan tools is the commercial world, the way in which the HDS outcomes relate to business organisations may need to be spelled out to the client.

It might be argued that the Hogan Personality Inventory (HPI) adds very little to what can be learnt from the instruments already mentioned, but there are several good reasons to use it. A 'dark-side' instrument like the HDS needs to be balanced by one that takes a more positive view of an individual's personality and the HPI does that in the same (business) context as the HDS.

Another extremely pragmatic reason for using the HPI with the HDS is that not only are all the Hogan reports produced branded so that they can be seen to be related, but the outcomes are seen as complementary and can be combined to form a number of useful composite reports. This is a trend that other publishers now also follow and in many cases there is the opportunity to personalise the suite of reports for your practice, though at prices likely to encourage you to be loyal to one publisher.

Another interesting suite of tools is Type Mapping, recently introduced by Team Focus. This combines Jungian Type with the Schutz/FIRO 'is/want' juxtaposing, which has been applied not only to the Type Dynamics Indicator, their version of the MBTI, but also to team situations with the launch of the Management Team Roles Indicator (MTR-i) and the Ideal Team Profile Questionnaire (ITPQ).

Particularly in the realm of personality self-reporting instruments, it needs to be emphasised that the results raise questions rather than making statements. Corroborative evidence, ideally from an external source, should always be sought. In an organisational situation this can usually be relatively easily obtained by means of a 360 degree questionnaire, but it may be necessary – and informative – to ask for relevant real-life situational evidence.

THE CLIENT

It seems appropriate at this point to stress that, particularly where someone other than the candidate is paying for the assessment, it is vital to ensure everyone is clear from the start who the 'client' is. Apart from reducing the chance of conflict over who is entitled to what information when, it improves the chances of being paid! Clearly agreed and observed boundaries are essential for trust and to optimise the quality of the information received, as well as indicating the way in which the resulting report will need to be phrased.

Even when there has not been a chance to talk to the candidate before the instruments have been completed it is important to establish what he or she thinks is going on. This may have been explained in writing, but instructions and explanations that would once have been given before administering a pen and paper test should be reinforced. Even with personality measures there seems often to be an assumption that there are good and bad answers, and some competitive types seem disappointed if they have not scored the maximum, almost regardless of how the scale is labelled. Irrespective of who the client may be, I see it as good practice to ensure the candidate benefits from the experience and I go to some trouble to let the client know this early on.

The labelling of traits is another fertile ground for misunderstanding. Unless the interested party is informed otherwise, there is a danger that an Extravert, for example, will be expected to be a loud party animal rather than someone who simply prefers not to spend too much time alone. Without adequate explanation, the Myers–Briggs labels of Intuition, Perceiving and Judging are also unlikely to be properly understood.

Whoever the actual client is, the aim should be an understanding of how strength or weakness in that particular trait or type would typically manifest itself in an environment with which the client is familiar. The process is particularly important where multiple instruments have been used, or where the one used is particularly complex. Relating the increasingly numerous trait permutations in such cases to situations familiar to the candidate can be challenging for the practitioner, but the consequence of achieving that level of understanding is the opportunity to get a reaction, an explanation or an example which can add more depth to the assessment. I recall a case where the results of tests completed over the previous weekend did not tie in with each other, or to what I had been told about the internal candidate's history. The feedback session gave me the opportunity to question this and to discover that a significant relationship had unexpectedly broken up that Sunday morning. I was then able to reschedule interviews and give the candidate time to recover from the shock.

Even where the candidate is not paying for the assessment, as practitioners we are professionally obliged to provide him or her with feedback and to explain the results. Particularly in the selection of external candidates the timing and extent of that feedback may come under pressure from the client. The expectation may be that the results will be explained to the panel before the interview and only fed back to the applicant afterwards. For unsuccessful candidates, the client may allow little or no time for feedback, feeling that a standard printed report should be sufficient. Even if it is to be conducted over the telephone, feedback and the opportunity to ask questions should always be provided.

I have occasionally, not entirely through my own fault, found myself interviewing a candidate before I have had time to familiarise myself thoroughly with their test results – and then had to brief a selection panel without further contact with the candidate. Even though the brief takes the form of suggesting areas which warrant further questioning, it tends to leave me with a suspicion that a closer study of the results in advance might have taken the initial interview deeper and enabled me to focus the panel's questions more tightly. As a practitioner it is not a comfortable position to be in and it is one which I go to considerable lengths to avoid.

SUMMARY

My intention in this chapter is to encourage practitioners (and through them their clients and candidates) to see the results of psychometric instruments and other assessment tools as prompting questions and posing hypotheses rather than making judgements. Outcomes should be seen as aids to diagnosis rather than diagnoses themselves.

To maximise the benefit to the client and to do the assessment process justice, the practitioner needs to be familiar with the limitations of and the assumptions underlying the instruments they choose to use rather than taking them at face value. Subjective decisions will necessarily have been made at various stages in their evolution and a competent practitioner needs to be aware of this.

It will be obvious that my approach is eclectic and it should come as no surprise that my preference is to work in a developmental capacity rather than in selection. This increases opportunities for me to be regarded as supportive, rather than risk being seen as transient and judgemental. Even in selection, however, it is possible to make the inevitably brief time together useful to all concerned by encouraging meaningful participation and commitment from the candidate.

Both people and situations are complex and multi-faceted, and allowance needs to be made for both contextual influences and the subjective perceptions of those involved at all stages in the process. A useful assessment requires the practitioner to use a variety of techniques and instruments but to have a sound understanding of what each is adding and to balance that against an allegedly ever-shortening, but increasingly expensive, span of attention. This should be regarded as an ongoing professional commitment.

REFERENCES

Appleyard, B. (1999). The battle of wits. *Sunday Times Magazine*, 13 June, pp. 44–50.

Boyatzis, R. E. (1982). *The competent manager: A model for effective performance*. Chichester: Wiley.

Brady, R., Bacon, J. & Ryves, D. (2000). A case study illustrating potential adverse impact using two popular psychometric ability tests. *Selection & Development Review*, 16(4): 10–15.

Cattell, H. E. P. (2007). *Exploring your 16PF profile*. Oxford: OPP.

Cattell, H. E. P. and J. M. Schuerger (2003). *Essentials of 16PF assessment*. Hoboken, NJ: Wiley.

Kelly, G. A. (1955). *The psychology of personal constructs. Volume 1: A theory of personality*. New York: Norton.

Lyons, G. (1997). Learning the hard way: Using competency-led assessment centres with head teachers. *Selection and Development Review*, 13(4), 12–14.

McClelland, D. C. (1973). Testing for competence rather than for intelligence. *American Psychologist*, 28, 1–14.

McLeod, A. (2003). *Performance coaching: The handbook for managers, H.R. professionals and coaches*. Carmarthen: Crown House Publishing.

Peltier, B. (2001). *The psychology of executive coaching: Theory and application*. Hove: Brunner-Routledge.

Raven, J. (1994). *Occupational user's guide: Raven's Advanced Progressive Matrices & Mill Hill Vocabulary scale*. Oxford: OPP.

Rushton, J. P., Bons, T. A. & Hur, Y.-M. (2008). The genetics and evolution of the general factor of personality. *Journal of Research in Personality*, 42(5), 1173–85.

Subich, L. M. & Billingsley, K. D. (1995). Integrating career assessment into counseling. In W. B. Walsh and S. H. Osipow (eds), *Handbook of vocational psychology: Theory, research, and practice* (pp. 261–93). Mahwah, NJ: Lawrence Erlbaum Associates.

Tupes, E. C. and Christal, R. E. (1961). Recurrent personality factors based on trait ratings. Technical Report No. ASD-TR-61-97. USAF, Lackland, TX.

19 When Profit Comes In the Door, Does Science Go Out the Window?

ROBERT FORDE

The purpose of keeping a register of test users is to try to maintain standards in the use and application of such tests. Commercial producers have generally co-operated by requiring that those who order tests meet a certain standard of training. They also grade tests for the degree of expertise required, and supply test materials only to those whose qualifications meet the standard.

However, commercial ventures exist to maximise sales and thereby profit. The originators of assessment instruments may also wish to maximise sales, as they collect a royalty. The originator of one popular assessment tool described it in my hearing as his 'pension plan'. He was joking (one hopes), but there is a serious point as well: is there a tension between the profit motive and the desire to maintain adequate professional and scientific standards? If so, could the desire to maximise profits lead to inadequate care in the choice and application of assessment instruments? What happens when the use of an instrument is challenged on technical grounds?

As an illustration of this point, this happened with the Psychopathy Checklist Revised (PCL-R) when its originator, Robert Hare, saw an advance copy of an article criticising it in 2007 (Carey, 2010). The PCL-R is widely used, not only as a research measure of psychopathic personality, but even more as a risk assessment instrument by professionals concerned with the release of offenders. Hare threatened to sue the authors, Skeem and Cooke (2010), citing commercial interests amongst other things. He was heavily criticised by fellow psychologists for allegedly attempting to 'stifle academic debate', but defended his action on the basis that he and his work had been misrepresented in the article.

The fact remains, though, that the PCL-R has many flaws as a risk assessment instrument. It has been shown that scores are not as reliable 'in the field' as they are in academic research groups (Boccaccini, Murrie, Rufino & Gardner, 2014). Also, scores are influenced by assessor 'allegiance', that is, whether they have been hired by the prosecution or the defence (Murrie, Boccaccini, Johnson & Janke, 2009). It has even been shown that scores depend partly on the rater's own personality characteristics (Miller, Rufino, Boccaccini, Jackson & Murrie, 2011).

I have carried out a more extensive critique elsewhere (Forde, 2014), but the crucial question is whether any assessment instrument should be defended on the grounds of commercial interest rather than its merits as an assessment instrument. The Skeem and Cooke article was eventually published three years late (Skeem & Cooke, 2010). However, had there been no agreement, criticism of undoubted flaws in the PCL-R might well have been suppressed, at least partly for the sake of commercial interests. There is currently no sign that the PCL-R's popularity is declining, despite its evident flaws, and its comprehensive marketing programme continues.

The PCL-R is not a test, but a checklist of 20 items, for each one of which assessors provide a rating based on their clinical judgement. The publishers provide not only the checklist itself, but also scoring sheets and standardised notebooks in which to record assessors' observations. This shows how marketing popularises a particular instrument: it is possible to do without the notebooks and scoring sheets, but much easier to use the complete package. This ease of use for a familiar instrument is essentially a marketing device which relies upon the idea that assessors are, if not lazy, at least so busy that they will tend to choose the most convenient option. This is not restricted to the PCL-R or to the forensic field in particular.

Some of the assessment tools which we use today have their origins in the 1950s, or even earlier, and some have been around for longer than the lifetimes of many assessors who use them. One example is the Myers–Briggs Type Indicator (MBTI), which is still widely used, especially in the occupational field. According to its publisher's website it is used in over two million assessments annually (CPP Inc., 2009) and is the most popular personality assessment in the world. Based on a development of Jung's idea of personality types, originally advanced in the 1920s and since republished (Jung, 1971), it purports to place people in one of 16 categories. As it has been in development since the 1940s, a great deal of work has been published on its development and psychometric properties. The website mentions some of the more favourable results, but not the fact that Myers and Briggs were qualified neither in psychology nor in test development. It also mentions that the company has been responsible for developing and marketing the MBTI since 1975, but not that it was previously published by the Educational Testing Service, which withdrew it after an internal report on its accuracy and psychometric properties (Stricker & Ross, 1962).

In retrospect, it seems curious that the MBTI was ever developed at all. By the time it appeared, there was already little support for the idea of personality 'types'. Modern thinking views personality as a series of dimensions, not a collection of boxes into which people can be pigeonholed (Kline, 2000). The MBTI looks rather like a dimensional personality test, as it asks a number of questions with yes/no answers, but it uses these answers to put people in a category rather than locate them on a dimension. One would therefore expect that answers to the questions would be distributed bi-modally (i.e., that they would 'clump' into two distinct groups, representing two categories) whereas studies have shown that in fact they are distributed normally, like the scores of more conventional tests (Pittenger, 1993). A cut-off is used in order to separate people into one category or another, which means that only a point or two may separate people in different categories. Consequently, it is not surprising that test–retest reliability is poor, so that assessments carried out only a few weeks apart may place the same person in different categories. Pittenger also cites validity problems, showing that MBTI assessments are not predictive of success in job placements or of personal satisfaction. Despite these failings, the MBTI has continued to sell well, although the flaws have frequently been debated in both academic and business journals (Krznaric, 2013).

Why do obviously flawed instruments continue to be widely used, and to sell? In both of these cases, an instrument was promoted by its developer(s), regardless of known flaws. In the case of the MBTI, it had already been withdrawn by one publisher because of technical inadequacies, but its authors went on to pitch it to another without addressing these. In the case of the PCL-R the flaws gradually became evident after it had been published. In neither case does there seem to have been any let-up in the marketing effort. Clearly, however, there are implications for ethically and technically justifiable practice in assessment. It is not popularity or commercial success that makes a test valid and useful: phrenology (measuring the skull and studying its shape in order to deduce character) and bertillonage (a scheme of anatomical measurements) were both used widely in their day.

Is there a way to avoid these problems? Clearly, there would be no problem if users chose a test on purely scientific criteria. For example, is it reliable and can it be validly applied to the population of interest? Equally clearly, some tests are still popular and strongly marketed despite failing to meet these standards. The answer is in our own hands.

NOTE

This chapter is reprinted from *Assessment & Development Matters*, Spring 2015, 7(1) by permission of the Senior Editor. *Assessment & Development Matters* is distributed to all those on the BPS's Register of Qualified Test Users.

REFERENCES

Boccaccini, M. T., Murrie, D. C., Rufino, K. A. & Gardner, B. O. (2014). Evaluator differences in Psychopathy Checklist-Revised factor and facet scores. *Law and Human Behavior*, 38(4), 337–45.

Carey, B. (2010). Academic battle delays publication by 3 years. *New York Times*, June 11. http://www.nytimes.com/2010/06/12/health/12psych.html. Accessed 9 January 2015.

CPP Inc. (2009). from https://www.cpp.com/products/mbti/index.aspx. Accessed 9 January 2015.

Forde, R. A. (2014). Risk assessment in parole decisions: A study of life sentence prisoners in England and Wales. Doctoral thesis, University of Birmingham. http://etheses.bham.ac.uk/5476. Accessed 9 January 2015.

Jung, C. G. (1971). *Psychological types*. London: Routledge.

Kline, P. (2000). *A psychometrics primer*. London: Free Association.

Krznaric, R. (2013). Have we all been duped by the Myers–Briggs test? *Fortune*, 15 May. http://fortune.com/2013/05/15/have-we-all-been-duped-by-the-myers-briggs-test/. Accessed 14 January 2015.

Miller, A. K., Rufino, K. A., Boccaccini, M. T., Jackson, R. L. & Murrie, D. C. (2011). Differences in person perception: Raters' personality traits relate to their Psychopathy Checklist-Revised scoring tendencies. *Assessment*, 18(2), 253–60.

Murrie, D. C., Boccaccini, M. T., Johnson, J. T. & Janke, C. (2009). Does interrater (dis)agreement on Psychopathy Checklist scores in sexually violent predator trials suggest partisan allegiance in forensic evaluations? *Law and Human Behavior*, 32(4), 352–62.

Pittenger, D. J. (1993). Measuring the MBTI... and coming up short. *Journal of Career Planning & Placement*. http://www.indiana.edu/~jobtalk/Articles/develop/mbti.pdf. Accessed 14 January 2015.

Skeem, J. L. & Cooke, D. J. (2010). Is criminal behavior a central component of psychopathy? Conceptual directions for resolving the debate. *Psychological Assessment*, 22(2), 433–45.

Stricker, L. J. & Ross, J. (1962). *A description and evaluation of the Myers–Briggs type indicator*. Princeton, NJ: Educational Testing Service.

Part IV Psychometrics and the Future

20 The Future of Psychometric Testing

Robert McHenry

This chapter attempts to examine how trends in consumer technology, the heightening of interest in the value of psychology and the willingness of consumers to forgo privacy will shape the psychometric testing industry, and perhaps transform it, within a decade. Another major driver of change will be the practices of the recruitment industry, currently a heavy user of psychometric tests, as it continues its relentless pursuit of speed and cost reduction in the identification of talent.

The portents for disruption of the psychometric testing industry have been around for some time. Big data methodology is already applied to the plethora of information that individuals reveal about themselves every day when they shop in supermarkets, surf the web, write emails and exchange information with others on Facebook. There are claims that it can already be used to predict behaviour with an accuracy similar to or greater than that of psychometric tests (Kosinski, Stilwell & Graepel, 2013). Influential psychologists like Robert Sternberg have lamented the lack of real innovation in the industry, claiming that cognitive tests have not fundamentally changed in their construction for over 70 years and that the industry is selling black-and-white televisions and rotary dial phones to its customers (Sternberg, 1997). The wide availability of smartphones that can record video and send and receive it now allows savvy and ambitious job applicants to construct digital CVs with footage of their behaviour in work contexts (Recruitment Grapevine, 2015). That has left some potential employers wondering why they should go to the trouble and expense of using psychometric tests to assess potential when such direct evidence is increasingly available to them.

This chapter will explore five assertions about the future of psychometric tests.

1. Smartphones will replace computers for employee assessment.
2. High-quality psychometric testing services will be sold direct to consumers.
3. Advances in the neuroscience of personality will reveal which are the most valid individual differences to measure and how best to measure them.
4. The digital badging movement, coupled to the use of big data and new forms of digital CV, will render many of the current applications for high-stakes testing redundant.
5. The basis for employee development will in the near future be derived from the data yielded by wearable devices and not from psychometric tests.

SMARTPHONES WILL REPLACE COMPUTERS FOR EMPLOYEE ASSESSMENT

There are three reasons for thinking that the smartphone will replace the desktop and the laptop – and probably the tablet – as the platform for delivering tests, exercises and feedback reports. First, there is the ubiquity of the smartphone; 1.5 billion people in the world own one. That is almost 20 per cent of the world's population, and in the US and Europe 60 per cent of the population own one (Smith, 2015). The smartphone is part of our daily lives. Many of us have it on hand at all times to check the weather forecast, get directions, access our text and email messages and read the latest news. Indeed, the average user spends three hours per day on a smartphone and 15 per cent of all global internet traffic originates from smartphones.

Secondly, there is the superior reach of the smartphone in emerging countries. In many parts of Africa and the Far East, the smartphone is greatly preferred to older devices like the laptop or the desktop for accessing the web. The third, and perhaps the most important, reason is that psychometric assessment via the smartphone can significantly reduce the costs associated with psychometric testing for the paying client. For example, the recruitment industry, so closely allied to the assessment industry, is already adapting its techniques to the popularity of the smartphone. In the US, over 40 per cent of candidates carry out their job searches on a smartphone, so big employers and some recruiters have made their recruitment sites mobile-friendly. At least one of the big US restaurant chains (see below) hires entry-level staff almost exclusively through smartphone campaigns, and prospective employees make their job applications through their own smartphone.

There are reasons to be cautious before rushing into the adaptation of current psychometric tests to a smartphone platform. The current situation is similar to the transition from paper-and-pencil to computer-based testing. Researchers first of all need to show that tests maintain their internal psychometric properties between smartphone and non-smartphone devices, and indeed this seems to have been demonstrated (Lawrence, Wasko, Delgado, Kinney & Wolf, 2013; Morelli, Illingworth, Scott & Lance, 2012; Morelli, Mahan & Illingworth, 2014). Researchers have also found that that non-timed measures take longer to complete on mobile devices (Arthur, Doverspike, Muñoz, Taylor & Carr, 2014). When the equivalence of test scores has been examined, research shows no difference in personality scores based on device type, but significant differences in scores for cognitive ability assessments (Arthur et al., 2014; Impelman, 2013; Morelli et al., 2014). The difference in cognitive ability scores was larger for verbal than numeric items between devices, possibly suggesting that using a smartphone increases the cognitive or memory load for verbal measures, perhaps due to scrolling and zooming. It can currently take up to 30 per cent longer to complete a test on a smartphone because of connectivity issues, distractions in the vicinity of the candidate, and the small screen size, and because these factors are more likely to affect performance on cognitive tests than on personality tests.

Numerous studies have now been conducted, to identify trends in mobile device use among applicants (e.g., McClure & Boyce, 2015), to explore the impact of different devices and device characteristics on assessment properties and applicant outcomes (e.g., Arthur et al., 2014; Illingworth, Morelli, Scott & Boyd, 2015; Morelli, Mahan & Illingworth, 2014), and to understand reactions to mobile assessments (e.g., Gutierrez & Meyer, 2013; Gutierrez, Meyer & Fursman, 2015). Where once little information was available about the impact of psychometric testing using the smartphone, there is now a diverse and continuously expanding database providing guidelines and recommendations for the delivery of mobile assessments.

It makes sense for test developers to focus on the smartphone and for employers who use tests to ask them to do so. Job candidates are making judgements on what they think a company is like to work for. Organisations whose processes and modes of recruitment fit the candidates' lifestyles are more likely to get the best applicants, and the company's branding gets a boost from being modern and easy to deal with. In a recent survey, (Gutierrez and Meyer, 2013) when given a choice of job application methods, a good proportion of women and minorities said they preferred a smartphone, so there could be an equal-opportunities angle here as well.

So, big organisations are already taking the plunge and offering cognitive and personality tests to smartphone applicants. Trends data suggests that smartphone use for completing selection assessments has steadily risen over the past five years (McClure & Boyce, 2015). As mentioned above, one example is a multinational restaurant chain that uses an adaptive personality test for the first stage of recruitment for entry-level and first-line-management jobs. It offers applicants for these positions the choice of coming to a nearby restaurant to take the test on-screen, completing it at home or at work on a desktop or a laptop, or accessing it on a mobile device. Three years ago, 91% of applicants preferred the desktop option, but that has fallen to 66%, while at the same time the popularity of the smartphone for taking the test has risen from 9% to 31%.

It remains to be seen how quickly the psychometric test industry will adapt to changes in the way prospective candidates want to engage at the recruitment stage. Even if the will is there, it is not just a matter of shrinking current assessments to fit a small screen. There are many graphic design and human interface issues to be considered. However, these changes may be forced on the test industry by their clients, because only by staying ahead and in tune with candidates' lifestyles can those clients expect to attract the best talent.

The author of this chapter has been experimenting with a free smartphone app specially written to measure personality and to make professional personality testing available to consumers. The app is called 'Practical Personality Test' and the website to which it is linked is called PersonaBubble. The website was originally created to find out how easy it would be to collect personality data from large samples across the world. Accessing large multinational samples during the construction and validation of personality questionnaires has hitherto been a time-consuming and expensive activity for researchers. It has already been argued here that the widespread availability of mobile devices such as smartphones makes such access possible even to areas of the globe where sizeable and representative subject samples have never before been measured.

This Practical Personality Test mobile app, downloadable to smartphones from the Apple Store and Google+, and also available via Facebook and for conventional devices at www.personabubble.com, can potentially answer several questions of interest to a researcher.

1. Is the delivery of personality assessments directly to consumers internationally popular?
2. How are pages featuring a personality questionnaire best presented to consumers on Web and smartphone platforms?

3. Which features of a free personality assessment increase its shareability with others and the number of respondents who complete it?
4. Can a personality assessment platform with unrestricted access be used for personality research in general, and test validation in particular?

When users log on to PersonaBubble, they are invited to give biographical information (sex, age, occupation, country of residence, etc.), provide their email address for identification and take a 55-item personality test. The test is the *16PF Express*, a proprietary short version of Cattell's 16PF (Gorsuch, 2006). PersonaBubble delivers only the US English version of the questionnaire.

After users take the test, they can generate their own personality report (in English) that covers Cattell's five global factors (very similar to the 'big five' personality scales) that have been renamed for consumers in non-technical language.

After the test taker views their personality report, they are encouraged to recruit other respondents by inviting friends and family to register and download the PersonaBubble app. Incentives such as a colour diagram (which can be uploaded to Facebook) displaying the scores of the whole group are offered.

When individuals have taken *16PF Express*, they can also elect to take a number of quick 'quizzes' on topics such as happiness at work, satisfaction with relationships, and work-environment fit. Their scores on these quizzes can be correlated with their personality results and described according to the biographical data that they have provided.

To date, almost 15,000 people have registered for PersonaBubble and new registrants are recruited at a rate of about 500 per month. These new registrants are discovering PersonaBubble despite the fact that few attempts have been made for some time to publicise its existence. Of the 14,598 people who have registered to take the test, 7432 (51%) have used the web and 7166 (49%) have used the phone app. Registrants represent over 40 countries and only the samples from the 11 countries with 80 or more registrants have been analysed in depth.

Significant personality differences have been found between those who used a smartphone to complete the questionnaire and those who used a desktop or a laptop. A significantly higher proportion of people who started the questionnaire on the smartphone app completed it – 99% as opposed to 75% for the web version. The latter finding may in part be due to the non-scrolling and other methods – arrived at by trial and error – used to present questionnaire items on the screen of a smartphone. In common with other researchers who have used the same questionnaire in multiple countries (Bartram, 2013), this study found only small total scale score variances that could be attributed to between-country effects. However, there were significant differences between nationalities in the extent to which they registered on the website but did not start the questionnaire. National differences in completing the questionnaire once started were also found. There were also national differences in the time taken to complete the questionnaire and these do not seem to be related to the first language of the person answering it. Additionally, there were significant differences in the time taken to answer certain individual questions and these seemed to be somewhat related to whether English was the first language in the country of the test taker.

The answers to the lifestyle and attitudinal quizzes available to users of the app enable the concurrent validity of the questionnaire scales to be measured. These validity coefficients are within the range generally found for personality questionnaires and they are independent of the country of the test taker. The main constraints on the present data lie in the number of countries sampled to date.

HIGH-QUALITY PSYCHOMETRIC TESTING SERVICES WILL BE SOLD DIRECT TO CONSUMERS

The experiment with the Practical Personality Test app and the associated PersonaBubble website has demonstrated how a smartphone-based platform targeted at consumers can recruit large samples. The resulting data can be used for the validation of scales on personality questionnaires, the analysis of individual questionnaire items and the exploration of best practices for creating new mobile app-based questionnaires and assessments.

There are reasons for believing that a proliferation of self-assessment smartphone apps based on psychometric tests will soon be available free or on a paying basis to consumers. The widespread use of the medium is making that business model attractive to test publishers but most have been reluctant to exploit the idea for fear of upsetting their current customers. In *Seeing what's next*, Christensen, Anthony and Roth (2004) define some of the market conditions that lead to the disruption of an industry and the demise of the professional expertise that may be associated with that industry. One reason is that lower-cost suppliers enter a market niche and start to commoditise it. Another is that relatively complex processes of supply become simplified and made more convenient for the consumer. Today, access to high-quality psychometric tests and their proper interpretation is expensive and inconvenient for consumers. Many people are only exposed to the benefits of psychometric tests if their employer or potential employer pays for the tests and associated services such as test interpretation. The average person who would like to know more about themselves, their capabilities and their potential, or to explore these on behalf of their partner or adolescent children, has to find a capable test practitioner and pay their fees, as well as for the test material, in order to get the results. The process for such a person is schematised in Figure 20.1

1. Consumer contacts qualified test user.
2. Qualified test user replies and makes a contract for services.
3. Qualified test user contacts test publisher to set up test administration for consumer.
4. Test publisher sends password and other administration data to consumer.
5. Consumer takes test online at test publisher's website.
6. Test publisher sends test results to qualified test user for feedback to consumer.
7. Qualified test user feeds test results back to consumer.

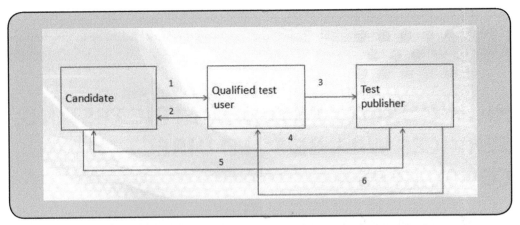

Figure 20.1 The steps currently taken by a consumer to gain access to the results of psychometric testing

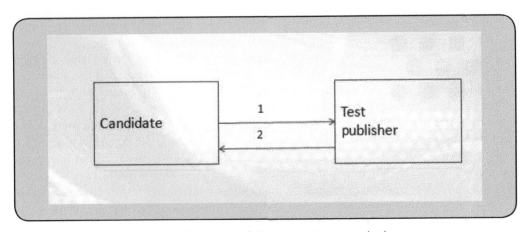

Figure 20.2 The two-step process the consumer follows to receive test results the new way

1. Consumer accesses test publisher's website directly and selects and pays for testing services.
2. Test publisher sends test reports directly back to consumer.

The process outlined in Figure 20.2 omits five steps from the procedure described in Figure 20.1. It is quicker and less expensive than the first procedure because a qualified test user does not have to be paid. The quality of service received by the consumer is undoubtedly less good but the conditions for a disruption of the standard practices of an industry and a professional practitioner are plain to see. Similar disruptions are at work in other consumer-facing areas such as medicine, where diagnostic tests that were once carried out by a qualified practitioner are increasingly becoming available directly to the consumer. It is likely that tests designed for the early diagnosis of Alzheimer's and other cognitive disorders will be marketed direct to consumers within the next five years.

The author has been investigating the popularity of high-quality psychometric testing services offered direct to consumers within the field of career choice and change. Using a smartphone app or a website called CareerClover, consumers can pay to take the full version of Cattell's 16PF personality test and for £30 receive four separate reports covering their competencies, their career preferences and the kinds of work environment that they would enjoy most. They can also receive a limited number of badges (see below) that show their clearest competencies. If they wish, they can post these competency badges on LinkedIn, Facebook or other social networking sites, where they can be viewed by potential employers.

ADVANCES IN THE NEUROSCIENCE OF PERSONALITY

One of the most exciting pointers to the future of psychometric testing is emerging through the rapid development of psychophysiological techniques such as functional neuroimaging. In order to understand the appeal of this approach, one has to acknowledge that the 'theoretical' basis for many of the currently popular psychometric tests of personality and ability is many ways superficial. In order to reveal the structure of personality or cognitive abilities, multivariate techniques, the most important being factor analysis, have been applied to phenotypical behaviour that is at the end of a long chain of causal and interacting forces. Many individual-differences psychologists see this approach as 'naming but not explaining'. The so-called 'big five' model of personality (Goldberg, 1981) is a prime example of a system that is basically descriptive and one-dimensional; it fails to explain what extraversion is or what any of the other major factors of personality are, what causes one person to be different from another, or what anatomical or neurological systems may be at work to produce the behaviour that others see.

For many years, researchers have sought to identify the causes of those behaviours that we currently use psychometric tests to measure. The pioneer of this movement was Ivan Pavlov (1927). In the modern era, the most prominent psychologists to be influenced by Pavlov's ideas are H. J. Eysenck and J. A. Gray. Eysenck (1947, 1947, 1960) identified, through factor analysis, two major dimensions of personality that he named Extraversion and Neuroticism. Later, he published a causal theory of personality, incorporating Pavlov's psychophysiological concepts (Eysenck, 1957, 1967). In Eysenck's model, Extraversion was aligned with the processes of cortical excitation and inhibition and neuroticism was aligned with the lability of the sympathetic branch of the autonomic nervous system. According to Eysenck, differences in Extraversion could be explained by the fact that Extraverts had under-excited brain systems that led them to seek thrills, want to be in the company of people and take risks. If they did not do these things, they would get bored and inattentive and have accidents. Introverts, on the other hand, had over-excited brain systems that could induce a feeling of discomfort when they interacted socially for too long and that is why they often sought solitude. The excited brains of introverts made it easier for them to avoid distraction, particularly when carrying out boring or repetitive tasks.

These ideas of Eysenck's, as well as some of the experimental methods he used to demonstrate their validity, were criticised by J. A. Gray (1981), who developed his own neuropsychological and causal theory of personality (Gray and McNaughton, 2000), which is now known as reinforcement sensitivity theory (RST). RST proposes three basic human individual differences of personality – openness to fear, orientation to pleasure and tendency to worry – all of which have an analogue in the brain or the nervous system. Unlike Eysenck, who was influenced by the technique of factor analysis, Gray derived his ideas about basic differences almost exclusively from experiments and observations of behaviour that were linked to cortical and nervous system differences in humans and animals. That is one of the reasons why Gray's descriptions of differences bear so little direct resemblance to the factors in the 'big five', whereas Eysenck's descriptions of Extraversion and Neuroticism do seem to map on to the 'big five' traits of Extraversion and Anxiety.

'Discovering' factors of personality and then searching for their causal bases may, in many instances, have been a flawed strategy. Following an independent path to discovering the basic, causal roots of human behaviour may have profound implications for psychometric tests and testing in the future. This is nowhere more evident than in the psychophysiology of personality. Instead of using factor analysis to discover the factors of personality and then searching for the causal basis of these factors, it is rapidly becoming possible to examine directly the way in which the brain works and identify the main pathways that determine behaviour. A taxonomy of these pathways may in the future replace the 'big five' as a descriptive system, and assessments based on these pathways may lead to better predictions of behaviour and allow assessors to use a wider and more valid range of measures than the ubiquitous self-report questionnaire or compendium of reasoning problems.

This work has already begun. Functional magnetic resonance brain imaging (fMRI) data is revealing neural networks that underlie individual differences in orientation to the self and orientation to others. Associated behaviours are likely to be a sensitivity or insensitivity to social cues and affinity with or difference from members of a team. Two complementary neural networks are involved. To be technical for a moment, the ventral medial prefrontal cortex is engaged in self-processing and the dorsal prefrontal network is involved in processing information related to others. It is obviously impractical for assessors in a work setting to use an MRI machine to measure this important individual difference, but it may be possible to develop simple stimuli which would excite the neural pathways that have control over self/other behaviour. The extent and the direction in which they are active in an individual could then be demonstrated. Such stimuli have been invented by Sui, Rothstein and Humphries (2013) and Humphreys and Sui (2015), who have subsequently developed a simple computer-based procedure which measures the speed with which an individual can associate three geometrical shapes with the self and with others. The results show massive biases on the part of individuals to respond more rapidly to self-relevant stimuli than to associations with other people. There are individual differences in the bias. These show trait-like stability across individuals over time and they are linked to a neural circuit.

Thus, we are already seeing the advantages of using new technology to map the brain and discover neural circuits that we had not anticipated either to exist or to be so prominent. These discoveries may allow us to form new models of basic individual differences in personality and intelligence from our more extensive knowledge of the brain. These models will almost certainly challenge current descriptive models like the big five or the multiple intelligences model which have been derived from factor analysis. They may also help us understand what causes certain behaviours and why some behaviours are so difficult to change. They will undoubtedly lead to the gradual demise of self-report questionnaire methods as ingenious new ways of stimulating these neural circuits are devised. If all of this comes about, it would be the equivalent for personality and ability measurement of turning a two-dimensional world into a three-dimensional one.

THE BADGING MOVEMENT AND HIGH-STAKES TESTING

Badges are logos that denote mini-qualifications. It is possible for anyone to create them using the Mozilla open badge initiative. A badge can be posted on a person's Facebook or LinkedIn page to tell others that they have a certain qualification or affiliation. Self-badging is of limited value to a job applicant and so commercial issuers of badges have emerged in the past few years which validate badges. Typically, they issue badges to individuals on behalf of credentialing organisations such as IBM or Microsoft who run training programmes for IT developers. So, instead of a qualified individual having to obtain and display a paper certificate or authentication for their skill or knowledge qualification, they can have a digital one instead. Information about the authenticity as well as the nature of the qualification is provided by the issuer of the badge and can usually be obtained by placing the cursor over the on-screen badge or clicking through to a website where fuller information is given. Badge issuers such as Acclaim (https://www.youracclaim.com/) are currently vying with each other to become the largest representative of credentialling organisations, as well as the one most trusted by third parties like employers.

Currently, most of the badges being issued and displayed are for 'hard' skills like computer programming know-how, and employers and recruiters are beginning to use search tools to trawl websites such as LinkedIn where individuals display their badges, in order to find candidates for job vacancies. As the issue and display of badges becomes more prevalent and search tools become more efficient, employers will not only want to search for 'hard' skills but also for 'soft' skills such as planning and organising or co-operative teamwork. The measurement of soft skills is an area where psychometric tests of personality and ability have always been pre-eminent, and there is little reason to think that they will not continue to fulfil this function for several more years. However, their importance will, in many cases, be shared with other measures of behaviour in the creation of badges. In order to validate the claims they make for the authenticity and validity of their badges, badge issuers will create systems of 'triangulation', where an individual's psychometric test results will be supported (or not) by data from other sources, like peer ratings and actual achievements. Thus, when an individual posts badges claiming to be competent at a range of soft skills, the worth of these claims will be judged according to the breadth and depth of the evidence that the badge issuer has demanded before issuing the badge.

One corollary is that in about five years, most professionals, whether job seekers or not, will have their own skills 'passports' which will be authenticated to the extent that a prospective employer will no longer have to conduct a fresh psychometric assessment of that professional. The current practice of pre-hire 'high-stakes testing' of talent by organisations will almost disappear. This will speed up recruitment by saving on 'time-to-hire', and it will also reduce costs considerably for employers, who will be able to conduct their own searches using a direct recruitment model that eliminates agency fees. Given that agencies charge up to 25 per cent of the recruit's first year's salary as a fee, the potential savings of the direct recruitment model for large organisations are staggeringly large and could easily run into tens of millions of pounds. The possibility of savings of that magnitude is bound to be a driver for change.

THE PROMISE OF DATA FROM WEARABLES, BIG DATA METHODOLOGY AND OTHER 'STEALTH ASSESSMENTS'

Electronic devices that clip on to a user's belt or are worn around the wrist to measure fitness and well-being are the first generation of new devices known as 'wearables'. The second generation of these devices is likely to be a little more invasive and they will monitor general brain activity (by means of an electroencephalogram (EEG)), body temperature, movements and posture and the correlates of the autonomic nervous system. Some employers are already asking volunteer employees to wear them at work so that fitness and stress can be systematically monitored and fed back to both employer and employee in real time (Waber, 2013). It is claimed that sensitive use of the data from monitors can result in increased employee productivity (by identifying an employee's most productive times of day) and better employee decision making (by redeploying temporarily an employee at the times of day when they are showing biological signs of heightened stress). Competitive sports teams already use analytics to track athletes on the field, off the field, at home, when they are sleeping and when they are eating, and there are small signs that the workplace is moving towards that model (Rackspace).

These forms of monitoring are known as 'stealth assessment' (Camara, 2015; Guszcsa & Richardson, 2014). According to one proponent, Chris Brauer (Rackspace, 2014), 'The depth and distinctiveness of profiles that can be built … is startling. Using just data gathered from wearable devices, it is possible to develop rich behavioural and lifestyle profiles of individuals.' In a paper on assessment practices in 2025, Jones (2015) states that 'Employees will become 24/7/365 data collectors known as "Terabyters". They will wear technology and/or implants that will produce an amazing amount of actionable data for ongoing, real-time validation and business impact studies.'

Applications of wearable technology in the workplace can easily be found. Employees working in oil and gas, and in mining and construction, have already started using military chest-mounted sensors that gauge heart rate, stress levels, breathing, skin temperature and body position. Equivital, the company that makes the technology, is currently working on systems that will flag up when someone is 20 minutes away from heat stress. The Bank of America has started using the products of another company, Humanyze, within its call centres. These are known as smart badges and they contain microphones which measure how much the wearer talks, how loudly they speak, and whether they interrupt or sound stressed. Using codified data from smart badges, they found that staff were more productive and less likely to leave when they had close bonds on the job with co-workers. Productivity was measured by the number of completed calls. Employees now have an additional 15-minute shared tea break, and productivity has risen by ten per cent, while staff turnover has dropped by 70 per cent.

John Coates, a neuroscientist at the University of Cambridge has hypothesized that as financial market traders make and lose money, they undergo physiological changes; most importantly changes in endogenous steroids. He suggests that these changes push traders between the extremes of irrational exuberance and pessimism, and thus alter their risk preferences. Coates has been exploring this hypothesis by monitoring via wearables the physiological systems of traders on the trading floor in the City of London, in particular their endocrine systems, the hormonal changes in the body; and their autonomic nervous systems. He has demonstrated that as traders experience market fluctuation, they undergo the physiological changes he hypothesized (Coates, 2012).

So, human optimisation and behavioural observation via wearables are already gaining traction. These devices are yielding psychological as well as physiological data. It is to be hoped that businesses will work within a social contract to collect and use these types of data sensitively and appropriately, because they have great potential for protecting the physical and psychological well-being of employees.

CONCLUSION

Disruptions to the current theory and practice of psychometric testing will come from many different directions over the next decade and they will occur at varying speeds. The fastest will be the digital badging movement and the most fundamental will be advances in the neuroscience of personality. This chapter, like many of the contributions to this book, has focused mainly on HR testing for recruitment and employee development. However, some of the changes that have been outlined will apply to the educational and clinical fields. There too, traditional tests will have to be adapted for new devices such as smartphones. Wearables are likely to be used more and more to collect longitudinal data for situational and lifestyle monitoring in the clinical field, and neurobiological discoveries are likely to reshape the description and categorisation of clinical disorders.

All this is a reminder that the popular questionnaire method of assessing individual differences is a proxy for repeated observation of behaviour and that new technology is enabling alternative methods of revealing the same data. Self-assessment questionnaires are unlikely to disappear completely from a practitioner's tool kit but those forms of measurement may soon be overtaken by better or more convenient methods. All these developments will be exciting for psychometricians and qualified test practitioners. Skilled test users need not have diminished roles. They will find themselves able to transfer their skills to the interpretation of new data and the construction of new assessments, and their competence in feedback to new measurement outputs. Although the medium may change, the psychometric fundamentals of test reliability and validity and good test practice will always apply. Let us welcome the challenge of the new era.

REFERENCES

Arthur, W., Jr, Doverspike, D., Muñoz, G. J., Taylor, J. E. & Carr, A. E. (2014). The use of mobile devices in high-stakes remotely delivered assessments and testing. *International Journal of Selection and Assessment*, 22(2), 113–23.

Bartram, D. (2013). A cross-validation of between country differences in personality using the OPQ32. *Journal of Quantitative Research in Education*, 1(2), 182–211.

Camara, W. J. (2015). Back to the future planning: Envisioning I-O assessments in 2025: Prognostications: School-to-work assessments and transitions. Paper presented at the Association of Test Publishers Conference, Palm Springs, CA, March.

Christensen, C., Anthony, S. D. and Roth E. A. (2004). *Seeing what's next: Using the theories of innovation to predict industry change.* Boston, MA: Harvard Business School Press.

Coates, J. (2012). *The hour between dog and wolf: how risk taking transforms us, body and mind.* London, Fourth Estate.

Eysenck, H. J. (1944). Types of personality: A factorial study of 700 neurotics. *Journal of mental science,* 90, 859–61.

Eysenck, H. J. (1947). *Dimensions of personality.* London: Kegan Paul, Trench, Trubner & Co.

Eysenck, H. J. (1957). *The dynamics of anxiety and hysteria.* New York: Praeger.

Eysenck, H. J. (1960). *The structure of human personality* (2nd edn). London: Methuen

Eysenck, H. J. (1967). *The biological basis of personality.* Springfield, IL: Charles C. Thomas.

Goldberg, L. R. (1981). Language and individual differences: The search for universals in personality lexicons. In L.Wheeler, L. (ed.), *Review of personality and social psychology* (vol. 2, pp. 141–65). Beverly Hills, CA: Sage.

Gorsuch, R. L. (2006). Manual for Personality Express: Big 5 and 16PF. Champaign, IL: Institute for Personality and Ability Testing.

Gray, J. A. (1981). A critique of Eysenck's theory of personality. In H. J. Eysenck (ed.), *A model for personality* (pp. 246–76). Berlin: Springer.

Gray, J. A. & McNaughton, N. (2000). *The neuropsychology of anxiety: An enquiry into the functions of the septo-hippocampal system* (2nd edn). Oxford: Oxford University Press.

Gutierrez, S. L. & Meyer, J. M. (2013). Assessments on the go: Applicant reactions to mobile testing. Paper presented at the 28th Annual Conference of the Society for Industrial and Organizational Psychology, Houston, TX, April.

Gutierrez, S. L., Meyer, J. M. & Fursman, P. (2015). What exactly drives positive reactions to mobile device administration? Paper presented at the 30th Annual Conference of the Society for Industrial and Organizational Psychology, Philadelphia, PA, April.

Guszcsa, J. & Richardson, B. (2014). Two dogmas of big data: Understanding the power of analytics for predicting human behaviour. *Deloitte Review,* 15.

Humphreys, G. W. & Sui, J. (2015). The salient self: Social saliency effects based on self bias. *Journal of Cognitive Psychology,* 27, 129–40.

Illingworth, A. J., Morelli, N. A., Scott, J. C., and Boyd, S. L. (2015). Internet-based, unproctored assessments on mobile and non-mobile devices: Usage, measurement equivalence, and outcomes. *Journal of Business Psychology,* 30(2), 325–43.

Impelman, K. (2013). Mobile assessment: Who's doing it and how it impacts selection. In J. Scott (chair) and N. Morelli (co-chair), Mobile devices in talent assessment: Where are we now? Symposium presented at the 28th Annual Conference of The Society for Industrial and Organizational Psychology, Houston, TX, April.

Jones, J. (2015). I-O Assessments in 2025: A futuristic perspective. Paper presented at the Association of Test Publishers Conference, Palm Springs, CA, March 2015.

Kosinski, M., Stilwell, D. & Graepel, T. (2013). Private traits and attributes are predictable from digital records of human behaviour. *Proceedings of the National Academy of Sciences of the United States of America,* 110, 5802–5.

Lawrence, A., Wasko, L., Delgado, K., Kinney, T. & Wolf, D. (2013). Does mobile assessment administration impact psychological; measurement? In J. Scott (chair) and N. Morelli (co-chair), Mobile devices in talent assessment: Where are we now? Symposium presented at the 28th Annual Conference of The Society for Industrial and Organizational Psychology, Houston, TX, April.

McClure, T. K., & Boyce, A. S. (2015). Selection testing: An updated look at trends in mobile device usage. Paper presented at the 30th Annual Conference of the Society for Industrial and Organizational Psychology, Philadelphia, PA, April.

Morelli, N. A., Illingworth, A. J., Scott, J. C. & Lance, C. E. (2012). Are Internet-based, unproctored assessments on mobile and non-mobile devices equivalent? In J. Scott (chair), Chasing the tortoise: Zeno's paradox in technology based assessment. Symposium presented at the 27th Annual Conference of the Society for Industrial and Organizational Psychology, San Diego, CA, April.

Morelli, N. A., Mahan, R. P. & Illingworth, A. J. (2014). Establishing the measurement equivalence of online selection assessments delivered on mobile versus nonmobile devices. *International Journal of Selection and Assessment*, 22(2), 124–38.

Pavlov, I. P. (1927). *Reflexes: An investigation of the physiological activity of the cerebral cortex.* Oxford: Oxford University Press.

Rackspace (2014). The human cloud at work: A study into the impact of wearable technologies in the workplace. Web report. Rackspace Ltd. https://www.rackspace.co.uk/sites/default/files/Human%20Cloud%20at%20Work.pdf. Accessed 20 October 2016.

Recruitment Grapevine (2015). Students ready to ditch the traditional CV for digital resume. 10 February. http://www.recruitmentgrapevine.com/article/51-of-students-are-ready-to-ditch-the-traditional-cv. Accessed 20 October 2016.

Smith, A. (2015). U.S. smartphone use in 2015. Pew Research Center report. 1 April. http://www.pewinternet.org/2015/04/01/us-smartphone-use-in-2015/. Accessed 20 October 2016.

Sternberg, R. J. (1997). Intelligence and lifelong learning: What's new and how can we use it? *American Psychologist*, 52, 1134–9.

Sui, J., Rothstein, P. & Humphries, G. W. (2013). Coupling social attention to the self forms a network of personal significance. *Proceedings of the National Academy of Sciences of the United States of America*, 110, 7607–12..

Waber, B. (2013). People analytics: How social sensing technology will transform business and what it tells us about the future of work. Upper Saddle River, NJ: FT Press.

Index

AAT (Approche Action Type)   153
ABAS-3 (Adaptive Behaviour Assessment System)   192
ability tests   17, 19, 67, 72, 95, 121, 122, 277
   cognitive   18, 43, 58n(1), 59n(6), 98, 254
ABLE Series Critical Information Analysis   67
Ablitt, H.   60n(17)
Acas (UK Advisory, Conciliation and Arbitration Service)   131
Acclaim (badge issuer)   277
accountability   103, 116, 126, 130
adaptation   135, 160, 207, 223, 230, 270
   good   222
   methods for monitoring   224–6
ADSC (British Army Development and Selection Centre)   12
advertising   216
affect   191–2, 197, 200
   cold   206, 207
African-Americans   257
AGCT (American Army and Navy General Classification Tests)   11
agreeableness   21, 35, 51, 92, 142, 163–6, 168–71, 207, 208, 252
agreement   30–1, 108, 177, 189, 264
Akhtar, R.   201
Alexander the Great, czar of Russia   4
Allison, J.   217, 218
Allport, Gordon W.   16, 22, 213, 252, 253, 256
altruism   207
American Football players   153
   see also NFL
Ames, R.   206
AMI (Athlete Motivation Inventory)   145
analytics   278
   blended   60n(20)
   image   56, 57
   predictive   43–63
   prescriptive   44
   talent   44, 47
   text   44
   see also HR Analytics; People Analytics; Workforce Analytics
Ancient Greeks   4, 5, 13
Ancient Rome   5
Anderson, H.   187–8
Anderson, N.   39
Anderson, P.   206
Ankersen, Rasmus   153–4
Anthony, S. D.   273
anti-social personality disorder   199, 200, 207, 209
anxiety   21, 30, 164, 198, 200, 219, 276
   CBT for   181
   controlling   27
   low levels of   207
   managing   15
   measuring   25
   reducing   135, 192
   see also Beck Anxiety Inventory-II; castration anxiety; Generalised Anxiety Disorder-7
AoEs (Areas of Expertise)   120, 123
APA (American Psychiatric Association)   189, 198, 201, 202, 230, 244, 249
   see also DSM
Apple   56, 271
aptitude   4, 66
   literacy replaced by   11
   special   158
aptitude tests   93, 95, 96, 98, 109, 121
   difficult   88
   highly reputable   158
   many have higher levels of validity   99
   numerical   90, 107
   preferred   153
   see also ASVAB
Arabic   225
Army Alpha and Beta tests (US)   11

Arnold, R.   149, 150
Aronson, J.   90
ARTD (British Army Recruiting and Training Directorate)   11–12
Arthur, W.   235, 270
artificial intelligence   44
Asian cultures   230
assessment   8, 9, 47, 54, 55, 58n(1), 122, 167, 188, 189, 276
   ability   13, 43, 69, 192–3
   basic   117
   benchmarking   123–6
   bespoke   126
   cognitive   109
   competency   59n(6), 104
   cross-cultural   224
   development centres and   105
   early models and their scope for psychometrics   157–8
   educated   3
   employment   45
   evidence from sources conducted by different assessors   105
   fairness and accuracy in   230
   full-day programmes   73
   generic British template   158
   gold standard approach to   187
   implications for ethically and technically justifiable practice in   265
   instant   84
   intra-individual   38
   limitations and assumptions implicit in   251–61
   mobile app-based   273
   neuropsychological   193
   non-forensic   201
   non-psychometric   99
   normative/ipsative   100–1
   occupational   213–20
   organisation-wide capability   119–21
   perceived organisational stressors in sport   149
   pragmatic   133–4
   presentation and organization of   247
   psychometrics can give a false level of   87
   quality of   107, 225
   questionable   109
   recruitment   48, 92
   reliability of diagnosis and   189–94
   risk   131, 263
   robust leadership   119–28
   school learning   253
   screening-style   84
   selection   123–6, 221
   simulation-based   43–4
   smart mobile technology and   44, 269, 270–3
   stealth   278–9
   team   133
   widening   6
   see also assessment centres; assessment instruments/tools; EAF; personality assessment; psychometric assessment; self-assessment
assessment centres   23, 69, 89, 95, 105, 126, 254
   army selection, two-day   12
   expense of   73
   off-job simulations in   172
   university   255
assessment instruments/tools   121, 133, 253, 255, 260
   deciding whether or not to use   74
   inadequate care in choice and application of   263
   looking at the overall use of   75
   originators/origins of   263, 264
   popular   263
   risk   263
   well-designed and psychometrically sound   201
   widely used   264
ASVAB (US Armed Services Vocational Aptitude Battery)   11
AT&T   12
ATS (applicant tracking system)   48, 106
attainment   49, 99, 158, 223
auditing   88, 94, 175
auditory stimulus   217
autonomic nervous system   278
avoidance   179
avoidant personality disorder   198, 200, 202

back translation   224–5, 226
badging movement   269, 275, 277–9
Bank of America   278
BARB (British Army Recruit Battery)   12
Barel, P.   153
Barnum effect   33

Barrett, P. T.   175, 177
Barrick, M. R.   169
Bartram, D.   43, 53, 106, 161, 163, 165–8, 241, 272
BDI-II (Beck Depression Inventory-II)   179, 191, 192
Bean, K. L.   217
Beauchamp, M. R.   148, 149
Beck Anxiety Inventory-II   192
behavioural issues   35, 36, 109, 130–2, 135, 137, 142, 147, 158, 178, 241
  coaching   126, 151, 240
  competencies   37, 160, 162
  disorders   202
  diversity   129, 143
  dysfunctionalities   170
  leadership ability   119
  observation via wearables   279
  patterns associated with unreliable, aggressive or dishonest activities   98
  personality assessments   254
  rich profiles of individuals   278
  traits   98, 202
  see also CBT
benchmarking   9, 44, 53, 55, 57, 58n(4), 59nn(15–16), 60n(17), 119, 120, 122
  assessment for   123–6
  predictive   46, 53
  standardised   125
Bennis, Warren   113
best practice   43, 101, 109, 128, 158, 180, 273
  recommendations in administration settings   228
  using a highly specific norm group makes for   107
bias   29, 36, 37, 109
  administration   227–8
  causes for concern about   257
  central tendency   31, 38
  conceptual   224
  construct   229–30
  instrument   226–7
  item   223–6
  linguistic   223
  opportunity   97–8
  positivistic   180–1
  psychological   224

sample   228, 229
selection   88
self-selection   229
social   105
subjective   18
big data   269, 278
  and predictive analytics   43–63
Big Five model   21, 38, 92, 136, 140, 142, 167, 194, 252, 275, 276
  Cattell's five global factors similar to   272
  Lumina Spark model draws on empiricism of   143
  major correlate of   208
  meta-analytical evidence for specific factors   169
  negative relation to   207
  rise of   163–4
  second-order   161
  utility of expanding   139
Big Five proxies   166, 172
  second-order   169
bilingual judges technique   225–6
Binet, Alfred   6, 9, 17, 19, 251–2
Binet-Simon IQ test   9, 10
black people   90, 257
Blinkhorn, S.   31, 38
Boddy, C. R.   216
Bohr, Niels   57
Bons, T. A.   253
borderline personality disorder   198, 200, 209
Boulder Conference (Univ. of Colorado 1949)   175
Bowen, Murray   240
Bowler, W.   48
Boyatzis, R. E.   102, 162, 254
  see also Competent Manager
Boyd, S. L.   270
BPS (British Psychological Society)   13, 66, 68, 70, 72, 109, 236, 239, 244–6, 248, 249
  assessment of learning disability   192
  Psychometric Test Centre   23
  Register of Qualified Test Users   65, 238, 265n
Bradshaw, Terry   153
brain injury/illness   193
brain systems   221, 242
  under-excited   275
  see also autonomic nervous system; neuropsychology

Branson, Sir Richard   31
Brauer, Chris   278
Briggs, Katharine Cook   137, 148, 252
  see also MBTI
British Ability Scales   192
British Army see ADSC; ARTD; BARB
Brook Reaction Test   215
Brown, A.   106
Brown, S. L.   207
Burisch, M.   34
Burke, E.   43, 48, 53–4, 59n(15), 60n(17)
Buros Institute   244, 245, 246, 248, 249
Busch, C. M.   167
Buzzard, R. B.   32
Byrne, B. M.   224, 229

Cambridge Dictionary   225
Cambridge University   44, 51, 278
  Cavendish Physics Laboratory   16–17
  Psychometrics Centre   57
Cameron, P.   206
'can do' category   50, 94–101, 124, 236
Canada   151
  see also CPA
CAPS (Clinician-Administered PTSD Scale)   190
CAQ (California Adult Q-Set)   167
career counselling   31
  coaching and   126–7, 202
career development   202, 251, 256
  high emphasis on   126
  running programmes   201
career guidance   87, 92–3, 237, 255
  school leaver receiving   107
careers   148, 157, 239, 240, 274–5
  advice on paths   59n(13)
  commitment to   119
  early stages of   98, 120
  inventories of   101
  leadership and   251
  management of   123
  planning   120, 122, 126
  predicting success   45
  progression in   117, 120
  school   11
  useful stimulus for discussions   218
CareerWhiz   59n(13)
Carlyle, Thomas   4

Carr, A. E.   270
castration anxiety   218
CAT (computerised-adaptive testing)   9, 48, 60n(19)
Cattell, A. K.   92
Cattell, H. E. P.   92, 257
Cattell, J. M.   6, 17, 19
Cattell, R. B.   21, 92, 159, 161, 163, 164, 252, 253, 256, 272, 275
Causal Flow Model   162, 165, 167, 172
CBT (cognitive-behavioural therapy)   181
CEB Talent Measurement   54, 59n(6)
cellphones see mobile phones
CEOs (chief executive officers)   139, 168
  high-profile   167
Chelladurai, P. see LSS
Cheung, F. M.   224
Cheung, G. W.   227
Christal, R. E.   163, 253
Christensen, C.   273
Christie, R. see Mach-IV inventory
CIA (US Central Intelligence Agency)   214
CIPD (Chartered Institute of Personnel and Development)   105
circumstances
  domestic   158
  questionable   158
  testing   3
CIT (critical incident technique)   101–2
clients   15, 18, 20, 43, 49, 68, 77, 165, 182, 253, 256–60
  analytics studies for   54
  approaches to   16
  assessment triangulation of   22, 23
  average mental health   180–1
  best interests of   188
  changes may be forced on test industry by   271
  clinical realities confronting therapists when they meet with   175
  collaborative understanding with   188–9
  confusion for   189
  costs for   270
  diagnosis of   187
  discharge of   179
  discussion of results with   193
  engagement and motivation of   178
  finding   50

forced to take a 'punt' 84
identity of 251
importance of hearing their own description of life 190
information gained from 194
measures of affect frequently used to track current mood state 192
orientation of 114
perceptions of series of patterned smudges 6–7
personal history, ethnicity, culture and educational opportunity 191
pre-screening 192
report writing for 241
resolution of issues 23
showing specific photographs of psychopaths to 6
usefulness of assessment to 255
clinical psychology 201, 214, 221
clinical settings/practice 213
  psychometrics in 175–84, 187–96
coaching 25, 93, 113, 132, 147, 150, 152, 209, 237, 242, 255
  behavioural 126, 151, 240
  counselling and 23, 126–7, 202, 255
  development and 45, 128, 201, 202, 203
  leadership 251
  substitution and 240
Coates, John 278
cognitive speed 252
Cohen, J. 167
Collins, D. 146, 147
colloquialisms 223
Color Code Personality Test 57
competencies 104, 275
  behavioural 37, 160, 162
  clustering of 166, 254
  commercial awareness 104
  commonly used/occurring 102, 254
  corporate 114
  developments in the use of 162
  genesis of 159–60
  group 116
  managerial 160, 167–70
  psychometric factors and 164–7
  relationships between psychometric factors and 164–7
  selected 12
  specific 158, 159, 160
  standardised set of 102
  supra- 166
  work-relevant 35
  see also Great Eight competencies
Competent Manager, The (Boyatzis) 159–60
computer-generated media
  images 218
  psychometric questionnaires 219
  reports 68, 70–2
computers 11, 50, 51, 96, 161, 162, 214, 217, 228, 240, 244, 256, 276
  access to 229
  analysis of results 18
  ownership of 44
  programming know-how 277
  smartphones will replace 269, 270–3
  written reports 18, 38, 107
  also CAT; internet; ITC; laptops; smartphones
conscientiousness 21, 51, 83, 92, 139, 141, 142, 163–6, 168–71, 199, 208, 252, 256
consumer psychology 216
Cook, M. 9, 12, 19, 23, 73, 88, 90
  see also ECCOS
Cooke, D. J. 263
COPS (criterion-focused occupational scales) 60n(17)
CORE (Clinical Outcomes Routine Evaluation) 181, 192
Costa, P. T. 21, 164, 194, 208, 228
counselling 23, 249, 255
  see also career counselling; counselling psychology
counselling psychology 240
Cox, Brian 33
CPA (Canadian Psychological Association) 238
Cramp, L. 32
Cripps, B. D. 9, 12, 19, 23, 73, 88, 90, 213, 237
  see also ECCOS
criterion validity 53, 108
  short-lived 49
Cronbach, L. J. 34, 38
Cronbach's Alpha 56, 108–9
cross-cultural psychology 221
Crump, J. 203

cultures   121, 153, 163, 177, 187
　empathy with other   219
　expectations of   197
　few idioms or metaphors translate
　　successfully across   36
　IQ tests tend to be specific to   253–4
　need of the individual self varies in   191
　organisational   93, 94, 101
　team   94, 101
　testing across   221–33
CVLT-II (California Verbal Learning Test)   193

Daniels, K.   149
Daouk-Öyry, L.   216
dark side   98, 258
　see also personality disorders
Dark Triad   197, 206–8
Darwin, Charles   5, 6
data collection   165, 190, 226, 278
De Fruyt, F.   201, 203
Deloitte   47
dependability   163, 170
dependent personality disorder   199, 200
depression   5, 51, 177, 189, 217
　CBT for   181
　clear pathway for treating   178
　differences in symptoms between
　　cultures   229–30
　see also BDI-II
derailment   122
　leadership   126, 197, 209
　potential   258
development
　assessment for   125
　behavioural   132
　coaching and   45, 128, 201, 202, 203
　gaining benefit from psychometrics in   127
　personal   92
　psychometric   132
　theoretical   7–9, 180
　see also career development; HDS; Personal
　　Development Analysis; team development;
　　test development
Dhurup, M.   152
diagnoses   32, 55, 134–5, 153, 178
　available directly to the consumer   274
　clinical and neuropsychological   221
　implications of   187–8

　outcomes should be seen as aids to   260
　reliability of   189–94, 202
　structured interviews   202
　uncertain   130
　vagaries of   182
　valid   202
　widespread use of   187
　see also DSM; ICD-10; self-diagnosis
dialect   215
Dichter, E.   216
Dickens, W. T.   11, 90
differential construct manifestation   229–30
digital divide   229
Dirty Dozen measure   208
Disabilities Act (US 1990)   109
DISC-based personality tests   235, 239, 241–4, 248
　Paltiel's examination of validity in   236, 245
DISC Classic   246–7
Discriminant Function Analysis   147
discrimination   17, 87, 148, 162–3, 178, 208
　cut-score   83n(2), 84
　disability   109
　ethnicity   109
　gender   90, 109
　law on   49, 158
　minorities   49, 106
　potential   46
　religion   109
　sexual orientation   109
Discus   242, 245
disposition   22, 158
　dysfunctional   202
distress   187, 192, 243
　distinguishing psychological from medical
　　approach to   188
　subjective   198
D-KEFS (Delis-Kaplan Executive Function
　System)   193
DMT (Defence Mechanism Test)   218–19
Dodo Bird verdict   178, 179
Donovan, J. J.   169
Doverspike, D.   270
Downey, K.   48
drawings   16, 158, 217, 218
drives   216
　fundamental   6
　motivational   130

DSM (*Diagnostic and Statistical Manual*)   176, 187, 188, 192, 197–203, 206, 209, 230
    PID-5 (Personality Inventory) for   201
    SCID-5 (Structured Clinical Interview) for   190
Dulewicz, S. V.   166

EAF (Executive Assessment Framework)   115–16, 118, 119, 121
    assessing against   123–5
    perceived benefits of   125
ease of use   106, 219, 264
Eber, H. W.   159
EBP (evidence-based practice)   176, 178, 179, 190
    dominance in Western care services   180
    strange and unintended consequence of   181–2
ECCOS (Eysenck-Cook-Cripps Occupational Scales)   16, 20, 25
ecological validity   145, 146, 150, 154
    issues of   151, 152
educational psychology   221
Educational Testing Service   264
Edwards Personality Preference Schedule   158
EEG (electroencephalogram)   278
EFPA (European Federation of Psychologists' Associations)   221
ego ideal   218
EI (Extraversion-Introversion) scale   19
Einstein, Albert   33
EIP (Emotional Intelligence Profile)   122, 124, 126, 127
Ekman, P.   153
Elferink-Gemser, M. T.   147
emotional intelligence   99, 115, 116, 119, 127, 254
    insights into   126
    see also EIP
emotional stability   21, 51, 163
empathy   140, 142, 219
    lack of   200
    low levels of   207
    see also IVE
Endicott, J.   189
English language   11, 223, 224–5, 252, 256, 257
    business   37
    US   37, 272
EPI (Eysenck Personality Inventory)   20, 158

EPQ (Eysenck Personality Questionnaire)   19, 20, 207–8, 214
EPS (Eysenck Personality Scales)   16, 20, 25
Equality Act (UK 2010)   109
E-RP (exposure and response prevention)   178
ERS (Extreme Response Style)   227
ethics   23, 114
    see also psychology ethics
ethnicity   36, 50, 90, 106, 191, 203, 230
    discrimination on the basis of   109
    measure that is remiss in lack of reliability and validity for   247
    see also minority groups
EU (European Union)   45
Europeans   215, 223, 227
    northern   31
    southern   31
    western   191
eustress   243
Evans, Chris   192
evidence *see* EBP; PBE
Exner, J. E.   218
extraversion   17, 19–22, 31, 51, 137–43, 148, 163, 164–6, 168–71, 222, 252, 259, 276
    correlation with narcissism   208
    differences in   275
    frequently broken into traits   92
    introversion may co-exist with significant contribution from   139
    see also EI; PEN
Eysenck, Hans J.   15, 16, 17, 19, 20, 31, 169, 213, 253, 275, 276
    see also EPI; EPQ; EPS; PEN
Eysenck, M. W.   20, 208
Eysenck, S. B. G.   16, 19, 20
    see also ECCOS

face validity   108, 236, 248, 249, 257
    importance in psychometrics   149
    lack of   36, 216
    low   218
    poor   150, 215
    quest for   241–2
    strong   121
    true validity requires moving beyond   244–5
Facebook   30, 49, 50, 247, 248, 269, 271, 272, 275
    Likes analysed   51

FACS (Facial Action Coding System)   153
factor alpha/gamma   30
factor analysis   5, 17, 21, 65, 164, 213, 252, 253, 275, 276
   Big Eight competencies emerging from   165
   confirmatory   19, 20
   constrained orthogonal methods of   163
   exploratory   20
Fairfax, H.   175
fairness   70, 109, 230
Far East   215
Faucher, L.   180
feedback   18, 19, 35, 70–2, 73, 75, 127, 219, 241, 242, 259, 270, 273
   accurate   147
   collaborative method of assessment and   193, 194
   competence in   279
   descriptive   147
   face-to-face   128
   indicative   147
   interpretation and   106–7, 121, 255
   line manager   124–5, 126
   negative   33
   positive   126, 151, 152
   skilful   258
   timely and skilled   128
Fetzer, M.   43–4
FFM (Five Factor Model) see Big Five
Fico, J.   203
financial services   102, 113, 115, 125
   see also Santander
Finn, Stephen E.   194
FIRO® (Fundamental Interpersonal Relations Orientation)   122, 133, 158, 252–3, 258
First World War (1914–18)   11, 252
Fischer, Constance T.   194
Fiske, D. W.   163
Five-Fold Grading System   158
Flanagan, J. C.   101
flashbacks   179
Fletcher, D.   149, 150
Fletcher, R. B.   152
Flynn, J. R.   11, 90, 253
fMRI (functional magnetic resonance brain imaging) data   276

football   31, 45, 147, 152
   see also NFL; Premiership Football
Forbes   47
forensic psychology   221
Forer effect   33
Forth, A. E.   207
Foucault, Michel   188
Four-Fifths rule   90
four humours   4–5
France   6, 11, 252
   universal education   9
Franklin, Benjamin   10
Freud, Sigmund   6, 7, 22, 35, 213, 214
Friesen, W. V.   153
Fuller, R.   152
functional impairment   198
functioning   131, 136, 242
   adaptive   192
   affective   197
   cognitive   197
   normal   197, 206
   social   192, 197
Furnham, A.   201, 202, 203, 208–9
Fursman, P.   271

Galen   4
Galton, Sir Francis   6, 17, 251
Gandhi, M. K. (Mahatma)   4
Geis, F. L. see Mach-IV inventory
General Factor of Personality   253
general intelligence   126, 158, 252
Generalised Anxiety Disorder-7   192
Gergen, K. J.   187–8, 192
Germany   11, 12, 207
Gibson, William   57
Glaze, R. M.   235
Glennon, R.   59n(15)
Goldberg, L. R.   163, 166
Google   56, 271
Gordon Personal Profile   158
graphology   215
Gray, J. A.   275–6
Great Eight competencies   165–6, 254, 255
grey markets   235, 236, 248, 249
   discourse of business creates   238–9
   ethical characteristics of   247
Guillaume, Y. R. F.   90
guilt feelings   218, 230

Guion, R.   244
Gutierrez, S. L.   271
Guttman, L.   182

Hadrian, Roman Emperor   4
Hall, C. S.   206
Hambleton, R. K.   222, 223, 224, 225, 226, 229
Hammer, A. L.   92, 148
Handler, C.   52, 55
Hanton, S.   150
Hardy, C.   90
Hare, Robert *see* PCL-R
Harley Davidson   51, 59n(11)
Harms, P.   207
Harré, Rom   16, 22
Harston, W. R.   159
Hart, S. D.   207
Harvard   241, 247
Harvey, William   5
HDS (Hogan Development Survey)   122, 197, 202–6, 209, 258
Henley Management College   159
Herbart, Johann   6
Hippocrates   4, 5
Hispanics   257
histrionic personality disorder   199, 200
Hodgkinson, G. P.   246
Hoffman, D.   105
Hoffman, L.   187–8
Hofstee, W. K. B.   166
Hogan, Robert & Joyce   197, 198–200, 203, 206, 209
    see also HDS; HPI
HoganLead   125
Holdsworth, R.   32
    see also SHL
Hong Kong   215
Hopton, T.   33, 39
Howard, J. C.   218
HPI (Hogan Personality Inventory)   122
HR (human resources)   17, 23, 29, 45–8, 50, 53, 57, 113, 119, 120, 128, 157, 249, 279
    applications of psychometrics   87–111
    diverse range of instruments   114
    ill-informed professionals   248
    strategic-level   55
HR Analytics   44, 55
HR Avatar   44

HRIS (HR information systems)   59n(7)
Humanyze   278
humour   32
    great men and   3–4
    see also four humours
Humphries, G. W.   276
Hunter, J. E.   164
Hur, Y.-M.   253
Hurtz, G. M.   169
hyperarousal   179

IAPT (Improving Access to Psychological Therapies)   178
IBM   47, 51, 277
IBM-Kenexa   59n(6)
ICD-10 (International Classification of Diseases)   176, 187, 188
idioms   223, 224
    avoiding   36
IES-R (Impact of Events Scale-Revised)   179
Illingworth, A. J.   270
incommensurability   177
Indian Ayurveda system   4
industrial psychology   109, 214, 221
    see also NIIP; occupational psychology
Insights Discovery   136, 147–9, 153, 242, 245
    findings for   246
intelligence   12, 16, 177, 225
    assessment of   192, 215
    crystallised   66, 252
    fluid   51, 66, 252
    individual differences in   276
    inflated self-insight and   31
    interpersonal   127
    major theories of   66
    measuring   6, 9, 17, 51
    personal   127
    popular explanation for rising scores   11
    see also artificial intelligence; emotional intelligence; general intelligence; IQ
intelligence tests   51, 55, 253
    highly reputable   158
    see also IQ tests; Wonderlic
interests   51, 95, 158, 203, 238
    assessment of   215
    business   249
    commercial   236, 263, 264
    leisure   108

International Telecommunication Union   229
internet   38, 228
   access to   229
   business disruption   235–51
   cybercrime and related fraud   96
   global traffic   270
   number of users   229
   online testing   43, 256
   see also ITC (Guidelines); UIT
interpersonal effectiveness training   93
interpretation   5, 8, 13, 21, 23, 37, 52, 97, 148, 154, 157, 165, 177, 178, 246, 254, 257, 279
   answer   72, 191
   complex and contested   7
   expensive   273
   face-to-face   70
   feedback and   106–7, 121, 255
   in-depth, detailed, of presenting difficulties   193
   interpretation complex and contested   7
   organisational   151
   personal world   16, 22, 25
   profile   147
   projective responses   214, 215, 218, 219
   proper   38
   reliability   69, 108–9
   scale   29
   score   43, 53, 68, 71, 228
   subjective narrative-report   77
   test result   67–9
   ugly   152
   variety of sounds   217
interviews   9, 12, 27, 29, 50, 68, 72, 78, 104, 105, 167, 218, 237, 260
   biographical   158, 159
   career development   256
   commonly afflicted by bias   88
   critical incidents   101–2
   extended   25
   extremely short notice   157
   feedback in conjunction with   255
   Four-Fifths rule and   90
   imprecision and unreliability of   189
   online testing candidate validity and   89
   personal characteristics emerging in   219
   reliable and comprehensive schedules   208
   rescheduled   259
   semi-structured   190–1, 194
   structured   95, 124, 125, 189, 190, 202, 256
   traditional selection   88
   unstructured   95
   visionary   102
introversion   5, 19, 20, 22, 26, 31, 137–43, 148, 169, 204, 252, 275
IPAT (Institute for Personality and Ability Testing)   110n, 167
ipsative measures   22, 37, 38, 100–1, 216
IQ (Intelligence Quotient)   10, 119, 166–7, 252
   average in the developed world   253
IQ tests   11
   culture-specific   253–4
   see also Binet-Simon; Stanford-Binet
IRT (Item Response Theory)   8, 9, 60n(19), 65
ITC (International Test Commission)   221, 240
   Guidelines on Computer-Based and Internet-Delivered Testing   43, 225, 228
item response   31, 37
   see also IRT
ITPQ (Ideal Team Profile Questionnaire)   258
IVE (Impulsiveness, Venturesomeness and Empathy) scales   19, 20, 25

Japan   215
Jensen, A. R.   90
Jensen, M. C.   133
jingle-jangle fallacy   206
job analysis   89
   example outputs from   102–5
   marketing of role   89
   methods of   101–2
   results of tests matched against   17
job description   101, 102–5
job performance   53, 66, 94, 164
   algorithm predicting   49
   dispositions that may impede   202
   expected   81–3
   negative correlations with   35
   predicted   79, 80, 95, 97, 100
   projected group-classification   79–82
   prospective   77
   psychometric test scores and   83n(3)
   very reasonable measure of   75
Johansen, Bob   128
Johnson, C. B.   38
Jonason, P. K.   207, 208
Jones, J.   278

Jones, J. L.   175
Jordet, G.   147
Judge, T. A.   169
Jung, Carl G.   15, 16, 21, 35, 132, 136–7, 139, 140, 142, 143, 148–9, 153, 214–16, 252, 258, 264

Kahneman, D.   170, 171
Kamin, S.   146
Karon, B. P.   218
Keller, J. W.   215
Kelly, George   15, 16, 22–3, 26, 102, 256
Kilmann, R. H. *see* TKI
Kline, Paul   16, 21, 67, 69, 215, 230, 235, 241–2, 244, 264
Knight, Craig   16
Korean War (1950–3)   253
Kragh, U.   218
Kroenke, K.   178
Kublai Khan   4
Kuder Occupational Interest Survey   257
Kuhn, T. S.   177
Kurz, R.   33, 35, 39, 92, 165–6

Lamiell, James Thomas   16
language(s)   57, 101, 121, 193, 215, 242
  adding words and phrases to   253
  common   16, 133, 142, 189, 257
  few idioms or metaphors translate successfully across   36
  first   257, 272
  idiosyncratic and nuanced   256
  non-technical   147, 272
  not appropriate for actual recipient   256
  representational   188
  shared   180
  shifting   244
  suited to the occasion   161
  test versions   221–6
  see also English language; Swedish language
laptops   96, 270, 271, 272
  ownership of   44
  see also tablets
latent trait modelling   8
Latino cultures   230
Lazare, A.   188
Lazarsfeld, Paul   8

leaders/leadership   12, 36, 53, 59n(6), 72, 102, 160, 166, 236
  advising on   251
  assessing the personality of   3
  blueprint for   114–16
  born   4, 5
  careers and   251
  challenges to authority   133
  clarity of   130
  corporate   237
  defining and assessing talent   113–28
  deployment of expensive development interventions   84
  derailment of   126, 197, 209
  development of   93
  effective   151, 152
  gift of   3–4
  implementing robust assessment   119–28
  increasing capabilities   239
  organisation-based measures of   151
  organisational   44, 55
  potential   71
  programme preparation   127
  supply of talent globally   59n(15)
  'thought'   241
  see also LEAP; LSS; Multidimensional Model; team leaders
LEAP (Leadership Excellence in Action Programme)   127
Lebanon   229
Lee, D.   190
Leonardo da Vinci   33
Levenson, M. R. *see* LSRP
Lewis, Michael   45
Li, N. P.   207
Lie scale   19, 20
Lievens, P.   43
Likert scale   30, 33, 38, 39, 78, 139, 227
linguistic equivalence   223, 224, 225
LinkedIn   49, 52, 59n(13), 239, 241, 275, 277
LMS (learning management systems)   48, 59n(7)
Lord, Frederic   8, 9, 60n(19)
Lothian, A. M.   148
LSRP (Levenson Self-Report Psychopathy) scale   208
LSS (Leadership Scale for Sport)   151–2
Luborsky, L.   178

Lululemon   240
Lumina Spark system   136, 139–43
Lyon, L. P. *see* AMI

Mabey, W.   32
Machiavellianism   205, 206, 207, 208
Mach-IV inventory   206, 207
MacIver, R.   32, 33, 35, 39, 92
Mackintosh, N. J.   11
MacLachlan, A.   148
Mahan, R. P.   270
Mahoney-Phillips, J.   48
make-up   6
   basic personality   214
   gender   168
   physical   158
   potential   117
management
   core   159
   first-line   271
   general courses   159
   talent   44, 46–7, 50, 94
   see also LMS
management selection   32, 157–74
managerial performance   160, 162, 167–8, 172
   generic psychometric predictors of   169–70
Manual of the Eysenck Personality Scales   19
Maravelas, A.   130
market research   13, 30, 31
   good   29
marketing   89, 216
Marston, William   241–6
Martorana, P. V.   167
Marx, Karl   4
mathematics and statistics   182
Maudsley Medical Questionnaire/Personality Inventory   20
MBTI (Myers-Briggs Type Inventory)   5, 16, 21, 25, 26, 33, 92, 93, 110n, 122, 132, 136–8, 143, 148–9, 153, 158, 193, 246, 252, 257–8, 264
McCaulley, M. H.   92, 148
McClelland, David   254
McCredie, H.   161–2, 164, 166–72
McDaniel, M. A.   98
McDowall, A.   226
McGinnis, E.   245
McLeod, A.   255

MCMI-III/IV (Millon Clinical Multiaxial Inventory-III/IV)   176, 193
McRae, R. R.   21, 164, 194, 208, 228
Meehl, P. E.   161, 170
megalomania   4
Mehr, S. L.   175
Meir, Golda   4
Mellalieu, S. D.   150
mental abnormality   188
mental health   36, 187, 189, 191–2
   diagnosis of conditions   32
   health EBP and   180
   quality and effectiveness of services   181
   stepped care   178
mental illness   189, 240
Merenda, P.   224
Merino, Dan   153
Merkel, Angela   4
mesomorphic types   153
meta-analysis   39, 90, 98, 100, 165, 169
   emerging use of   164
   reliability of   95
metaphors   36
method bias   226–30
Meyer, J. M.   271
Michell, J.   6, 8, 177
Microsoft   51, 277
Middle Eastern cultures   230
Milner, R.   201
Minnesota   246
   see also MMPI; University of Minnesota
minority groups   271
   disadvantaged   90, 108
   discrimination against   49, 106
   opportunities for   90
   selection of members   90
   vast majority rejected   91
misinterpretation   36
mistranslation   223, 225
MMPI (Minnesota Multiphasic Personality Inventory)   32, 193, 203, 214, 224
mobile phones   44, 106
   see also smartphones
mood state *see* affect
Morelli, N. A.   270
Morgeson, F. P.   34, 35
Morris, L.   198, 199
Mosaic Test   217

Moscoso, S. 170, 198, 199
motivation 17, 27, 87, 99, 100, 103, 121, 122, 130, 137, 177, 243, 254
   achievement 216
   engagement and 94, 178
   high 35, 135
   interpreting as malevolent 199
   low 35, 131
   problem with 35
   purpose and 227
   see also AMI
Mottram, R. D. 159
Mount, M. K. 169
MRI (magnetic resonance imaging) 276
MTR-i (Management Team Roles Indicator) 258
Multidimensional Model of Leadership 151
Muñoz, G. J. 270
Munro, Andrew 239, 242, 243, 246, 247
Murray, H. A. see TAT
music 158
Myers, Isabel Briggs 137, 148, 252
   see also MBTI

Napoleon Bonaparte 10
narcissism 207, 208
   see also NPD; NPI
narrative 51, 57, 72, 107
   computer-generated 71
   counter 181
   dominant 180
   free-flowing 190, 191
   subjective 77
Nathanson, C. 207, 208
National Service (UK) 11
Nelson, Horatio 4
NEO-PI-R (NEO-Personality Inventory-Revised) 21, 92, 164, 166, 193, 208, 227
Net Index 229
Netherlands 215
neuropsychology 192, 193, 221, 275
   see also RBANST
neuroticism 19, 92, 164–6, 168–70, 199, 200, 208, 252, 275, 276
   see also PEN; SN dimension
New York Times 50
NFL ([American] National Football League) 145, 153

Nguyen, N. T. 98
NHS (UK National Health Service) 180, 181
   Adult Mental Health Secondary Care 175
   progress of therapy and outcomes 192
NICE (UK National Institute for Health and Clinical Excellence) 180, 181, 189
NIIP (UK National Institute of Industrial Psychology) 158
Noguchi, Hideyo 153
non-psychometric procedures 78–81, 99–100
norm groups 9, 67, 69, 71, 106–7, 237
   imitation of 68
Norman, W. T. 163
North America 54
NPD (narcissistic personality disorder) 199, 200, 202, 209
NPI (Narcissistic Personality Inventory) 206
numerical reasoning tests 74, 89, 96
   sample 97
   see also RANRA
Nyfield, G. 32

Occam's razor 34
occupational psychology 17, 100, 109, 214, 216, 242, 251
   decline in use of projective measures in 219
OCD (obsessive-compulsive disorder) 178, 199, 200
Ogawa, T. 215
Ogilvie, B. C. see AMI
Oldham, J. 198, 199
openness 21, 51, 92, 124, 163–5, 168–70, 208, 252, 276
OPQ (Occupational Personality Questionnaire) 21, 36, 39, 92, 122, 124, 127, 136, 165, 167, 253, 255
   CM7 version of 38
organisational context 129–30
organisational psychology 109, 221
OSI-SP (Organisational Stressor Indicator for Sport Performers) 149–51
OSS (US Office of Strategic Service) 214
   see also CIA
Owens, P. D. 167

Paltiel, L. 236, 239, 244, 245, 247, 248
paranoid personality disorder 198, 199
Pareto 77

passive-aggressive personality disorder   198
Patsula, L.   225
Paulhus, D. L.   30, 206, 207, 208
Pavlov, Ivan   275
PBE (practice-based evidence)   181
PCL-R (Hare Psychopathy Checklist-Revised)   190, 207, 263–5
Pelham, B. W.   228, 229
Peltier, B.   255
PEN (Psychoticism-Extraversion-Neuroticism) model   164, 207–8
People Analytics   44
performance *see* job performance; managerial performance; performance outcomes; performance psychology; team performance; test performance
performance outcomes   25, 77, 83
   computer algorithm   51
   ratings of   78
   successful   15, 23
performance psychology   15
   applying psychometrics in   25
   uncritical push for more organisational psychology in   151
Performax Systems International   245
Persia   5
PersonaBubble (website)   271, 272, 273
Personal Construct Psychology   16, 22, 26, 256
Personal Development Analysis   242, 245
personal profiles *see* Gordon; PPA; PPS
personality
   advances in the neuroscience of   275–6
   dark side of   98, 258
   differences in   272, 276
   five domains measured   164
   four humours and   4–5
   normal functioning   197
   psychometrics and   136
   psychopathic   208
   psychophysiological theory of   19
   typology of   148
   see also under following headings prefixed 'personality'
personality assessment   3, 4, 13, 43, 59n(6), 100–1, 104, 106, 193–4, 201
   most popular in the world   264
   triangulating nomothetic and idiographic approaches to   15–27

   very well-established and valid   108
   see also Society for Personality Assessment
personality disorders   175
   higher-order classification of   199–200
   labels for   198–9
   measuring   176, 197–211
   second most widely used test of   176
Personality Insights (application)   51
personality research   16, 146, 164, 270, 272
   group   149
   psychopathic   263
   wars and   252
personality scales   17–18, 19, 33, 38
   Big Five   272
   measuring   34
   writing items for   34
   see also EPS
personality testing   19, 277
   competition and   247
   workplace   235–51
   see also under various titles, e.g. Big Five; Color Code; DISC; General Factor of Personality; MBTI; Sixteen Personality Factor
personality theory   252
   Big Five   194
   Marston's   243–4
   see also MBTI
personality traits   18, 21, 51, 71, 93, 146, 152, 208
   abilities and   254
   Big Five   207
   broad   92
   divined   3
   enquiries designed to uncover   20
   identifying the presence of   20
   inspecting   16
   measured   92, 100, 121, 223, 237
   opposing   139
   overt behaviour and   164
   perceived   4
   personality disorders must be distinguished from   198
   predictive of job performance   100
   psychologists are interested in   197
   stable   164
   valuable for competitive sports person   25
personality type   5, 16, 21, 121
   broad indications of   92

Jung's idea of   264
  tests that measure   237
  see also MBTI
Peterson, R. S.   167
Pfizer   178
PHQ-9 (Patient Health Questionnaire-9)   178, 192
physiology   34, 153, 230, 278, 279
  brave if flawed attempt to synthesise developments in   243
  see also psychophysiology
Piotrowski, C.   215, 217
Poortinga, Y. H.   226, 227, 229
potential   52–5, 67, 97, 120, 128, 153, 160, 236, 257, 273, 279
  aptitude tests measure a wide variety of   96
  assessment methods help to identify   95
  awareness of   133
  defining   117–19
  demonstrating   39
  fairer way to evaluate   99–100
  future   99
  high   59n(6), 117
  indication of   93, 256
  key aspects of   118
  leadership   71
  low   117
  medium   117
  performance   162–3
  psychometrics can provide clues about   94
  realising   46, 56
  using psychometric tests to assess   269
  'will do'   101
PPA (Personal Profile Analysis)   242, 245, 246
PPI (Psychopathic Personality Inventory)   208
PPS (Personal Profile System)   242, 243, 245–6
Practical Personality Test (app)   271
practitioners   56, 151, 157–74, 176, 191, 208, 221, 230, 242, 244, 251–8
  applied   150
  capable   273
  credentialed   235
  discourse of psychology provides certain rights to   236
  experienced   65
  indicator of potential value to   149
  insights from   75
  obvious challenge facing   226
  psychological   182, 249
  qualified   235, 239, 274, 279
  scientist   175, 180, 189
  useful tool for   145
Predictive Index   242, 245
Premiership Football (UK)   45, 153
Primary Psychopathy   208
PRIME-MD (Primary Care Evaluation of Mental Disorders)   178
problem-solving   58, 66, 134, 253, 256
  distrust of intuition in   138
  imaginative ability   205
  real-world   127
profit   178, 237, 238, 240, 247, 263–6
projectives   213–19, 254
PSC (Profile Similarity Co-efficient)   161, 163
psychoanalysis   6, 214, 215
  elimination of teaching at undergraduate level   219
psychoanalytic concepts   35
  cards designed to assess   218
  direct link between   216
psychodynamics   22, 136, 188, 214
psychological research   30, 48, 181, 182, 230
  good   175
  mixed methods   182
psychology *see* BPS; clinical psychology; consumer psychology; counselling psychology; cross-cultural psychology; educational psychology; EFPA; forensic psychology; industrial psychology; neuropsychology; occupational psychology; performance psychology; Personal Construct Psychology; psychological research; psychology ethics; quantitative psychology
psychology ethics   235–50
psychometric assessment   12, 25–7, 99–100, 102, 175, 222, 277
  basis of   194
  can be administered through a variety of media   106
  clinical practice and   176–81
  crucial quality of   106
  early days of   31–2
  HR applications of   87–98
  pioneering approach to   194
  results of   107, 176
  smartphones and   270
  specific, sources of information about   109
  split between preferred types of   7

Psychometric Society 6
psychometrics 121–4
   challenges of developing and using for other languages and cultures 222
   clinical/clinicians' use of 178–80
   early assessment models and their scope for 157–8
   evaluation and development of team performance 129–44
   father of 6
   further developments in 163–4
   gaining benefit from use in development 127
   history of 3–14
   HR applications of 87–111
   importance of face validity in 149
   in-house developments in usage 162–3
   modern, beginnings of 5–6
   more systematic use of 161–2
   organisational impact of 181–2
   personality and 136
   sport and 145–56
   use and misuse in clinical settings 187–96
   using to make management selection decisions 157–74
   war and peacetime dividend 11–12
psychometrics research 47, 51, 57, 60n(18), 94, 175
   serious 50
psychopathy 6, 206
   subclinical 207
   see also LSRP; PCL-R; PEN; PPI; Primary Psychopathy; SRP; YPI
psychophysics 5, 6, 65, 152, 153
psychophysiology 19, 20, 275, 276
psychoticism 19, 31, 198
   see also PEN
Psytech International 13, 21
PTSD (Post-Traumatic Stress Disorder) 179
   see also CAPS

quantitative psychology 221
Quenk, N. L. 92, 148
questionnaires 29–41
   computer-presented 219
   culture fit 101
   emotional intelligence 99
   mobile app-based 273
   motivation 17, 94, 101, 122, 254
   other-report 202
   personality 17, 18, 43
   self-assessment 279
   self-regulation 147
   self-report 202, 276
   trait-based 93
   unconscious 219
   see also under various titles, e.g. EPQ; ITPQ; Maudsley; OPQ; PHQ-9; Sixteen Personality Factor; Sport Values; TDEQ

Raad, B. de 166
Rackspace 278
Randall, K. 153
RANRA (Rust Advanced Numerical Reasoning Appraisal) 257
RAPM (Raven's Advanced Progressive Matrices) 257
Rasch, Georg 8
Raskin, R. 206
Raven's Progressive Matrices 192
   see also RAPM
Rawling, K. 158
Raymark, P. 244
RBANST (Repeatable Battery for the Assessment of Neuropsychological Status) Update 193
RCTs (randomised control trials) 180
recruitment 3, 13, 45, 49, 54, 68, 69, 94, 99, 100, 105, 145, 242, 269, 279
   assessments not suitable for 92, 101
   challenging regimes 11
   direct model 277
   employer enabled to easily manage and monitor 106
   entry-level 271
   executive 120
   first-line-management 271
   frequently used methods in 88
   funnel of 89
   graduate 98
   high-volume 157
   inept 11
   information collected by company during 106
   managerial 12, 167
   military 11–12

mobile-friendly sites   270
personality profile of candidates   162
public sector   257
sample of convenience   228
selection and   59n(6), 72–3, 88, 89–92
senior   120
specialized worker   50
think tests or assessments embedded in   45
top end of the market   12
website trawling for   277
reliability   104, 38, 68, 71, 74, 104, 105, 176, 235, 255
   alternate form   109
   classic   219
   diagnosis and assessment   189–94
   inter-measure   177
   internal   56, 60
   internal consistency   108–9, 244
   interpretation of   69, 108–9
   inter-rater/scorer   218
   measures under specific conditions   9
   questionable   247
   removing test supervisor can result in a drop in   241
   subtest   67
   see also reliability and validity; test-retest reliability
reliability and validity   8, 36, 66, 107, 108, 213, 221, 249, 279
   classic   216, 219
   good   237, 246
   high   121
   importance of supervisor for   241
   independents who confirm   245
   measure that is remiss in lack of   247
   projective measures   216
   questionable   236, 239
   true   242
Rensvold, R. B.   227
Repertory Grid   16, 22–3, 26, 102
reports   25, 26, 55, 102, 121, 127, 128, 135, 179, 215, 216, 246, 272, 274, 275
   ability to standardise   256
   candidate performance potential   162
   complementary   257
   composite   258
   computer-generated   70, 72
   computer-written   18, 68
   confidential   194
   direct   101
   expert   107
   feedback   270
   final/full assessment   124, 125
   internal   264
   narrative   51, 72, 77, 107
   need of editing   256
   official   243
   product sales   97
   research and professional   131
   standard   256, 259
   workplace   218
   writing for client or referring third party   241
   see also self-reports
research
   academic   202, 263, 278
   advertising   216
   Big Five   139, 140, 194
   clinical   176
   comparative   221, 222
   consumer   216
   critical tool for   149
   Dark Triad   206, 207
   diagnostic categories   188, 189, 197, 198
   empirical   160, 179, 241
   high-quality   180
   idiographic and nomothetic styles in   16
   lie detector   243
   organisational practice and   203
   parallel   8
   prestigious   153
   scientific   49, 227
   selection methods   95
   semi-structured and structured interviews   190–1
   see also CIPD; market research; personality research; psychological research; psychometrics research; research and development
research and development   52
   analytics   55
response format/style   227
retrieval capacity   252
risk-taking behaviour   25, 98, 160, 166, 200
Rivera, L. A.   88
Roberts, M. H.   152

Robertson, I. T.   95, 164, 172, 221
Robertson, S.   246
Robins, E.   189
Rodger, A.   158
Roman Empire   4
Rorschach, Hermann   6, 7
Rorschach inkblot test   6, 7, 215, 217–18
Rose, D.   206
Roth E. A.   273
Rothstein, P.   276
Royal Air Force   11
RST (reinforcement sensitivity theory)   275–6
Rushton, J. P.   90, 253
Russell, J. T. *see* Taylor-Russell approach
Rust, J. *see* RANRA
Ryan, A. M.   227

Saleh, S. D. *see* LSS
Salgado, J. F.   39, 170, 198, 199
sample convenience   228
sampling sequence   79–84
Santander   113, 114, 115, 117–28
Saville, Peter   19, 21, 31–3, 35, 36, 38, 39, 168, 253
   see also SHL
Saville Consulting Wave   34, 35, 37, 39, 92, 236
schizoid/schizotypal personality disorder   198, 199, 209
Schmidt, F. L.   164
Schmit, M. J.   227
Schmitt, M.   244
Schmitt, Neal   34
Schuerger, J. M.   257
Schutz, Will   253, 258
scientist practitioners   175, 180
Scott, J. C.   270
screening out   18
Second World War (1939–45)
Seïtai   153
selecting in   92
selection
   assessment for   123–6, 221
   bias in   88
   cost-effectiveness of   88
   management   32, 157–74
   recruitment and   89
self-assessment   279
   accurate   159
   smartphone apps based on psychometric tests   273
   well-organized   247
self-deception   30
self-diagnosis   202
Self-Directed Search   257
self-reports   32, 71, 88, 168, 191, 192, 202, 258
   ubiquitous   276
   see also LSRP; SRP
SEM (standard error of measurement)   8, 19, 68–9, 71
Sentence Completion   214–15, 216, 217, 219
Seven-Point Plan, The (Rodger)   158
shell shock   11
Sherman, C. A.   152
SHL (Saville & Holdsworth Limited)   13, 21, 239, 255
show jumpers   25–7
sifting   88, 89–91, 92
   see also screening out
Sik, George   21
Simon, Théodore   9, 17
   see also Binet-Simon
Simoneit, Wolfgang   12
situational judgement inventories/theory   254, 255
   see also SJTs
Sixteen Personality Factor (16PF)
   questionnaire   21, 35, 39, 92, 110n, 158, 159, 161, 162, 164, 166–9, 172, 252, 253, 272, 275
   Reasoning (Scale B) factor   257
SJTs (Situational Judgement Tests)   43, 58n(1), 59n(6), 89, 95, 98, 101, 121
   behavioural   109
   cognitively loaded   109
Skeem, J. L.   263
small organisations   77–84
smart badges   278
smartphones   44, 56, 247, 269–75, 279
Smith, D. B.   167
Smith, G. S.   218
Smith, M.   88, 95, 164, 172, 221
Smith, P.   88
SN (Stability-Neuroticism) dimension   19
snowballing technique   228
Social Desirability scale   19, 20
social media   57, 59n(7), 113
   see also Facebook; LinkedIn; Twitter

social support   151, 152
Society for Personality Assessment   7
soft skills   277
solid objects   217
Sorenson, E. R.   153
Southern Africa   215
Spearman, Charles   6, 8, 9, 17, 167, 252
Spearman-Brown prophecy formula   34
Speed, H. D.   152
spelling   96, 107
   differences in   37
   grammar and   66
Spencer, L. M. & S. M.   162, 165, 167
Spielberger, C.   224
Spitzer, R. L.   178, 189
Splash signature   142
sport   15, 23, 25, 27, 249, 278
   linking predictive analytics to success in   45
   psychometrics in   26, 145–56
   see also AMI; football; OSI-SP
Sport Values Questionnaire   26
Spry, D.   237
SRP (Self-Report Psychopathy) scale   207, 208
standard deviations   17, 68, 78, 150
standard error of the mean   68
   see also SEM
Stanford-Binet IQ classification   9, 10, 252
Stanford University   51
Steinman, R. B.   216
Stevens, Stanley Smith   8
stimulation   136, 137, 205, 276
stimuli   218
   auditory   217
   idiographic   213
   oral   217
   projective   214
   self-relevant   276
   structured/unstructured   213
   verbal   215
   written   217
Strategic Assessment System   242, 245
StrengthScope   127
stress   12, 15, 141, 188, 202, 218, 219, 258, 259
   calm under   103
   climate free of   241
   heat   278
   injury-based   150
   measured   192
   mental   187
   non-organisational   151
   organisational   149, 150
   performance might be affected by   228
   poor coping responses   198
   systematically monitored   278
   tolerance of   161
   work-related   203, 243
   see also distress; eustress; PTSD
Strong Interest Inventory   257
Style Analysis   242, 245
substitution   240, 242, 247, 248
Sui, J.   276
Surujlal, I.   152
Suzuki, L.   90
Swedish language   223
Szondi, Leopold   6

tablets   44, 270
talent   36, 43, 48, 56, 143, 158
   best   271
   development of   147
   fantasized   204
   identification of   145, 153, 269
   ignored   204
   innovation   59n(15)
   latent   12
   leadership   59n(15), 113–28
   low   35
   recruitment of   145
   special   205
   testing for   11, 154, 277
   utilising   130
   unusual   204
   see also TDEQ
talent management   44, 46–7, 50, 94
talent metrics   54, 55, 59n(15)
Tanzer, N.   224
TAT (Thematic Apperception Test)   214, 215, 217, 218–19
Tatsuoka, M. M.   159
Tauriz, G.   39
Taylor, J. E.   235, 270
Taylor-Russell approach   72–3
TDEQ (Talent Development Environment Questionnaire)   146–7
team building   87, 93, 242
team context   130–1

team development   122, 137, 237
  broad-based   120
  fundamental component of practice   131
  psychometric context   131–6
Team Focus   258
team formation   93, 138
team leaders   116, 142, 162
  customer service   102, 103
team performance   129–44
Teicher, E. A.   207
Terry, H.   206
test development   52, 221, 225, 226, 230, 244
  effective   45
  funding   45
  independents employed in   245
  influencing the flow of finances to   47
  innovation in   45, 57
  persons not qualified in   254
  smartphones and   271
  standards of psychology in   249
  technology that is shaping   44
test instructions   228
test performance   11, 17
  maximal   58n(1)
test results   9, 73–5, 194, 253, 259, 273, 274
  ability   17
  cognitive   193
  feeding back   70–2
  interpreting   67–9
  psychometric   277
  ranked   17
  validation of   241
test-retest reliability   109, 203, 218, 246
  poor   148, 264
test theory   75
  classical   8–9, 230
test users   23, 228
  accredited   249
  intentions identified   17
  lower costs on quality products for   249
  PPA qualification courses   245
  practical application of knowledge and skills   65–76
  purpose of keeping a register of   263
  qualified   273, 274; see also BPS
  responsibilities assumed by   238
  skilled   279
  training of   248
  unqualified   238, 239
tests/testing
  across cultures   221–33
  analytics as platform for the evolution of   56–7
  candidate-friendly   49
  choosing   65–7
  clinical practice   191
  computer-based   228
  context for   43–5
  educational   239
  evaluating   105–9
  forensic   239
  future of   43–63, 269–81
  high-quality services direct to consumers   273–5
  job knowledge   97
  occupational   236–7
  online   43, 89, 256
  potential disruption challenges for   240–1
  putting forward the case for   72–4
  scenarios in a big data and analytics world   52–7
  utility for small organisations   77–84
  value-add to analytics   55–6
  work sample   97
  see also ability tests; aptitude tests; CAT; intelligence tests; numerical reasoning tests; personality testing; validity; verbal reasoning tests; also entries above prefixed 'test'
Thatcher, Margaret   4
Thomas International see PPA
Thomas, K. W. see TKI
Thurstone, Louis   6
Time magazine   46–7
TKI (Thomas-Kilmann Conflict Mode Instrument)   122, 134
tough-mindedness   19, 20, 25, 252
traits   23, 35, 37, 65, 122, 125, 128, 148, 162, 193, 201, 218, 257
  abilities and   194
  adaptive   5, 6
  behavioural   98, 202
  Big Five   276
  coherent   108
  common   22

concealed   8
concern about breadth   253
descriptions of   244
detailed   92
dysfunctional   126
labelling of   259
latent   8
long-lasting   192
lower-order   165
narrow   36
source   163, 166
see also ECCOS; personality traits; YPI
translation   36, 37, 113, 124, 147, 230
accurate   224
achieving equivalence in   223
assessing/checking quality of   224, 225
back   224–5, 226
difficulties of   191
forward   225, 226
good   224, 230
literal   225
meaningful context across languages   223
mistakes in   223, 226
poor   222
triangulation   22, 23, 27, 277
Trickey, G.   203
Tuckman's five-stage model
adjourning   132, 135–6
forming   132–3
norming   133–5
performing   135
storming   133
Tupes, E. C.   163, 253
Turner, S.   190
Tutko, T. A. *see* AMI
Tuzinski, K.   43–4
Twitter   247
Tynke Toering, T.   147
Type Dynamics Indicator   258
Type Mapping   258

UIT (unproctored internet testing)   43, 48, 58n(1), 235–6
UK (United Kingdom)   215
access to computers   229
see also BPS; British Ability Scales; British Army

unconscious   18, 137
core   214, 219
covert   214
key feelings   216
means of accessing   218
University of East London   255
University of Minnesota   243
Urry, V. W.   164
US armed forces *see* AGCT; ASVAB
US Navy   253
utility analysis   23, 84
financial cost-benefit   88

validity   13, 79–81
consequential   74, 75, 108
construct   74, 108
faith   108
high   39, 97, 121
moderate   39, 84
see also criterion validity; ecological validity; face validity; reliability and validity
Van Scoyoc, Susan   194
Vaughan, C.   59n(15), 60n(17)
verbal reasoning tests   69, 74, 254
sample   96
tests well-used   68
Vijver, F. J. R. van de   222, 224, 226, 227, 228, 229
Villado, A. J.   235
Vineland-II (Vineland Adaptive Behaviour Scales)   192–3
Visscher, C.   147
visualisation   44, 55, 58, 252, 254
VUCA (volatile, uncertain, complex and ambiguous) environment   113, 114, 128, 130

Wall Street Journal   59n(8)
Wampold, B. E.   178
Watkins, D.   224, 229
wearables   56, 57, 269, 278–9
Webster, G. D.   208
Wellington, Arthur Wellesley, 1st Duke of   11
WGCTA (Watson Glaser Critical Thinking Appraisal)   257
Whetzel, D. L.   98
Widiger, T. A.   208
Wiener-Levy, D.   218

Wilhelm II, German Kaiser   12
'will do'/ 'will fit in' categories   94, 100–1
Williams, J. B.   178
Williams, K.   206, 207, 208
Willson, E.   38
Windelband, W.   16
Wonderlic Intelligence Test   153, 154
Wood, R.   38
Woods, S. A.   90

word association   215, 216
Workforce Analytics   44, 52, 55
Wundt, Wilhelm   6

Xerox   59n(8)

yoga wear   240
YPI (Youth Psychopathic Traits Inventory)   208

Printed and bound by CPI Group (UK) Ltd, Croydon, CR0 4YY
21/05/2023

03220643-0002